H

Patrick and Henry Counties
Virginia

BY

VIRGINIA G. AND
LEWIS G. PEDIGO

*With a New Preface
By Richard P. Gravely, Jr.*

CLEARFIELD

Originally Published
Roanoke, Virginia
1933

Reprinted with a New Preface
and a List of Illustrations
Regional Publishing Company
Baltimore, 1977
Genealogical Publishing Co., Inc.
Baltimore, 1990

Reprinted for
Clearfield Company, Inc. by
Genealogical Publishing Co., Inc.
Baltimore, Maryland
2002

Library of Congress Catalogue Card Number 76-53104
International Standard Book Number: 0-8063-8010-1

Reprinted from a volume
in the Virginia State Library

THIS BOOK IS DEDICATED

TO

CAPTAIN HARDEN W. REYNOLDS

HIS WIFE

MRS. NANCY COX REYNOLDS

AND

THEIR SONS AND DAUGHTERS

PREFACE

Henry County, Virginia, is situated in the south-western Piedmont section of the state along the North Carolina border, on the upper drainage system of the Dan River. Formed from Pittsylvania County to the east in the climactic year of 1776, Henry originally included all of what is today Patrick County and that part of Franklin County which lies to the south of Blackwater River, in addition to the area now encompassed by the Henry lines.

In the past the name "Henry County" on manufactured tobacco products denoted absolute top quality; today the county is a major producer of furniture, textiles, and fibers.

Patrick Henry lived here for a time and was the owner of plantations totalling nearly 20,000 acres in extent. The county itself, and its daughter county of Patrick to the west, was named for the fiery Revolutionary War patriot and orator. Brigadier-General Joseph Martin, who probably contributed more than any other individual to preventing the Cherokee Nation and its southern neighbors from joining with the British against the Colonists, had his home in Henry County for almost forty years prior to his death in 1808. George Hairston, at one time the owner of over 235,000 acres of Virginia and by repute the largest landowner in the state, was an early settler and life-long resident of the county.

No definitive history of Henry County has been written. However, there are two histories by amateur historians with family roots deeply embedded in the origins and development of the county which are of considerable value and interest.

In 1925 Miss Judith Parks America Hill, a retired school-teacher, was the author of a 300-copy edition of a book entitled *History of Henry County, Virginia*. Long out of print, the *History* is much sought after and brings very high prices when found, which is seldom; an excellent reprint edition with an added guide to contents was issued in 1976 by the Regional Publishing Company, affiliate of the Genealogical Publishing Company of Baltimore, and can still be obtained.

Although entitled a *History*, "Miss Judy's" book is actually a compilation of sketches, anecdotes, reminiscences, legends, and lengthy family genealogies, with a few photographs and no index. The author accurately and fairly describes her work in its Preface: "This History was not begun with the intention of writing a book for the public but merely to produce a family booklet.

As time wore on and I found myself connected with so many families of the County, I determined that I would use my best endeavors to get as much information about the facts and families as I could." Miss Judy should be taken at her word, and her book read in that light.

Eight years after the publication of Hill's *History,* in the Depression year of 1933, a lesser-known but probably an overall more valuable history of the county appeared, which is today virtually unobtainable at any price in the original edition. It is *History of Patrick and Henry Counties, Virginia,* by Miss Virginia Pedigo of Martinsville and her distant cousin, Dr. Lewis Gravely Pedigo. The Pedigo history drew largely from Hill, and is quite derivative, but it is better organized, shows considerably more research, covers a much broader range of topics, and contains a useful index. The genealogical section still bulks large in the overall format, filling 278 of the volume's 360 pages, but it includes many families of Henry and Patrick counties that received little or no attention from "Miss Judy." Pedigo does not supersede Hill; it complements and enlarges upon Hill, fills many of the lacunae found therein, and answers many questions of local history which Hill leaves unanswered. Of its genre (the amateur genealogico-historical compendium), it is a good example. Most important, it is surprisingly interesting reading, particularly so to anyone connected with the section of Virginia and neighboring North Carolina which it depicts. It is most unfortunate that this book has not been more generally available to students of the area and of the times with which it deals.

The Regional Publishing Company has rendered a real and lasting service to genealogists, local historians, and those simply tied by relationship, birth, or otherwise to Henry and Patrick Counties, Virginia, by adding this reprint edition of Pedigo's *History* to its growing list of similar publications.

Richard P. Gravely, Jr.
Martinsville, Henry County, Va.
August 15, 1976

LIST OF ILLUSTRATIONS

INDEX

INTRODUCTION

PATRICK AND HENRY COUNTIES existed for so many years as one county that it would seem almost impossible to give an account of the sons and daughters of one of these counties and ignore those of the other, their history being so closely related.

In writing the annals of the people of these two counties, therefore, we are giving an account of those especially who, in the realm of the professions, in statesmanship, and in the establishing of business enterprises of various kinds, have rendered humanity a great service.

In this history we have included those who, for a number of years, have cast their lots with our people as well as those born and brought up within the borders of the two counties. We have followed those, whose records are available, who have gone forth into other sections of the state or into other states and accomplished something really worth while.

It is a little singular that some one has not written a complete history of these two counties before this time. Those extant that have come within our knowledge are limited in scope, so in considering just adding to what has already been written of these great counties, we are reminded of the story Benjamin Franklin told when the revision of the Articles of Confederation was under consideration. The story is as follows: "A very decrepit old man, who could scarcely hobble along on crutches, constantly used the exclamation, 'God mend me! God mend me!' A young lad who heard him said, 'Mend you, why, I think it would be easier to make a new one!'"

So we hope what we have gathered in our research, having used every available means for securing the best knowledge of these counties and their splendid people, will prove to be of interest to our readers.

TERRITORY ONCE INCLUDED IN LUNENBURG COUNTY

Lunenburg occupies a very prominent place in the list of counties of southern Virginia, as so many of them were formed from subdivisions of that county.

An Act creating Lunenburg County from territory taken from Brunswick County, was passed by the House of Burgesses on March 26, 1745, during the administration of William Gooch, Esq., Governor. Lunenburg County thus created and which was to have its legal existence and name "from and immediately after the first day of May, 1746, was princely in domain and extent. It embraced the territory later to be laid out into the present Counties of Halifax, Bedford, Charlotte, Mecklenburg, Pittsylvania, Henry, Campbell, Franklin and Patrick.

In February, 1752, Halifax County was created to be effective May 10, 1752. The Act provided that the said County of Lunenburg be divided into two counties, that is to say, that all that part thereof lying on the south side of Blackwater Creek and Staunton River, from the said Blackwater Creek to the confluence of the said river with the River Dan, and thence to Aaron's Creek to the county line, shall be one distinct parish and county and called and be known as the County of Halifax and parish of Antrim, and all that other part thereof on the north side of Staunton River from the lower part to the extent of the county upwards shall be one other distinct county and retain the name of Lunenburg and parish of Cumberland.

In quick succession after Halifax, Bedford was formed from Lunenburg, November, 1763. "On November 12, 1762, a petition of divers inhabitants of the County of Lunenburg praying that the said county be divided into three distinct counties, and that an Act may pass for that purpose" was presented to the House and read. The bill was reported November 7, 1764. Thus Charlotte and Mecklenburg were formed from Lunenburg. Pittsylvania was formed from Halifax in 1767. Henry from Pittsylvania 1776. Campbell from Bedford 1782. Franklin from Bedford 1786. In May, 1777 (first year of the Commonwealth), a part of Charlotte County was restored to Lunenburg, this was the final change in the area and boundary of Lunenburg.

The group of counties including Lunenburg which trace their descent from Charles City and Prince George illustrate in their naming a wealth of Virginia history.

Charles City (1764), originally the name of a town, was the designation of a very large territory. It was named for Charles, afterward King Charles First.

Prince George (1703) was named for Prince George of Denmark, the husband of Queen Anne, who was on the English throne when the county was formed.

Brunswick (1720-1732) was named in honor of King George II, one of whose titles was Duke of Brunswick Luneburg.

Amelia was named for the Princess Amelia Sophia, the youngest daughter of King George II, who came to the English throne in 1727.

Lunenburg was also named in honor of King George II (Luneburg being the German form of Lunenburg).

Halifax County (1752) was named for George Montague Dunk, the second Earl of Halifax, of the distinguished family of Montague, who was first Lord of the Board of Trade about the time the county was formed, and greatly interested in the trade with the colonies.

Dinwiddie (1754) was named in honor of Robert Dinwiddie, lieutenant of the colony 1751 to 1758.

Bedford (1754) was named in honor of John Russell, the fourth Duke of Bedford, who was the Secretary of State of Great Britain, from February 13 to June 20, 1757.

Prince Edward (1754) was named for Edward Augustus, a son of Frederick, Prince of Wales.

Charlotte (1765) was named after Princess Charlotte Sophia, of Mecklenburg, the young Queen of George III.

Pittsylvania (1767) was named for Sir William Pitt, Earl of Chatham, the great English orator-statesman.

This was the last of this group of counties created before the Revolution. Up to this time the counties generally had been named in honor of some one connected with the royal family of England or the royal government of the colonies. Upon the achieving of independence the counties thereafter created were given names significant of the new era.

Henry County, created in 1776, was named in honor of the great orator of the Revolution who did so much to overthrow the royal establishment in Virginia.

Greenville (1781) was named for General Nathaniel Greene, who fought the Battle of Guilford Court House.

Campbell (1782) was named for General William Campbell, the hero of King's Mountain.

Franklin (1786) was named in honor of the philosopher and statesman, Benjamin Franklin.

Nottoway County (1789) took its name from the Indian tribe which inhabited the territory along the Nottoway River.

Patrick County (1791), the last of the group, like Henry County, was named in honor of Patrick Henry.

After the formation of Henry County, Patrick Henry made large purchases of land in the county and subsequently the county was divided and the new county named Patrick.

SUMMARY

Isle of Wight and James City County were two of the original eight shires under royal government.

Surry was taken from James City County in 1652.

Brunswick from Isle of Wight and Surry in 1720.

Lunenburg from Brunswick in 1748.

Halifax from Lunenburg in 1752.

Pittsylvania from Halifax 1767.

Henry from Pittsylvania 1776.

Patrick from Henry 1791.

EARLIEST INHABITANTS AND THE BUILDING OF FORTS

There are evidences that Henry and Patrick Counties were the homes of numerous Indians of the Algonquin family. The Cherokees were their neighbors on the south in North Carolina. The flints and other implements of Indian warfare prove that many conflicts took place along the banks of the Marrowbone and Smith Rivers. Crockery remaining intact near Ridgeway, Henry County, around soapstone hill, indicates some skill in that handiwork.

The General Assembly, March, 1776, ordered a chain of forts to be built along the frontier, the last, of course, near the state line. George Washington left Winchester, September 29, 1756, to visit these forts and wrote later that he visited Fort Trial on Smith River. The fort is situated on an eminence that commands a very fine view of Smith River for several miles and of the confluence of Beaver Creek with that river, but at the time it was built only the low ground along river and creek could be perceived, the lofty timber on the opposite bank of the river effectually preventing any greater distance being seen.

The fort was built in the form of a square, the walls were made of split trees planted in the earth four feet deep and very close together, the height was sixteen feet above the ground, with holes cut at the proper height to use firearms. There was a bastion at each corner, and a log house, bullet proof, at each side of the gate. Within the area of the fort near the center was a common framed house and between the outer and inner walls it was filled with stones and earth to the height of six feet as an additional defense.

The fort was not used by soldiers alone in protecting the frontier but, in time of serious alarm, to this the entire population scurried for protection. A distinguished British traveler and writer traversed the country in 1774, and described the appearance of the central section when the people were in a panic over a report that the Indians had taken up the hatchet. He wrote, "There were several large plantations on the rich low grounds of Leatherwood and Beaver Creeks deserted, not a single inhabitant to be seen; the cattle, horses and other animals were wandering about their master's habitations, conveying the most mournful, melancholy and dismal ideas that can be easily conceived." He told of finding a mill on Beaver Creek with the hopper half full of corn, the miller having left in such haste, and finally finding the populace in Fort Trial, on Smith River, huddled together in the most woeful and unsanitary condition. It was only by searching the country for miles around without finding an Indian that he could allay the fears of the inhabitants. The same writer reported traveling a long distance prior to reaching Sauratown settlement, on Dan River, opposite Leaksville's present site, without seeing a habitation.

In those days land was cheap in that section and it was an age of pioneers, so men, through love of adventure or desire to own homes, gradually made their way into this region, braving dangers, difficulties and hardships.

The settlers, as far as our knowledge goes, escaped serious trouble with the Indians, though reports of Indian raids caused such consternation as that described by the English traveler. Later on the Indians were driven back and the Fort (Trial), being needed no longer, was abandoned with the other fourteen of its era. As the site of Fort Trial is across the creek from the National highway, about four or five miles northwest of Martinsville, it is destined to be one of the county's places of historical interest. A marker has been placed so that travelers may read the inscription.

COLONEL BYRD'S SURVEY

In 1728, during the month of October, Colonel William Byrd wrote of locating the state line between Virginia and North Carolina. They crossed the River Irvin, so named in honor of the professor in his party, and surveyed six miles during the day and camped on the west side of Matrimony Creek, so called by an unfortunate "mary'd" man because it was exceedingly noisy and impetuous. From here, looking to the northwest about four miles, he saw a round point which he named Wart Mountain. This was evidently Holt

Knob, the last spur of the Chestnut Knob highlands. He made no note of any inhabitants along here nor at any place to the Stokes line. The following day they traversed five miles, killed a turkey and a bear, and camped next about where Price, North Carolina, is to-day. After describing the rough hills at the junction of north and south Mayo, named in honor of one of the engineers, he stated that they brought into camp six bears. He said they pitched their camp on the west side for the purpose of being lulled to sleep by the cataract.

THE DIVIDING LINE

As Patrick and Henry Counties both border on North Carolina, the history of the "dividing line" has always been of much interest to the people of these counties.

To the London Company, by the second charter, was granted all lands in that part of America called Virginia, from Point Comfort along the seacoast two hundred miles northward, and from Point Comfort along the seacoast southward two hundred miles and between these lines westward to the sea. This territorial description included most of what we now call North Carolina and Tennessee.

Succeeding kings thought that, by divine right and royal prerogative, they were not bound by precedent or any act of predecessor, and although Virginia had won the title of "Old Dominion" by her loyalty to Charles I and Charles II, during the Cromwell regime, yet in 1663 Charles II, of England, inexcusably ungrateful and forgetful of the loyalty of his faithful colony, in disregard of the grants to the Virginia Company, issued a charter to Edward, Earl of Clarendon, and seven others of his courtiers to the colony of Carolina, describing the lands therein granted as being all the lands between thirty-one degrees and thirty-six degrees north latitude and running westwardly from sea to sea. This would have placed the northern boundary line of the grant approximately forty miles south of the present line between Virginia and Carolina.

In 1665 Charles II enlarged the grant to the Carolina colony by making it cover all the lands between twenty-nine degrees and thirty-six degrees thirty minutes north latitude—describing particularly the northern boundary line, the one with which we are now concerned as follows:

"All that province and territory within America extending north and eastward as far as the north end of Currituck River or inlet, upon a straight westerly line to Wyonoke Creek which lies within or about thirty-six degrees thirty minutes, northern latitude and so west, in a direct line as far as the south seas."

Thus an interlock more than a hundred miles wide running from ocean to ocean was formed between the Virginia and Carolina colonies, and thus, for the first time, was introduced into our geography and history the most famous parallel of latitude running east and west across the United States.

Whether the junior grant to the Carolina colony operated as a repeal of the senior grant to the Virginia colony in so far as concerned the interlock, was a question which never reached serious consideration, for Virginia, in 1776, out of the goodness of her generous soul, by an act in constitutional convention, released to North Carolina all claim to lands within the charter of the Carolina colony, but both recognized that by royal power and intent the dividing line westward from the Atlantic Ocean between the two colonies should be on thirty-six degrees thirty minutes north latitude.

There had been no real effort prior to 1711 to locate the line between Virginia and Carolina colonies, but in that year commissioners were appointed to do so. They met, looked over the ground at the starting point, disbanded and reported that they did not have sufficient means and instruments for locating and running the line.

Within the next few years frequent and disturbing conflicts arose between the colonists of Virginia and Carolina in the neighborhood of the probable location of the line. Wyonoke Creek, called for in the Carolina charter, had lost its name. Virginia contended that it was Wiccacon Creek; Carolina that it was Nottoway River. Most of the settlers were procuring grants from the Carolina proprietors, chiefly because it was a simpler procedure and because taxes were less burdensome. Sometimes grants were made by both sides for the same tract of land. Something definite became immediately necessary to be done in fixing the limits of the two colonies. In 1727, Governor Alexander Spottswood, of Virginia, and Governor Eden, of North Carolina, entered into negotiations and conferences for the settlement of the troublesome situation and reached an agreement as to how the line should be located, as follows:

"From the mouth of Currituck River, setting the compass on the north shore thereof, a due west line shall be run and fairly marked, and if it happen to cut Chowan River between the mouth of Nottoway River and Wiccacon Creek, then the same direct course shall be continued toward the mountains and be forever the dividing line between Virginia and Carolina; but if said westward line cuts Chowan River to the southward of Wiccacon Creek, then from the point of intersection the line shall continue up Chowan River to the middle of the entrance of Wiccacon Creek and thence a due west line. If said west line cuts Blackwater River to the northward of Nottoway River the line shall from the point of intersection run down the middle of Blackwater to the middle of the entrance into Nottoway River, thence a due west line."

Provisions were also made for the inclusion of islands and where natural water boundaries made it more convenient to include small slips of land in one colony rather than in the other this should be done. The line when run, did cut Blackwater one hundred and seventy-six poles north of the entrance into Nottoway River and the line was made to follow Blackwater down to the Nottoway. This agreement was transmitted to England for ratification, was approved by the King, Privy Council, Lords and Earls and others concerned, and returned by King George II to the Governors for execution. Governor William Gooch appointed as commissioners for Virginia, Colonel William Byrd of Westover, William Dandridge and Richard Fitzwilliams. The Governor of North Carolina appointed four commissioners for that colony. In 1728, these commissioners ran the line westward a distance of two hundred and forty-one miles from Currituck Inlet to a point near the mountains. According to their report they ran it on thirty-six degrees thirty-one minutes north latitude, equivalent to more than one mile north of thirty-six degrees thirty minutes called for in the Carolina charter, the reason assigned in the report being that they found the north end of Currituck Inlet in that latitude. As a matter of fact they were farther north than thirty-six degrees thirty-one minutes as the line now on the ground is about four miles north of thirty-six degrees thirty minutes.

In the writings of Colonel Byrd, his narrative of the running of this line is as charming and romantic as is the story of Governor Spottswood and his Knights of the Golden Horseshoe, in their expedition across the Blue Ridge Mountains. He says that in the party of seventeen, they had with them a chaplain to keep their souls nourished with spiritual food, their conduct that of gentlemen, and to give the people along the line an opportunity to be baptized into the Kingdom of God. After running through the Dismal Swamp, a distance of fifteen miles, one of the Carolina commissioners begged to be released from further service, giving no better reason than that he had lately married. At the Meherrin River, which Colonel Byrd says was about as wide as the River Jordan (forty yards), they decided to adjourn until fall, because the warm sun was bringing out rattlesnakes in uncomfortable numbers although they had with them a snake bite remedy, and in addition they discovered that by rubbing the juice of the rattlesnake weed on their hands and on their dogs' noses they could even handle the snakes with impunity. The bear, the deer, the buffalo, the wildcat, the beaver, the wolf and the Indian kept up continual excitement and entertainment all along the way.

In the fall, work was resumed and at the Hico River, a branch of the Roanoke, at one hundred and seventy miles west of the starting point, the Carolina commissioners decided to go no farther. In their report to the Governor of North Carolina they said that at this point, they had already run fifty miles west of any habitation and that it would probably be a generation or two before the settlements would reach this point. Colonel Byrd, in all seriousness, states the real reason for their quitting to be that all the good liquor had given out. Over the protest of the Carolina commissioners Colonel Byrd and the Virginians continued the line for a distance of seventy miles westward to the shadow of what he terms the Chariky Mountains, and stopped because of the fear of deep snows and swollen streams of winter. The King of England and council approved the whole line as surveyed by Colonel Byrd.

Contrary to the supposition of the Carolina commissioners, when they stopped at Hico River, that it would be a generation or two before settlements would reach that point, only twenty years elapsed until settlers pushed beyond the end of the Byrd line at two hundred and forty-one miles west of Currituck. Conflicts arose in the same way as before—grants from both sides for the same land, allegiance and military service demanded by both colonies, North Carolina being favored by the inhabitants, and the urgent necessity for extending the line farther westward, the governors agreed upon the appointment of commissioners for this purpose, Weldon and Churton for North Carolina, Joshua Fry and Peter Jefferson for Virginia. These commissioners located and extended the line, in 1748-49, for a distance by surface measurement of three hundred and thirty miles from the beginning or three hundred and twenty miles by horizontal measurement ending, as they reported, at Steep Rock Creek, which is in the neighborhood of the present corners of North Carolina, Virginia and Tennessee.

Patrick Henry, Governor of Virginia, with the approval of the legislature, in 1778, appointed Dr. Thomas Walker as one of the Virginia commissioners and the Governor of North Carolina appointed at the head of the North Carolina commission, Colonel Richard Henderson, their instructions being to run the line on thirty-six degrees thirty minutes. By an Act of Assembly in December, 1790, North Carolina adopted the Walker or southerly line as the boundary line and Virginia adopted it in 1791, and from that time to the present both states have carried it in their codes as the true boundary between them.

FORMATION OF HENRY COUNTY

Henry County was formed by an Act of October, 1776 (first year of the commonwealth), which enacted "That from and after the last day of December next ensuing the said county of Pittsylvania be divided into two counties, by a line beginning at the mouth of Blackwater on Staunton River and running parallel with the line of Halifax County till it strikes the county line, and that all that part of the said county which lies to the westward of the said line shall be one distinct county and be called and known by the name of Henry, and all the other part thereof which lies to the eastward of the said line shall be one other distinct county and retain the name of Pittsylvania."

The surface of Henry County is hilly with a few high points such as the Chestnut Knob, Nance's Mountain, and bluffs along Smith River. From the summits of eminences, especially the latter, views of the surrounding country with its farms and valleys are very beautiful.

The county lies in southern Virginia, a little west of the center; its southern line bordering North Carolina. The soil conditions are most favorable, hillside and meadow yielding most bountiful returns to husbandry, bringing forth fruits, flowers, grains, grasses and the choicest tobacco of the southland.

By an Act of the Assembly of October, 1776, the county court of Henry County was held at the home of John Rowland on the third Monday in January. The records show that six hundred and thirty citizens took the oath of allegiance to the United States and about forty refused to renounce their allegiance to Great Britain. Many had joined the army under Washington, many were away hunting or trading at this time, for there was a much larger citizenry in the county than these figures would indicate.

From the scattered homes the county furnished only one organized body of troops to the nation. This was (as noted in another chapter before) under Colonel Abram Penn and began the march from Beaver Creek, March 11, 1781, crossed Rowland's Ford just below Fontaine, about two miles from Martinsville's present site, following the old road (deep cuts now show the location) up the Marrowbone Valley, crossing the creek where Ridgeway now stands, thence along the ridge two miles, then crossing Matrimony Creek half a mile to the state line.

From the line south, their route is not known, however they marched so rapidly they soon reached General Greene and took part in the Battle of Guilford Court House, March 25, 1781.

FORMATION OF PATRICK COUNTY

Patrick County was formed by an Act of November 26, 1790, which enacted "That from and after the first day of June next, the County of Henry shall be divided into two distinct counties, that is to say, that all that part of the said county lying west of a line beginning on the line dividing the County of Henry one mile above where it crosses Town Creek, a branch of Smith River, thence a parallel line to the Pittsylvania line to the county line, shall be one distinct county and called and be known by the name of Patrick County, and all the residue of the said county retain the name of Henry County."

By an Act passed November 30, 1791, a part of Henry County was added to Patrick. The Act provided "That all that part of Henry County lying to the south of a line beginning one mile above Town Creek on the line dividing the Counties of Franklin and Henry and running thence a direct course to the North Carolina line at the lower crossing of Crooked Creek, a branch of Mayo River, shall be and the same is hereby added to, and made a part of the County of Patrick."

By an Act of March 13, 1848, a small triangular portion of Patrick County was added to Franklin County.

Patrick County is twenty-five miles long with a mean width of twenty miles and is watered by the Dan River and its branches. The face of the country is broken and it has the Allegheny Mountains on the western boundary and the Bull Mountain and other ranges running across it from east to west. There is great diversity of soil. The bottom land on the water courses is generally of good quality and a large portion of the upland is strong though rocky. On the south side of Bull Mountain the staple is tobacco; iron ore abounds.

Stuart, on Mayo River, is the county seat.

COURT OF PATRICK COUNTY

In 1808, an Act was passed dividing the state into twelve judicial districts. There were no circuit superior courts in existence. The state, soon after the close of the war, had been divided into judicial districts, some central point being selected for holding the district courts. The district court for the district in which Patrick was embraced was held in New London, a very ancient town in the County of Bedford, about twelve miles from the City of Lynchburg, and one hundred miles from the County of Patrick. Here Patrick Henry delivered his famous "Beef Speech."

The first superior court for the County of Patrick, under the provisions of the Act of 1808, was held at the present county seat on the sixth day of October, 1809, by Judge Paul Carrington, an able lawyer of unblemished reputation, who had been a member of and taken a prominent part in the proceedings of the Virginia Convention of 1788, convened for the purpose of deliberating on the constitution adopted and recommended by the memorable Federal Convention of 1787.

HENRY COUNTY

Henry County was formed from Pittsylvania in 1776. The clerks of the county have been:

John Cox, from 1777 to 1808.............................. 31 years.
Waller Redd, from 1808 to 1825........................... 17 years.
Sanford Reamey, from 1825 to 1831........................ 6 years.
A. M. Dupuy, from 1831 to 1845........................... 14 years.
Jerry Griggs, from 1845 to 1864.......................... 19 years.
George D. Graveley, from 1864 to 1869.................... 5 years.
T. E. Donegan, from 1869 to 1870......................... 1 year.
George D. Graveley, from 1870 to 1875.................... 5 years.
J. H. Matthews, from 1875 to 1887........................ 12 years.
Reëlected in May, 1887, for six years. Served until 1912.

Thomas C. Matthews was elected in 1912, and is now (1932) the clerk of the Henry County Court.

Clerks of Patrick County from the time of its separation from Henry County in 1791.

Samuel Staples, from 1791 to 1826........................ 34 years.
Abram Staples, his son, 1825 to 1852.
In 1844, he resigned the clerkship of the circuit court and was succeeded in the latter by his son, Samuel G. Staples.
Samuel G. Staples held the office from 1844 to 1852.
Abram Staples, nephew of Abram Staples above mentioned, was circuit clerk from 1852 to 1869............................... 17 years.
He was removed by military authority and John Anglin appointed.
John L. Anglin held the office to January 1, 1871.
Henry Tuggle (county court), from 1862 to 1869.
Larkin G. Rucker (county court), from 1871 to 1887.
Thomas Clark (circuit court), from 1870 to 1871.
When the amended constitution went into effect Larkin G. Rucker, having been elected clerk of the county court, became ex officio clerk also of the circuit court and continued as such to 1887.
Charles Reade Martin followed Larkin G. Rucker.
John S. Taylor was next elected, at the expiration of whose term T. Lee Clark became clerk.
John S. Taylor was again elected and is the present incumbent.

EARLY SETTLERS OF THE TERRITORY NOW OCCUPIED

BY

PATRICK AND HENRY COUNTIES IN VIRGINIA

———

By JOHN REDD SMITH

———

THE people of the Blue Ridge and Appalachian Ranges laid deep the foundations of this republic and were the largest contributors to the prosperity of our institutions.

Their contributions were threefold, they cleared the track through the wilderness and here they were wedged in between kingly oppression and savage brutality, the one on the east, the other on the west, but with heroic courage and sacrifice unsurpassed in the annals of mankind they brought thereout a civilization that has elicited the applause of the world, and has caused downtrodden humanity in all lands to look up with inspiration and hope. Such was the patriotism manifested by the people in southern Piedmont Virginia in the first one hundred years of this republic.

In the unsettled times antedating the American Revolution, many sturdy colonists with rare vision, seeing the coming storm and hearing the mutterings of distant thunder, wishing to place themselves in the most strategic position to successfully meet the inevitable conflict, moved their all to the mountains of Virginia and it was these people who formed Henry County in 1776, and named it in honor of Patrick Henry who lived here in his latter days on a farm six miles east of Martinsville.

At this time the eastern boundary was well defined, but as was the custom in those days the western frontier extended to the heads of the water courses and it was not until 1854 that, by an Act of the Legislature, the western boundary was accurately fixed. The Act, however, provided that the same was not to be established by law until the voters of Penn's Store and Blackberry precincts approved it.

The first courthouse was on a hill just northeast of where the Stanley

Furniture Factories now stand, a few miles northwest of Martinsville, and the clerk's office was two miles across the river therefrom. At the meeting of the courts, presided over by five justices, the clerk brought the court papers across the river in a basket, and if the river was past fording there was, of course, no clerk and no court. While the justice then administered was delivered amid crude surroundings, yet it came from the rock of integrity, prompt, pure and undefiled.

The contributions of these people, under the leadership of such men as Abram Penn, George Waller, Joseph Martin, John Redd and George Hairston, not only to the fortunes of the Revolution but also to the establishment of local peace and order, were large. Indeed, the prayers made by the Methodist circuit rider, rendered in laying the foundation of our civilization, what cannot be estimated, nor has such patriotism been confined to the activities of the Revolution but in every fight for constitutional liberties since those days, Henry County men have participated and the bones of some of them are now resting in the war-worn fields of France.

The original settlers were of English and Saxon blood. Abram Penn and George Waller formed a company and took the lead in the formation of a settlement.

Many descendants of these pioneers still live within the bounds of the county. Both were Revolutionary patriots and participated in the Battle of King's Mountain, claimed by Thomas Jefferson, as "the joyful turning of the tide." Bancroft, the historian, observes that "the Battle of King's Mountain changed the aspect of the war."

The remains of George Waller lie at present in an unmarked grave in Fieldale, while two of his descendants, George and Stuart Pannill, volunteers from Henry County to the World War, "sleep the sleep that knows no ending" at Chateau Thierry, France.

Major John Redd, Henry County pioneer and one of the strongest men of his time, was a witness to the surrender of Cornwallis at Yorktown.

Among the earlier settlers of Henry County were the Penns, Wallers, Redds, Minters, Hords, Laniers, Joneses, Hairstons, Roysters, Martins, Gravelys, Bassetts, Stultzes, Burches, Spencers, Dillards, Bondurants, Richardsons, Dyers, and others, many of whose descendants still reside in the county of their forbears of colonial days.

Henry County, Virginia, is considered of enough geologic importance to warrant an extensive survey, which is now being carried on by the United States Geological Survey in coöperation with the State of Virginia. The purpose of this survey is to determine the mineral and hydraulic resources of the area, and to aid in the development of enterprises of this nature.

FARMING IN THE EARLY DAYS

After the Revolutionary War agriculture made steady progress. From the first settlements in Virginia till the mountains were reached the tendency was to take up large boundaries of land, the plantations usually embraced hundreds or even thousands of acres. Under the slave system they were cultivated and made profitable.

The surface of the farming land in Henry and Patrick Counties varies from steep hills to rich bottom land. Preparing the hillsides for planting crops was, of course, a difficult matter; oxen, horses and mules were used to draw the plow.

We learn that at first two men were required to manage a one-horse plow, one to lead the horse and the other to hold the plow, and that furrows were run up and down hill instead of circling around.

George King, an early settler in the Leatherwood neighborhood, learned to guide the horse with plow lines and hit upon the plan of running furrows around the hill instead of up and down.

Leatherwood has the distinction of being one of the most progressive sections of Henry County, one citizen of that community is credited with having built the first rock flue by means of which the beautiful, fragrant yellow tobacco was cured, the kind that made Henry County famous.

Upon the large plantations the landlord had an overseer who superintended the slaves, and the landlady, with the help of the brightest and most capable of the female servants, looked after the household affairs and reared the sons and daughters of the family according to the traditions of her ancestors, many of whom were of royal blood.

After the Revolution the population, both white and black, increased amazingly. Better homes were built and the big house ideally located, with the groups of smaller houses located about the premises, gave the place the appearance of a village. There were the kitchen, smokehouse, weaving house and other places in which the work of the household was carried on. In the smokehouse hundreds of pounds of bacon and tubs of snow-white lard were always on hand.

A few hundred yards distant was the "cabin row" where the slaves lived. From amongst these the cooks, butlers, maids, coachmen, weavers, spinners and seamstresses were chosen and trained, their specialties being often handed down from one generation to another.

In the wealthy families each young lady had her own particular maid, usually a gift from her parents, and each young gentleman his "body servant" (valet).

The mistress of the mansion kept her basket of keys always at hand in her sitting room, and, with the cook, went into the smokehouse and store rooms and gave out supplies for a meal or for a day.

As the houses were usually built on high ground and the water supply obtained from springs several hundred yards distant, bringing up sufficient water for household use was a Herculean task and required the services of one or more servants almost constantly. The laundry was done in the summer under the shade of trees near the spring. A fire was made under a big iron pot, which rested on legs several inches from the ground, so that the fire could be replenished by thrusting dried limbs of trees gathered from the surrounding forest under it. The linen was washed, boiled in the big pot, rinsed and dried in the sun on bushes. Before the corrugated washboards came into use, the garments, if much soiled, were laid upon a flat, smooth rock and paddled to loosen the dirt. The paddles were made of very hard wood and were very smooth. In winter the water for laundry work was hauled to the house in barrels.

The telegraph apparatus came into use at a later period, but was installed by only a small percentage of the people. This apparatus consisted of a wire cable, on which a bucket could be sent sliding down hill and plunged into the spring, then by some arrangement of wires the dripping bucket, full of water, could be drawn to the starting place.

Ice was a luxury, practically unknown in the very early days, but after a time people dug ice houses after the fashion of a deep cellar with a roof over it and from a pond ice was cut and stored, well covered with straw and sawdust, for the summer. The spring house was a splendid substitute for ice. It was a small structure built across the branch that drained the cool water from the spring. Boxes were arranged so that jars of milk and crocks of butter could be kept in water at just the right temperature.

Until the introduction of cooking stoves, cooking was done in heavy iron utensils before an open fireplace in which beds of red hot coals had been prepared by burning plenty of well-seasoned wood. A broad hearth in front of the fireplace furnished space for the skillets and ovens in which baking and frying were done. These utensils were on legs and had covers or heavy lids

HOME OF JOHN REDD SMITH

Home of John Redd Smith, Martinsville, Virginia, built by his grandfather, James M. Smith, in 1841, from brick made by hand on the adjoining land and from timber cut from the adjacent forest. The boxwood and cedar planted by his grandmother about the same time. Never belonged to but three men, the builder, his son, the late Dr. James M. Smith, and the present owner. Was used for a hospital by the Federal forces, under General John A. Palmer, in the latter part of the Civil War, while for a short time quartered in Martinsville, and two of the Federal soldiers are buried in the garden in the rear.

so that coals could be put on top as well as underneath. Pots in which meat and vegetables, hominy, etc., were boiled were hung on cranes or set securely on the logs. Pot hooks were an indispensable adjunct to the kitchen equipment, as the ovens, pots and skillets had places in which these could be hooked and the utensils lifted conveniently.

Corn pone and ash cake were delicious when made by a real cook. Ash cake was made just as any other corn bread—meal with a little salt mixed with cold water. The flat stones that formed the bottom of the fireplace were raked clear of the red hot coals, embers being left upon sufficient space upon which to put the cakes of dough, after being patted into shape by the brown hands of the cook, with a grace and skill which were inimitable. Then standing some distance from the scorching heat the round cake of dough was "flung" into the right spot, covered with hot embers and coals heaped on top. At just the right time the cake was taken out, washed in cold water while very hot and a nice, brown, thick-crusted cake was ready to be eaten with butter and a glass of cool milk—a meal fit for a king!

In later years one of the negro men made a trip to the Middle West with some traders, and while there married and brought back a wife—a tall mulatto woman said to have some Indian blood in her veins. On one occasion she was told by her husband to make an ash cake for supper. After puzzling over the matter she concluded that an ash cake must contain ashes as an ingredient, so she mixed part meal and part ashes and baked it, much to the amusement of the other colored folk and disgust of the husband.

There was in the household usually a black mammy or chief nurse who took a leading part in caring for the white folks' children and was loved by them next to their own parents.

The weavers made, besides the jeans (woolen cloth for the men's clothing), cotton checks and "linsey woolsey" for the women's dresses, plain cotton cloth as well as brilliant colored blankets woven in intricate patterns, some of which are in use at the present time, though the old ones are kept as souvenirs. There was some flax raised, especially in Patrick County, and the cloth woven from it is exceedingly strong and durable, pieces of it over a hundred years old still retain its strength.

TRAVEL AND TRANSPORTATION

In another chapter we have an account of rolling tobacco to market many miles distant in hogsheads, prepared with shafts fastened to the ends of the hogsheads so that they would turn after the fashion of a wheel, the mule or horse hitched as if to a wagon. Wagons, carts and plows were drawn by oxen to a large extent about the farms. Until the advent of rail-roads and motor vehicles, covered wagons were the principal means of hauling tobacco and other produce to market, bringing back goods of every description to supply the storekeepers or private families. The wagons were strongly built, roomy and the thick covers provided a good shelter and sleeping quarters when camp was made.

Travel was necessarily slow as a two or four-horse wagon, loaded heavily, drawn by horses or mules, could make only thirty or forty miles a day over roads frequently washed out in deep ruts and heavy with mud. Horseback was the earliest and most popular mode of travel. A man with a good horse, equipped with saddle and saddle bags, was considered well prepared for a journey of almost any length. He could stop when night overtook him at any farmhouse and food and lodging were freely given.

Carriages and buggies were in use also, especially for the well-to-do families, but doctors went from place to place to visit patients, lawyers rode from one county seat to another to attend court, young men and women rode for the pleasure of it and often went visiting or to church on horseback.

The side saddle was used by women and girls; to sit astride a horse in early times would have shocked the community almost to the point of hysterics, although the side saddle was a clumsy affair, much more danger-ous than the well-balanced saddle used by men and much harder on the horse, as the weight had a tendency to pull to one side. To add to the in-convenience for women, long riding skirts were considered absolutely indis-pensable, for, by no chance must a lady's ankle be exposed to view. The ordinary riding skirt was made of straight widths of denim or alpaca sewed to a belt, which was buttoned around the waist and the skirt closed with buttons down the side. The riding habit was a better looking affair, worn by those who could afford something better than the riding skirt. The habit consisted of a long skirt with a basque which fitted snugly; this worn with a becoming hat made a costume which was pretty and picturesque.

SOCIAL LIFE

Social life in Henry and Patrick Counties kept up a standard equal to any in this, or any other country, for let it be remembered that the early settlers were descended from noble or highly respectable English, French, Scotch, Welch or Irish families.

On the large plantations the people were well prepared and enjoyed dispensing hospitality, so, naturally, the home was the social center and what could be gayer than the gatherings of young people for house parties. There were always fiddlers and banjo players available and dancing could be indulged in until the morning hours. During the day before the party dispersed, horseback riding was enjoyed and frequently all hands joined in following the hounds in a real fox hunt. Fox hounds in large numbers were almost always an adjunct to every gentleman's premises.

Visiting among the older people, as well as among the young, was a very different matter from that of the present time. People went for visits and usually spent the day. An unexpected guest was a source of pleasure as people with well-filled larders, trained servants and time to spare, enjoyed entertaining their friends. News traveled slowly in those days; writing and receiving letters were events of importance. Mail was carried on horseback in leather pouches, and people had to go or send to the post office for their mail, in many cases several miles distant. Usually, however, the post office was located in a country store, which carried groceries and general merchandise and going for the mail could be combined with a shopping expedition.

The country church was also a real social center. There was time before and after services for the young people to meet and enjoy each other's society, but the climax was the "protracted meeting." There were two services a day with an intermission of an hour or two for lunch and social intercourse. Families went with well-filled lunch baskets and a real picnic lunch was spread underneath the trees. After lunch all returned to the church for the afternoon service.

THE TOURNAMENT

Although the Tournament—relic of the days of chivalry—has been relegated to the past, many of the Henry and Patrick people can recall the pleasure and excitement of these gala occasions, even as late as sometime in the "seventies."

A place was chosen for the track—a long stretch of level ground. Heavy poles were set firmly along the side, at intervals, with arms upon which rings two or three inches in diameter were placed. These arms extended over the track within reach of the rider's lance, which was a long, well-finished rod, perhaps four or five feet in length. In those days horseback riding was a real accomplishment, men, women, boys and girls were usually skilled riders.

For weeks and even months before the event, the Tournament was discussed by the young people and the girl who had an admirer who was to enter the lists, was envied by the less fortunate, and what better means could there be for a young man to win the admiration of a young lady than by making such a gallant appearance, win a crown or wreath and choose her for the "Queen of Love and Beauty."

When the eventful day arrived the young people for miles around appeared in carriages, buggies, etc., and took the best positions they could find along the track. The knights mounted on the finest horses the country afforded, wearing picturesque riding clothes, with broad sashes of brilliant colors, passing over one shoulder and under the arm on the opposite side, to float upon the breeze as they passed in splendid array to the starting point.

The field marshal, with much dignity and ceremony, took charge of the program and when all was ready called the knights by their titles which they or their lady loves had chosen. The knight whose name was announced dashed along the track at full gallop, catching the rings upon his lance. This was repeated until each knight had been given an opportunity to show his prowess. The one catching the greatest number of rings, while making the fastest time, was declared victor and, riding to the place where his chosen one sat, dropped the rings from his lance at her feet. The knight catching the next largest number, the third and fourth repeated the ceremony of seeking out the one upon whom they wished to bestow their favor.

The grand ball followed in the evening and upon a sort of dais in the ballroom the ladies chosen by their knights appeared in their order. The first gallant placing a glittering crown upon the head of the one he had chosen "Queen of Love and Beauty," making an appropriate speech. The other knights followed in turn, placing wreaths less ornate upon the heads of their chosen ones.

Then the "Royal Quadrille" was led by the first knight and his queen, this being participated in only by the successful knights and their partners, after that the other guests joined in the dancing.

OUR GREAT STAPLE—TOBACCO

The cultivation of tobacco has always been a long, tedious process, and only in recent years have labor-saving devices been invented and they are not perfected even yet.

For the beginning of the crop plant beds are prepared in very early spring and the seed sown, tobacco seed so tiny that in order to handle them they must be mixed with dry earth or ashes.

In early times there was no well-known protection for the little plants against the frosts or especially the flies that delight to devour them. These flies are amongst the most persistent of pests. Planters now use thin, white cotton cloth for covering the plant beds. This is a great protection against frosts and puts the tobacco fly entirely out of business. Traveling through the country these cloth-covered beds on the rich hillsides have the appearance of patches of snow. One planter in early times hit upon a plan most unique, by which he saved his tobacco plants. He made two plant beds close together and when the tender plants began to show themselves and the flies were getting ready for a feast, the planter would take a hen with a newly hatched brood of chicks and put the hen in a coop between the plant beds. The baby chicks having the freedom of the premises, as is their wont, would swarm over the beds like animated puffballs keeping up such motion that the flies could not settle down and get in their deadly work. When this brood grew large enough to injure the plants another newly hatched brood was put on duty, and the plants saved until transplanting time. Transplanting was then done entirely by hand but a device is now in use, which makes the work of planting easier and more rapid. This device, a funnel-shaped implement, with a hole through which the plant passes, is inserted into the ground. Water contained in the implement is forced around the roots of the plant and with a twist the earth is pressed close. No mechanical device has yet been invented to rid the growing tobacco plants of the worms which invariably appear. Some planters have again resorted to the barnyard for aid. Turkeys when allowed the freedom of the tobacco patch will walk about under the plants, casting an appraising eye underneath the beautiful broad leaves and pick off and devour the destructive worms. Worming for the most part, however, must be done by hand. The worms are of a bright green color just the shade of the growing tobacco and grow to the thickness of a lead pencil or larger, and two or three inches long. Unless the plants are kept free from them, they get in their "chewing" before the other fellow has a chance, leaving holes in the leaves which injure the tobacco materially.

In order to develop the full richness of tobacco, the tops of the plants must be plucked out at a certain stage of the growth and leaves near the ground must be pulled off.

It is essential to keep the fields well cultivated as weeds must be kept out.

Late summer and early fall are also anxious times for the tobacco grower; he must know just when the plants are ripe for cutting and curing. Frost is a deadly enemy of the plants, turning the leaves dark and injuring the sale of the tobacco.

Until recently the entire stalk was cut, a portion of it split, so that it could be put astride the sticks and hung upon rafters in the barn several feet above the flues. The later method is to pluck the leaves from the stalk, and tie them in bundles by a sort of weaving process with cord. Flues have been improved and thermometers aid the curers in keeping the right temperature, a very important point in curing tobacco. The work is still unfinished. When first cured the tobacco is very dry and must be handled with great care. In early times the planters had to wait for a season of rain, so that the tobacco would absorb enough moisture to render handling it without injury possible. Now there are other means of bringing it "in order."

As much fertilizer must be used to produce fine tobacco and that is very expensive, the planter is decidedly out of luck if he does not receive a good price for his crop.

HENRY COUNTY TOBACCO

Some time ago the inimitable and lovable Henry Grady was rambling through Lancaster County, Pennsylvania, when he met an intelligent looking man on the highway and asked him this question. "What is the explanation of the fact that Lancaster County is the richest agricultural county in America?" Came the swift and terse answer, "Tobacco." Some time later, when wandering through a desolate region of North Carolina where (with apologies to Gen. Sheridan) a crow would have to take his knapsack if he flew across it, he met a down-and-out looking man and fired this question at him, "Brother, what is the matter with this God-forsaken country?" "Tobacco."

Grady contended that both answers were correct. The difference was this: in Lancaster County they raised almost everything else that they needed, and the fine or high-priced cigar tobacco was the "apex" of the "pyramid." In current English it was their money crop. In the North Carolina district they raised tobacco, sold it, bought bacon and ate it, bought grain and fed it, bought whiskey and drank it, and undertook to buy everything else with the little money left after the annual settlement with the merchant who furnished supplies or overhead expenses.

For many years the Henry County farmers have conformed too closely to the methods of the North Carolina district farmers, as described above. The gospel of diversified crops has been preached to them in season and out, but has usually fallen upon deaf ears. Thus, the Henry County tobacco grower has missed a great opportunity. Nobody that knows or has ever questioned the statement that the very finest chewing tobacco in the world grows in Henry County.

When I (the writer) was an undergraduate medical student in New York City, something over a half century ago, I walked into a fashionable tobacco store on Broadway and requested the proprietor to show me a plug of the very finest chewing tobacco. Without the slightest hesitation he reached up to a shelf and took down a plug of B. F. Gravely's "Superior," and laid it on the counter with an air of finality, as if there could be no room for discussion. The sample that he showed me was raised and manufactured in my native district of Henry County.

Some years later, in Jacksonville, Florida, I approached a retail dealer in tobacco, and in a business way showed him some samples of tobacco manufactured in Martinsville, wholly out of the genuine Henry County leaf. A tired expression came over his face and he said, "Oh, everything is Henry County, Henry County!" The plain implication was true, namely, that all over the country the name of this famous tobacco region is counterfeited on tobacco that was never even shipped through Henry County. "Imitation is the sincerest flattery."

Many years ago, when the great explorer, Henry M. Stanley, forced an expedition through six hundred miles of seemingly impenetrable forests to the rescue of Emin Bey, and when he and Emin met formally on the shore of the lake, it seemed the proper thing for them to exchange diplomatic presents. Emil Bey's gift to Stanley included a pound of Peyton Gravely's "Honey Dew" tobacco.

ORIGIN OF ONE OF THE GREATEST TOBACCO MANUFACTURING ENTERPRISES IN THE WORLD

By MAJOR A. D. REYNOLDS

WHEN my father was eighteen years of age, my grandfather had him roll his crop of tobacco in a water-tight hogshead over an Indian trail, through the mountainous country to Lynchburg, Virginia, to be gone about ten days. He returned very much discouraged by the prices received and induced his father to let him chisel a hole in a chestnut tree and put a beam through it something like a cider press; this he did and manufactured his tobacco into twists which he carried off to South Carolina in peddling wagons.

He did so much better than he did with his leaf that he put two of his negro men on what we called the Rich Hollow where they grew about six thousand pounds of tobacco, and he raised about twice that at the home place, then bought as much more from the negroes, all of which he disposed of in South Carolina.

Seeing the cotton presses down South made from wood on beams and threaded with wooden threads with roofs over them, he saw that this was a greater protection to the tobacco than the tree press, and quite an improvement on the latter. This press had two levers, each forty feet long, with a mule hitched to one end of the lever and the factory hands at the other.

While this was a great improvement over the cider press, being of a progressive nature, he bought the iron screws with the iron lever which he said to me he did not mind investing in as he did not think they could make any further improvement over the iron press, but before his death we introduced hydraulic pressure which was a great improvement over the other processes.

I ran his factory as a partner for five years and made sufficient money to move to Bristol, Tennessee, and start a factory on my own account, leaving my father with greatly increased capital.

I sold out to my brother, R. J. Reynolds, and he ran the business for three years, then sold out to my brother, H. H. Reynolds, who ran the business several years, and sold out to Walter Reynolds and Robert Critz (my youngest brother and brother-in-law). A few years later, after my father's death, they closed out and moved to Bristol, Tennessee, where they remained for a few years, then brother R. J. induced them to wind up the business in Bristol and take stock in the R. J. Reynolds Tobacco Company in Winston, North Carolina.

DEVELOPMENT AND GROWTH OF THE R. J. REYNOLDS TOBACCO COMPANY

The R. J. Reynolds Tobacco Company was established in 1875, with a capital of $7,500 and incorporated under the laws of New Jersey, in 1899, the capital stock had then reached the figures $2,100,000.

Afterwards the American Tobacco Company obtained control through the acquisition of more than half of the outstanding capital stock. The company thus came, to some extent at least, under the control of the old tobacco trust until the dissolution, in 1911, of the old American Tobacco Company, under court order resulting from the suit of the government against that company under the antitrust laws.

In compliance with the ruling of the court, the American Tobacco Company divested itself of its holdings of Reynolds Tobacco stock through distribution of such holdings pro rata among its common shareholders.

Since its reëstablishment in the field as an independent, the R. J. Reynolds Tobacco Company has experienced a truly remarkable growth. Each year it has succeeded in securing its full share, and more, of the constantly increasing demand which the industry as a whole has experienced.

As the first company to sense the developments which have so completely revolutionized the tobacco industry during the past two decades, when cigarette production has increased enormously, while consumption of other forms of tobacco has declined or remained stationary. The R. J. Reynolds Tobacco Company introduced, in 1915, the Camel brand cigarette, the first to have the inexpensive blended cigarette which has proved so popular, and which is to-day by far the most important branch of the tobacco industry.

At the present time the most powerful companies in this field are the ones which recognized this development, and who were aggressive in the marketing and advertising of this particular brand of cigarette. As the pioneer in the popular-priced, blended cigarette field, the R. J. Reynolds Tobacco

Company has been foremost in this branch of the industry and has maintained a leading position in the face of constantly increasing competition.

While the company is best known for its commanding position in the cigarette field, it occupies a leading place as a producer of both chewing and smoking tobacco. Prince Albert smoking tobacco was the outcome of many years' patient study and exhaustive experiments. When the manufacturing process was perfected, and the brand placed on the market, in 1908, it was an instantaneous success, which has been enormously augmented with the passing years.

From a comparatively modest beginning, the R. J. Reynolds Tobacco Company has grown to such stupendous proportions that the name and fame have reached to the uttermost parts of the civilized world.

INDIAN CORN

Indian corn has always been the crop next in importance to tobacco, the latter being the crop that brings the farmer cash if he has good luck. Some wheat, rye and oats have been produced but to a limited extent.

Fruits, especially apples and peaches have been plentiful in Henry and Patrick Counties; some cherries are produced and quantities of berries grow wild and can be had for the picking.

In times past, in the fall of the year, gathering and shucking the corn, especially the latter, was a real festival. Fodder pulling preceded the gathering of the corn by some weeks, the blades were pulled off of the stalks by hand, tied into bundles, dried and stacked so that the top of the stack formed a cone and the rains would not soak in. Some time in October the corn was gathered, hauled to a place near the corncribs and piled upon the ground. Each family had an evening set apart for the shucking. Neighbors both black and white were called in and soon after supper time the work and fun began, and was kept up until a great pile of gleaming corn was on one side and a mountain of shucks on the other, no matter how late the hour.

Singing corn songs was an indispensable part of the program. The songs were given out, and led by a colored man who could cut more "monkey shines" than any one else. He stood on the crest of the big pile of corn, waving his arms and urged on the work by the words of his song, while the crowd as they joined in the singing tore the shucks from the ears, which they sent whizzing through the air to the growing mound, all to the accompaniment of the songs and the capers of the leader.

Mill situated on North Fork of Leatherwood Creek, near Belmont, the Martin estate. This picture was made from a negative taken by L. G. Pedigo, thirty-three years ago, and still preserves the wonderful contrasts and minute detail.

The drinks were a great feature of the occasion and jugs and flasks were passed at intervals all through the evening. The closing ceremony consisted of catching the plantation owner, whether he resisted or not, swinging him to the shoulders of two of the huskiest of the men and marching around the house three times to the tune of the closing song.

All that is changed now, the corn is pulled from the shuck which is left on the stalk, hauled to the storage place and the stalk cut with fodder and shucks (or husks), stacked and used for winter food for cattle.

CORN SHUCKING SONG (*Uncle Remus*)

Oh, honey, w'en you year dat roan mule whicker—
(Hey O! Hi O! Up'n down de Bango!)
W'en you see Mister Moon turnin' pale an gittin' sicker—
(Hey O! Hi O! Up'n down de Bango!)
Den it's time fer to handle dat corn a little quicker—
(Hey O! Hi O! Down de Bango!)
If you wanter git a smell er ol Marster's jug er licker
(Hi O! Miss Cindy Ann!)

Oh, work on boys! Give dese shucks a mighty wringin'—
(Hey O! Hi O! Up'n down de Bango!)
Fo de Boss come aroun' a dangin' and a dingin'
(Hey O! Hi O! Up'n down de Bango!)

Git up en move aroun'! Set dem big hans ter swingin'
(Hey O! Hi O! Up'n down de Bango!)
Git up'n shout loud! Let de w'ite folks year yo singin'!
(Hi O! Miss Cindy Ann!)

Fer de los' ell an yard is a huntin' fer de mornin'
(Hi O! Git along, go 'way!)
En she'll ketch up wid us fo we ever git dis corn in,
(Oh, go way Cindy Ann.)

THE PARTISAN LEADER—
A Prophesy

By JUDGE BEVERLY TUCKER (1836)

NO history of Patrick County would be complete without a somewhat elaborate review of a famous novel the scenes of which were laid in the high mountains of that picturesque region. I allude to the "Partisan Leader," written by Judge Beverly Tucker, in 1836, and printed serially in Washington City until it was suppressed by the government authorities under the old "Alien and Sedition Laws" of that time.

This book, written in the form of a novel, is the most remarkable instance of fulfilled political prophesy in the history or literature of this country. The story was projected twenty years into the future. It foreshadowed a secession movement among the southern states, led at first by the states south of Virginia, the hesitation of Virginia to join the movement, the development of parties and factions in Virginia, based upon the issues involved. There were original Union men, whose hearts were torn between their devotion to the Union and their lifelong belief in the doctrine of state sovereignty. A striking prophetic detail is this: That one prominent citizen of this kind, as a pledge of his love for his own state, named a daughter born in this period of stress, Virginia. As a matter of historic fact a very prominent citizen of Virginia, an original Union man who followed his state into the Confederacy, named a daughter born at this time "Virginia Secessia." Her intimate friends to this day call her "Secie." A remarkable feature of this entire bit of prophesy is that the author, in predicting the secession of the southern states and the organization of a Southern Confederacy, missed the date of the actual event by only five years.

The original printing of this remarkable book was conducted somewhat secretly and was intended to be circulated in the South.

The details of this plan were intrusted to a man by the name of Duff Green. The surname of this adventurous man is common and familiar in all parts of any English-speaking country. The Christian name, Duff, is far less common and the combination is probably rare, therefore, I am strongly under the impression that I met and conversed with this highly interesting character in Richmond in the winter of 1881-2. He was about old enough to have done this secret printing job in 1836, had iron gray hair and beard, seemed to be about seventy-five years of age, but was still active, energetic and aggressive. He was a representative in the Legislature from some county in the extreme northern part of the state, and he was serving as General Mahone's "lieutenant" in the command of the readjuster caucus.

L. G. P.

THE WAR BETWEEN THE STATES, 1861–1865

IN the War Between the States Henry and Patrick Counties contributed honorable parts to the history of Virginia. At the beginning there was a strong sentiment against secession and in this feeling the people were in strict accord with General Lee.

When Virginia cast her lot on the side of the South and the Confederacy, a great majority of the people followed the gallant Lee or gave aid and comfort to the armies of the Southland.

As brave a company of soldiers as ever drew sword in defense of their country went out from Martinsville, on June 3, 1861, under the leadership of Peter R. Reamy.

For a short period Martinsville was invaded by a Federal force under command of General Palmer who ran for president on the gold standard ticket in 1896. He had headquarters on Church Street and established a hospital.

Henry County furnished another unit designated as Company A, Virginia Infantry, with the late Cabell Hairston as Captain.

WAR EXPERIENCES OF MAJOR A. D. REYNOLDS OF PATRICK COUNTY, VIRGINIA

I was something less than fourteen years of age in April, 1861, yet I was anxious to volunteer in the first company that left the county.

My father suggested that if I wanted to be a soldier I should go to the Virginia Military Institute and prepare myself to be a good soldier, but I could not get an appointment there until I was about fifteen years of age.

After being there a year I returned home, expecting to return to the Institute, but the enrolling officer insisted on my going to the court house where the reserve forces were organizing a company. I was elected captain of the company when I was a little over sixteen years of age. We were ordered to report to Dublin, Virginia, where I drilled my company for about thirty days, then the regiment was ordered to Christiansburg to march across through Giles County and meet about three hundred Federal soldiers with a lot of recruits with the deserters of that country, who had been ordered to burn New River bridge.

MAJOR ABRAM D. REYNOLDS

From a photograph taken in later life, many years after the close of the War Between the States.

When we reached Pilot Mountain I was ordered to take my company and one other and deploy a skirmish line and come in on the opposite side of the mountain, as we had been informed that they were in the trenches. Taking them by surprise they ran like wild animals and not a single one of our guns would go off, as the government had issued us old guns that had caps, and we had been marching through the woods in the rain, so we chased them to New River, about six miles and found that they had crossed the river so long before we reached there that we gave up the chase and were ordered back to Dublin, our regular camp.

The prospective colonel was a dissipated man and I feared he might be elected, so I applied for a transfer to an eastern army, which was granted, and I was ordered to Danville, Virginia. As I had my company well drilled I had them out the next day on parade ground and Colonel R. E. Withers, Commandant, saw me drilling my company and as the regiment was organized the next day, Lieutenant Davis of my company was anxious to become the captain of the company, so to my surprise he nominated me for major when the colonel was nominated. Colonel Withers put the vote without any remarks and the same when the lieutenant was nominated, but when Lieutenant Davis nominated me for major, Colonel Withers pointed to me and said, "I second that nomination," which I always thought he did because he saw how well I had my company drilled. There were two other candidates for the office who had been out for several weeks, but I received more votes than both of them.

Our duties at Danville were to guard the prisoners, and when our armies needed reënforcements, we were ordered to different places. I was in Richmond at the close of the war, and passed over the bridge with the last troops after President Davis passed over to Danville, Virginia, where we were ordered. This was after General Lee had surrendered. President Davis remained in Danville several days. While I was down in the city my colonel called the regiment together and disbanded them, so when President Davis called for volunteers to go with him to the Trans-Mississippi Department, I with my other volunteers agreed to go with him. So many of us volunteered that he did not have transportation enough for all of us. President Davis came to the platform and congratulated us on our loyalty and ordered the quartermaster to issue each one of us a horse and saddle, and for us to organize ourselves into a regiment and proceed to Salem, Virginia, and unite with General Lomax' command. We rode all day to get to Martinsville, but I am sorry to say that a great many of the volunteers did not proceed with us all the way to Martinsville, where we met a great many of Lomax' command who said that the whole command had been disbanded.

I put my horse in the livery stable and fed him and had my supper and rode all night to my father's home in Patrick County. I arrived there about sunrise where I found my horse that I had sent home by a colored boy that had been with me in the army, hitched to the rack just ready to start to Greensboro to try to intercept me. He had a letter from my father saying "My dear son, can't you see that the war is over? Don't be foolish, but come home and let us try to rebuild our lost fortunes." I never knew until that morning that my father loved me so much; he had always been such a good disciplinarian that I thought that he was most too strict with me, but when he saw me ride to the gate he ran to meet me and threw his arms around me and said, "My son, Stoneman's raid has been here, carried off all my able-bodied negro men and mules, and tore up my crops and things generally, but since you have come home alive, it is all right, I could never have replaced you but we can rebuild our lost fortune."

I remember one of our neighbors coming home with us from church. In talking about the war and his losses he said to my father, that there was no hope for them to rally and regain their lost fortune. My father said, "Joe, it is with you as it was with a Mississippi farmer when the flood covered up the cotton and corn in June. One said he was ruined and grieved over his losses and did nothing to regain the same, until it was too late to do anything, while his neighbor set his plows going and in a short time you could not tell that the crop had been covered up. The sediment was so rich the crop soon recovered." Father said, "Just so it is with us, Joe, for we never had such a rich sediment for making money. We have the experience and both have boys to do the work. Let us plan for them and in ten years we will have money equal to what we have lost." This was true with us, in ten years father, brother R. J. and myself had a hundred thousand or more.

The next morning after I returned from the army one of our soldiers called to see me and told me of the death of Mrs. George Hylton, who had given birth to twins. Her husband had returned to the army and had been captured so she was left almost helpless and supposed that her husband was dead. A dozen stragglers from Stoneman's raid had organized a battalion of deserters and was raiding over the country taking the horses, feed, what little grain and bacon there was, killing stock, and causing great terror. This raiding party had visited Mrs. Hylton's place several times, but this trip they entered her home and took her blankets, bedquilts, pillows, and such household things as they could carry with them. Mrs. Hylton's babies were only ten days old at this time, but this was more than she could endure so she rose up in bed and said, "Men, you have carried off my horses, my corn, my meat and fodder, and I never opened my mouth, but I can't live and see my bedding and quilts that I made with my own hands taken away." Just then a neighbor she knew, who was one of the raiders, rushed in and presented a pistol in her face—she fainted, but before she died, she said, "Tell Mr. Hill (the raider) that it is my religious duty to forgive him although I know he has murdered me, the law can deal with him as it should."

When he told me this I jumped to my feet and said, "If we have surrendered to a government that is going to tolerate such outrages as this I don't want to see it." So I got my horse and rode from house to house trying to make up fifty men to capture the three hundred, mostly deserters, who we did not fear, but the fathers and mothers would not let the soldiers go with me. Mothers would throw their arms around their sons and say, "My dear boy, you must not expose your life any more." So after several days we secured four more, we went to Center Meeting House in Henry County and, after preaching, I got the consent of the preacher to allow me to call for volunteers to join us in suppressing this lawless gang of robbers. Some thirty-five ex-soldiers joined us, and we rode to Harrison Floyd's and remained until midnight, as we wanted to reach the camp at sunrise. In going up the turnpike we were told that three hundred Yankees had gone on to reënforce Major Scott, who organized the battalion. It would have been foolhardy to have gone on with only forty men to capture six hundred, but I did not believe the Federal Government was going to back up such a gang as Scott had organized, however, if they left the pike and turned off to go to Scott's camp we would go to my father's and feed our horses and get our breakfasts. Just then, in passing Mr. Pryor Tatum's, I saw a light burning. I halted our command and inquired if it was a fact that three hundred Yankees had gone to reënforce Scott's raiders. He said that Captain Edd Penn with about forty men were going to arrest the Scott crowd, being the same mission we were on. So we found them at Mrs. Hylton's place waiting for the proper time to reach Scott's camp at sunrise.

When we reached a place near the camp we divided our forces with the agreement that at sunrise we would deploy our forces and charge the camp. When we got in sight of the camp we saw the United States flag floating and as half or more of our men were paroled, we decided that three of us had better approach the camp with a white flag and demand a surrender. An officer dressed in a Federal captain's uniform met us. Just then our men formed in line in sight of the house so this officer said, when we demanded a surrender, he would see what his men said. Instead of doing so he ran for the woods and I supposed he was Major Scott and I was anxious to capture him. I had my saber just ready to capture him, but the other squad under Captain Penn thought I was Major Scott and they fired a volley of shots at me, but the party I was pursuing fell as if he were dead. I raised my hat and no more shots were fired. One of the command rode up to me and said that I ran a great risk. They supposed I was Major Scott until I raised my hat. He said this officer they shot down had on a new pair of boots which this soldier who rode up to me pulled off and threw his away. I said, "Is he really dead?" He said, "Yes, so dead he can't kick." There was also a dead negro near by.

After we captured the crowd, I took some men down to bury the dead, but to my surprise the officer, who was one of the Brown boys, had crawled off, and only the negro remained. We marched our prisoners to Penn's Store and then turned them loose making them swear they would go home and be "good children." We sent our sheriff and two others to Richmond to see General Orr, military commander of the state, and reported the crimes that this band of robbers had committed, so he authorized the sheriff to organize a military court and have the criminals arrested and tried for the crimes committed.

We arrested those that had committed crimes and tried them for same. The one that murdered Mrs. Hylton was condemned to be shot and the others sent to prison. Many of them fled from the country.

Patrick County is divided by Bull Mountain. After we arrested the criminals on the south side, Major Acres, who was in charge of the north side, sent me to take my company to the north side where he was having trouble in arresting men who had organized another band of robbers similar to the one on my side. When we reached the neighborhood, after a night on Shooting Creek, our company came to a halt and Murray Turner, who had been commissioned as the leader of our two companies, called to me to pick five of my men to surround the house where six sons and a son-in-law resided. Four other squads were ordered to come on either side of the house, I was ordered on the south side. It had been the custom for the squad coming on the side the door was on to enter the house and arrest the criminals. As my company had volunteered to assist Major Acres, I was surprised to find we had been ordered to the side the door was on, so I halted my squad of men to rally them by saying that if the north side boys were afraid to enter the house, let us show them that the south side boys were not afraid. I said, "I will lead you, you follow me and one other by my side." So three of us jumped the fence, and Washburn and myself walked up the steps and Samuel Penn just behind me, the others from fear, I suppose, failed to cross the fence. Our commander said to us just as we were starting not to expect to take these men alive; they had been hemmed in during the war and had shot their way out a number of times. This excited us all but when we entered the house we found they had just gone out. We heard them say, "Yonder they come," so we ran and reached the house much quicker than Mr. Turner expected and he took us for the robbers. We knew his voice when he called for us to halt, but we supposed he saw the robbers on the outside and we naturally raised our pistols and watched to see the blaze of his guns. Sam Penn being just behind me caught most of the load, and no doubt saved my life. Mr. Penn said very loud, "Oh Lord, I am killed by one of my friends." I saw that he was going to fall down the steps and I tried to catch him, but could not raise my right arm as I was shot within my right side and, trying to raise my arm, I said, "Sam, I think I am killed, too." So I fell over on a bed at the door to keep from falling. My comrade would have fallen down the steps but Mr. Turner ran and caught him and laid him down, he seemed to die before he laid him down.

My shock passed off. I rode home the next day twenty miles. My father met me with a carriage, but I could not stand the jar. This ball lodged against my shoulder blade and for years I could not raise my right arm, but I forced the use of it until the ball worked down and is just below the shoulder blade where it can be felt now.

This is a part of my life history that I have never given out before, but I am sure I did my native county a great service in ridding it of many of its worst men. Many of them left the county before we arrested them and several broke jail and left. Reconstruction days were darker in many respects than during the war. In other localities, where these marauders were allowed to dominate the community, they went so far as to sell the Confederates' land which was restored later, but many good families had to flee from their homes just as we would have done if they had been allowed to go on.

CIVILIZATION AND PROGRESS HANDICAPPED BY WAR

WELL may it be said:

"Give me the money that has been spent in war, and I will clothe every man, woman and child in raiment that kings might envy. I will build a schoolhouse in every valley and a church on every hill."

The original white settlers evidently followed the streams, Smith's and Mayo Rivers, as the easiest mode of reaching a place for a settlement. These settlements were scattered miles apart as the backwoodsmen wished large ranges and were full of the spirit of independence and adventure.

We have no record of any Indian massacre in Henry or Patrick Counties, but a great fear hung over the settlers and as told in another chapter, the forts afforded protection when an Indian raid was feared.

Until 1750 the country was sparsely settled, after that the population increased rapidly. Large land buyers began to come in and tracts of thousands of acres were, in some instances, purchased by one man, among them George Hairston who bought 30,000 acres and Patrick Henry 10,000. Then before agriculture was established on a firm basis the Revolutionary War called the men to arms. Hundreds left their homes, responding to the call, many never to return—taking from a sparse population some of the country's best builders.

After the close of the war the people, proud of victory and independence, turned in earnest to the cultivation of the soil. The leading crop was tobacco which, with slave labor, could be produced with little cost and great profit.

A great advance in real estate values had taken place, many fortunes were made or increased and better homes were built. Then again the war cry! England had persistently encroached upon the rights of Independent America, and there seemed to be no solution of the difficulties but to fight it out, thus the War of 1812 resulted. Men of Henry and Patrick responded, as was their wont, and many lives were blotted out.

The blight of war fell upon the country again in 1845, but the most disastrous of all was the horrible calamity of the War between the States. A large proportion of a generation of men hewn down, families divided in sentiment, brother's hand turned against brother, farms neglected, in many instances the work carried on only by slaves who were still faithful enough to work. There are many instances of the faithful service of the slaves in these two counties but the unrest caused by the talk of freedom had its effect. In her dire need the Confederate Government accepted the services of old and young—mere boys in many cases joining the ranks. (See war experiences of Major A. D. Reynolds.) All the innate courage of the women of our counties was brought out and strengthened. Women accustomed to every luxury of that time ate rough fare and wore homespun clothes if necessary. Throughout the South the refrain was heard,

> *"Our dress is plain and homespun*
> *Our hats palmetto, too,*
> *But then it shows for southern girls*
> *What southern girls can do."*

Sugar was scarce and extremely hard to get, salt, still more necessary, was so scarce at times that the earthen floors in the smokehouses containing the drippings from salted meat were dug up and boiled to secure what salt the earth contained. Rye was parched and ground to be used as coffee.

After the close of the war, with the sudden and almost unconditional freeing of the slaves, the whole scheme of life had to be readjusted. The men, those who came back, found a dreary and discouraging outlook, although many of the slaves were glad to retain their homes as hired servants of their former masters, and the work on farms and in households was resumed and gradually became more or less systematic, but four years of warfare left its impress which it took time and stout hearts to overcome.

From 1865 to 1914, unexampled progress was made, advancement in every line, then again thousands of Americans were called upon to face the horrors of modern, more than savage warfare, this time to leave home and country to fight a foreign foe in foreign lands, and a number went never to return. The Spanish War, in 1898, had cost dearly, short as it was, but the War between the States and the World War cost beyond human calculation.

SLAVERY IN OUR COUNTRY FROM DIFFERENT
POINTS OF VIEW

RESEARCH has proved that the first negroes landed at Jamestown in 1619, and others brought by early privateers were not reduced to slavery but to limited servitude, a legalized status of Indian, white and negro servants preceding slavery in most, if not all of the English mainland colonies.

Statutory recognition of slavery occurred in Virginia in 1661, in some of the New England colonies before that time. Perpetual slavery resulted gradually, the slaves being regarded as property just as any other possession and were inherited along with the land, ownership of which passed from one generation to another. They were valuable and such an important part of every gentleman's property that the very mention of disturbing the status of affairs aroused every fiber of his being.

They did the labor, attending to the personal wants of every member of the family, till labor was thought to be the especial business of the slave's life and not the white man's, especially in the high classes of society.

The cultivation of tobacco, which went so far in enriching our people, depended in a great measure upon slave labor. The plantation owner could ride over his broad lands, take a general view of the work being done under the supervision of an overseer; he then had leisure to read, discuss politics and entertain his friends with such hospitality as had never before been seen.

The sons and daughters had the best advantages for an education. Private instructors were engaged and many young men attended the University of Virginia and other colleges and universities. The girls in great numbers went to Salem Academy in Winston-Salem, North Carolina. For something like eighty years this life of ease and elegance existed under the plantation system.

Mills operated by water power increased in number, roads were built by slaves, fine dwellings were erected, the bricks of which they were built being made on the place, generally, and the lumber sawed in the near-by forest. Tobacco factories were operated, some very successfully, but agriculture was the greatest industry when the eternal question of States' Rights came up for solution and war jeopardized the nation. No wonder that when their age-old institutions were threatened and their ideals about to be sacrificed, they rushed to arms and fought as only men fight for homes and rights.

There were, on the other hand, men owning slaves who believed that the institution was fundamentally wrong, but were unable to do much to change the accepted customs of the majority. William F. Mills, of Horsepasture, Henry County, emancipated slaves by will and sent to Liberia seven slaves.

John Calloway living on his Smith River estate, eight miles from Martinsville, about that time, 1850, sent seven slaves to Liberia, "staking" them. He started about twenty more the next year but an injunction against sending them out was put into effect and they were arrested in transit and returned. Mr. Calloway's estate was involved in litigation and the slaves were never sent.

William M. Schoolfield, of near Horsepasture, Henry County, willed their freedom to about seven or eight slaves, mostly women and children, provided they elected to go to Liberia.

In the same district Francis Bannister had emancipated unknown numbers before this time.

HENRY COUNTY

By John Redd Smith

HENRY COUNTY men with characteristic courage and fortitude met the political convulsion of 1860–1866. Loyal Virginians they were, but with prophetic vision they could not fail to see the fallacy and hopelessness of secession and the strong men like C. Y. Thomas, J. M. Smith, George D. Gravely, C. W. Jones and many others who, with a fidelity to duty and a wisdom that could see beyond the clouds of the passing storm, stood like the rock of ages shielding our people from the hatreds of fanatical abolitionists and adventurous reconstructionists.

While the dear things of the North were spilling large quantities of sob stuff over the condition of the negro in "Uncle Tom's Cabin," it appeared that their tears blinded them to the fact that the South was only protecting property purchased from Yankee trade ships, and following the example set by New England, nor was South Carolina to be censured for making profitable an institution that Massachusetts had made a failure of. Though most people everywhere agree that the hand of Heaven was in the abolition of slavery and the preservation of the Union, yet the fact will ever remain that the attitude of the South in the matter of slavery was in obedience to a constitution that all Federal officers had sworn to hold inviolate.

In the same spirit and with the same wisdom they have adjusted the race question and there has never been any racial disturbances in Henry County. They felt like Paul, the preacher, and Calhoun, the publicist, that there must be a master class and a serving class in all well-ordered societies, and though man-made laws might make the negro the white man's political equal, yet it was God-made law that made the white man the intellectual and social superior, and without noise but with a determination that allowed no uncertainty, the superior race has maintained this law, but with such fairness that the racial differences are easily adjusted and without friction and industrial disturbances.

It being written that no man liveth to himself, these folk felt that no community could live alone, and so they early bestirred themselves in the matter of communication with the outside world. The first outlet to which they contributed was the Danville and Wytheville turnpike (often mentioned in the land records of the county) that entered the village in 1851. About 1880, Major W. T. Sutherlin, of Danville, knowing the richness and resources of this section, became interested in a railroad and with the encouragement of many of the leading citizens of Henry and Patrick Counties, built what was then called the Danville and New River Railroad, which extended from Danville, by Martinsville, to Stuart, and which has been taken over by, and is now a part of the Southern System. Ten years later our people feeling the need of further railway outlet, the late C. B. Bryant interested such men as Moomaw, Terry, Trout and Fishburn in Roanoke, and Reynolds, Fries, Haynes and Blair in Winston, and out of this came the Roanoke and Southern Railway that is now a part of the Norfolk and Western lines. With that eagerness to keep in the front of the outward march of progress, this people caught early the spirit of good roads, and while other counties were agitating state bond issues and asking other folks to do for them what they should do for themselves, Henry County went on at its own expense and built good roads leading to the center from all points, and to-day from Martinsville the State Capital can be reached in five hours and the National Capital in eight hours over a smooth public highway, and this year, by Martinsville, the most direct scenic and historical route through Virginia will be completed connecting Washington with Atlanta.

Tobacco being traditional in Virginia and at one time the currency, Henry County early developed its growth to such perfection that its production here became world known and while men like Ben Gravely, of Leatherwood, Will Spencer, of Spencer, Henry Lester, of Martinsville, Dick Reynolds, of Winston, Frank Penn, of Reidsville, and Jim Penn, of Danville, lived, the industry flourished here because these highly successful men shared with the producer their profits. With the passing of the old-time industry of tobacco, our leaders turned their attention to the development of other industries and there is now in Martinsville a diversity of industries that afford investment and employment in many lines of human endeavor.

MARTINSVILLE AND ITS BUILDERS

The town, located in 1793, and named for Joseph Martin, was built on land donated by George Hairston. The town struggled on as a village suffering many adversities, one of which was being victimized by the northern army in 1865, and was not incorporated until 1873, but now with soil, climate, raw material, labor, transportation and power facilities most favorable, the town has gone forward by leaps and bounds, increasing its population and business activities one hundred per cent. in the last few years, until to-day it is one of the most progressive centers in Virginia, owning its public utilities.

Cotton, tobacco, glass, silk, furniture, brick, milk production and electric power offer a variety of investment and employment equal to the demands of any community.

Through the foresight of the late A. D. Witten and J. D. Bassett, aided by many other able local men, our community occupies first place in the furniture industry of the Commonwealth of Virginia and a close second in all the south.

THE BUILDERS OF MARTINSVILLE

Mr. Sigmund Putzel was one of the early merchants, opening a general merchandise establishment about the year 1850. He was very successful and accumulated property.

Mr. Roland Bryant had a cabinet shop on Fayette Street, where excellent work was done in serving the public.

Dr. Clarence P. Kearfott was a druggist locating in Martinsville in 1882. Throughout his life he had the confidence and esteem of the people of the entire community.

Mr. Jesse Ben Lavinder was one of the successful merchants of the town.

Mr. John P. Lavinder also kept a general mercantile establishment and erected the best business building in town at that time.

Joe Gregory, son of Mrs. Roland Bryant and her former husband, kept a confectionery.

The Peoples National Bank was the first establishment of that kind in the town.

The tobacco factory of Lester and Griggs has been mentioned. Those following were: The Browns, Dudleys, Englishes, from Franklin County, the Spencers, from the Spencer Community in Henry County, the Penns, from Patrick, Henry C. Lester, from Figsboro, Henry County.

Other business men who came a little later were: A. D. Witten, from Tazewell, C. B. Keesee, from Danville, S. S. Stephens, from Montgomery, J. C. Greer, from Franklin, C. D. Keffer, from Franklin, John Read, from Bedford, and many others.

HENRY COUNTY COURT HOUSE AND CONFEDERATE MONUMENT
Martinsville, Virginia

Along in the nineties more than a thousand people were engaged in working tobacco here, paying to the government an annual revenue of around half a million dollars.

Colonel Pannill Rucker and his father-in-law, B. F. Stephens, built largely in the tobacco industry which about 1905, along with the Spencer interests, were taken over by the Reynolds Company.

After the decline of the tobacco business, Messrs. Stephens, Witten, Keesee, Burch and others turned their attention to the furniture business, then began the remarkable revival of industrial life which we now enjoy.

THE HENRY COUNTY BAR

By JOHN REDD SMITH

THE Henry County Bar, a quarter of a century ago, had brilliant members and is still noted for men of that type.

George L. Richardson (Guinea) was noted for splendid oratory and was once a member of the Legislature.

Colonel C. B. Bryant was a member of the bar. (See sketch.) Mr. C. Y. Thomas, George W. Booker and Colonel William Martin were the older members. Messrs. Thomas and Booker had been members of the Legislature and Colonel Martin had been a member of the Constitutional Convention of 1851.

Mr. George D. Gravely was at the bar about this time and later practiced with his son, George L. Gravely, under the firm name of George D. Gravely and Son.

Samuel A. Anderson began the practice of law here, later moved to Richmond and was soon recognized as a leading lawyer, enjoyed a large practice as consulting attorney and was one of the revisors of the code with Judge Burke, of Lexington, and Judge Hutton, of Abingdon, all of whom died about the same time a year or so ago. At one time Mr. Anderson was associated with Judge Stafford G. Whittle in Martinsville.

Judge S. J. Mullins, then living upon a large estate on Mayo River, later moving to Martinsville, was at one time judge of the county court. His son, Henry G. Mullins, was later judge of that court.

Judge Mullins was succeeded by George L. Dillard, son of Dr. John R. Dillard, of Spencer, Virginia. Judge Dillard moved to Bluefield, West Virginia, and is now a judge of a court in that state.

Henry M. Ford was the judge of the circuit court here under the readjuster régime. He moved to Lynchburg where he died many years ago. He was an uncle of the Ford Brothers, of Martinsville.

Judge N. H. Hairston was judge of the county court here for a number of years. Later he moved to Roanoke where he died in 1927.

During the last years of his practice in Martinsville he was associated with W. H. Gravely.

Herbert G. Peters began the practice of law here. He was a member of both Houses of the Legislature and while in the Senate he formed a partnership with W. F. Rhea, of Bristol, Tennessee, and for thirty years he there engaged in a most successful career. He died in 1926.

Wythe M. and William M. Peyton, of Salem, Virginia, were members of the bar. The former was more interested in education than in law. He was one time principal and later superintendent of schools in Martinsville.

John W. Carter, a native of the county and father of the present member of the bar of that name, began the practice of law here in the eighties. He held a leading position until his death in 1914.

Jack Dillard, son of a distinguished jurist of North Carolina, and uncle of our townsman, W. L. Pannill, was here for a while at the bar, about 1890, but returned to his native state and is now one of the leading lawyers in western North Carolina, located at Murphy.

A. P. Staples, a native of Patrick, began the practice of law here, later moving to Roanoke, and then taking the position of professor of law in Washington and Lee University. He was a good lawyer and a man of charming personality. Mr. Richardson called him the "Prince of Technicality."

L. S. Thomas was a member of the bar and referee in bankruptcy. He was interested in the development of his father's estate and in public welfare. It was largely through his efforts that the school on Brown and Cleveland Streets was built.

Mr. G. H. Marshall has been a member of the bar for some time and has gained the confidence of tne people of the community.

Mr. J. R. Taylor was commonwealth's attorney for a number of years.

Mr. John H. Matthews was county clerk from 1875 to 1912. His popularity was almost unprecedented.

Mr. Henry Tuggle was sheriff for many years, having moved from Patrick County to a large farm on Leatherwood Creek which he purchased. Later his family moved to Martinsville. He was succeeded by J. P. Davis, father of J. Mitchell Davis, the present sheriff.

Mr. Jesse Noel brought the mail from Danville twice a week and at election times would get upon a box and read the news.

ORIGIN OF THE TWO GREAT POLITICAL PARTIES
OF THE UNITED STATES

THE Democratic Party is the oldest political organization in the United States and was inspired by the principles laid down by Thomas Jefferson. From the time of Washington's Administration it was known as the Democratic-Republican Party, and soon after 1829, the Democratic Party.

The party had its origin with the question of the adoption of the Federal Constitution. Before then all men were united in their effort to establish order, following the trying days of the Revolution. However, on the question of adopting the Constitution public opinion was divided. One group led by Alexander Hamilton advocated its acceptance by the state without alteration; another group declared against such centralization of power as the Constitution threatened to impose upon the country and maintained that the states should be invested with almost sovereign authority to assure local self-government. The faction led by Hamilton won, but the opposition obtained a promise that Congress, as one of its first acts, should propose a series of constitutional amendments guaranteeing certain inalienable rights to the people. Hamilton and other spokesmen for the Constitution in the form in which it was adopted, became known as the Federalists. The natural designation of the opposition headed by Thomas Jefferson was the Anti-Federalist, and this party was in every essential the beginning of the present Democratic Party.

After the adoption of the Constitution the distinction between the Federalist and the Anti-Federalist parties became almost meaningless. All united in the effort to get the government established as quickly as possible, and for a few years party names were forgotten.

On the eve of the second presidential election in 1792, there sprang up two active groups, the old Federalist wing becoming known as National Republicans and the followers of Jefferson as Democratic Republicans.

Since the days of Jefferson the Democratic Party has come down to the present time closely associated with figures of Andrew Jackson, Samuel J. Tilden and Grover Cleveland.

The name "Republican" as used by the followers of Jefferson about 1792, and by the adherents of Henry Clay and John Quincy Adams about 1825, was current in each case only a few years, but in common usage the name "Republican" is given only to the party which elected Lincoln to the presidency in 1850.

The Republican Party owed its existence to the effort to extend slavery into the territories and to the inability or unwillingness of the Whigs, as a party, to take vigorous steps in opposition. The northern Whigs were already displeased by the passage and enforcement of the fugitive slave law of 1850, but the Kansas-Nebraska Bill led to open revolt in 1854. Three months before the latter bill was passed a local mass meeting of voters opposed to slavery met at Ripon, Wisconsin, and adopted resolutions declaring that if the bill became a law they would throw old party organizations to the winds and organize a new party on the sole issue of nonextension of slavery.

The local party was soon organized and the name "Republican" was suggested as suitable for the new party. It was in Michigan, however, on July 6th, that the opposition to the extension of slavery first led to a real organization which formally adopted the name "Republican." In Maine, Massachusetts, Ohio, Illinois, Wisconsin and other states, conventions were held during the summer of 1854, and almost at once the Republican Party became a power in the north.

In the fall of 1854 the Republicans elected eleven United States Senators and secured a plurality in the House of Representatives. This sudden growth was due to the fact that nearly all opponents to the extension of slavery at once joined the party. Amongst the Republicans were most of the antislavery Whigs, including Lincoln, Seward and Greely, all the Free Soilers, most of the Know-Nothings, including Nathaniel F. Banks and Schuyler Colfax, and a few Abolitionists who felt the new party offered the best means of real opposition to slavery. Besides these complex elements, there were a few northern antislavery Democrats, among them being Simon Cameron, Hannibal Hamlin and William Cullen Bryant, who favored the Republican cause.

SCENERY IN PATRICK COUNTY PICTURESQUE AND BEAUTIFUI

THE scenery in the mountainous sections of Patrick County is wild and romantic. A late publication thus describes the passage of the Dan River down the Allegheny and "Bursted Rock": "The scenery presented by the passage of the Dan River down the mountain and into the flat country is awful and sublime in the highest degree. The river rises in a plain, traverses it for eight or ten miles until it reaches the declivity of the mountains, dashes down it by a rapid succession of perpendicular falls and winds its solitary way unapproached by any footstep save that of the mountain hunter and hemmed in on every side by immense mountains, descending almost parallel to the water's edge for a distance of seven miles before its banks afford room for settlements."

The Pinnacles of Dan are found in this interval. To approach them you must ascend the mountain at some convenient gap. Upon reaching the top of the mountain the country becomes comparatively level. The visitor goes along the top under the guidance of some mountaineer who knows the location of the Pinnacles. He meets with no obstruction, except fallen logs and a most luxuriant growth of weeds, till suddenly he reaches the declivity of the mountains.

An immense basin presents itself to his view surrounded by lofty mountains almost perpendicular, of which the ridge on which he stands forms a boundary. The depth of the basin is beyond his view and appears to him to be incalculable. From the midst of the basin two pinnacles in the shape of a sugar loaf rise to a level with the surrounding mountains and, of course, with the beholder.

They appear to be masses of rocks rudely piled on each other with hardly soil enough in the crevices to nourish a few bushes.

There is no visible outlet to the basin, the narrow chasm through which the river makes its escape being out of view.

If the visitor wishes to ascend the main pinnacle (one being much larger than the other), he descends from his station, the face of the mountain which is very steep, to a distance which he imagines sufficient to carry him down the mountain, when he reaches a narrow ridge or passway, not more than

PINNACLES OF THE DAN

thirty feet wide, connecting at the distance of thirty or forty yards the pinnacle to the main mountain, and to his astonishment, the river appears at an incalculable distance below him.

The ascent of the pinnacle then commences and an arduous and somewhat perilous one it is. A narrow pathway winds up among the rocks, and in many places the adventurous climber has to pull himself up a perpendicular ascent of five or six feet by the bushes.

When he reaches the top, however, he is amply repaid for his labor in ascending. The prospect though necessarily a limited one, is picturesque and sublime in a high degree. The view of the basin is then complete. The mountains surrounding it are nearly of a uniform height, no outlet visible, and the beholder perches upon the summit of an immense natural pyramid in the center. The river is seen occasionally as it winds around the base of the pyramid. It attempts to pass on the west side where the narrow ridge passes between the two pinnacles. It then passes around the western and southern sides of the smaller pinnacle and makes its escape as best it can from its apparently helpless imprisonment.

The summit of the pinnacle is about twenty or thirty feet square and, strange to relate, small bushes of aspen grow upon it, which is found nowhere else growing wild in this section of country.

The echo produced is somewhat remarkable. If a gun be fired off on top of the pinnacle, you hear nothing for several seconds, when suddenly in the distance of the narrow pass through which the river flows a rushing sound is heard which although not a correct echo seems to be the sound of the report escaping through the pass.

OTHER CURIOSITIES

The other natural curiosity to which reference is made is the "Bursted Rock," which is not very far from the Pinnacles and forms a part of the frowning and sublime scenery which overhangs the Dan in its passage through the mountains. You approach it as you do the Pinnacles along the level top of the mountain, till suddenly your course is arrested by a perpendicular descent of many hundred feet. The face of the precipice is a smooth rock. Far below, everything appears in ruins, rocks piled on rocks, the timber swept from the earth and every appearance indicates that a considerable portion of the mountain has been, by some great convulsion of nature, riven and torn from the rest and precipitated into the valley or rather chasm below.

A MOST REMARKABLE STONE FORMATION. LO, THE FAIRIES WEEP!

This story is a fairy story, and, strange to say, it was not born in the hills of old Scotland, the traditional home of all fairies, but in the hill country of Henry and Patrick Counties, Virginia.

Most of the fairy tales which come to us from the past speak of the joyful mood of the fairies of all lands. They were thought to be a kind of intermediate being, partaking of both the nature of man and of spirits, having material bodies and yet possessed of the power to make them invisible. Small in stature with fair complexions and clothed in green, they were said to inhabit groves, verdant meadows and the slopes of hills. The traces of their tiny feet were supposed to remain invisible on the ground and grass long afterward, and they were called fairy rings. They are described as being so delicate in form that a dewdrop, when they chance to dance upon it, trembles, indeed, but never breaks. The traditional fairy was always happy.

But this is a story of a little group of fairies who cried; so bitter was their grief that their tears, falling to the ground, turned to stones of a definite formation suggestive of the cause of their grief.

And now the story: "Centuries ago when the Cæsars sat upon the throne, the whole of the Roman world was startled by the announcement of the birth of a new prophet in Israel, who, coming to mature years, was now transforming the whole of society by his wonderful speech and his purity of character. Far removed from the scenes of the labors of the New Teacher, in a quiet, sunny glade nestled among the foothills of the Blue Ridge Mountains in Henry and Patrick Counties, Virginia, there lived a little group of fairies who spent their days as all other fairies had done before and since, in dancing around a spring of limpid water, playing with the naiads and wood nymphs and occasionally laboring in their little workshops, creating the most beautiful of gems. They little dreamed at the time that with their tears and not with their hands they were to produce these gems.

"One day when the mirth of the fairyland was at its height, when the very air was vibrant with the rollicking strains of their music and the little spring mirrored forth each graceful movement of the gleeful dancers, an elfin arrived from the far distant land of the Cæsars where the New Teacher was born and told the fairies the sad story of the untimely death of Christ on the Cross.

"Of a sudden their music ceased, their little heads drooped, their bodies became riveted to the earth—Lo, the fairies wept! And as their tears fell to the grass they became crystallized into little stones, on each of which was formed the figure of a cross. It is not known how long the fairies wept, nor have we ever learned if they returned to their workshops to spend a single moment afterwards. Years later, when it was discovered the fairies had disappeared from the enchanted spot, the spring and valley where their little feet had tripped to the strains of sweetest music, were now strewn with little crosses, a unique memento of that melancholy hour when the Teacher died whose story had been brought to them by the elfin."

To-day hundreds of pilgrimages are made to this scene of the fairies' first and only home in America where these stones are found in shapes representing the four well-known crosses of the world, Maltese, Roman, St. Andrew and the five-cross Maltese.

As you gather them you are impressed with their uniqueness. Beautifully formed are they as though the tools of a master artisan had shaped them and, to-day, thousands all over the world wear these gems, some in superstitious awe and still others ignorant of the legendary origin of this somber reminder of the death of the New Teacher—THE FAIRY STONE.

MURAL RECORDS OF THINGS LEGAL AND HISTORICAL
IN PATRICK COUNTY COURT HOUSE TO GO

———

THE criminal archives of Patrick County during the past half century, reflecting the blood and thunder days when the moonshiners battled with the "revenooers" over the right to convert apples and corn into ardent spirits, are threatened with extinction.

Probably no more unique method of keeping the chronicles of crime is to be found than in the two jury rooms which open into the churchlike interior of the Patrick County Court Room, for upon the four plastered walls of each chamber has been written, in pencil, the names of jurors in cases celebrated and otherwise until, to-day, the handwriting on the wall constitutes a mural fresco making many of these mural records indecipherable.

Perhaps it is recognition of the fact that the records constitute an accurate chronicle of the famous court trials in Patrick County that has caused the county supervisors to refrain from wiping them out for all time by having the walls "done over," but the time has come now when this necessary work cannot be longer postponed, and this spring will see the records buried for all time under fresh coats of paint.

RECALLS STORMY TIMES

The mural testimony brings to the fore the stormy life that once was in the hills, when Shooting Creek was a frequent battlefield between the freemen of Patrick, who with their squirrel guns disputed with the representatives of the law the tax required on spirituous liquors, and of more recent years the actual prohibition of the making.

Patrick was settled by English and Scotch stock. For years it was isolated somewhat for lack of roads. The people had their own traditions and viewed with concern, if not with suspicion, new faces in their midst. All of the clannishness of the Anglo-Saxon race was manifested, in some localities, until an age of progress brought first a winding railway, then good roads, which have put one of the centers of real rustic beauty of Virginia in touch with the rest of the world.

Twenty years ago, a pilgrimage on horseback into the recesses of the fir-clad Bull Mountain or Bald Knob was to enter a belated civilization. All of that has passed now and the mountain girl of to-day has her dorine, wears up-to-date clothes and drives the family flivver with ease and grace.

SINISTER INTERIOR

The Patrick Court House has a sinister interior. The walls are painted gray, and marked off with lines of imitation mortar, which give the impression of a castle keep in hewn rock. It seats not more than sixty persons, though more than a hundred can be accommodated. The high chamber is divided by the wooden bar, and the judge sits behind a wooden railing on an elevated dais dominating the well-worn witness chair set upon a platform, whence has come words sounding the doom of many a man. Two rooms opening from the court chamber, are for the juries, one for the petit jury and the other for the grand jury, though both are used for the petit jury deliberations.

The wall inscriptions date back to 1875, when men were lured by the opportunity to write their names for posterity in a slender and sloping hand. Some of the writings reflect the emotions of the juries irritated by stubborn men holding out against the majority. There are even some obscenities. Thus, for a certain crime that is not divulged there follows a list of the twelve jurors and as a postscript, "The biggest set of fools that was ever sworn as jurors." In another case in which a jury was called upon to deliberate, during a long winter night, one of the jurors wrote beside the list of names "Cold as hell."

POETIC FANCY AROUSED

In at least one instance a juror turned to poetic fancy. The following lines neatly penciled in 1878, observe:

> *"Underneath this marble stone*
> *Lies the body of Billy Mahone*
> *Large in mind and small in figger,*
> *He died (politically) of swallerin' too much 'nigger'."*

Again high on one wall is the heavily chalked significant phrase, "Eat, drink and be merry for to-morrow ye die."

Ten of the inscriptions recall vivid days in Patrick's history, one of them is the case of Charles McBride under the date of December 7, 1896, with the following verdict: "We, the jury, find the prisoner, Charles McBride, guilty of murder in the first degree as charged in the indictment and fix his punishment at eighteen years in the penitentiary."

There is record also of The Hollow lynching case of thirty years ago when a white man was taken from the hands of a sheriff, removing him to jail for a dastardly crime, and shot to death in his tracks. This was one of the rare cases in Virginia, in which convictions were secured. J. Murray Hooker, now chairman of the State Democratic Committee, was then commonwealth's attorney of the county and he secured the conviction of six men, the ringleader being sent to the penitentiary for six years and the other five for five years. The jury verdict was sustained and Governor Tyler offered special congratulations to Mr. Hooker for his work, in a legislative message. The date of the trial is not given, but the names of the jurors are bracketed together.

In one of the inscriptions there is the shrewd suspicion that there was trouble in the jury. A murder case jury has the words, "A damn rascal and a dog," written after the name of one of the jurors, in what is obviously the same calligraphy and apparently written at the time the wall record was inscribed.

OTHER FAMOUS CASES

Among the famous cases discerned is that of Gilbert Boswell, tried in 1875, and the Oliver Reynolds case in 1914. The joint trial of Thomas and Luther Chapman. The Monroe Lawson case which resulted in an acquittal and, of more recent vintage, the sharp legal-political battle—the election contest between Charles Gilbert and T. L. Clark, which saw the Democrats and Republicans, who in this county are evenly matched, fighting for the court clerkship with Clark as winner.

Many other interesting records are lost because they have been written over and could be deciphered only with the greatest difficulty. There is enough, however, to suggest that the bar of Patrick County has not been lacking in retainers in famous cases, murder trials, many of these being paid in kind.

THE SCENES CHANGE

All of these grim reminders are destined to go and will soon be forgotten. Patrick County is living down its early notoriety in feuds and shootings in which life and death were always the issue. Its scenic beauties are luring an increasing number of tourists each year. Stuart is now a summer resort with a growing fame. The county has a growing apple industry with a demand for its products extending as far as Great Britain, and a lumber business which is becoming more and more important.

To Patrick County belongs the distinction of having within its borders the furnaces in which armor plates were made for Confederate cruisers. The Confederate Government was the first power that ever used an armored vessel in actual warfare.

Major W. H. Werth, chemist and soldier, owner of Patrick Springs, was employed by the Confederate Government, 1864–65, to take ore from the mines, take it to a crucible where it was made into blistered steel for the battleships. The furnaces were about ten miles from Patrick Springs and were operated by a man named Barksdale, from Halifax County.

The ore was placed underneath boxes in which iron bars were placed, the spaces between the bars of iron were filled with chemicals, which produced blistered steel.

The Yankees tore up the furnaces near the close of the War.

EARLY CHURCHES OF VIRGINIA

VIRGINIA, being an English colony, the church of England was established by law as a form of worship for the people of the colony. Parishes were laid out coextensive with the counties which were later divided and subdivided as settlement increased.

The administration of the affairs of each parish was under the control of a local body of men known as the vestry, which was composed of the foremost men of the parish, whether from their standing of intelligence, wealth or social position.

At first, gentlemen in the country, from the prestige they derived from being principal guardians of the public morals, were looked up to as the models of all that was most polished and cultured in their respective parishes.

Besides arranging and providing for religious worship for the people of the parish, and safeguarding the morals of the community, it was also incumbent upon the vestry to collect taxes and mark the boundary lines of land. Occupying positions of such trust and authority, the members of the vestry were obligated, on their part, to be exemplary in their conduct.

The colonial church labored under a great disadvantage in that there was no resident Bishop in Virginia, the care of the church in the colonies being assigned to the Bishop of London, a man whose time was already filled with the demands of the churches of that city. The Bishop was represented in Virginia, in the person of the Royal Governor and Commissary. Those who ministered to frontier parishes had to ride scores of miles over rugged upland country to reach their appointments. The scarcity of ministers was due to the fact that the Virginians refused to "induct" their ministers into the parishes, an English custom which made the parish the minister's for life and the people were unable to dismiss him no matter how unpopular or undesirable he became. Meade declared that in the history of vestries can be traced not only the origin of religious liberty but of civil liberty as well. The vestries were the intelligence and moral strength of the land and had been trained up on the defense of their rights against governors and bishops, kings and cabinets.

The life of the church in this section began with the organization, in 1746, of Lunenburg County and Cumberland Parish, extending westward to the

Blue Ridge Mountains. A grant to John Ray, in 1750, records that there is a church, "a building," on Peter's Creek in Patrick County. Lay readers held services when ministers were not available and received three hundred pounds of tobacco a year for their services.

The Rev. Alexander Gordon, of Halifax County, agreed for sixteen thousand pounds of tobacco a year, to preach at Peter Copeland's, Henry County, Hamon Critz', Patrick County, and five other places.

Churches were built in 1770, with former locations changed, sextons engaged and books bought. Sandy River Church, Stinking River Church, Leatherwood Church, Snow Creek Church, Stony Creek Chapel (Henry County), and a chapel built near Captain Critz', in Patrick County.

DECLINE OF THE EPISCOPAL CHURCH

The Church of England and the English Government were so closely associated in men's minds that the people of the country with patriotic fervor turned from the established church and embraced the new faiths of the Baptist and Methodist churches. This is evidenced in the minutes of the vestrymen which now began to appear.

For nearly twenty years the Baptist faith had been preached through the country by able and earnest men. At the close of the Revolutionary War the glebes (land belonging to a parish church upon which the minister made his home) were ordered sold by the General Assembly.

Leatherwood being the first settled region of Henry County, the earliest churches were built there. From old letters and data collected, apparently the Leatherwood Church was built just before or just after the Revolutionary War. John King was pastor for a long time and died while still serving this congregation in 1821.

Reed Creek Church was built about 1850. Old Center later. Ridgeway about 1850. Goodwill a little later. Horsepasture Church was built as a free church. The Methodist Church at Ridgeway in 1893, George O. Jones gave the site and most of the funds to erect the edifice. Mrs. Sue Garrett was the prime factor in building the Baptist Church in the same town.

Prior to 1806, the Methodists worshiped in private houses, schoolhouses and courthouses, but in that year John Travis deeded, for five shillings, an acre of land to the trustees, John French, John Abingdon, James Patterson and W. F. Mills. On this was a building called Travis' Meeting House. Eighteen years later the Rev. J. C. Traylor deeded two more acres to the old plot and built a church which was named Mt. Bethel.

The trustees, French and Patterson, were succeeded by W. A. Taylor and Thomas I. Wootton.

In that day the men sat on one side of the aisle and the women on the other. Seats in the rear were reserved for the colored people. Among the leading members of the church were the Schoolfields, Baileys, Hunters, Mills, Bakers, Bouldins, Hills, Wells, Pannills.

Among the pastors were Pines Allen, Alfred Norman, James Moore and others. Class meetings were held every Sunday and its leaders almost always got happy before the meeting was over and often you might hear shouts of joy issuing from that church, not only from the leaders but the members joined their leaders, and many sinners were converted.

In 1858, the present Mt. Bethel Church was built.

The Methodist Church in Martinsville was erected in 1838, on a site deeded by George Hairston to the following trustees: Anthony Dupuy, William Martin, J. C. Traylor, John Redd, James Smith, Sr.

A handsome new church has been built upon the site of the old building which was removed. The corner stone was laid July 4, 1922, and the building was finished May, 1923, at a cost of $65,000.

The Missionary Baptist Church was organized in Martinsville in 1884, in the home of Dr. C. P. Kearfott. There were fifteen charter members. The Broad Street Church was built in 1890. A handsome new church has been erected at the corner of Broad and Church Streets.

The Episcopal Church was erected on West Church Street in 1847, on a lot donated by George Hairston. The trustees were Anderson Wade, William Clark, Hughes Dillard, Jesse Wootton and George Hairston. The latter's wife was the first one to be confirmed in this church. In 1900, a new Episcopal Church was erected on East Church Street, the lot being donated by Miss Ann Hairston.

PATRIOTIC SOCIETIES

THE society of the Daughters of the American Revolution has for many years been an outstanding organization in Henry County, and its national importance and influence has been incalculable, therefore, a brief history of the society and an account of some of its activities may be of interest to our readers.

The Cincinnati was the first patriotic society formed in this country following the Revolutionary War. (This society was not approved by Thomas Jefferson. See letters to Washington.) Then came the society of the Sons of the American Revolution, organized in California, October 22, 1875, composed of men and women, the latter called Daughters of the American Revolution. The organization was practically unknown in the east.

In 1883, Mr. John A. Stevens, of New York, organized the Sons of the American Revolution in New York, and in 1890, Mrs. Ellen H. Walworth assisted in founding the Daughters of the American Revolution in Washington, District of Columbia, the Sons having been organized independently of Mr. Stevens in 1889.

On April 30, 1890, at a general meeting of the Sons in Louisville, Kentucky, after a discussion in the convention, a vote was cast excluding women. This was telegraphed to various papers throughout the country and the American women were filled with indignation. Among these was Miss Eugenia Washington, a great grandniece of George Washington, so with a number of other influential women the work of organizing a society of the Daughters of the American Revolution was started. The actual organization took place August 9, 1890, but the work was continued on October 11th, which has been claimed to be the date of organization—that being the date of the discovery of America by Columbus and the connection between the two dates gave added interest to the former.

Only three women were present at the first meeting, Miss Eugenia Washington, Miss Mary Desha and Mrs. Ellen H. Walworth. Eighteen women signed the formal draft in 1890. In 1929 and 1930 there were 175,157 members and 2,394 chapters.

Mr. William O. McDowell, a great great grandson of Hannah Arnett, Revolutionary heroine, assisted in planning and organizing the society from the beginning and much credit is due him for its success.

The design for the badge was made by George Barton Goode and patented September 22, 1891.

The numerous activities in which the Daughters of the American Revolution are engaged would make a list too long to be included in this work. A few of them are as follows: To have better films, encourage conservation and thrift, teach the use of the flag, publish the D.A.R. magazine, provide a student loan fund, provide employment and help for foreigners detained on Ellis and Angel Islands, genealogical research, instruction in home-making for girls, historical and literary reciprocity, furnish means for historical research, legislation in United States Congress, send out manual of citizenship of the United States for immigrants, national defense, marking national old trails, and many other lines of endeavor.

Continental Hall, a magnificent building in Washington, District of Columbia, stands as a lasting monument to the members of this great society.

THE PATRICK HENRY CHAPTER D. A. R.

On June 15, 1905, under the leadership of Mrs. Keziah Drewry Carter, Mrs. Essie Wade Smith and Mrs. Faith Thomas Parrott, the Patrick Henry Chapter was organized. Those who have filled the office of Regent are: Mrs. Essie Wade Smith, Mrs. Faith Thomas Parrott, Mrs. Alice Williams Gravely and Mrs. Olivia Simmons Keesee.

The members of this chapter have been untiring in their efforts to accomplish worth-while work. A monument was erected in 1922, in honor of Patrick Henry, at the entrance to the estate formerly owned by this gifted statesman, about six miles from Martinsville, owned and occupied for some time by the great statesman. The shaft of granite of imposing proportions was the gift of Mrs. Olivia Simmons Keesee. A bronze plate appropriately inscribed was placed upon it. A suitable plot of ground was given by the present owner of the estate, Mr. Samuel Hooker.

An oil portrait of Patrick Henry, by Edward Rosenthal, of Philadelphia, was placed in the Virginia Room in Continental Hall during the thirty-third annual Congress in Washington, District of Columbia. The presentation being made by the beloved Regent of the chapter, Mrs. Faith Thomas Parrott.

UNITED DAUGHTERS OF THE CONFEDERACY

The Mildred Lee Chapter of the United Daughters of the Confederacy was organized April 3, 1896, with the following charter members: Mrs N. H. Hairston, president; Mrs. H. C. Smith, vice president; Mrs. M. M. Mullins, secretary; Mrs. S. L. Waller, treasurer; and the following members: Mesdames M. L. Zentmeyer, O. C. Smith, Peter Hairston, T. A. Ranson, H. S. Williams, C. P. Kearfott, H. G. Mullins, L. L. Gravely, B. H. Ingles and C. R. Preston.

Many others joined the organization and much patriotic work has been accomplished. A handsome monument was erected in memory of the Confederate soldiers on the Court House Square, in Martinsville, Virginia, and was unveiled June 3, 1901.

After serving as president for seven years, Mrs. Hairston moved to Roanoke, Virginia, and was succeeded by Mrs. O. C. Smith, whose devotion to the cause and unbounded enthusiasm were proverbial. She served almost continuously until the time of her death in 1930. Short terms of office being filled by Mrs. J. T. Marshall and Mrs. J. W. Carter, respectively.

The work of the society has included placing markers at the graves of Confederate soldiers, in Oakwood Cemetery, giving name and regiment of each. These graves are decorated with flags and flowers on Decoration Day each year. The funeral of every Confederate veteran is attended by the chapter in a body. The sick and needy are cared for and an annual dinner given the Stuart Hairston Camp members when they meet to reorganize, making April 30th a day for a happy celebration.

Education is encouraged by the chapter by gifts of books to the public schools, medals for essays on southern history and literature and other patriotic work.

THE HENRY COUNTY RED CROSS SOCIETY

The Henry County Red Cross Chapter was organized in June, 1917. W. B. Gates was elected president, Miss Janie H. Lavinder, vice president, Miss Bessie Tuggle, secretary and John R. Smith, treasurer.

During the World War this chapter made a splendid record in carrying out the work allotted to the organization. The work includes assisting ex-service men and their families, adjusting compensation claims, and health work in schools.

Mrs. Frieda Drewry has filled the position of public health nurse most acceptably for a number of years. Clinics are held in the county for crippled children, tuberculosis patients, and baby welfare is an important branch of the work.

THE BUSINESS AND PROFESSIONAL
WOMEN'S CLUB OF MARTINSVILLE, VIRGINIA

ON Friday, the thirteenth of April, 1923, the initial meeting, out of which grew the Martinsville Business and Professional Women's Club, was held in the Sunday school room of the First Baptist Church.

Mrs. J. K. Bowman, of Richmond, Virginia, then State President, Misses Sallie Haskins, Ellen Harvey and Ruth Burch, of Danville, Virginia, came to Martinsville, Virginia, to meet with a group of women who were interested in organizing a club. These women were so filled with enthusiasm that it proved contagious and a committee, composed of Misses Bessie Tuggle, Virginia Pedigo, Lucy Stovall and Loula Carter, was appointed to consider the expediency of such an organization, and to ascertain if the women of the town were sufficiently interested to support it.

The committee did its work well, and on April 23, 1923, the Martinsville Business and Professional Women's Club was organized, and Miss Loula Carter was elected president and Miss Bessie Tuggle, vice president. The following is a list of the charter members:

Misses Loula Carter	Misses Kathleen Hite	Mrs.	Laura Penn
May Carter	Mamie Hundley	Misses	Virginia Pedigo
Mary Childress	Louise Kuykendall		Julia Self
Mrs. May Campbell	Mrs. Fannie Kolofny		Virginia Self
Misses Gertrude Fulfeld	Blooma Leaderman		Elsie Shumate
Esther Fulfeld	Misses Mary Long		Mary Stovall
Sabina Fulfeld	Elizabeth Marshall		Lucy Stovall
Myrtle Grogan	Maude Moore		Bessie Tuggle
Margaret Heiner	Lelia Nelson		Elma Williams
Pattie Holt			Sadie Warren

The club quickly attained prestige and influence in the community, and when not taking the initiative its coöperation has always been sought in civic matters.

The office of president of the club has been held by prominent, capable women, who fulfilled every duty and obligation connected with the work. Miss Loula Carter holds and has held for a number of years an important position in the American Furniture Factory. She was ever ready to promote the interests of the club and attended the state and national conventions.

Mrs. Laura H. Penn has filled the offices of president of the local club, regional chairman of the *Independent Woman*, the official organ of the National Federation, vice president and president of the Virginia Federation, each two years, and, in the latter capacity, member of the National Executive Board. Mrs. Penn has for a number of years been a teacher in the public schools of Martinsville, and is now principal of the Joseph Martin School.

Following Mrs. Penn's administration, Mrs. J. W. F. Beckner was president of the club for two years, she was also treasurer of the local club for two years. While representing the Martinsville club on the state board, Mrs. Beckner was appointed the first health chairman of the Federation.

Miss Hilda Marshall, a popular teacher in the Martinsville schools, has been a faithful member of the club since its organization. From being a leading member in the local club she has been chosen president of the state organization.

PUBLIC SCHOOLS OF PATRICK AND HENRY COUNTIES

WITH the advent of public schools in 1870, an almost unbelievable change has come over the country but the change has come gradually it is true. Could one have gone to sleep in a Patrick or Henry County schoolhouse in 1875 or '80, and awakened in one of the present time, his bewilderment would make that of Rip Van Winkle seem mild.

The earlier schoolhouses were, for the most part, little better than cabins, indeed, in many localities log cabins were used as schoolhouses. The furniture consisted of rude benches and desks. A very few were supplied with blackboards, maps and charts.

Fireplaces, with wood cut from the forests, furnished heat. Later on stoves replaced the open fireplaces, and were much more satisfactory as the heat could be much more evenly distributed.

As time went on better equipment replaced the rude furniture and now the comfortable one-teacher schools are passing and the "consolidated" schools are taking their places. There are many advantages, of course, in the latter, as better classification can be accomplished, and transportation by "busses" furnished, whereas in the past, each family furnished transportation for their own children when they were not within walking distance of the school. In winter the roads were muddy, at times almost impassable, so horseback was the usual method of transportation. The school session was five months in duration.

The old Masonic Hall (abandoned as such) close by Mt. Bethel Church, was one of the best-known schools in Henry County, and the district was especially fortunate in securing good teachers, outstanding amongst the number were Miss J. P. A. Hill, Joseph R. Pedigo and others. A large number of boys and girls, some of them eighteen or twenty years of age, attended that school. Many horses were tied to the limbs of the trees in the grove during the long school hours and fed, if at all, from boxes nailed to the tree trunks. Many of the students, who for years have made their homes in other states, will remember "The Old Hall School" and the romances originating there—love affairs, some of them lasting through years of separation as, like driftwood, the boys and girls are carried down the stream of time.

The Old Well School, close by the church near Spencer, Henry County, was another popular school, especially as some unusually efficient and accomplished teachers had charge of the school for a number of terms. Amongst them were Mrs. John R. Dillard and her sister, Miss Helen Lee, both formerly of Lunenburg County.

The Old Well School is now a modern, graded school with a high school department. The building is of the most modern type and the name "Spencer-Penn" has been given it in honor of the two prominent families who have been its sponsors and aided in making the school a great success. Mrs. Mary Spencer Buchanan donated the land upon which the building was erected and Mr. Jefferson Penn, of Reidsville, whose parents were from that locality, has made handsome donations to the school.

THE HARDEN REYNOLDS MEMORIAL SCHOOL OF PATRICK COUNTY, VIRGINIA

The public school of Critz, Patrick County, Virginia, with a very modest beginning, is one of the outstanding institutions of learning in that section of the country.

It is now The Harden Reynolds Memorial School and through the munificence of Mr. W. N. Reynolds, large, modern buildings, providing ample room for primary, grammar and high school departments with the addition of a dormitory, have been erected.

HIGH SCHOOLS

Reference has been made to the employment of governesses and tutors in the families of the well-to-do planters and manufacturers of Patrick and Henry Counties. Sometimes these teachers were provided with schoolhouses near the homes of the employers and other pupils from neighboring families could attend by paying tuition. In many cases, however, the governesses and tutors gave their time exclusively to the children of the household.

Sylvan Retreat, located between Rangeley and Mt. Bethel Church, was built by the Rev. W. W. Hill for the benefit of his own and his neighbors' children. Located in a pleasant grove, this school was well attended by both boys and girls, many of the students coming some distance on horseback.

Dr. G. W. G. Estes was the teacher of this school, he was a teacher of unusual personality and ability. He was educated at Hollins College when that school was co-ed, then attended Jefferson Medical College, Philadelphia, but preferred teaching to the practice of medicine.

Dr. Estes left his school, being succeeded by Miss Judith P. A. Hill, and joined the forces of the Civil War where his knowledge of medicine was invaluable and where his ministrations to the sick and wounded were a mercy to many a sufferer.

After the war Dr. Estes took up railroad work, at Drakes Branch until his health failed. His last days were spent at the home of his brother at Danbury, North Carolina, where he died in 1882.

DENNIS MARSHALL'S SCHOOL

The oldest school for higher learning was conducted by Dennis Marshall, whose parents came from Mecklenburg County and settled near the head-waters of Leatherwood Creek. The family was related to Chief Justice John Marshall.

Dennis Marshall was born in 1768, and was the eldest of seven children. He was highly educated and spent about forty years in teaching. His home was near Nance's Mountain and his school building near his home. The latter was converted into a tobacco factory in 1843.

JOSHUA SMITH'S SCHOOL

Another high school, of a much later period, was taught by Joshua Smith, near Ridgeway, in Henry County. Few distinguished men, after the Civil War, reared in the south side of the county, failed to attend this school.

Professor Smith was a scholarly man and knew how to control as well as teach the young. He managed them by the honor system and was very successful. Many young ladies sought his instruction; he taught languages and prepared the students to take up professional studies, law, medicine, etc. The pupils from a distance boarded in the neighborhood.

His student list included many who became leaders in various walks of life. Among the number are the names of Dr. John R. Dillard, of Spencer, Judge Peter H. Dillard, of Rocky Mount, Virginia, Judge N. H. Hairston, of Roanoke, formerly judge of Henry County Court, Judge P. G. Trent, of Alabama.

PATRICK HENRY ACADEMY (1813)

Patrick Henry Academy was located on a road leading from Mt. Bethel Church to Spencer, near the south central part of Henry County.

Little definite information is now obtainable regarding the beginning of the school—a very small beginning it must have been, but it reached proportions that were imposing for its time and location. The last building was of brick, plain and substantially built. The location was attractive—a knoll with a view of the Blue Ridge Mountains as a background.

The fame of the Academy was not confined to Virginia. Many students came from distant communities to attend. Those within reach coming on horseback and others boarding with families in the neighborhood. Many of the early settlers, after moving west, brought their sons back here to be educated.

In the early days, when the building consisted of two stories, it is said that on account of rough settlers and roving bands of Indians, school property was taken to the upper story after school hours, which was reached by means of a ladder and the ladder then drawn up.

In 1770, Francis Asbury was sent by John Wesley from England to America as a missionary. In 1784, he was made the first Bishop of the Methodist Episcopal Church in America, and Virginia was in his diocesan jurisdiction when he died in 1816.

In 1813, the Bishop sent the Rev. J. C. Traylor as a circuit rider to Henry County with instructions to build a Methodist Church, a school from which to feed a college in the western part of the state and another to feed Patrick Henry Academy.

Mt. Bethel was the church he built, Patrick Henry Academy was the school and the smaller one in his yard for his neighbors' children was the feeder. The reference was to Emory and Henry College beyond the mountains that stand like a great monument.

ALUMNI OF PATRICK HENRY ACADEMY

Colonel Lewis Neale Whittle, leader at the bar and member of the Legislature from Macon, Georgia.

Stephen Decatur Whittle, lawyer and clerk of the House of Delegates of Virginia, and member of the Convention of 1849–50.

Francis McNiece Whittle, D.D., LL.D., the fifth Bishop of the Protestant Episcopal Diocese. These are uncles of Judge Stafford G. Whittle.

Samuel and Waller Staples.

Judge Henry Clay Pedigo, distinguished jurist of Hardin County, Texas.

Alexander Stuart, brother of General J. E. B. Stuart.

General Jubal Early, noted Confederate general.

INTERESTING NOTES

OATH OF ALLEGIANCE

I DO swear that I renounce and refuse all allegiance to George III, King of Great Britain, his heirs and successors, and that I will be faithful and bear true allegiance to the Commonwealth of Virginia as a free and independent state and that I will not at any time do, or cause to be done, anything injurious to the freedom and independence thereof as declared by Congress, and that I will discover and make known to some justice of the peace for the said state all treasons or traitorous conspiracies which I now or shall hereafter know to be formed against this or any of the United States of America.

QUIT RENTS

The Quit Rent Rolls for Virginia which listed the land ownership in each county on which a tax of one shilling for each fifty acres was payable directly to the Crown, were sent annually to England. Only the Rolls for the year 1704 have been found and they constitute an excellent source for tracing early Virginia families.

SMITH'S RIVER FORMERLY CALLED IRVIN

Smith River had been called Irvin by Colonel Byrd's surveying party in honor of a member of the party, but as early as 1743 we find the name being changed, for in that year William Bertram was granted 400 acres of land on the north side of Smith River beginning at the lower end of the Indian field, and also 400 acres on the south side, including the "bent."

BATTLE ABBEY

On the 4th of October, 1066, the Battle of Hastings was fought and William of Normandy was seated on the throne of England as "William the Conqueror." Close by the field of Hastings, William caused a stately pile to be erected, which was named Battle Abbey, in commemoration of his victory.

A roll or catalogue was prepared in which was carefully recorded the names and titles of the Normans who had followed his banner in the enterprise. This was the famous "Roll of Battle Abbey."

HOSPITAL

A hospital for the sick and wounded of Morgan's Command was established at Henry Court House.

HURRYING TO THE ASSISTANCE OF GENERAL GREENE

In Henry County, when troops were called for to go to the assistance of General Greene in North Carolina, Major Waller reported to the Governor that his order calling the militia out to General Greene's assistance had been received, but the approach of the enemy being so alarming had caused the militia to assemble, and they had already joined General Greene in greater numbers than called for.

NAMES OF THOSE WHO HAD BEEN IN SERVICE BEFORE THE BODY OF TROOPS LEFT IN MARCH, 1781

ELISHA ARNOLD
MICHAEL BURNS
DAVID BURCHELL
MAJOR THOMAS CARPER
GEORGE DYER
WILLIAM DESHAZO
COLONEL JOHN FONTAINE
LEWIS FRANKLIN
THOMAS FLEURMAN
PETER FRANCE

GRIFFIN GRIFFITH
WILLIAM HOPPER
DOCTOR BENJAMIN JONES
JAMES JOHNSON
JOHN KING
JACOB KOGER
JACOB MCCRAW
DAVID MULLINS
NEWSOME PACE

JOHN PRICE
CHARLES PHILPOTT
BENJAMIN STRATTON
SAMUEL SHUMATE
MOSE SPENCER
JAMES SHELTON
JOHN SALMON
WILLIAM SHACKLEFORD
MAJOR JOHN REDD
AXTON WHITECOTTON

NAMES OF MILITIAMEN WHO MARCHED TO THE ASSISTANCE OF GEN. GREENE

AT

GUILFORD COURT HOUSE

ABRAHAM PENN, *Colonel Commanding*

MAJOR GEORGE WALLER, *Adjutant*
JONATHAN HAMBY, *First Captain*

DAVID LANIER, *Second Captain*
GEORGE HAIRSTON, *Third Captain*

LIEUTENANTS

First Lieutenant, EDWARD TATUM
Second Lieutenants, ISAAC CLOUD, JOSIAH SHAW, JOSIAH RENTFRO

SERGEANTS

First Sergeant, ROBERT WATSON   *Second Sergeant,* GEORGE BELCHER

Ensigns, JAMES PRATHEY, JESSE CORN

HAMON CRITZ' COMPANY

PATTERSON CHILDERS
CHARLES DOTSON
WILLIAM DOTSON

PATRICK EWELL
DEVERIX GILLIAM
WILLIAM GOING

WILLIAM LOCKHART
WILLIAM SMITH
S. DANIEL SWILWANT

JOHN CUNNINGHAM'S COMPANY

William Beal
Joseph Cunningham
Thomas Hollinsworth

Samuel Packwood
Mumford Perryman
Daniel Smith

Josiah Turner
William Turner
Reuben Webster

JAMES COWDIN'S COMPANY

John Arthur
William Cheek
Josiah Channel
William Hodges

Jesse Hall
Stephen Hurd
Charles Summerfiels
Thomas Watson

Dudley Mileham
Jordan Mileham
John Robertson

S. TARRANT'S COMPANY

Philip Brashears
William Cox
John Carrol
John Davis
Thomas Edwards

John Gray
Richard Gilley
Jacob Stalings
Archie Murphy
William Moore

John Pharis
John Rea
Humphrey Scroggins
John Wilson, Sr.
John Wilson, Jr.

BRICE MARTIN'S COMPANY

James Billings
John Burchell
James Barker
John Cox
Archibald Hatcher

Thomas Jones
Peter Mitchell
Abraham Moore
John Prytle
Joseph Piper
John Pursell

John Rea
Peleg Rogers
Michael Rowland
Henry Tate
Nathaniel Tate

JOHN RENTFRO'S COMPANY

Thomas Bell
William Dunn
Robert English
Samuel Fox

James Grier
Thomas Harris
Abraham Jones
Isaac Jones

John Kelly
John Miles
Ebenezer Pryatt
Thomas Welch

OWEN RUBLE'S COMPANY

John Atkins
David Atkins
William Bohanan

John Brammer
Richard Copeland
Joseph Davis
Robert Grimmet

Philip Massey
William Mullins
John Stanley

LANIER'S COMPANY

Fisher Allen
John Alexander
Joseph Anglin
John Bowling
Charles Denham

John East
Howell Evey
Hans Hambleton
William Hays
Noble Johnson
Joyce

Shadwick Keziah
David Mays
Ham McCain
James Pratley
John Richardson

GEORGE HAIRSTON'S COMPANY

LEWIS BRADBERRY
JOSEPH BRACKLEY
ARISTOPHUS BAUGHAN
JOHN CROUCH

JAMES DAVIS
JESSE ELKINS
THOMAS FINCH
JOHN JONES
JOHN JAMERSON

SAMUEL JAMERSON
JOHN KITCHEN
RICHARD PARSLEY
JOHN RIVERS

JAMES DILLARD'S COMPANY

JOHN ATKINS
JOHN DEPRIEST
WILLIAM FEE
THOMAS HAMBLETON

MORRIS HUMPHREYS
WILLIAM ROBERTS
JAMES ROBERTS
BARTLETT REYNOLDS
JOSIAH SMITH

JOSEPH SEWALL
AUGUSTINE SIMS
JOHN TAYLOR
JESSE WITT

TULLY CHOICE'S COMPANY

NOAH ATKINS
MOSES BROOKE
WILLIAM BENNETT
NATHAN DAVIS
JOWEL ESTES

ELISHA ESTES
SAMUEL LUTTRELL
WILLIAM LONG
DAVID PRUITT
JAMES PRUNTY

DANIEL RICHARDSON
NATHAN RYAN
ISAAC SKILMORE
JOHN WILKES

THOMAS HAILE'S COMPANY

PETER ANDERSON
JOSEPH COATS

JESSE COOK
JOSEPH HAILE

JOSEPH RICHARDSON

JOHN FONTAINE'S COMPANY

ALEXANDER BARNES
WILLIAM BLEDSOE
THOMAS DOOLINGS
WILLIAM GRAVES
STEPHEN KING

THOMAS LEAK
HENRY MANNINGS
ABRAHAM PAYNE
THOMAS PARSLEY
GEORGE POOL

JAMES REA
JOSEPH RICE
JOHN WILLINGHAM
SAMUEL WEAVER

THOMAS SMITH'S COMPANY

DAVID ATKINS
JESSE BURNETT
GEORGE BOWLES
JOHN HURD

THOMAS HURD
HENRY LAW
JONATHAN PRATT
JAMES STRANGE

WILLIAM STEWART
HENRY SMITH
GEORGE STEWART
FRANCIS TILLSON

PETER HAIRSTON'S COMPANY

JOHN ARAGAN
WILLIAM BOWLING
JOSEPH BOWLING

WILLIAM BROWN
NATHAN JONES
JARRATT MARTIN

JOHN NANCE
JOSEPH PEREGOY
JOSEPH PEARSON

JAMES TARRANT'S COMPANY

JAMES BRYANT
JOHN BURCH
JAMES COX
CHARLES DICKERSON

JOHN DOYAL
WILLIAM ELKINS
JOSEPH GRAVELY
EDWARD SMITH

ROBERT TATE
SAMUEL WANE
HENRY WARREN

THOMAS HENDERSON'S COMPANY

MOSES ARMS
MICHAEL BARKER
JOHN BRANHAM
WILLIAM BRANHAM
WILLIAM BRAINBRIDGE

BARNABAS BRANHAM
JAMES CRAWLEY
JOHN EDWARDS
GEORGE FOLLY
JOHN GIBSON
JOSEPH HURT

SAMUEL HOOF
JOEL HARBOUR
ALEXANDER JONES
RICHARD REYNOLDS
THOMAS SMALL

ELEPHAS SHELTON'S COMPANY

JACOB ARNOLD
JACOB ADAMS
JOHN BARRAT

FRANCIS BARRAT
SHADRACK BARRAT
JOHN CARROLL
THOMAS HARRISBY

HEZEKIAH HARRIS
THOMAS HUDSON
WILLIAM McGHEE
MATHEW SIMMS

JONATHAN HANBY'S COMPANY

JOHN BOWMAN
JOHN CARTWELL
JOHN CHANDLER

NELSON DONOTHAN
BENJAMIN HENSLEY
HICKMAN HENSLEY
HENRY HENSLEY

JOHN HOWELL
DUDLEY STEPHENS
JOSHUA STEPHENS

JAMES POTEET'S COMPANY

PETER BAYS
AQUILLA BLACK
WILLIAM ELLIOTT
BEN HUBBARD
CHARLES HIBBERT
JOHN MULLINS

AMBROSE MULLINS
GEORGE NEVIL
RICHARD POTSON
NINON PRATER
JOSEPH PEREGOY
JOSEPH STREET

JOHN SNEED
THOMAS TINSON
PETER TITTLE
JOHN RATFORD
STEPHEN WATKINS
JOSEPH WALDEN

SWINFIELD HILL'S COMPANY

SOLOMON DAVIS
GEORGE FARGASON
AMBROSE WARREN
WILLIAM STEWART
ANDERSON McGUIRE

JOHN HOLLODAY
DOZIAR GRIMMETT
JOSIAH WOODS
JEREMIAH HOLLODAY
WILLIAM DELLINGHAM
WILLIAM THOMPSON

WILLIAM BARTEE
DAVID PEAKE
OBEDIAH GRAVES
JOHN GRAHAM
JOHN WOODS

Copied from Muster Roll in Colonel Penn's handwriting. This Muster Roll is in the possession of Mr. John Penn, of Martinsville, Virginia.

RIDGEWAY, HENRY COUNTY, VIRGINIA

IN preceding pages of this book Ridgeway has been mentioned in various connections, but the History of Henry County would be incomplete without a fuller account of this interesting and unique town.

The founders were two cousins, George I. Griggs and George C. Jones, the former a descendant of Michæl Griggs and the latter of George King. On account of their relationship and similar ideals the two cousins formed a partnership and engaged in the mercantile business, in farming, and in the manufacture of tobacco with great success. In earlier times these activities were usually carried on in connection with each other. The day of specializing came later.

These two cousins married sisters, Misses Churchill, descendants of the well-known and distinguished Churchill family of England. They survive their husbands, and their daughters, sons and sons-in-law hold the following positions in the civic, business, professional and religious life of Ridgeway:

Postmaster.
Assistant Cashier.
Depot Agent.
Magistrate.
Hotel Proprietor.
Insurance Agent.
Physician.
Chairman of the W. C. T. U. in Henry County.
Owners of the Two Leading Stores.
Owner of the Garage and Automobile Repair Plant.
Manager of the Town Hall; also farmer and cattle raiser.
Four Members of Town Council.
Superintendent of Sunday School.
Cashier of the Only Bank in Ridgeway.
Directors of the Bank.

Real Estate Dealer.
Notary.
Red Cross Chairman, Ridgeway Auxiliary.
Chairman of Drought Relief Work in this District.
Chairman of the Health Relief Work for Ridgeway District.
Owners of the Cemetery, and the greater part of the real estate of the town.
Town Treasurer.
Town Sergeant.
Owner and Operator of Mica Mines.
Undertaker.
Chairman of Junior Red Cross.
Two Members of the Board of Stewards of the Methodist Episcopal Church, South, the largest church in the town, and they take up the collections at each service.

EARLY DAYS IN WINSTON-SALEM

ALONG in the late "seventies" the City of Winston was young, and like the young was full of the spirit of jollity, intermingled with the serious affairs of business activities.

Salem, the near-by sister city, had long been established and lay in quiet dignity with her splendid people, schools, churches and business enterprises.

The tobacco manufacturing business brought an influx of young men, those from Patrick and Henry Counties being the outstanding ones considered in this volume. R. J. Reynolds had established the tobacco manufacturing business in 1875, which has since assumed such colossal proportions, and he was joined by other members of the family.

Other lines of business brought in many young men from Virginia and North Carolina communities, and all merged into a citizenry well fitted for the building of a wonderful and prosperous city.

A friendliness that scorned petty resentment permitted practical jokes being played and when opportunity offered retaliation in the same kind.

One young man owned a fine mule which a leading business man wished to purchase. Offering the owner a good price, the offer was refused but some time later the owner of the mule went to the business man and told him that, needing some money especially at that time, he had decided to sell the mule at the price offered. The money was paid and a negro was sent with a halter to bring up the mule, but soon reappeared wild-eyed and open-mouthed, stammering "Mars . . . . dat mule—he am layin' in de stable done daid!"

A young man who was interested in buying and selling horses and mules sold a customer a horse. The purchaser was not quite satisfied with the appearance of the horse's eyes, but was reassured by the seller saying, "Why, that horse's eyes are as good as mine." After a short while the man who bought the horse brought him back and complained that the horse was blind in one eye. "Well, so am I," replied the seller, which was true.

The same young man had a beautiful pair of horses brought in from Patrick County, horses of course unaccustomed to the sights and sounds of city streets. Being a reckless, daring driver, he gave no thought to danger and, without warning, invited a friend to go for a drive. The invitation was accepted, as the friend was a great admirer of fine horses, but at the same time more cautious in risking his neck. After driving a short distance the friend said, "Say, M— are these horses afraid of the street cars?" "Well," replied the driver with all the nonchalance imaginable, "we'll soon see," so cracking his whip and starting off at terrific speed, the horses, catching sight of the street cars, became absolutely frantic and dashed along the streets in the most terrifying manner, and as the friend relates "fairly tried to climb the buildings" before being stopped. Many years have elapsed, but that ride has not been forgotten and the recital of the incident by the victim is most amusing. Strange to say, no one was hurt.

PROGRESS

As the years are passing, Winston, having joined hands with the sister city, Salem, has developed into a wonderful, progressive city. Many of the Patrick and Henry County people, who came here in the early days, have been amongst the city's builders.

The R. J. Reynolds manufacturing business has given employment to countless thousands and large fortunes to many. New residential sections have been, and are constantly being developed, and many magnificent homes built. A number of large and beautiful estates occupy hundreds of acres within a few miles of the city. The outstanding ones are Tanglewood, the estate of Mr. W. N. Reynolds; Reynolda, the estate of the late Mr. and Mrs. R. J. Reynolds; Forest Hills, the beautiful estate of Mr. and Mrs. R. E. Lasater; Wilshur, the estate of Mr. S. Clay Williams; and Reynolda Park, an exclusive section containing many beautiful, spacious homes surrounded by lovely gardens.

THERE IS A MORAL AND PHILOSOPHICAL RESPECT FOR OUR ANCESTORS WHICH ELEVATES THE CHARACTER AND IMPROVES THE HEART. NEXT TO THE SENSE OF RELIGIOUS DUTY AND MORAL FEELING, I HARDLY KNOW WHAT SHOULD BEAR WITH A STRONGER OBLIGATION ON A LIBERAL AND ENLIGHTENED MIND THAN A CONSCIOUSNESS OF ALLIANCE WITH EXCELLENCE WHICH HAS DEPARTED AND A CONSCIOUSNESS, TOO, THAT IN ITS ACTS AND CONDUCT AND EVEN IN ITS SENTIMENTS IT MAY BE ACTIVELY OPERATING UPON THE HAPPINESS OF THOSE WHO CAME AFTER IT.

—DANIEL WEBSTER

THE AARON FAMILY OF HENRY COUNTY

The Aaron brothers, Jacob D. and John R., are not only prominent business men of Martinsville but have done much towards the upbuilding of the town, some of the best rental property for homes being owned and kept up by the former.

The Aaron Flour Mill is an extensive plant, its products being shipped to many points in large quantities. Mr. J. D. Aaron has also been a metal worker and owner of a shop for years, which has been well known throughout the community.

The first of this family known in Virginia were Jacob Aaron and his wife, Juda. There were three children, a daughter married a Mr. Oakes and lived in an adjoining county. One of the boys was kidnapped when eight years of age and taken to Missouri. He never returned. The other son, John B., located in Henry County. He was born in 1826 and in 1855 married Sarah Jane Oakes whose family came from England and located in Guilford County, North Carolina. Her grandfather served in the War of 1812 and her father was a gallant soldier in the War Between the States.

The children of this family are: Jesse Filmore, Christopher Columbus, Jacob Davis, John Read, Talitha Jane, Alice Laura, Malinda Carr, Lucy Evelyn and Nocolas.

Jesse Filmore married Sallie Giles; Christopher C., Loula Giles; Talitha J., John Carter; Alice Laura, James Smith; Malinda Carr, Frank King; Lucy Evelyn, Frank B. Powell.

John Read Aaron married Jessie Roberta Stanley, daughter of Captain Crockett Stanley, of Henry County. They have an attractive home in Martinsville and their two sons, Jacob and John, are fine, intelligent young men. Their only daughter, Jessie Read, passed away several years ago.

THE ABINGDON FAMILY

The family of William Abingdon lived near Horsepasture, in Henry County. Mrs. Abingdon's maiden name was Philpott, member of a Henry County family.

There were three children, one son and two daughters. Lucy, one of the daughters, taught school near Horsepasture for a number of years.

THE ALLEN FAMILY

William Allen (1725-1788) was the founder of the Allen family in Henry County. His first wife was Mary Lewis, of Campbell County, Virginia. They were parents of thirteen children, the only names of the children available are as follows: Reuben, Meredith, Pleasant, Darling, William, James, Mrs. Mary Morgan, of Alabama, and Mrs. Jarred, of North Carolina.

The second wife of Mr. Allen was Miss Beverly, of Essex County, Virginia, who died after a short while and was survived by one son, Beverly.

Mr. Allen's third wife was Sarah Ann Smith, of Prince George County, Virginia, who with six children survived him. The names of the children were: Robert, Joseph Smith, Pines, Susan, Ellen and Fannie.

The home of the Allens was a small village called Lewiston, now Brengle's Place. Mrs. Allen's second husband was John Bailey and they established a home near the present site of Mount Bethel Church. Mr. and Mrs. Bailey were the parents of one daughter, who married Rev. J. C. Traylor.

Robert Allen, son of William Allen and Sarah Ann Smith, married Celia Mullins, daughter of David Mullins, a Revolutionary soldier; Joseph Smith Allen married Sarah Wade, his second wife was Rachael May. Pines Allen married Charlotte Bailey, his second wife was Nancy Hughes. Susan Allen married William F. Mills; Ellen Allen married Edward Carter, of Pittsylvania County; Fannie, the youngest daughter, married first, James Shelton, soldier of both the Revolutionary War and the War of 1812. Their children were Pines Henderson, Nancy, Polly and James. Mr. Shelton died during the War of 1812 and his widow married William Abingdon.

David Allen, son of Robert Allen and Celia Mullins Allen, married Sally Ann Spencer, daughter of William Spencer and Sallie Parks Hill Spencer. They were the parents of eight sons and four daughters. Amongst these were: Spencer, James, John Mills, Brooks, Eliza Dabney, Forest and America.

Eliza Dabney Allen married James Matthews, of North Carolina, and reared a large family. Coleman Allen married Frances DeShazo, daughter of William DeShazo, of Leatherwood, and moved to Missouri.

After the death of his wife he returned to Henry County with their one child, a daughter who married a Minter and was the mother of two sons namely, Coleman and Lethridge, and a daughter.

Jones Allen, another son of Meredith Allen, married Nancy Cooper and their two children were Nancy and Obediah.

Other members of the various branches of the Allen family have moved to other states. Mrs. William Cox, formerly Forest Allen, of Baldwin, Mississippi, occasionally visits relatives in Henry County.

OBEDIAH ALLEN

Obediah Allen, a veteran of the Civil War, spent many years of his life in Martinsville, Virginia. He held the rank of captain and was honored by the United Daughters of the Confederacy, always receiving the attentions accorded the surviving soldiers by that organization. Mr. Allen's first wife was Eliza J. Martin, whose mother was a sister of Joseph Dickerson, enrolling officer of Henry County and niece of Wash Dickerson.

Mr. Allen's children were, Anna, who married J. R. Bondurant; Nannie married Joseph H. Stultz, prominent business man of Martinsville, Virginia; Sallie married J. H. Hairfield; Lucy, Edd Bondurant; Fannie, J. D. Jones; Jones Allen, Nancy Eggleston; Peachy, Mary Bell.

Late in life Captain Allen married Mrs. Mary Williamson.

THE ANDERSON FAMILY

The founder of this distinguished family was Leonard Anderson, of Prince Edward County, Virginia. His wife was Mary Morton, a granddaughter of Captain Morton of the Revolutionary Army. There were five children, John, Leonard, Robert Campbell, Virginia and Mary.

Robert Campbell Anderson, born in Campbell County, Virginia, came to Henry County and in 1854 organized the first Presbyterian Church in the county, with three members.

Rev. Mr. Anderson's home for many years was near Ridgeway and he built Cedar Chapel as a place of worship near his home. About the time of the Civil War he built a church at Ridgeway. These two churches merged with the one in Martinsville and is now the Anderson Memorial Church. A handsome new building has been erected near the site of the former less pretentious edifice. Mr. Anderson was connected with this church for forty years. He was noted for his implicit faith in the dispensations of Providence and was a devout believer in the efficacy of prayer. He was a graduate of Hampden-Sydney College and Union Theological Seminary of New York.

He married Justinia Armistead, daughter of Rev. Samuel Armistead, a Presbyterian minister and Mary Madison Armistead, of Campbell County, Virginia. Ten children were born to them, all reaching maturity. Samuel Armistead, Mary Morton, Nannie Madison, Katherine Virginia, John Rice, Leonard W., James Lewis, Robert Campbell, Henrietta Alice and Lucy Frances.

Samuel A. Anderson began the practice of law in Martinsville, Henry County, but later went to Richmond, Virginia, where he became a noted lawyer. (See Henry County Bar.) He married Pauline Daniel, of Virginia. Four children were born to them, Pauline, Samuel, Lavillon and Elizabeth. Both Mr. and Mrs. Anderson passed away several years since.

Mary Morton Anderson married Samuel Cole Fontaine. Their children are as follows: Robert, married Genevive Kearfott; William Hale, Gretchen Welty, later Annie Coan Sheffield. One son was born of the first marriage, to whom was given the distinguished family name, Madison.

Samuel C. was accidentally killed while operating an electric plant and Henry was killed accidentally while hunting.

Justinia married Arthur Richardson, of Roanoke, Virginia. She inherits a talent for art for which the Anderson family was noted.

Nannie Madison Anderson married E. L. Williamson, one of Martinsville's most prominent and respected business men.

Katherine Virginia Anderson was a woman of splendid character, unusual talents and was greatly beloved for her works of charity and helpfulness in all good causes. Both she and her sister, Mrs. Fontaine, were artists of recognized ability. Their portrait work has taken high rank. She has passed away.

John R. Anderson graduated from a medical school in Baltimore, and practiced his profession in Henry County for a number of years. He died a few years since.

Leonard W. Anderson became a lawyer and practiced successfully in Rocky Mount, Virginia, for a number of years.

James L. Anderson received his degree at the University of Virginia, and practiced law in Richmond, Virginia. He died January, 1921.

Robert Campbell Anderson graduated at Hampden-Sydney College and at Union Theological Seminary. He has been pastor of the following churches: San Antonio, Texas, Second Presbyterian Church, Roanoke, Virginia, a church in Shelbyville, Kentucky, and in Gastonia, North Carolina. He was elected, by the General Assembly of the Southern Presbyterians, president of the Montreat Association, where he has rendered great service for a number of years. A beautiful auditorium has been named in his honor. Mr. Anderson has been twice married, his first wife was Miss Kate Walker, of Virginia, second, Miss Sadie Gaither, of Charlotte, North Carolina.

Henrietta Alice Anderson married Eugene Richardson, of Farmville, Virginia. They have six children, Katherine Virginia, Robert Anderson, Eugene, Horace Leonard, Hetty Lowery and Louise.

Lucy Frances Anderson married Daniel M. McIntosh, of North Carolina.

Mrs. Justinia Anderson, mother of this large family, was of English descent and was related to four presidents of the United States. She was much honored and beloved by a large circle of relatives and friends. She died in her ninetieth year in her home at Martinsville, Virginia.

THE ANGLIN FAMILY OF HENRY COUNTY, VIRGINIA

The founder of the Anglin family, a family well known and highly esteemed, was Philip Anglin who came to this country, from France, about the year 1750. His son, Philip, was born about 1742 and came with his father to this country.

Philip Anglin II married Miss Frances Cox and spent many years in Henry County, on their farm on North Mayo River.

Philip Anglin III was born in Patrick County, Virginia, in 1797, and lived and died on his farm about eight miles northeast of Martinsville. The members of the older families were farmers and in the days of slavery bought and sold slaves for use on the southern plantations.

JOHN B. ANGLIN

John B. Anglin, son of Philip Anglin III, was born in Patrick County, but moved to Martinsville where he established a home and reared a large family. His first wife was Miss Mary Athey, granddaughter of Peter and Sallie Athey, of Henry County. She was connected with the Hay and Scales families, of North Carolina. There were three children of this union, Mrs. Mattie Ramsey, of Martinsville, Virginia; Mrs. S. N. Rangely, of Bluefield, West Virginia, and Dr. John T. Anglin, of Dover, Oklahoma.

The second wife of J. B. Anglin was Miss Pocahontas Houchins, of Patrick County, Virginia, a woman of fine Christian character and intelligence. She passed away after their removal to Holdenville, Oklahoma, being survived by her husband and six children, W. T. Anglin, Benjamin H. (Harry), Arthur, Charlie, Agnes and Grace.

Few men of the community were better known and more beloved, as friend and neighbor, than John B. Anglin. Shrewd business sense or native ability brought to him a large measure of success. Kindhearted, his never-failing friendliness and cheerfulness endeared him to his neighbors, and sincere was the regret of all when, after their children married and left for homes of their own, Mr. and Mrs. Anglin moved to Holdenville, Oklahoma. During the years after reaching an advanced age, Mr. Anglin was noted for his cheery disposition, and enjoyed life, took a lively interest in business affairs and occasionally visited his friends and members of his family in Virginia and North Carolina. His death occurred in 1932.

DR. JOHN B. ANGLIN

Dr. John B. Anglin was born in Patrick County, Virginia. He was a graduate of Milligan College, Tennessee, and of a Medical College of Richmond, Virginia. He located in Dover, Oklahoma, for the practice of his profession and has been very successful. He married Miss Burleson, who was also a student of Milligan College.

MRS. MATTIE ANGLIN RAMSEY

Mrs. Mattie Anglin Ramsey has made her home in Martinsville, Virginia, since the death of her husband. She has two sons, John A. and Benjamin, to whom she has been a most devoted mother, giving them the best educational advantages obtainable.

Hallie Anglin (Mrs. Sam Rangely) has lived in Bluefield for a number of years. Mr. and Mrs. Rangely are the parents of five sons.

W. T. ANGLIN, OF OKLAHOMA

W. T. Anglin, eldest son of J. B. and Pocahontas Anglin, has become one of the outstanding citizens of his adopted state. He was graduated from the high school of Martinsville, Virginia, Milligan College, Tennessee, and the Law School of the University of Virginia. Having had splendid educational advantages and possessing a brilliant mind, he soon became a leading lawyer of Holdenville and has served his state in many important positions. He was State Senator for three terms, Speaker *pro tem.* of the Senate, Lieutenant Governor and acting Governor of Oklahoma for some time.

Mr. Anglin's wife was Miss Claudia Reed, of Allen, Oklahoma, they have one son, Philip Reed.

BENJAMIN H. (HARRY) ANGLIN

Benjamin H. Anglin was born and reared in Henry County, Virginia, and received his education in the schools of Martinsville. He was one of the brave young men who gave their services in the World War and died of pneumonia in Camp Meade.

ARTHUR ANGLIN

Arthur Anglin was attending a business college in Richmond, Virginia, when the World War began. He joined the army and served in France for four years. After his return he married Miss Hundley, of Calvin, Oklahoma, and is carrying on a successful mercantile business.

CHARLIE ANGLIN

The youngest son, Charlie Anglin, also joined the army to serve his country in the aviation corps. He was called and ready to embark for France when the armistice ended further expeditionary forces being sent over. He continued in the service as a pilot, carrying mail from New York to Chicago, but was compelled to give up flying after being in a crash in a blinding snowstorm. He joined his father in Holdenville, Oklahoma, where they engaged in the motor car business.

Agnes Anglin, the elder of the two daughters, married Charles Cargille, of Johnson City, Tennessee. Mr. Cargille is a successful business man of that city. They have one daughter, Martha Stuart.

The younger daughter, Grace, married William Gresham who has held a place as educator in the schools of Roanoke and Richmond, Virginia, for a number of years.

THE ANSON FAMILY OF MARTINSVILLE, VIRGINIA

The Rev. Alfred W. Anson, for twenty-eight years the esteemed and beloved rector of Christ Church, in Martinsville, Virginia, was born in

HONORABLE W. T. ANGLIN
OF
Holdenville, Oklahoma

Windsor, England. He belonged to a family many of whose members were churchmen, his father being one of the canons to Queen Victoria.

At the age of twenty-one Mr. Anson came to this country and bought a farm in Augusta County, Virginia, but later decided to enter the ministry. His first charge was a congregation in Norfolk, Virginia, then accepting a call to Christ Church in Martinsville, he remained there as rector until ill health forced him to retire a short time before his death. He was twice married, his first wife was Miss Georgiana Green, and his second wife was Mrs. Lena Moore Green.

Having a large family of daughters, the rectory became one of the social centers of the town and weddings were frequent occurrences.

The children of Mr. Anson and Georgiana Green Anson were: Caroline, who married William H. Gravely, an attorney at law, of Martinsville; Mary married Mr. Thomas G. Burch, a prominent business man, now congressman from the Fifth Virginia District; Grace married Mr. John Jamison, an attorney at law, of Roanoke, Virginia. Misses Ethel and Lucy Anson make their homes in Martinsville, but spend much of their time with relatives in England. The only son, William Anson, passed away in 1916. His wife, who was Miss Vera Seay, survives him and makes her home in Roanoke, Virginia.

Frances R. Green, daughter of Mrs. Lena Green Anson, married Mr. Arthur Barr, of Washington, D. C. He died several years since. Mary Green married Dr. Taylor, also deceased. Both Mrs. Barr and Mrs. Taylor make their homes in Martinsville and take leading parts in social activities and work connected with the church. Mrs. Anson's only son, Joseph Green, died a few years since.

Hilda, the elder of the two daughters of Mr. Anson and Mrs. Lena Green Anson, died after a lingering illness just as she reached womanhood. Edith Vernon, the younger daughter, married Mr. Osborne Taylor, of Roanoke, Virginia.

THE ANTHONY FAMILY OF HENRY COUNTY

Joseph Anthony was the original Anthony in Henry County. The original deeds show that he had property on Beaver Creek and Marrowbone Creek near Martinsville.

The names of his children are: Elizabeth, Mark and Bolling Anthony.

The family of Benjamin Anthony lived in Patrick County and after his death moved to Henry, having bought the home and farm near Spencer, Virginia, formerly owned by the France family.

The Anthony family consisted of Mrs. Anthony, two sons, Virgil and Homer, and five daughters, Sarah, who married Mack Bradley; Columbia died after a lingering illness; Nettie married James Walters, of Richmond, Virginia; Morgiana married Dr. Lester, a dentist of Roanoke, Virginia, and Susan who was unmarried.

THE BARBOUR FAMILY OF HENRY COUNTY, VIRGINIA

Thomas N. Barbour, one of Martinsville's most prominent business men, was a native of Campbell County, Virginia. He came to Martinsville in 1889 and engaged in the hardware business in which he continued successfully for a period of forty years. Mr. Barbour was born about the close of the Civil War, six months after his father was killed in battle.

He married Elizabeth Smith, youngest daughter of the late Dr. James M. Smith and Mrs. Corinna Smith, of Martinsville.

Mrs. Barbour is a woman of unusual intellectual ability and has taken a leading part in social, church and literary activities.

The children of Mr. and Mrs. Barbour are: Charles, Thomas N., Elizabeth, Mary and Martha. The eldest son, Thomas N., lost his life in a distressing accident—a gun being discharged in the hands of a playmate. The unusual and beautiful tribute to the eldest son was giving his name which was also his father's to a younger son born several years later.

Elizabeth, the eldest daughter, married Mr. Jervey, of Jacksonville, Florida.

THE BARKER FAMILY OF HENRY COUNTY

J. M. Barker, of Axton, is one of Henry County's successful business men, having acquired a large area of land which he improved to such an extent that it brought rich returns. By gradually adding to his estate he became one of the largest land owners and planters in the county.

Mr. Barker also has taken great interest in public affairs. He served as supervisor for his district for a number of years and was a very efficient officer. He was appointed a member of the State Board of Agriculture a second time by Governor A. J. Montague.

Mr. Barker's wife was Miss Roach. The children are as follows: James Monroe, Jr. (deceased), married Maggie Haley; William Henry, Lizzie Haley; Christey Gordon, Lily Gravely.

Margie, daughter of Mr. and Mrs. Monroe Barker, married Donald Arnold, of Vermont. Mr. Arnold is a brother-in-law of Governor Case, of Vermont.

THE BARROW FAMILY OF HENRY COUNTY

The first Henry County home of the Barrow family was in the Leatherwood section. The founder of this family was William Barrow. His wife was Susan Marshall, daughter of Dennis Marshall. Their children, two sons and five daughters, were: Benjamin, William, Cassandra, Mary, Julia, Ann and Susan.

William Barrow married Elizabeth King. His second wife was Mary Cahill. There were five children, George, Columbus, Ferdinand, Tippie and Jennie.

Cassandra Barrow married first, Armistead Jones. Her second husband was Gresham Choice. They moved to Texas and their only son returned to Virginia and married Loula Griggs, daughter of Colonel Jerry Griggs, of Martinsville, but returned to Texas where they spent their lives.

Mary Barrow married Charles Stockton, and their children were: Peter, John, Edward, Molly and Virginia. Julia Barrow married James Arnold, and they made their home in St. Clair, Missouri. They were the parents of six children, William, Sam, Marshall, Edd, Eliza and Susan.

Ann Barrow married Willis Gravely who was a member of a firm of very prominent tobacco manufacturers. (See Gravely Family.) Susan Barrow married William Stockton.

Benjamin Barrow married Susan Watkins who was of French Huguenot descent. They were the parents of nine children, Robert, Orrin, John A., Watkins, Pete Tom, Benjamin F., Mary, Nannie and Cassandra.

Robert Barrow never married, Orrin also remained unmarried. He was a distinguished soldier in the Civil War, serving as captain of volunteers in the Confederate ranks. He was twice wounded, but nothing daunted, led his command to victory while suffering from a severe wound which he had received some time previous. His uniform is being kept in the Smithsonian Institute in Washington, D. C.

John A. Barrow married Mary Smith and they were the parents of two children, Albert and Mabel.

Pete Tom Barrow made his home in Danville, Virginia. His wife was Dora Guerrant. Their children are: Ben, Nannie, Tom, George, John and Elva.

Mary Barrow married Dr. Jesse H. Turner and their home is the old family homestead, "Barrow's Mill." The names of their children are as follows: Walter, Lelia, Edd, Ella, Orrin, Lottie, Jessie, Watt and Irvin.

BENJAMIN F. BARROW

Benjamin F. (Nib) Barrow was one of Henry County's popular and influential citizens. His genial disposition and kindness of heart won for him many warm, lifelong friends. Mrs. Barrow was Judith Sheffield, daughter of Colonel William Sheffield, of the Ridgeway community. Mr. Barrow owned and managed large farms, but for many years prior to his death made his home in Martinsville, driving out each morning to look after the work being done on his estates.

The family consisted of Mr. and Mrs. Barrow, three sons and two daughters, William, Pete S., Benjamin F., Susan W. and Kate.

William died just as he reached maturity. Pete S. married Corinne Brown, daughter of the late John Andrew and Pattie Smith Brown. They make their home in Bluefield, West Virginia. Susan W. married James H. Mongel, of near Abingdon, Virginia. Kate occupies the Barrow home in Martinsville and is interested in church and social activities.

Benjamin F. Barrow is a successful business man of Roanoke, Virginia, and is highly esteemed in his community. His wife was Hazel Middaugh, an accomplished and talented violinist.

Nannie Barrow married Captain William F. H. Lee, of Franklin County. (See Lee Family.)

Cassandra Barrow married Clack Stone, who died in early life. (See Stone family.)

THE BASSETTS OF HENRY COUNTY, VIRGINIA

The Bassetts trace their lineage to ancestors of early English families who were distinguished as statesmen, many of them belonging to the nobility.

The first of the name in America was William Bassett, who came over in 1621. He was a man of education and brought with him a library of unusual proportions for that time. The first known of the Virginia Bassetts was William of the Isle of Wight.

J. D. BASSETT, Sr.
OF
Bassett, Henry County, Virginia

Burwell Bassett bought a tract of land of Colonel George Hairston, of Revolutionary fame, in 1790. This land is still owned by a descendant of the purchaser.

Burwell Bassett married Mary Hunter, 1794. There were four sons and two daughters born to them. Alexander Hunter, William Nathaniel, George Hairston, Burwell, Mary and Martha. Alexander Hunter married Mary Koger; William Nathaniel, Jane C. Staples; George Hairston, Columbia Staples; Burwell, Malinda Waller; Mary, Charles Philpott, second, Woodson Morris; Martha, Burwell Bassett.

The mother and all except Alexander Hunter moved to Missouri. He settled in the home built by his father. The children of this family were: Martha A., who married John Dyer, son of David Dalton Dyer, and moved to Missouri. Woodson married first, Julia Prunty, second, Mary Price. John Bassett married Nancy Spencer. Their children were as follows: J. D., C. C., Joseph, Samuel, Mary and Nancy.

Eliza Bassett, second daughter of Alexander Hunter Bassett, married Allen Hopper. The third daughter, Mary Catherine, married William W. Hill. Harden died while in the Confederate Army.

THE BASSETT BROTHERS OF BASSETT, VIRGINIA

Among the men who have aided in "making Henry County famous" are J. D. and C. C. Bassett, sons of John and Nancy Spencer Bassett. They are founders of a thriving town about ten miles northwest of Martinsville, which is in itself a monument to the industry, foresight and business ability cᶠ these two men. The furniture factory, starting on a small scale, now ships a large amount of furniture each year to various points from the Atlantic to the Pacific.

The town has several department stores, a bank, hotel, and a good graded school with high school departments, and the building is modern and well equipped. There are nice, comfortable homes for employees as well as the handsome and commodious homes of the two Bassett families.

J. D. Bassett married Pocahontas Hundley and they are the parents of two sons and two daughters, William, J. D. Jr., Blanche and Anne. C. C. Bassett married Roxy Hundley. The tragic death of these two in an automobile accident, as they were on their way to their winter home in Florida, caused great sorrow in the community. They are survived by three daughters and one son, Mabel, Avis, Doris and Edwin.

THE BOOKER FAMILY

The Bookers of Henry County, while distantly related, are of two distinct families. They are descendants of Edward Booker, a large tobacco manufacturer of London, England. His son, Captain Richard Booker, came to Virginia and obtained large grants of land in Gloucester County, about 1685. He married Rebecca Leake and they reared one son, Richard, who married Margaret Lowry, daughter of William and Frances Purefoy Lowry.

In 1732 a patent of 970 acres of land in Prince George County (now Amelia) was granted to Richard Booker, "Gentleman," of James City County. He was justice of the court of James City County in 1730, and died in York in 1743. There was one son, William. (1714–1755.) His son, Lowry, married Phoebe Cox, of Charlotte County, Virginia. A son of Lowry Booker and Phoebe Cox Booker settled in Franklin County, Virginia, near the Henry line at Shady Grove.

Edward Booker was born about 1810. He married Martha Sheffield, sister of Colonel William Sheffield. Their children were: John, who married Julia Hamlet; Leonard died in the Civil War; Edward married Judith Carter, daughter of James Carter, of Spencer, Virginia; Lowry was unmarried; Mary married W. E. Haynes, of West Virginia; Martha married John O. King, of Henry County, and Jesse Wootton Booker married Sallie C. Cook, of Franklin County, Virginia (see sketch), and for many years have made their home in Martinsville in which place Mr. Booker and his sons have been engaged in business. The children of this family are: Samuel Edward, Lowry Sheffield, Jesse Wootton, Fletcher Clement, Mildred Ann and Mary Catherine.

Samuel E. Booker married Mildred E. Smith, of Culpeper County; Lowery C. not married; Jesse W., Jr., Claude Clanton; Fletcher C., Mildred Ashforth; Mildred Ann, Dr. George P. Dillard, son of Samuel Dillard and grandson of Dr. George Dillard, of Henry County.

Mary Booker, the younger daughter of Mr. and Mrs. J. W. Booker, married R. Sydney King.

MRS. SALLIE COOK BOOKER

Mrs. Sallie Cook Booker has the distinction of being the first and up to the present time the only woman to represent Henry County in the House of Delegates. She was a native of Franklin County, Virginia, and after her marriage made her home in Martinsville, her husband being engaged in business in that place.

Mrs. Booker is a woman of marvelous energy, wide intelligence and was deeply interested in affairs pertaining to the government and welfare of the country. She was a member of the Fifth District Congressional Committee, and later was a member of the Democratic Executive Committee. She was elected to the Virginia House of Delegates in 1925, without opposition, and served through 1926, and again in 1927 in an extra session called by Governor Byrd on account of governmental reforms inaugurated by himself. She was again nominated in 1927 for the 1928 session with no opposition at first, but later was opposed by R. L. Stone, a Republican, of Bassett, whose campaign slogan was "Membership in the General Assembly is a man's job." The voters evidently did not coincide with him in that opinion as Mrs. Booker was reëlected. When asked about the election some time since, Mrs. Booker said, "Mr. Stone made a gentlemanly campaign—entirely free from 'mud slinging' and when defeated was too gallant to 'sulk in his tents'."

Mrs. Booker did not seek reëlection to the 1930 session, having served three terms including the extra session. She was the third Virginia woman to be elected to the General Assembly. She says further, "The House members were very kind and considerate of Mrs. Sara Lee Fain, of Norfolk, and myself, the only two women in the 1926–27 sessions. On the closing night the elder woman of the two members (Mrs. Fain) was presented with a sterling silver pitcher.

"I spent twenty-five years of my life in the teaching profession and I do not think it impossible for a woman to have a career and at the same time be a home maker. I believe a woman's greatest work is in the home and the bulwark of the nation is the quiet home maker whose name is never seen in print."

All who know Mrs. Booker and the sons and daughters reared by Mr. and Mrs. Booker need no further evidence of the ability of at least one woman in the community to combine a career with home making.

THE BOOKER FAMILY OF PATRICK AND HENRY COUNTIES, VIRGINIA

Edward Booker, a cousin of Edward Booker, of Shady Grove, was born in Cumberland County, Virginia, in 1794. He moved to Patrick County when twenty-five years of age, after serving in the War of 1812. His wife was Elizabeth Anglin and their children were: George W., Richard A., John, Marshall and Elizabeth.

George W. Booker was born in 1822. He studied law and practiced his profession for many years. He represented Henry County in the Legislature just after the Civil War, and in 1868 was elected to Congress from the Fifth District of Virginia. His wife was Maria Philpott, daughter of David Philpott, of Henry County. The family included four children, George William, John Minor Botts, Ruth and Sallie.

GEORGE W. BOOKER

George W. Booker was one of the most interesting characters that ever lived in Martinsville or Henry County. He was endowed with a superior intellect, cultured and enriched by a lifetime of reading. His brain was stored with the treasures of English and American literature. His memory was simply prodigious. It was not only gripping in its character and habit, but it was also accurate in its deliveries. His quotations from the classics of the English language were always word perfect. For this and other reasons he was altogether one of the most interesting conversationalists I have ever encountered. For one thing, above most others, I liked him; he never attempted to improve on Shakespeare. For example, ninety-nine men out of a hundred will make a loose, vague effort like this: "He that hath no music in his soul," etc. Shakespeare said nothing about a soul in this connection. The subject of this sketch would quote the entire passage crisply and accurately,

> " *The man that hath no music in himself,*
> *Nor is not moved with concord of sweet sounds*
> *Is fit for treasons, stratagems and spoils*
> *The motions of his spirit are dull as night*
> *And his affections dark as Erebus.*
> *Let no such man be trusted.*"

With the possible exception of one or two tragedians I have had the pleasure of knowing, he could quote Shakespeare more fluently and more accurately than any other man I have ever met.

His answers to questions were prompt, definite and usually edifying, one illustration of this trait will suffice. Once upon a time when he was sitting in an easy chair in front of the Lavinder store, engaged in quiet conversation with a small group of his friends, a half grown boy approached him and fired this at him: "Mr. Booker, do you believe these people in a camp just outside of town are real sure enough gypsies?" "I don't know, do they say they are gypsies?" "Yes, sir." "Well, I suppose they must be gypsies then, I can't imagine any man acknowledging he is a gypsy unless he is one." No silly idealizing there, you can read between the lines his opinion of the average gypsy character.

Many years ago before conversation was a lost art, Mr. Thomas E. Donnegan, the brilliant and eccentric school master, described elsewhere in this volume, made the following unusual and reckless proposition to a friend of his: "Let's go over and visit George Booker and outtalk him on English Literature." The friend bravely accepted the invitation, the visit was made and a frank and full report was made by Mr. Donnegan on his return. He said, that Mr. Booker did not seem to know that any contest was going on, but that naturally he was very much interested in the subject under discussion and that first and last he quoted fifty English authors of whom neither of his visitors had ever heard! The experiment was never repeated.

A character sketch of George Booker would be incomplete without a record of one outstanding trait. He was not a forgiving man. He was as relentless towards his enemies as he was loyal to his friends. The Sermon on the Mount did not appeal to him. Not only this, but when opportunity offered he did not hesitate to avenge an injury, this always in a quiet manner and in perfect fairness. He had about three favorite enemies. It seems that in his earlier and more active years he had saved up some thousands of dollars as a provision for support of himself and his wife in old age. He accused these three men of inveigling him into some sort of business and swindling him out of all his possessions. After many years one of these men was nominated for the State Senate, to represent Henry and Patrick Counties. Here was the long awaited opportunity, he could not afford a horse but he was a good walker, so he dropped everything else and undertook a patient, strenuous, house-to-house canvass in behalf of the opposing candidate. He said he would enter into a "covenant with death and an agreement with hell" in order to compass this man's defeat. The political party whose interests he was incidentally serving saw that he was doing uncommonly effective work, and wisely invested part of their fund in a horse, saddle and bridle, turned this outfit over to him for his exclusive use, and furnished enough money for horse feed, currying and other incidental expenses and told him to go forth. He went forth. Whether walking or riding in that memorable campaign, he had with him a walking cane designed and fashioned by himself. He was an amateur wood carver—could have made his living by following this trade. Once, in the latter half of the campaign, I was sitting with him on somebody's front porch listening to his review of the political situation. I reached for the cane to inspect the beautiful work he had done on it, and found carved in perfect capitals and small letters a famous quotation from Byron's Mazeppa—

> *"For time at last sets all things even*
> *And if we do but watch the hour,*
> *There never yet was human power*
> *That could evade, if unforgiven*
> *The patient search and vigil long*
> *Of him who treasures up a wrong."*

The campaign ended to Mr. Booker's entire satisfaction. His candidate was elected over his ancient enemy by four hundred majority. Quite a mob of us gathered in around the *Herald* office to hear the returns. When the result became assured, I endeavored to start a conversation with Mr. Booker, but for once in his life the experiment failed. Something in the situation seemed to take away his power of speech, but he circulated speechlessly around through the crowd with a smile on his face that for inscrutability would have faded Mona Lisa's feeble effort off the map. There was an expression also of deep and abiding satisfaction, the equal of which I have never seen before or since.

THE BOULDIN FAMILY

John Bouldin was a citizen of the Grassy Creek locality. He was a landowner and after his death the family, consisting of Thomas C., Anna G. and Mary, moved to Martinsville, where Thomas Bouldin engaged in business. The family is of English descent and came to this country about 1760.

THE BROWN FAMILY OF HENRY COUNTY

Among the prominent families that came to Henry County and cast their lot with our people were the families of Frederick R. and John R. Brown, who came from Franklin County to Martinsville in 1882, and engaged in the manufacture of tobacco. So successful were they that they became a potent factor in the upbuilding of the town.

The Browns are of English descent, Frederick Brown, the ancestor of this family, was born in 1745. His children were: Frederick, Reuben, John and Tarleton.

John married Sarah Rives Brown, their children were: John Spottswood, Reuben Skelton, Frederick Rives, William Alexander, Nancy, Gorman and Sarah.

Frederick Rives Brown married Jane Prunty Brown, their children were: Eliza Jane, John R. and Nancy. His second wife was Elizabeth E. Brown and their children were: Lucy, who married Henry Lester, Tarleton and Millard Filmore.

Frederick R. Brown occupied a prominent place in Franklin as well as in Henry County. He was a representative in the Virginia Legislature from Franklin County.

Colonel William Z. Brown, son of John and Sarah Rives Brown, married Susan Finney. Their children were: William, Walter, Lula and George Akers. Colonel Brown manufactured tobacco for forty-three years. One of his famous brands of plug tobacco was Brown's Log Cabin. He was not only a successful business man but took great interest in political affairs. He was elected to represent his county in the Legislature and was also State Senator.

John R. Brown, son of Frederick R. Brown, married Eliza Vial. The following children were born to them, viz.: Nannie, Alice, Frederick R., William, Rosa, Kate, May, Annie, John Andrew and Lula. Nannie married Dr. Charles P. Smith. Their children are: John and Charles P., Jr. Alice married Edward Gaines, of Gainesville, Georgia. She died in 1921, leaving a large family. Frederick R. Brown married Etta Burge. Willie and Rosa died in infancy. May married George M. Finley (see Finley family). Kate married C. E. Van Pelt, who died in 1929. John Andrew Brown married Pattie Smith, daughter of Dr. James M. Smith. He died in 1893 and was survived by his wife and the following children: Pattie, who married A. N. Hodgson; Corinne, P. S. Barrow; John Andrew, Mary Elizabeth Jones; James Moss died in early manhood.

Several years after the death of John Andrew Brown, Sr., Mrs. Brown married E. M. Dickinson; she died a few years after her second marriage and was survived by Mr. Dickinson and several children.

Tarleton F. Brown married Annie Eliza Brown. Their children were: Elizabeth, who died in infancy; Mattie married G. M. Andes; Lucy, Dr. M. E. Hundley; Rives, Cornelia Gregory. Rives Brown is one of Martinsville's most successful young men and owns one of the handsomest homes in a town noted for beautiful homes.

William B. Brown, son of Colonel William Brown, married Lula

Dudley, one daughter, Doris, was born to them. Walter Spottswood Brown married Virginia Williams, granddaughter of Senator R. E. Withers of Virginia.

Sarah Brown married G. A. Dudley (see Dudley family). Lula married George William Coan, son of John O. Coan and Mary Jones Coan (see Coan family). George Akers Brown married Minnie Matthews. He has been one of Martinsville's most prominent citizens for many years, was a successful merchant and after retiring from that business was elected mayor of the town for several successive terms. The family consist of Mr. and Mrs. Brown and five daughters.

Henry Taylor and Millard Fillmore Brown were sons of John Spottswood Brown, of Franklin County. They came to Henry County and entered into business about 1882.

The children of Taylor Brown were: Susan, who married Joseph Schartza and lives in Washington, D. C.; Mary and Clark, the latter married Dona Marshall, of Martinsville, Virginia.

Mary J. Lucy Brown married A. C. Poindexter and they made their home in Martinsville, Virginia. Mr. Poindexter died a few years since and is survived by his wife.

The daughters of George Akers Brown and Minnie Mathews Brown are as follows: Catherine married John Randolph, of New York; Sue, Wayles Harrison, of Danville, Virginia; Mary, C. L. Boothe, Jr., of Danville, Virginia; Lucy Akers, J. D. Bassett, of Bassett, Virginia. Minnie May Brown, the youngest daughter, is engaged in educational work in Martinsville, Virginia.

THE BRYANT FAMILY

Major Roland Bryant came to Martinsville, Virginia, from Rockbridge County. He had at that time one son, Charles B. Bryant (see sketch).

Major Bryant married Susan Wells Gregory, daughter of Frank Wells and Sarah Smith Wells. Mrs. Gregory was a widow whose husband died in the Civil War. She had five sons, namely: Overton, who married Eliza J. Hill, daughter of Rev. W. W. Hill; J. R. Gregory married Josie Rierson, of North Carolina, and they were the parents of a son and daughter: Robert, who married Mildred Stephens, and Cornelia, who married Rives Brown (see Brown family); Tom Gregory married Minnie Walker, and two sons were born to them; Joseph Gregory married Mary Norman, and they make their home in Roanoke.

The children of Major Roland and Mrs. Bryant are as follows: William F., Rowland, Norvell and Sallie.

CHARLES B. BRYANT OF HENRY COUNTY, VIRGINIA, 1842–1915

Charles B. Bryant was one of the most brilliant men and unique characters that ever lived in Henry County. He was the son of Major Roland Bryant, who came to Martinsville, from Rockbridge County. He studied civil engineering and later law. Chancery practice was his specialty. When the Civil War broke out he enlisted and was made a colonel of the Virginia Militia. He served in the quartermaster's department being an adjutant in the army.

Later he was called from his military occupation to accept the clerkship of the Henry County and Circuit Courts, holding this office until the close of the War. For a short while he did civil engineering, but was elected mayor in 1881.

Colonel Bryant's mind was unusually alert and his wit well known. His vision and efficiency in planning improvements, and influencing others to advance the interests of Martinsville are well remembered. The promotion of railroads, water power and inventions claimed his attention and to him the county is greatly indebted for many improvements.

He was the engineer and negotiator of the town's water rights, Secretary of the Phospho Lithia Springs Company, and Secretary of the Henry County Historical Society.

Colonel Bryant married Miss Malinda Waller, member of a prominent Henry County family, and they maintained a handsome home in Martinsville. No children were born to them but they adopted two, Joseph and Annie Oakes, who took the Bryant name and were cared for and reared by Colonel and Mrs. Bryant as if they had been their own. Colonel Bryant passed away in 1915 and Mrs. Bryant only a few years later.

MAJOR BRYANT'S COURT

Preliminary to any thing like a character sketch of Major Roland Bryant it becomes necessary to clip a strange chapter from the history of Martinsville. The town had a new charter, that is it had been new. It had been somewhat used and abused for several years. That charter provided as plainly as the English language could express it that the voters should elect a council to be composed of nine members and that the council should elect one of their own members as mayor. Surely no citizen of the town had ever taken the time or trouble to read that charter. At any rate we went serenely on electing our mayors year in and year out by direct vote of the people. Eventually, there was a close election followed by a cry of "fraud" and then a contest. The attorneys, before presenting the two sides of the case to the court, thought they might as well wake up and read that charter once, so the breath-taking discovery was made, and of course the court could only say that there had not been any election. Indeed, there had not been a lawful election of mayor for several years. How the official acts of these unlawfully elected mayors were ever legalized this deponent sayeth not. However, I do say that we pulled ourselves together and did things in perfect technical form in all the years that followed.

Soon after this something else happened, nothing exceptional this time, we started the usual "citizens'" movement to oust the equally familiar "court house ring." It was a hard fought campaign. When the returns came in we found that we of the citizens' movement had elected four members of the council and the court house ring had elected four. Major Roland Bryant was elected independently of both factions. In the parlance of that time, "he stood on his own platform." Major Bryant had the mayoralty bee in his bonnet. In addition to the salary that office carried with it the judicial functions and authority of a magistrate's court. Major Roland Bryant was duly elected Lord Mayor of Martinsville, and as some local wit expressed it "we had a year of it."

There was little or no employment for boys and young men in Martinsville in those days. Youth must have some outlet for its superfluous energy; when there is nothing else for them to do they turn hoodlum. The boys under consideration developed a code of ethics, the chief provision of which was that it was entirely legitimate and honorable to swear to anything in Mayor Bryant's court.

After a night of stupendous devilment he would corral a bunch out of the usual gang and you could not tell for the life of you which were culprits and which were witnesses. He treated them with judicial impartiality. The boys, by a certain diabolical ingenuity, would becloud the issues with perjured and contradictory testimony until they would get the case into a hopeless tangle which would have puzzled King Solomon himself in his best days. Not so with Mayor Bryant. His treatment of the problem was simplicity itself. He would fine the whole crowd, prisoners and witnesses alike, and thus would be sure to get the guilty ones. His usual fine was one dollar. He knew they could not appeal against so small a penalty. On one such occasion he caught in his dragnet his stepson, the late Robert Gregory. His victim arose in the court room and said "Please your Honor, I wasn't in town when this thing was done. I spent the night in Ridgeway, ten miles from Martinsville." He produced two thoroughly competent witnesses and conclusively proved his alibi. The Mayor looked thoughtfully into his pocket memorandum book for a moment and said, "Well, I'll not remit the fine any way, if you had been here you would have been with that gang." Bob afterwards commented to the effect that he thought the old gentleman's opinion on that last point was probably sound. If he had been in Martinsville he guessed he would have been with the boys all right, and he would have paid his fine cheerfully, but he hated awfully to part from a good American dollar for fun he might have had if he had been in town.   L. G. P.

BULLARD

Dr. Chester Bullard, of Snowville, Virginia, was the first to organize the Christian Church in Henry County. He married Mrs. Lucy Redd Wootton and lived for many years near Ridgeway.

THE BURCH FAMILY OF HENRY COUNTY, VIRGINIA

John W. Burch was a citizen of the Leatherwood community in Henry County. His wife was Sarah Frances Minter.

Mr. Burch's family included four sons and one daughter: Thomas Granville Burch (see sketch), Waller P., Mary E., William G. and John J.

HONORABLE THOMAS G. BURCH, OF MARTINSVILLE, VIRGINIA

Thomas Granville Burch was born in the Leatherwood district of Henry County, Virginia, and in early life came to Martinsville and entered into a most successful business career; first in the insurance business which is still carried on under the name of Burch-Hodges-Stone, Incorporated, and is one of the oldest insurance agencies in southside Virginia. His business activities have been enlarged until its ramifications extend to many institutions in Martinsville and Henry County, particularly in furniture, banking, building companies and agricultural development.

A citizen of his character, integrity and industry could not remain in private life and soon he was called to public service as an officer in the public schools, in the governing bodies of local institutions, and as mayor of the city. Under the Wilson administration he served as marshall of the Western District of Virginia in a manner that invoked the highest praise from those high in the federal service. This position placed him in touch with the state at large and his talent for business administration was soon seen by those high in the positions of the state, who called him to service in the agricultural and educational departments of the Commonwealth.

In 1930, Mr. Burch succeeded Joseph Whitehead as Congressman from the Fifth Virginia District and has taken a most honorable stand in the House of Representatives and is recognized both in Washington and Richmond as one of the leading Democrats of Virginia. He married Mary Anson, daughter of the late Rev. Alfred Anson. They reside in a most delightful home in Martinsville, Virginia.

THE CALLOWAY FAMILY

The history of the Calloway family dates back to the Fourteenth Century. The name in early times was spelled Callway. In a list of books taken from the library of the British Museum, written by the members of the family, there is evidence of superior literary attainments. An interesting connection of the family is Marian Caloway, of Stratford-on-Avon, who is the only living descendant of Anne Hathaway.

The ancestry of the Calloways in America is traced to William (Gulie) Calloway, born 1624. The original ancestor of the Calloways in Virginia was William Calloway, of Bedford County. He married Elizabeth Tilley and they were the parents of five sons.

John or Jack Calloway came to Rocky Hill, Henry County, from Horse Shoe Farm, on the Yadkin River, in North Carolina. He was a descendant of Colonel James Calloway, of Bedford, or Campbell County. From a miniature picture of John Calloway painted in London, there is enclosed a stamp resembling a king's seal. The design contains the crowned head and name of George III, and an inscription in Latin, "Shame on him that evil thinks" also "God and My Right." The former is the same adopted by the old English Knights of the Garter.

America Hairston, daughter of Elizabeth Letcher and Colonel George Hairston, married John Calloway and their children are: George Hairston Calloway and Bethenia Ruth Calloway who married George Pannill (see Pannill family).

THE CARTER FAMILY OF HENRY COUNTY, VIRGINIA

Mr. James H. Carter, well-known citizen of Henry County, owned and lived upon a farm between Horsepasture and Spencer.

His first wife was Elizabeth Hill and they were parents of two daughters and one son, viz.: Judith who married Edward H. Booker; Sallie, William A. Latimer, and John Waddy who became a prominent attorney at law and practiced his profession in Martinsville, Virginia. His first wife was Mary Smead, of Salem, Virginia. Two sons were born to them, John W. and Louis.

Several years after the death of Mrs. Mary Smead Carter, Mr. Carter married Keziah Drewry, daughter of Dr. Henry M. Drewry. They were the parents of two daughters, Keziah and Ruth.

John W. Carter married Mary Picket, of Canada. Louis married Sara Morgan and they make their home in Philadelphia. Keziah has taught in the Martinsville and county schools several sessions and she and Ruth Redd, who married Edd Whitener, formerly of North Carolina, make their home in Martinsville.

THE CLANTON FAMILY

The Clanton family came from Brunswick and are of English descent. William Clanton, born in 1779, came to this county when a young man and acquired about 3,000 acres of land. His wife was Polly Thornton, of Cascade, and their children, George, Jesse and Dolly.

George W. Clanton was born in 1818 and his wife was Mary Hylton. He was a planter and owned a large boundary of land in the western part of the county and a large number of slaves.

Jesse Clanton was twice married, his first wife was Kinnie King and one son was born to them, Willie C. His second wife was Columbia King and their children are: Mary, Lillie, Nannie, Bessie, George, Robert and Jesse.

The children of George W. and Mary Hylton Clanton are: Mary E., Nancy Hylton, George W. and Hylton Claude.

Eliza Clanton married John Salmons, she lived to the unusual age of over a hundred years. Their children were: Edward, George, Jesse, Lou and Dolly. Dolly Clanton married Franklin Griggs; Mary married John Gravely; Betsy married Garnet Philpott.

The children of George W. Clanton are as follows: Nancy married William Rangely; Mary K. and George William unmarried; Hylton married Mary Bennie Jones, their children are: Claudia, Lucille, William and George.

Claudia married Jesse W. Booker, a prominent business man of Martinsville; Lucille married Claude A. Turner, a successful business man also of Martinsville.

THE CLARK FAMILY OF PATRICK COUNTY, VIRGINIA

Dr. George R. Clark was a prominent physician of Russell Creek, Patrick County, Virginia. He was twice married, his first wife was Bettie Ross and his second Sallie Dalton.

The children of Dr. Clark are as follows: Nora, who married H. I. Tuggle; Emma; Carrie; Sue, who married Bob Shelton, of Winston-Salem; George, who married Jean Waller, daughter of Dr. George E. Waller and Mrs. Sarah Putzel Waller, of Martinsville, Virginia.

Mr. and Mrs. George Clark have made their home in Taylorsville, California, where Mr. Clark is engaged in business.

The two sons of Dr. George Clark and Mrs. Sallie Dalton Clark are Samuel and Charles.

The Clark family are of English descent and have been for many years one of Patrick County's leading families. The home of Dr. Clark was noted for real Virginia hospitality. Before the advent of automobiles when "Old Dobbin" could make only twenty-five or thirty miles a day over roads more or less rough and often heavy with mud, travelers through Patrick County will long remember the splendid hospitality accorded them in the home of Dr. George R. Clark.

THE FAMILY OF DR. JOSEPH CLARK, OF PATRICK COUNTY, VIRGINIA

Dr. Joseph Clark, one of Patrick County's prominent physicians, lived near the county seat, Stuart, and, like many of the practitioners, looked after a large farm and attended the sick of the community as well.

Mrs. Clark was Ella Jefferson, also of Patrick County and they were parents of five sons and three daughters. John R. Clark engaged in the mercantile business in Stuart with great success. He married Viola Massey and they have a most attractive home.

Edward L. Clark, also a successful business man of Stuart, married Anna Massey. Walter E. married Mabel Lawson; William H., Mary Howard; Lillian married W. E. Shelton; Bessie, W. E. Simmons; Joseph J. Clark and May Clark live at the family home.

THE COAN FAMILY OF HENRY COUNTY, VIRGINIA

John O. Coan came from South Carolina and became a business man of note in Ridgeway, Henry County, Virginia. He was engaged in the mercantile business and in farming. He was also a popular teacher and later in life was the first Mayor of Ridgeway, being reëlected to that office successively for a number of years. His wife was Mary Jones and their children, Betty, Loula, George William, Posey, Bird and John O., Jr. Betty Coan married Leonard Sheffield, of Henry County; Loula Coan married A. H. Bouseman, Mayor of Ridgeway; George William married Loula Brown, of Franklin County, later of Henry County; Posey D. Coan married J. J. Cox, of Tennessee; John O., Jr., married Mary Montague, of Winston-Salem, North Carolina.

GEORGE WILLIAM COAN

George W. Coan, Sr., was an energetic, popular and successful young business man of Henry County, Virginia. In 1899 he accepted a position as Postmaster in Winston-Salem. Later he became connected with the R. J. Reynolds Tobacco Company in which he rose steadily until he was recognized as one of the leading members of that tremendous organization.

Mr. Coan's wife was Miss Lula Brown, of Martinsville, Virginia.

(From the society column of a local paper)

"Cards are out for the marriage of Miss Lula M. Brown, one of Martinsville's most popular belles and Mr. G. W. Coan, one of Danville's young business men. The marriage will take place in the Broad Street Christian Church on Wednesday."

The family circle of Mr. and Mrs. Coan consists of Mr. and Mrs. Coan, George W., Jr., and Mrs. May Coan Mountcastle.

GEORGE W. COAN, POPULAR MAYOR OF WINSTON-SALEM, NORTH CAROLINA

George W. Coan, Jr., was born in Henry County, Virginia, but most of his life was spent in Winston-Salem, having come to this city when a lad in 1899. Mr. Coan, although still a young man, has had a remarkable career. He graduated from the Winston-Salem public schools in 1907 and entered Davidson College from which he was graduated in 1911. After working one year in the offices of the R. J. Reynolds Tobacco Company he completed a special postgraduate course in Commercial Law and Business Administration at Harvard 1912-13, and occupied the position as clerk at the R. J. Reynolds Tobacco Company offices until 1915, at which time he entered the real estate business. In 1917, he organized and became active manager of the first industrial bank operated in Winston-Salem, becoming president and controlling stockholder. He withdrew from this business in 1928 and organized a private investment and banking business in 1928.

Mr. Coan was elected mayor in 1929, being the youngest man to be chosen for this important office. (Winston-Salem being a city of over 70,000 inhabitants.) After serving for two years he was reëlected for another term (two years). He has been elected president of the State Municipal League, whose membership consists of city officials, mayors, councilmen and city managers of various cities and towns of North Carolina.

During Mr. Coan's industrial banking experience, he indicated a partiality for realty investments, having built and sold a number of attractive small homes and likewise having constructed for himself three very attractive small-type apartment buildings, which are of great convenience to small families and a very satisfactory investment for the owner. Mayor Coan is a pioneer in the industrial banking and financial fields of Winston-Salem, and likewise a pioneer in the apartment house business as he was without question the first operator in both fields.

Mr. Coan is affiliated with the Fourth Street Church of Christ, has served as a trustee as well as on the board of deacons; was chairman of the building committee some ten years ago when the present modern church building was constructed. He was campaign director of the Community Chest drive in the spring of 1928, the amount of funds secured to finance the various charitable agencies exceeding $120,000.00. Under his leadership, this goal was reached in one day's drive. Since 1928 Mr. Coan has served on the Board of Directors of the Winston-Salem Community Chest, which is a big organization, raising annually from $120,000.00 to $150,000.00 to finance the various associated charity agencies in Winston-Salem.

Another welfare work the Mayor has rendered conspicuous service to during the last dozen years is, as a member of the board of the Salvation Army, having served as treasurer of the local post for several years, and having also been chairman of the building committee about 1921–22 when the modern Salvation Army home in Winston-Salem was constructed.

For the last several years Mayor Coan has served on the executive committee of the Associated Charities, which is the largest charitable organization in Winston-Salem, composed of a staff of some fifteen or eighteen persons. This organization has expended over $100,000.00 during the last two years for the needy. The Mayor is likewise a board member of the Rescue Mission Home which is doing fine work among the colored folk in the city. By virtue of his office the Mayor is chairman of the Miller Airport Commission, and also is general chairman of the Inter-Club Council of Winston-Salem, which Council is composed of the presidents of the various civic clubs in Winston-Salem. He has been president for more than one term of the two social clubs, the Twin-City and the Forsyth Country Club. He is likewise a member of the Winston-Salem Kiwanis Club, having been a charter member and served this club as vice president. He is also Alumni Trustee of Davidson College.

The Mayor has fulfilled every promise made to the citizens, when elected, to give them an honest, economical and efficient administration. He has stood for faithfulness and honesty in public officials, has encouraged citizens to become home owners, and is a leader in the "back to the farm" movement which has had an effect upon unemployment in the cities.

Mayor Coan's wife was Miss Mary Wiggins and they occupy a beautiful home on Arbor Road, one of the lovely residential sections of the city. The family circle consists of Mayor and Mrs. Coan and three children, Billie, James and Mary Spottswood.

THE COLEMAN FAMILY

The family of James Coleman lived near Spencer, Virginia. They were landowners and farmers.

THE CRAGHEAD FAMILY

Mrs. Lucinda Craghead, widow of Thomas Lodowick Craghead, who was born in 1819 and died a prisoner at Point Lookout, Maryland, 1864, made her home near Preston, Henry County, Virginia. Mrs. Craghead's family consisted of four daughters, namely, Sallie, who married John H. Matthews; Pocahontas, John Coleman; Ruth Angeline, Morgan A. Coleman, and Loula, who married Samuel C. Hill.

The Craghead family is of English descent.

THE CRITZ FAMILY OF PATRICK COUNTY, VIRGINIA

The Critz family originally came from Alsace. Hamon Critz, one of the ancestors of the family of Patrick County, settled on Spoon Creek, Patrick County, Virginia, then Pittsylvania, in 1747, where he became a leading citizen. He was one of the first Justices of the Peace of Pittsylvania County (Justices of the Peace at that time were men of rank and importance), and was Captain of Militia from 1767 to 1770.

Before church buildings could be provided services were held in private homes, and we note that Hamon Critz's home was one in which meetings were held, also a chapel was built near his home at a place conveniently near a good spring.

Captain Critz not only took a leading part in the religious life of the community, but in the political life as well. He led a company to the assistance of General Greene at Guilford Court House, and has been honored and respected as one of the distinguished men of the community.

ROBERT C. CRITZ

Robert C. Critz was a native of Patrick County, Virginia, an only son of William Critz. He inherited extensive tracts of land in that county. He married Lucy B. Reynolds, daughter of Harden W. Reynolds, whose loveliness and charm gave her an enviable place in the social life of the community.

Mr. Critz was connected with his father-in-law in the tobacco manufacturing business and later moved to Bristol, Tennessee, where he was interested in the business promoted by Major A. D. Reynolds. After several years he became connected with the R. J. Reynolds tobacco manufacturing business, of Winston-Salem, North Carolina, and moved to that place where he spent the rest of his life.

Mr. Critz was a man who was greatly beloved for many noble qualities, some of which were strict integrity, loyalty in friendship and kindness to all with whom he came in contact.

The hospitable home of Mr. and Mrs. Critz will long be remembered by those whose privilege it was to visit there.

Mr. Critz passed away in 1926, and since the marriage of her children Mrs. Critz has made her home at Kentwood, with her daughter, Mrs. C. A. Kent. No one in the entire community is more beloved and admired for splendid qualities than Mrs. Lucy B. Reynolds Critz, whose benevolence, sympathetic helpfulness, and sunny disposition are widely known.

Mr. and Mrs. Critz were parents of seven children reaching maturity.

Nancy, the eldest daughter, married Mr. E. W. O'Hanlon, a widely known and popular druggist of Winston-Salem. They have a beautiful home in Reynolda Park and three charming daughters, Lucy Amelia, Nancy and Margaret, complete the family group. Their only son died in infancy.

Mary Critz married Robert E. Follin, of Winston-Salem. Mr. Follin, after his graduation from the University of North Carolina, went to New York where he was assistant editor and special writer on the staff of the *New York Herald*. His fine intelligence, versatility and keen understanding of humanity brought his splendid stories very close to the hearts of hundreds of readers. Later Mr. Follin was editor of the *Winston-Salem Journal*, and was also at one time connected with the *Charlotte Observer*. Leaving newspaper work, Mr. Follin entered the insurance business with his father, which he continued until his death in 1928. He was survived by his wife and two daughters, Lucy Reynolds and Estelle Marion.

Mrs. Follin possesses unusual musical talent and as a pianist has given great pleasure to her friends. The elegant home of Mr. and Mrs. Follin on Country Club Drive attest their artistic taste in their plans and furnishings.

Senah H. Critz married Charles A. Kent a successful business man who was for many years connected with the R. J. Reynolds Tobacco Company, and later with the Brown-Williamson Tobacco Company, of Winston-Salem, and was a director of the Merchants Bank of that city.

Mr. Kent was a Virginian by birth, and was noted for kindness and generosity to all seeking help in any good cause. The home of Mr. and Mrs. Kent, Kentwood, is one of Winston-Salem's most beautiful places. The location in Reynolda Park is unusually attractive, and the exquisite taste of the owners in beautifying the grounds and gardens has added much to the natural beauty of the location. Mrs. Kent's brightness, vivacity and charm have made her very popular. Mr. Kent passed away in 1930, after a long and trying illness.

Ruth Critz married Wilson Gray, of Winston-Salem. Mr. Gray is a prominent wholesale merchant dealing in paper supplies, toys, etc. They have a lovely home in the Country Club District and Mrs. Gray is a charming member of the younger social set and Mr. Gray is very popular.

Charlotte Critz, youngest daughter of Mr. and Mrs. Robert C. Critz, even in early youth took a leading part in church and Sunday school work. She is a devoted member of the Presbyterian Church. She married James Harper, of Lenoir, North Carolina. Mr. Harper is connected with a furniture manufacturing firm and is a leader in musical circles of that city.

Robert Critz, only surviving son of Mr. and Mrs. Robert C. Critz, is a young man of splendid ability. He has been connected with the R. J. Reynolds Tobacco Company for several years. When the World War called the young men of our country to arms, Mr. Critz became an aviator and entered the service of our country. After the close of the War, he resumed his business activities. He married Alice Dunklee, of Winston-Salem, who on her maternal side is a descendant of the Hairstons, one of the most prominent families of Virginia and North Carolina.

Just upon the threshold of a happy and successful manhood, Harden Reynolds Critz' life was lost through a most distressing accident upon a railroad train. Evidently leaning from a window, he was thrown to the ground and the life of this young man was taken with heart-breaking suddenness.

THE DALTON FAMILY

There is so much of vital interest connected with the Dalton family, of Rockingham and Stokes Counties, North Carolina, close to the borders of the counties whose history forms the principal contents of this book that some account of that family should be included. Much interest centers around Mary Dalton Hughes, wife of Archelaus Hughes, of Patrick County, Virginia. The long life and marvelous personality of Mrs. Hughes would fill a volume.

The name Dalton in the days of William the Conqueror was written D'Alton, and from Count D'Alton, one of the followers of William the Conqueror, the American family descends.

The colonists, John and William Dalton, came to America between 1685-90, settling in Gloucester County, Virginia; some of the family later settled in Westmoreland County, Virginia, before 1722, and still later we find that they showed the restless spirit of the day, some of them settling in the vicinity of Goochland County, Virginia.

Records show that the members of the Dalton family were influential and important from their entry into the New World. Their contacts were with the greatest men of the ages in which they lived, Washington, the Madisons, Jefferson and others. Alexandria, Virginia, was founded by one of the Daltons.

Mrs. Lucy Henderson Horton gives a most comprehensive history of the family and its various branches in her book on the genealogy of the Hughes, Dalton, Martin and Henderson families, having secured her data from the world's most reliable sources.

One of the most remarkable members of the family was Samuel Dalton, of the Mayo River vicinity, Rockingham County, North Carolina, known as Samuel Dalton of Mayo. He has the unusual distinction of having seen the light of three centuries—born in 1699 and lived until 1802. He was a son of William Dalton, the colonist, who came first to Gloucester County, Virginia.

Samuel Dalton was also remarkable for his wonderful success in accumulating riches. He was the wealthiest man in all the country round, owning large areas of land and many slaves. His wife was Anne Dandridge Redd, and they were the parents of four sons and six daughters, one of whom, Mary, became the wife of Archelaus Hughes, of Patrick County, Virginia.

The Daltons intermarried with the most important families of North Carolina, Virginia and other states including the Winstons, Martins, Fulkersons, Dillards, Redds, Hendersons, Stovalls, Scales and others, and descendants of the various members of the families have moved to various states of the union.

An interesting paragraph from Mrs. Horton's book, in which she quotes Thackeray, is as follows: "History tells us that the younger sons of noblemen came to America." (The English law of primogeniture no doubt influenced them to seek their fortunes in the New World.) Mrs. Horton goes on to say, Thackeray in his Virginian corroborates the statement, he says, "The resident gentry was allied to good English families. Never were people less Republican

(Democratic) than those of the great province which was soon to be foremost in the memorable revolt against the British Crown. The gentry in Virginia dwelt upon their lands after a fashion almost patriarchal, their hospitality was almost boundless, no stranger was ever sent away from their gates. The gentry received one another and traveled to each other's houses in a state almost feudal." Again he says, "Even after the establishment of independence, there was no more aristocratic country in the world than Virginia. It was a custom in old families at that time to have a little servant assigned to each boy at his birth. This custom prevailed up to the time of the Civil War."

THE DANDRIDGE FAMILY OF HENRY COUNTY, VIRGINIA

The Dandridge family trace their lineage back to Scotch, English and French royal families; also to the Indian princess, Pocahontas.

The ancestor of the Dandridge family of Henry County was Colonel William Dandridge of the British Navy. He and his brother, Colonel John Dandridge, the father of Martha Washington, came to Virginia about the same time and settled on opposite sides of the Pamunkey River. Colonel John in New Kent County and Colonel William in King William County, near Westpoint, which was named for the ancestors of his wife, Unity West.

William Dandridge, born in Hanover County, Virginia, 1812, settled in Henry County near Martinsville, Virginia. His wife was Sarah Nickols, sister of Greenberry Nickols.

Five children were born to them, Thomas West, Robert Bolling, Clay, John and Sarah Virginia. In 1847, he married his second wife, Mary Jane Hamner, of Brunswick County, Virginia. After his second marriage he moved to his plantation, Locust Grove, near Spencer, Virginia.

His second son, John, died in service in the War Between the States. The children of William Dandridge and Mary Hamner Dandridge were: Nannie Anderson, Mary Pocahontas, Emma Louise, Martha Washington, Bessie Lee, James Spottswood, Samuel Hamner, George Gilmer and Walter Alexander. All of the children of William Dandridge were born in Henry County.

Dr. Thomas West Dandridge, eldest son of William Dandridge, graduated in medicine at the Richmond Medical College and attended lectures at the University of Virginia. He was in Texas at the outbreak of the

Civil War, and served with the Texas Rangers. Later he was transferred to Salisbury, North Carolina, as one of the surgeons in charge of the Federal Hospitals. After the War, Dr. Dandridge located at Madison and soon built up a large practice.

Sarah Virginia Dandridge was educated at a girls' school in Richmond, Virginia. She taught school in Virginia and North Carolina and also spent some time in nursing the sick and wounded in Richmond.

She married Samuel Wall, of North Carolina. Five children were born to them, Thomas, Elizabeth, Roseboro, Samuel S., Nannie Spottswood and Robert Edward.

Nannie Anderson Dandridge married Peter Washington Dalton, of Patrick County, Virginia, son of James Hunter and Nancy Critz Dalton, and grandson of Colonel Hamon Critz, who was an officer in the Revolutionary War. Mrs. Dalton died in 1922.

Mary Pocahontas Dandridge married James Wilborn and moved to Mississippi. She died in 1815, and was survived by her husband and four children. James Spottswood moved to Mississippi. He married Mary Cathey. Six children were born to them. George Gilmer Dandridge moved to Mississippi. Their children were: Merle, Jessie, Beatrice, Edward, George Gilmer, Samuel Clark, Mattie, Martha Washington, Zelia Lightfoot and James Spottswood. Emma Louise and Walter Alexander also moved to Mississippi.

Martha Washington Dandridge was reared in Mississippi. She married J. W. Thornton, of Littleton, North Carolina. There were three children, Dandridge, Martha and Mary. The latter died in infancy. Bessie Lee, the youngest child of William and Mary Hamner Dandridge, married Walter Compton, of Paris, Arkansas. They have four children, Dandridge, Mary Anna, Lou and Walter George.

Dr. Robert Bolling Dandridge graduated in medicine at the Virginia Medical school in Richmond, 1860, after which he took a postgraduate course at the University of Virginia. He established a practice in Henry County, but when the Civil War broke out he enlisted for service as a private in Company B, 24th Regiment, Virginia Infantry. He was promoted to Hospital Steward and in 1862 was discharged from service. His home was near Horsepasture, Virginia, and he practiced medicine for many years but always took a vital interest in politics. His wife was Susan Rangely, a daughter of John Rangely, a prominent citizen of Henry County. Their children were: William R., John Thomas, Harry C., Una and Annie.

Una Dandridge married Kelsey Puckett.

ANNIE DANDRIDGE

Among the many young women who have gone to other fields to seek their fortunes, Miss Annie Dandridge deserves more than a passing notice. She was born in Henry County, Virginia, and is the daughter of Dr. Robert B. Dandridge and Susan Rangely Dandridge.

After finishing her studies in school and having developed a taste for literary work she taught school a number of terms in the country near her home, later going to Washington City where she secured a position in one of the Federal offices and has held that position for a number of years. The accomplishment, possessed by few, of perfect penmanship has proved to be of inestimable value in some of her work.

THE DAVIS FAMILY OF HENRY COUNTY, VIRGINIA

The Davis family, well known in Henry County, is of English descent. Coming to this country about 1768, they settled in Charles County, Maryland. Charles Davis, the founder of the family, married Sarah Morehead. Their children were: Moses, Rachæl, Lydia and Joshua. The second wife was Anne Dent and they came to Virginia prior to 1785, and settled on Reed Creek, Henry County. Their children were: Benjamin, Thomas Blackburn, Eleanor, Anne and Peter.

Peter Davis married Mary Heard, their children were: Jonathan, who married first, Nancy Turner, second, Elizabeth Turner, third, Nettice Smith. Mary Dent married Captain Tom Draper.

Peter Perkins Davis married first, Emily Wade; second, Mary Frances Holland. He was prominent as a merchant, tobacconist and landowner and was also Captain of Detail in the Civil War, his duty being to look after deserters and also to furnish supplies for soldiers' families.

Thomas Blackburn married Martha Coleman; William Beard married Bettie Napier; Laban J. married Talitha Pedigo; David H. married Nancy McGee; Margaret Carr married Joseph Jones; Jane Hickey, Jesse Lavinder; Benjamin S., Anne Hunter.

John Peter Davis, son of Peter Perkins Davis, married Mary J. Mitchell. He was popular and was elected sheriff of Henry County for three terms and died while in office serving his third term. Their children were: Emily

Wade, Sarah Jane, Charles, Peter, Robert, Mary Elizabeth, Anne Ursula and J. Mitchell.

Emily Wade married Ernest L. Kelly; Sarah Jane, James W. Kelly; both deceased. Charles P. Davis married Kate De Cotton. Mary Elizabeth, Anne Ursula and J. Mitchell make their home in Martinsville and include in the family the daughters of the late James and S. Jane Kelly.

J. MITCHELL DAVIS

Among the outstanding young men who have filled official positions in Henry County, J. Mitchell Davis has enjoyed a large share of popularity and success. He was the youngest man to be elected sheriff in the county, and has served in that capacity for several terms.

ROBERT E. DAVIS

Robert E. Davis, son of Peter Perkins Davis, was elected to fill the unexpired term of his brother, J. Peter Davis, sheriff of Henry County. He was also elected as sheriff for another term. His wife was Lillian Trent, of Martinsville.

EVERETT J. DAVIS

Everett J. Davis, son of Jesse H. Davis, is a prominent business man of Martinsville. He has conducted a large tobacco warehouse and engaged in other business activities for many years, and is known and highly respected as a business man, winning many friends by his unvaried cordiality.

His first wife was Sallie Elizabeth Davis and their children are: Frank Payne, Harry Holland, Maude Wall, Mary Sue, Walter E. and Jesse Guy. His second wife was Minnie Heard Davis, and their children are: Evelyn, Elizabeth and E. J., Jr.

D. S. DAVIS

D. S. Davis, son of Benjamin S. Davis, has been elected to the office of Treasurer of Henry County for six consecutive terms. James P. Davis, his brother, who moved to Indiana, was a prominent business man of Kokomo. He has represented his county both in the Legislature and Senate. He died recently in Kokomo, Indiana.

HONORABLE BEVERLY A. DAVIS

Beverly A. Davis, son of David H. Davis, is a prominent attorney of Rocky Mount, Franklin County, Virginia. He has represented his county both in the Legislature and Senate and was a member of the Constitutional Convention which met in Richmond, in 1898. His sons are prominent attorneys and his brothers, Charles J. Davis and Raymond Davis, are prominent business men, both cashiers of banks.

THE DESHAZO FAMILY

William DeShazo (1759) came to Leatherwood when a young man and acquired about 600 acres of land adjoining the land of Patrick Henry on the north. He lived upon this land and reared his family. In the spring of 1777, he joined the Second Virginia Infantry and served with Lafayette under Washington during the northern campaign. He was in many battles, the most noted were that of Monmouth and with General Wayne at Stony Point when it was captured. He was honorably discharged in 1780. His death occurred in 1839 and he was survived by the following children: George King, Tabitha Jane, Sallie, Fannie and Richard. His wife was Jane King, of Leatherwood, she belonged to the family of Kings that came with the first settlers to Virginia. She died in 1864.

Tabitha King married first, a Conway; second, Dr. Gaffenried; third, an Albritton. Her only child was a son, Robert Albritton, of Bowling Green, Kentucky.

Sallie DeShazo married a Pace; Fannie married an Allen; she died in Missouri and her daughter returned to this county and married Obediah Minter, 1851. She had three sons, Leftridge, Coleman and William, who were the last of the line in this county. One daughter, Mrs. Devan.

Richard DeShazo was born in this county in 1794. He married Elizabeth Conway and moved to Missouri, making his home in St. Clair County. They reared eleven children. He was a Baptist minister.

George King DeShazo was born in this county in 1794. He married Susanna, daughter of John and Diana Garner Cahill, his home was on Reed Creek where he reared his family of eight children, John, Sallie, William T., Larkin, Nathaniel, George, Richard T. and Mary.

Richard Tazewell DeShazo married Mary Napier and lived on a farm on Mayo River. The children of this family were William T., G. B. and Mary Reid.

George DeShazo, born in 1839, was a brave Confederate soldier. He was wounded at Gaines Mill and died.

Nathaniel C. DeShazo married Virginia, daughter of Walker Smith, of Rockingham County, North Carolina. He was in the Forty-Second Virginia Regiment and fought in many battles.

Larkin DeShazo married Susan Dalton. He owned a fine farm on Horsepasture Creek. He was First Lieutenant in May's Company in the Forty-Fifth Virginia Regiment, and saw much service in the war. The children of the family were: Mary Virginia, who married Judge George P. Pell of the Corporation Commission of North Carolina; Annie D., who married W. P. McMichael; Minnie who married Sam Watkins; Dora and Mattie.

Dr. Dalton DeShazo graduated in medicine in Richmond, Virginia, and located at Stokesdale, but died within a month.

William Thomas DeShazo served in the Tenth Virginia Cavalry under William Henry Lee, and was captured at Five Forks, April, 1865, and imprisoned at Point Lookout until summer. He returned to his farm on Reed Creek, and engaged in raising tobacco. He accumulated considerable money which he invested in land, and manufactured tobacco for several years. There were five sons, Robert Noble, accidentally killed in boyhood, Homer K., William T., J. Beverly and Dameron.

Sallie Finney, wife of William T. DeShazo, Sr., was the daughter of John Finney, of Franklin County, and was descended from the earliest settlers of Virginia.

Rev. J. E. DeShazo, a Methodist minister, whose family lived in King and Queen County, married Mary Lou Zentmeyer, of Patrick County. Their children were: Edwin Penn, John E., Florence, Peter H. and Mary Hunter.

Dr. J. Beverly DeShazo, son of William Thomas DeShazo, occupies a prominent position as physician in Ridgeway, Henry County, Virginia, where he maintains a modern, well-equipped office and has practiced his profession successfully for a number of years. He married Annie S. Jones, daughter of George O. Jones, a prominent citizen of Ridgeway.

William T. DeShazo, of Martinsville, married Nona Pratt, of the Mayo Community, of Henry County, Virginia. Their family includes three sons and five daughters, namely: Henry, Buford, Napier, Myrtle, Nannie, Hallie, Louise and Virginia.

_____

DR. JOHN REDD DILLARD, OF HENRY COUNTY

Few men deserve to be remembered with greater affection and admiration than Dr. John Redd Dillard. He was a man of brilliant intellect, unusually attractive personality, strong character and courtly manners. He gave his life and unusual talents to the practice of medicine in a rural community—riding horseback over frozen or muddy roads in winter, often in the darkness of night to help and comfort the suffering. His never-failing kindness and cheerful presence gave hope and confidence to sufferers and to anxious families.

He was born about 1830, and when he decided upon medicine as his profession he attended the Jefferson Medical College in Philadelphia, from which he was graduated. He lived on a fine farm near Spencer, Virginia, and his practice extended over portions of both Henry and Patrick Counties.

Dr. Dillard was twice married, his first wife was Miss Margaret Brown, of Charlotte, North Carolina. She died in a few years and was survived by her husband and three daughters, viz.: Elizabeth, who was married three times; first, to Tyler Hairston; then to Charles Angle, and later to L. Ayers.

The second daughter, Martha Hughes, married Mr. Robert Jordan, of Charlotte, N. C., and after his death returned to her former home in Henry County, and later married Mr. Penn Watson. Mrs. Watson has made her home in Philadelphia for a number of years since Mr. Watson's death, but returns to Henry County frequently and spends some time with her relatives in Martinsville.

Lucy, the youngest of the three daughters, married Mr. Brown, a Lutheran minister.

Dr. Dillard's second wife was Miss Adele Lee, of Lunenburg County (see sketch). Dr. and Mrs. Dillard were the parents of six sons and four daughters, George L., Peter, John, William, Robert Jordan and Charles. The daughters are, Caroline, Annie, Helen and Adele.

The home of Dr. and Mrs. Dillard was one of such gracious hospitality that any one who had the pleasure of being a guest there took away the most delightful memories of the visit.

After a long and useful life Dr. Dillard passed away in 1913, and was laid to rest near the home and in the neighborhood in which he was beloved and honored.

MRS. ADELE LEE DILLARD

Mrs. Adele Lee Dillard was a woman of great beauty, accomplishments and charm. She taught school in private families before her marriage to Dr. John R. Dillard and afterwards, in addition to her duties as the head of a large household, continued teaching for many years. So great was her popularity as an educator and the appreciation of the people of the community whose children she had uplifted and educated, that one of the district schools was located at her home in a good building on the grounds and she taught there for some time. She was an accomplished and talented musician and many young girls were indebted to her for instruction so patiently and graciously given.

Mrs. Dillard was a member of the distinguished Lee family. Their earliest ancestors appeared in England in 1066, when William of Normandy —The Conqueror—landed on the shores of that country with a Norman army, fought the battle of Hastings and won the crown of England. Among his followers from Normandy were Hugh de la Lee, and Lionel his brother both of whom had fought in crusades and were distinguished for their bravery. The Conqueror bestowed on them the Earldom of Litchfield and Ditcherly besides their share of the rich provinces he distributed among his followers.

Among their descendants were Thomas and Richard. Stratford, the ancestral home, was built by Thomas Lee, fifth son of Richard, whose father, Colonel Richard Lee, was the first of his family to come to the colony of Virginia. He came from his English home to Shropshire in 1614, forced by his loyalty to the royal cause to abandon his native land. Thomas Lee built Stratford, in Westmoreland County, in the early years of the Eighteenth Century, naming it for his English estate. It was burned but with the aid of a gift from Queen Charlotte it was rebuilt in its original pattern.

Thomas Lee was president and commander in chief of the colony and after serving for some time in this capacity the King made him Governor by royal appointment. Colonel Lee died before the appointment reached him.

Thomas Lee had six sons all of whom grew to honorable manhood, their names have gone down in history as synonyms of patriotism, culture and high character; they were: Philip Ludwell, Thomas Ludwell, Richard Henry, Francis Lightfoot, William and Arthur.

William Lee, great grandfather of Mrs. Adele Lee Dillard, had sons who came to Lunenburg and Charlotte Counties. They were as follows: Edward Lee (grandfather of Mrs. Dillard), Thomas and Ambrose. General Harry Lee known as Light Horse Harry, father of General Robert E. Lee, another brother did not come to the same counties, but fought throughout the Revolutionary War with his brother Captain Edward Lee. George Henderson Lee, father of Mrs. Adele Lee Dillard, died the third year of the Civil War, having volunteered in the first company formed in Lunenburg County. He was captain of an artillery company stationed at Norfolk, Virginia.

George L. Dillard, eldest son of Dr. John R. Dillard and Mrs. Adele Lee Dillard, chose law as his profession and practiced for some time in Henry County, where he served as Judge of the County Court. He moved to Bluefield, West Virginia, where he has practiced his profession successfully and occupies the position of Judge of the Criminal Court there. He married Florence Echols, of Bluefield, and they have an attractive home in that city.

Peter Dillard, the second son, chose medicine as his profession and practiced in Martinsville for some time. His death occurred while he was still a young man and he was survived by his wife who was Margaret Penn, daughter of the late Joseph Penn, and one son.

John Redd Dillard, prominent in politics in West Virginia, at one time member of the House of Delegates from Mercer County, is an attorney at law in Bluefield, West Virginia. His wife was Nellie Prince.

Caroline Lightfoot Lee Dillard spent her girlhood at the family home in Henry County. Her first marriage was to Charles Wilmut, of Dallas, Texas. After his death she returned to Henry County and later was married to Walter L. Penn, a business man of Spencer, Virginia. Mr. and Mrs. Penn moved to Martinsville, Virginia, where they have an attractive home. The family consists of Mr. and Mrs. Penn and two sons, Walter L., Jr., and John Redd.

Helen married Thomas Morris and died while quite young being survived by her husband and one son, John D.

Annie married Murray Hooker, an attorney at law, of Patrick County (see sketch), and their home is at Stuart, Virginia.

Adele Lee married William Pannill, a successful textile manufacturer, of Martinsville (see Pannill family).

THOMAS E. DONEGAN

This brilliant and eccentric man, who in the old time before the present public school system was thought of, became one of the outstanding "old field" school teachers of Henry County, had an unusual, thrilling history.

The extremely casual manner in which he became a citizen of this county, mixed up as it was with the law of chance, is worthy of record.

To start with, Mr. Donegan was the son of a full-blooded Irish family in the City of New York—not the Tammany type of Irish with the unmistakable potato mouth as Mark Twain expresses it, but the thin-lipped, sharp-featured, well-educated type. His father was well off in this world's goods, and he would have given his son a good opportunity to finish his education to whatever limit of scholarship he wished, but there was one temperamental obstacle in the way. It is familiar to us all—how a young fellow develops what some one has aptly called "the malady of being eighteen years of age." This is a time when a youth is prone to cherish a notion that all the world is against him. This delusion of conspiracy and persecution applies with especial emphasis to his own family.

Thomas Donegan in his early days had an acute attack of this interesting malady and had it bad. Not only this, but he acted upon it with prompt and decisive resolution which being interpreted means that he did not threaten but did actually run away from home, and refrained from writing back to inform the homefolk of his whereabouts. He tramped southward. When he had made about five hundred miles, the impression came over him that he was about far enough from New York City and that he had better anchor somewhere. The question was where? He found himself standing on the crest of Turkey Cock Mountain, the boundary between Henry and Franklin Counties. He looked east and west and his eyes encountered a smiling and beckoning valley in either direction. He could not decide the momentous question. In the language of a locomotive engineer he was "on a dead center." He held in his hand a straight walking stick which he had selected, cut and trimmed on his way. He balanced this stick between his thumb and index finger, let it down carefully to the ground and turned it loose, whichever way it fell he would go, thus he submitted the issue, Biblical fashion, to the law of chance. The stick fell southward towards Henry County so that our wanderer descended into Leatherwood District. He began casting about for some way of making a living. He was a pretty well educated young man so he found that one opportunity was open to him and only one, he could teach a country school. He canvassed the community and by hard labor succeeded in getting up a subscription for a small school of the old field type. This determined his career and fixed his vocation for life. He taught and strongly impressed his ideals upon some generations of the youth of Henry County. Directly and indirectly thousands of men and women have had their characters, their conduct and their destinies decisively influenced by the fall of that stick "east or west."

One illustration shall be given showing this emanation of large effects from small causes. This at the risk of making the writer the rather insignificant and innocent hero of his own story. Our wanderer, after anchoring in Henry County and after establishing himself in his chosen profession, was married to one of the first generations of his pupils, and reared a large family. In the latter half of the Civil War period it fell to my lot to sit for two sessions under his piercing grey eyes and in plain view of his minatory ferrule. Being an uncle of mine by marriage, he showed a rather special personal interest in me. Among other interesting discoveries he announced that I had some Daniel Webster and Henry Clay stuff in my makeup, which he undertook to develop by teaching me the art of declamation. He put on a special Friday afternoon program to recite the peroration of Webster's reply to Hayne. When I reached the climax of that memorable passage (without an idea of what it all meant), I squeaked out in my little boyish, almost infantile voice, those immortal words which were once thundered out in the United States Senate Chamber, in the profound rolling basso of Daniel Webster: "When my eyes shall be turned to behold for the last time the sun in heaven, may I not see him shining on the broken and dishonored fragments of a once glorious union, on states dissevered and discordant, on a land rent with civil feuds, or drenched, it may be, with fraternal blood." At this thrilling juncture a handsome old gentleman in the audience leaned towards his next neighbor and made inquiry, "Whose son is that?" "John F. Pedigo's." Um-m-m-m this patrician was the owner of broad acres and many slaves, lived in a beautiful colonial home in Pittsylvania County about seven miles away. He was an ardent secessionist, moreover he was dogmatic in his views, overbearing in temperament, and intolerant of any differences of opinion. He inferred that my father had taught me this speech, which was not true.

Friends were estranged, enmities engendered, personal difficulties were developed, all hinging on a possible small pebble under the west side of that stick on the crest of the mountain. However that may be, I submit this entire incident as my Civil War record, quite a little rumpus for a seven-year-old boy to kick up in two large counties.

School discipline is one of the unsolved problems of the ages. The hero of this story had his own methods and it is scarcely necessary to add that they were in the highest degree original. By various and ingenious measures, he could make a half-grown boy so ridiculous and humiliate him so thoroughly in the presence of the school that the victim would be glad to trade the whole situation off for a good, sound, wholesome thrashing with a twisted hickory switch. I hold no cards for any particular method. Alfred Williams, the cleverest editor in Virginia, in his time, once said that there are two problems that the human family had never solved, "how to keep a hillside from washing into gullies and how to rear a boy." I take no responsibility for even suggesting a solution of either of these unsolved and unsolvable problems, but I do say this much, that this teacher's method of mental punishment seemed very effective.

A sketch of this man's life would not be complete without some allusion to avocations. He was an exquisite penman and was employed as an assistant in the County Clerk's office in an emergency when an accumulated mass of papers needed to be copied into the records. At other times he was a valuable helper in writing up the books of a merchant. At one time he built a log factory on his little plantation and tried an experiment of manufacturing tobacco on a small scale. He succeeded with this as men with small capital could do in those irreclaimable days. In this period of comparative prosperity it occurred to him that his father must be growing old, and that possibly he needed some financial assistance so he slipped off to New York City, visited his father's home, was ushered by a stylish butler into a very fine parlor, and while waiting for some member of the family to come in, he made a critical inspection of his surroundings. He estimated that one French plate mirror cost more than his entire estate was worth. Evidently, his father did not need his help. At the first decent opportunity he sneaked out and went home.

The subject of this sketch lived all the active years of his life in Henry County. He was regarded on all hands as a highly interesting and highly respected citizen.

When increasing age forced his retirement, he moved to Winston-Salem, North Carolina, and spent his last few years with his wife and some of his children.

THE DREWRY FAMILY OF HENRY COUNTY, VIRGINIA

Dr. Henry M. Drewry was born in Chesterfield County, Virginia. He was graduated from Princeton in 1855, then studied at the University of Virginia, and was graduated also from the Jefferson Medical College in 1858, and located at Martinsville, Virginia, where he practiced his profession through a long period of years.

The Drewry family belong to a distinguished family whose lineage is traced to the time of William the Conqueror.

Mrs. Drewry who, before her marriage, was Flora Redd, daughter of James Madison Redd and Ruth Staples Redd, members of Virginia's very prominent families. She was born at Stuart, Patrick County, and received her education at Dr. Dame's school in Danville, Virginia, and Madam de Fere's school in Richmond. She was endowed with great beauty and charm and had a coterie of friends and admirers. Being a devoted member of the Episcopal Church she was always ready to do her full duty and was the first to be confirmed in Henry County.

Dr. and Mrs. Drewry reared six children, four daughters and two sons. Ruth, the eldest daughter, married Stafford G. Whittle, one of Virginia's most distinguished citizens (see sketch). Mrs. Whittle inherited her mother's beauty and charm and in her community was greatly beloved. Flora Drewry married John A. Wright and has made her home in South Boston, Virginia. Amelia married James P. Lewis, a successful banker of Martinsville. Keziah married John W. Carter, an attorney at law who was a member of the Martinsville bar for many years. Madison Drewry chose medicine as his profession and practiced in Henry County for a number of years; he married Mary Starling.

Plummer, the younger son, was an attorney at law and practiced in Martinsville for some time; he married Freda Williams, a woman of unusual talents who has done much work in connection with the Red Cross Society of Henry County.

Dr. and Mrs. Drewry and all six of their children have passed away.

THE DUDLEY FAMILY

About 1882, when Martinsville, Henry County, Virginia, seemed to have a new awakening in business development, G. B. and A. M. Dudley, of Franklin County, became citizens of the growing city and have been important factors in its development and growth. Gustave B. Dudley was a successful tobacco manufacturer for many years. His wife was Sarah Brown. They were parents of four children, two sons and two daughters. The two sons, Dr. Brown Dudley and Dr. G. B. Dudley, have been successful in the practice of their professions. Dr. Brown Dudley doing for the most part a general practice and Dr. Gustave specializing in diseases of the eye, nose and throat.

Ruby Dudley, the elder daughter, married J. E. Howard, who has been connected with the tobacco manufacturing business and distribution of manufactured products for some years. Mr. Howard has during past years taken a great interest in the advancement of education in the community, and as a member of the Board of Education, a position he held for several years, he had the confidence and esteem of all with whom he came in contact.

Virginia Dudley, younger daughter of G. B. Dudley, married Samuel S. Walker, who has been for a number of years connected with the textile industry of Martinsville.

M. H. Dudley established a large wood, coal and feed business in Martinsville, Virginia. His wife was Miss Ada Hancock, of Franklin County, Virginia. They were parents of two sons and two daughters, Albert, Harrison, Corrie and Mabel.

Corrie married Zack Drake, of Bennettsville, South Carolina, and Mabel married C. W. Holt, one of Martinsville's most popular and successful merchants.

THE DYER FAMILY OF VIRGINIA

The Dyer family is of English-Scotch origin and came to this country in the Seventeenth Century. The progenitor of the family in this country was George Dyer, who was born in Prince George County, Maryland, in 1753 and died in Henry County in 1827. He was a lieutenant in the Revolutionary War, going from Maryland in 1778 in Captain Charles Williamson's Company.

After settling in Henry County, he married Rachael Dalton and their children were: James, Benjamin, Francis, Phoebe, Joel, David Dalton, Elizabeth, Louisa, Rachael and Martha.

James Dyer married Sarah Reynolds. Their children were: Coleman, Joseph Fountain, James, Benjamin, Hugh, Elizabeth, Ann, Mary, Grief and George.

Benjamin Dyer married Mary Gravely (1801). Their children were: George, Eleanor, Rachael, James, Jabez, Sackville and Benjamin. He was in the War of 1812 and represented the county in the Virginia Legislature in 1822. He died in 1823.

Frances Dyer married Edward de Lazier; Phoebe, Arnold Thomasson; Joel Dyer, Mary Salmons; their children were: Nancy, Mary, Sallie, Martha, Susan, Joseph, George, Benjamin, Fanny and Rachael.

David Dalton Dyer was born in 1791; he married Nancy Reynolds Salmons. Their children were: George W., Joseph F., Martha, John, Sarah, James, Nancy, Elizabeth, Mary, Louisa, Rachael and David P. Martha Dyer married Lewis Gravely (1822); Joab Dyer married Mary Salmons, and they were parents of the following children: Margaret, Ann, Rebecca and Rachael. His second wife was Nancy Harvey.

The children of David Dalton Dyer, were: George W. Dyer, who married Mary Philpott. Their children were: Martha, Nancy, David, Sinai, Mary, Virginia, Fredonia, Trusten and Minnie.

Joseph F. Dyer married Elizabeth Dyer, the names of their children follow: Mary, Sarah, Martha, Joseph, Harriet, Nancy and James.

Mary B. Dyer married Bailey Martin; Martha C. married Nathaniel Spencer.

John S. Dyer (1813) married Martha Bassett. Their children were: Mary, Nancy, David A., James, George, Cherokee, Choctaw, Pocahontas, Louella, Cora, Ida and Eloise.

Sarah Dyer (1822) married Albert Mason; James D. Dyer (1824) married Martha Combs, and they were parents of David A., George, Joseph, John H., Leonidas, Mary, Nancy, Anne, Virginia and Emma.

Nancy J. Dyer married Douglas Wyatt; Elizabeth married John E. Ball; Louisa married first, W. L. Carter; second, J. E. Carstarphen; Rachael M. Dyer married D. J. M. Foreman; David P. Dyer married Lizzie C. Hunt, their children were: Ezra, Emma, Grace, Lizzie, Logan, David P., Horace, Levi and Maria Louise.

The children of Benjamin Dyer and Mary Gravely Dyer were as follows: Benjamin Franklin Dyer married Martha Walker, their children were: Mary, Sallie, Fannie, George, Alice, Henry, Gustavus, David and Lula. His second wife had one daughter, Kate.

Benjamin Dyer was a gallant soldier in the Civil War. He was promoted to a captaincy, and also represented the county in the Legislature in 1875–76. He died in 1914.

Jabez Dyer was born about 1823. He married Martha Eliza Ivey; their son, Willis, married Harriet Jones.

Mary and George were unmarried; Ben married Agnes Strong, of Rockingham, North Carolina; Susan married a Taylor; Eliza married Dr. Franklin King.

James Dyer, son of Hugh and grandson of George Dyer, married Lucy J. Holt. They reared a large family. Sallie Ruth married Hughes Oakley; Ella, Benjamin B. Hundley, of Martinsville, Virginia; J. Ballard engaged in business with the R. J. Reynolds Tobacco Company, Winston-Salem, North Carolina. He died in 1929 and was survived by his wife, who was Diana Mouze, and four children, Diana, Elizabeth, J. B., Jr., and Joseph L.

John married Julia Williamson; Hugh married Katherine Garrett; Holt married Annie Bone; Tom and Ira are the other sons of James and Lucy Holt Dyer.

DAVID DALTON DYER

A distinguished member of the Dyer family was David Dalton Dyer, born 1791. His father, George Dyer, was a lieutenant in the Revolutionary War. He married Nancy Reynolds Salmons when he was only nineteen years of age. He was called to arms when the War of 1812 began and, leaving his young wife and child, fought through the war. When peace was declared he returned home and became a successful and influential member of the community. For twelve consecutive years he was a representative in the House of Delegates or Senate from Henry County, and made an official record of which his descendants will always be proud. He died in 1844.

Mrs. Dyer was of Irish descent, a woman of strong mind and wonderful constitution. They moved to Missouri in 1841, five of the sons having gone to that state the year before. On the trip she traveled over a thousand miles in a four-horse wagon. She was the mother of twelve children and had the unusual experience of living under every presidential administration from Washington to Benjamin Harrison. She had in all 277 descendants before her death.

DAVID PATTERSON DYER

Henry County can boast of no more distinguished son than James Patterson Dyer, youngest of the twelve children of David Dalton and Nancy Salmons Dyer. The name Patterson was given in honor of a colleague of his father with whom he served in the Legislature.

In 1840, the five eldest children emigrated to Missouri and settled in Warren County and in St. Charles County, all engaging in farming. In 1841, the father and mother with the seven remaining children and a few slaves, left the old home in Henry County, Virginia, and after six weeks of hardships reached Missouri. The means of transportation was two four-horse wagons made by the convicts in the penitentiary at Richmond, Virginia.

Arriving in Lincoln County, Missouri, Mr. Dyer purchased a farm of 260 acres upon which was a cabin and "living water." Houses were built and other improvements made. After three years of hard labor in improving the land and building the houses a disastrous flood swept everything away and, worse still, left malaria in its wake, of which the father of the family died. The wife and mother who was also a sufferer from the dread disease finally recovered, and assumed the burden of managing the farm and rearing the family as only the heroic pioneer women could do.

After attending such of the country schools as could be reached, David Patterson Dyer went to the St. Charles College for a year, then engaged in teaching and studying law. In 1857 he went to Bowling Green and entered the law office of Honorable James C. Broadhead as a law student. In 1859 he was admitted to the bar and opened a law office. Naturally, his practice was not very lucrative for some time, but the future held great success for him.

Mr. Dyer's life work was so varied and important that we here give a summary of his career.

Entered law office of Mr. Broadhead in Bowling Green, Missouri, 1857. Admitted to the bar in 1859, and opened a law office in a small room of the Court House. Practiced with reasonable success. Married Lizzie Chambers Hunt. Was Lieutenant in Home Guards of Bowling Green. Became Colonel of a Missouri regiment. In 1862, moved from Bowling Green to Louisiana, Pike County, Missouri, and entered the law office of John B. Henderson. Practiced law and performed duties as State's Attorney. Was elected to the Legislature in 1862.

There were three factions in the Legislature—Charcoals, those who favored the immediate emancipation of slaves, Claybanks, those favoring gradual compensating emancipation and Snowflakes, those opposing emancipation in any form.

In 1864 Mr. Dyer was authorized to recount and organize the regiment thereafter known as the Forty-Ninth Missouri Infantry, and was commissioned Colonel of the regiment. Mustered out in 1865. Returned to the Legislature in 1865. Was elected Secretary of State in 1866. Was delegate from the Ninth District to the National Republican Convention at Chicago, 1868, which nominated U. S. Grant for president and Schuyler Colfax, of Indiana, for vice president. Elected to Congress (Forty-First) 1869. Introduced and succeeded in having a bill passed authorizing the building of a bridge across the Mississippi River at Louisiana, Missouri.

In 1872 he was a delegate from the Ninth Congressional District to the Convention which met at Philadelphia, and nominated Grant and Wilson. His colleague was Theodore Bowers, of St. Charles. It was a remarkable coincident that twenty-eight years later he was again delegate with Bowers at the National Convention at Philadelphia, and nominated McKinley and Roosevelt. He was appointed United States Attorney by President Cleveland in 1887, and prosecuted those involved in election frauds. He was delegate at large, from the State of Missouri, to the National Republican Convention that met in Chicago in 1888, and voted for Greshan, but Harrison was nominated. He was elected as one of a committee of three to supervise drawing of homesteads when Oklahoma was opened. He was delegate at large to the National Republican Convention at Philadelphia in 1900, nominated William McKinley the second time for president and Theodore Roosevelt for vice president. He was United States Attorney for the Eastern District of Missouri.

Mr. Dyer numbered among his friends distinguished men in public life, among them President Roosevelt.

He was appointed Judge of the United States Supreme Court of Appeals.

THE ENGLISH FAMILY

Two brothers, J. L. and S. D. English, came to Martinsville and entered the business field of the growing community. They are sons of James L. English and Pamela Tyree English, of Franklin County, Virginia. Their emigrant ancestors are from England and Ireland.

S. D. English engaged in the tobacco business. His wife was Lucy Brown, daughter of John R. Brown, and they were the parents of two sons and a daughter. The elder son, James, is in business in Lexington, North Carolina. The younger son, John Brown, makes his home in Martinsville, and the daughter, Purnell, married M. H. Schottland.

J. L. English has held the official position of Department Collector for a number of years. He married Gertrude Whittaker, of New Market, Tennessee. Mrs. English's ancestry on her mother's side were of English and French extraction, and among them were several generations of soldiers; one, John Stark, of Flanders, New Jersey, her great-great-grandfather, being a Colonel in General Washington's Brigade. Her father's people were from

Lancaster, England, and at the present seat of the family, Symonstone Hall, there is an unbroken record of their pedigrees as far back as 1326. Many members of this family came to America at different periods, one being Alexander Whittaker, the Episcopal minister, who baptized Pocahontas and married her to John Rolfe.

Mr. and Mrs. English are the parents of four children, viz.: Whittaker, who married Roberta Perry and lives in Asheville, North Carolina. Dorothy married Thomas M. Ford, of Martinsville. John Letcher, Jr., married Hazel Deane, of Miami, Florida, and they make their home there. Frank makes his home in Martinsville.

GEORGE M. FINLEY

George M. Finley, one of the business men and city builders of Martinsville, is a grandson of Mr. John Jamison, one of Henry County's prominent citizens. Mr. Finley is well and favorably known and has done much for the promotion of the growth of Martinsville.

He married May Brown, daughter of the late Honorable John R. Brown, of Henry County. Their family consists of Mr. and Mrs. Finley and four daughters, May, Ellen, Katherine and Virginia. The eldest daughter, Elizabeth, died in infancy.

May Finley married N. S. Schottland, and they have a very attractive home in Martinsville. Ellen married William Andrews, of Roanoke, a member of a very prominent family of that city. Mrs. Andrews is an accomplished violinist, and for many years delighted her friends by playing at social functions. Katherine married Robert Fagg, a rising young druggist of Martinsville, whose popularity has given him a prominent place in business.

Virginia is a musician of unusual ability and possesses a beautiful soprano voice. She graduated recently from Breneau College, Gainesville, Georgia.

THE FONTAINE FAMILY

The Fontaine family is of French origin. The Reverend de la Fontaine, of a Huguenot family, came to this country in 1716, and became rector of King William and Westover Parishes. His son, Peter Fontaine, was also a minister and Lieutenant of Halifax before that county was divided. He married Elizabeth Winston and their family included six children.

John Fontaine, son of Peter Fontaine and Elizabeth Fontaine, married Martha, daughter of Patrick Henry. Their children were: Patrick Henry, Charles, Martha, William Winston and Rev. John I. Fontaine.

John Fontaine was a soldier in the Revolutionary War, and was promoted to the rank of captain. He died not long after this and his widow was given the Leatherwood home by her father. The children of this family were: Patrick Henry, the eldest son, married Nancy Dabney Miller, and their eldest son, who became the Reverend Edward Fontaine, was born at Leatherwood about 1800.

William Winston Fontaine, another grandson of the orator, married Martha Dandridge, and their children were: William Spottswood, Patrick Henry and Anne.

Martha Dandridge was a descendant of Governor Spottswood, also of Governor John West whose administration was in 1635. She was a first cousin of Mrs. George Washington. Her husband died and she married a Perkins and lived in Martinsville, Virginia.

Patrick Henry Fontaine, son of William Winston and Martha Dandridge Fontaine, married Sarah Miller Cole about 1830. Their children were: Samuel Cole, Watson Hale, Nathaniel Cole, Katherine and Unity.

Samuel Cole Fontaine was a gallant Confederate soldier. He was promoted to lieutenant, was captured and imprisoned at Cincinnati. After the war, he was liberated and returned to his home near Martinsville, Virginia. His wife was Mary Morton Anderson.

William Hale, son of Patrick Fontaine, died while serving his country in the Civil War.

Nathaniel Fontaine distinguished himself as a soldier of the Confederacy. He is noted for capturing a whole squad of Union soldiers single-handed, by some ruse of quick-witted action, without sustaining a wound.

Katherine Fontaine married Overton better known as "Tobe" Wootton. They lived in Henry County and reared the following children: Eva, Nora, Lucy, Sallie, Maude, Nathaniel, William, John and Hale.

Unity Fontaine married Ed Estes and they spent their lives in Henry County, near Martinsville.

THE FORD FAMILY OF HENRY COUNTY, VIRGINIA

The Ford family occupies a prominent place in Henry County and members of the family are leading business men of Martinsville.

Hezikiah Ford came to the county about 1870 from Charlotte County. He was the only son of Samuel Calvin Ford and his mother was a Pentecost. Mr. Ford taught school for many years, and exerted much influence for good in his community. His wife was Sarah Armistead, of Campbell County, Virginia.

The children of Mr. and Mrs. Ford were: Samuel C., James, Joseph, John, Lena, William and Henry.

Samuel C. Ford married Susan Janie Dillard, and they were parents of the following children: Overton Dillard, who is a prominent business man of Martinsville being connected with The American Furniture Manufacturing Company. He married Cecil Witten, daughter of the late A. D. Witten. Hezikiah (Heck) married Martha (Pattie) Packard. Tom married Dorothy English. Both the last named are the leading real estate men of Martinsville. The firm name is H. A. Ford & Company. Pete Ford married Blanche Walker and they make their home in Martinsville. He is an active business man taking great interest in all business and club work affecting the welfare of the town. Ingles, the only daughter, passed away just after reaching womanhood.

James Ford married Elizabeth Dillard and moved to Florida. They reared a large family. John Ford was unmarried.

Lena Ford married Sidney Hamlet and they make their home in Charlotte County, Virginia. Their children are: Sarah, Joe and Ella.

Joseph Ford married Margaret Lavinder. Their children are: Annie, Joseph, Jesse, Jane Hickey and Mary.

Henry Ford studied law and practiced in Martinsville for some time. He was Judge of the County Court for some time, and later moved to Lynchburg.

Willie Ford made his home in Axton and engaged in farming. He married a widow, Mrs. Tom Dillard, and reared the following children: Sarah, Annie, John, Lewis and Lena.

THE FRANCE FAMILY

The France family is of German origin but the name as spelled in this country retains no suggestion of that origin.

COLONEL CARTER HARRISON FRANCE

MRS. CATHERINE PENN FRANCE
WIFE OF
Colonel Carter Harrison France

The first of the family of whom we have a record was William France, whose wife was Nancy Carter.

William France, Jr., married Harriet Harrison and lived at The Cedars in Patrick County, Virginia, a mile west of the present Village of Stella.

William France, Jr., and Harriet Harrison France had only two children, Susan Lee France (1813–1893) and Harrison Carter France.

Susan Lee France married first Gabriel Penn, son of Greensville Penn and Anna Leath Penn, of Penn's Store, Patrick County, Virginia. Of this union there were only two children, William Leath Penn, born July 29, 1834, and Edward Penn, born July 3, 1837. Her second marriage was to William Murphy and they were parents of one son, William.

HARRISON CARTER FRANCE married CATHERINE (or KITTY) PENN FRANCE
    b 1818—d 1896   1842   b 1821—d 1914

ISSUE

1. James Penn.................m Sara Elizabeth Schoolfield
2. Susan Barbara, d July 4, 1927..m John Harrel Schoolfield
3. Ruth Ann Kelly McCabe.....m James Mitchel Alexander
4. Mary Alice.................m Parry Ansom Cummings
5. Harriet Harrison, d 1931......m George Watkins Martin
6. Lucy Dillard, b Dec. 6, 1850...m James Edward Schoolfield, b Sept. 18, 1850, d Aug. 6, 1902
7. William Starling
8. Peter Shelton
9. John Gabriel...............m Daisy Wayne (of Cincinnati)
10. Katie died an infant
11. Minnehaha.................m Henry Fitzhugh Vass, b 1855
12. Annie Redd, d 1897.........m Robert Addison Schoolfield, d 1931

Harrison Carter France was born in Patrick County, Virginia. His forbears came from Amherst County. He and his wife, Catherine (Penn) France, were distant cousins, both being descendants of Moses and Katherine (Taylor) Penn. His father was William France (d 1811), the son of Peter and Susan (Carter) France. His mother was Harriet Harrison (d 1876), the daughter of Richard (d 1816) and Suzannah (Lee) Harrison (d 1832). In 1842 he married Catherine (Penn) the daughter of James and Mary (or Polly) Shelton Penn. He had one sister, Susan Lee, who married Gabriel Penn. His estate in Henry County was called Fairview. The original house was burned. Fairview was situated on an elevated site in Henry County, Virginia, and commanded a beautiful view of the Alleghany Mountains and the Blue Ridge and of the stately peak of Pilot Knob, lying far to the south.

Carter France was an extensive planter and manufacturer of tobacco and owned a number of slaves. After the closing of the old PATRICK HENRY ACADEMY, named for its founder, Carter France bought the building and used it for a tobacco factory.

He was Captain of the Militia in Henry County. After the Civil War he was forced to give up his plantations in Virginia. Accordingly he moved his family to Asheville, North Carolina, where he engaged in the tobacco business. The family lived in the Patton House on what is now Biltmore Street, and which has since become the local headquarters of the Young Women's Christian Association. Later Captain France moved to Danville, where he and his wife are buried.

Captain France was tall and commanding in appearance. He had blue eyes and brown hair. His manner was characterized by the quiet and noble dignity of the old-fashioned Virginia gentleman. In the latter years of his life he bore a striking resemblance to the portraits of General Robert E. Lee.

Katherine (Penn) France or "Miss Kitty" as every one loved to call her, was a woman of rare charm and beauty. She lived to be ninety-three years of age, and never lost her sense of humor or her love of the society of people, young and old. She had a round, plump figure, blue eyes and brown hair, and a skin remarkably smooth and fair even in her old age. To the day of her death, her hair fell in thick ringlets around her shoulders, which was unfortunately concealed by the quaint cap she wore, a custom she adopted in her early thirties, when caps were the symbol of the dignity of matronhood.

The France home was a center of Virginia hospitality in their neighborhood. Their visitors were frequent and numerous. The halls of their home resounded with the merriment of the young beaux and belles of that day.

MISS ANNETTE FULLER OF MARTINSVILLE, VIRGINIA

Few women in Martinsville, Virginia, or elsewhere who have engaged in educational work and whose influence in the promotion of culture occupy a higher place or whose work has been more appreciated than that of Annette Fuller.

Miss Fuller and her sister, now Mrs. J. F. Carey, conducted very successfully for several years a select school for girls, instruction in music being one of the outstanding features. Since closing the school Miss Fuller has given her time exclusively to her music classes, her work includes instruction in piano, violin and voice culture. She and her pupils are in constant demand for concerts and social functions, and to the numerous requests for her services, she responds with unvarying graciousness.

SENATOR W. ALLEN GARRETT OF HENRY COUNTY, VIRGINIA

Senator W. A. Garrett, one of Henry County's most distinguished citizens, is the son of W. S. Garrett and Mary Eliza Price Garrett, of Rockingham County, North Carolina. The family included four daughters and three sons.

Senator Garrett came to Ridgeway about forty years ago and for several years engaged in the mercantile business. Being a public-spirited citizen of the old school of Virginia gentlemen, his talents and ability were soon recognized by the people of the community and he was elected mayor of Ridgeway. Later he was elected member of the House of Delegates from Henry County (1897–98). His popularity and recognized ability as the people's representative secured his election to the State Senate, which position he still holds.

For twenty-one years he has served as senator from what was the Twenty-Third and is now the Thirteenth Senatorial District consisting of Henry, Patrick and Pittsylvania Counties.

Many times he has been elected senator without opposition, and for sixteen years he has been Chairman of the Finance Committee of the Senate. This position is of great importance and gives him state-wide influence.

Senator Garrett was twice married. His first wife was Susan Trent and his second wife was Emma Garrett.

J. P. Garrett, a former citizen of Henry County, made his home in Salem, Virginia, for a number of years, where he died in 1932. Mr. Garrett's wife was Anna Lee Mitchell and the family included the following children: J. P. Garrett, Jr., and W. S. Garrett, of Roanoke; P. G. Garrett, of Richmond, Virginia; Mrs. G. W. Coltrane, of Greensboro, North Carolina; Mrs. H. N. Dyer, of Martinsville, Virginia; Mrs. G. W. King, of Charlotte, North Carolina; Mrs. T. G. Tinsley, of McKeesport, Virginia, and Mrs. T. G. Shannon, of Tampa, Florida.

Thomas J. Garrett, another son of W. S. Garrett, is a citizen of Price, North Carolina.

THE VISITATION OF HERTFORDSHIRE, made by Robert Cook, Esq., Clarencieux, in 1834, and Sir Richard St. George Clarencieux, in 1572. With Hertfordshire Pedigrees from Harlean MSS 6147 and 1546, edited by Walter C. Metcalf, London.

EXCERPT FROM THE VISITATION OF HERTFORDSHIRE 1572, GRAVELY OF GRAVELY.

ARMS—SABLE A CROSS POINTED ARGENT IN THE DEXTER POINT MULLET OF THE LAST.

THESE ARMS WERE TAKEN OUT OF A WINDOW IN GRAVELY CHURCH.

ROBERT GRAVELY KT—BEATRICE DAUGHTER OF—AND E FILIA REGIS EDWARD. A DEED OF BEATRICE AFTER THE DECEASE OF HER HUSBAND E FILIA REGIS EDWARD.

William did give to Rafe—his son.
Rafe, the son of William 14 E 3.
John Gravely of Grave to Hertfordshire descended of Rafe Gravely-Oson of William-Son of Robert.
Thomas Gravely—Agnes, daughter of Atwill or Lathill, of Hill Land.
John Gravely—Elizabeth, daughter of 2 Henry.
Gravely Thomas Core of Core ob S. P.

Thomas Gravely	Elizabeth 3 Edw James		Jno. Gravely
of Gravely son	daughter of Hollins 4 Edw 6 George		These sons
and heir	north of Cheshire		daughter of Thos.
			Hutton of Co. C
Francis Gravely	2 Thomas		
son and heir is	3 Rowland	Winifred	Anne
8 years old	8 months old	Julian	Mary

THE GRAVELY FAMILY OF HENRY COUNTY

WRITTEN BY "OMECRON," MAY, 1878

Perhaps there is not in all the land another family so remarkable for length of days as the Gravely family of Henry County, Virginia. I presume more of them have lived to a very great age than any other family in this part of the state.

Let me give you a few facts and figures. Mr. Joseph Gravely, the ancestor of all the persons bearing that name in the county and the father of the older members of the family now living, was of English descent. He emigrated from the county of Culpeper to Henry County quite a number of years ago, and settled on Leatherwood Creek. He cultivated the soil for a living. He was a soldier in the Revolutionary War. He was very temperate and methodical in all his habits. One great peculiarity with him was that he never ate any warm bread. In his last days he could read the finest print without the aid of spectacles. He lived to the great age of ninety-six years. His widow survived him a number of years, attaining the unusual age of ninety-eight. Her life was marked by great strength and force of character.

They were the parents of ten children, eight sons and two daughters. Of the sons four are now living, Jabez Gravely, the oldest son, the father of Mr. B. F. Gravely, of Leatherwood, was born in the ever memorable year of 1776. He died in April, 1872, of paralysis, being ninety-six years of age. Joseph Gravely, the next brother, died a few years ago of pneumonia at the age of ninety-three years. He was more irregular in his habits than any of his brothers and during his long life performed a great deal of hard manual labor and was much exposed.

Mrs. Polly Dyer, one of the sisters, the mother of Captain B. F. Dyer, died in January, 1878, of no well defined disease. She was ninety-two years old. Of the surviving brothers, two, Captain George and Edmund Gravely, are twins. They are now in their ninetieth year. They are comparatively active and retain all their faculties to an almost perfect degree. Lewis Gravely, the next brother, is eighty-four years of age. He walks to the post office, a distance of two miles, almost every week for his mail. He is very fond of reading and in doing so does not use glasses. In him the faculty of hearing is much impaired. He does not see well at a distance, otherwise he is a healthy old gentleman.

Willis Gravely, the youngest of the brothers, is seventy-eight years old and is a stout, active man. I believe, however, his hair is grayer than that of any other member of the family. He labors in the field every day and in this regard he puts to shame many who are on the sunny side of life's meridian. As a successful gardener he scarcely has a rival.

These are very extraordinary instances of long life in the same family. The united ages of the father and mother and the seven children here enumerated make for each one of the nine an average age of ninety years and seven-ninths of a year.

What was and is there in the quiet and unobtrusive lives of these persons by which they have thus spun out life's brittle thread? What fortunate star was in the ascendency at their natal hour? Did they inherit better conditions than other persons, or did they and do they husband with more care than others life's waning taper? Who will solve this enigma? Such length of life is truly wonderful. It seems almost to contravene the physiological laws of our being and to force one to the conclusion that they have really well nigh discovered the long sought for "Elixir of Life."

Joseph Gravely, referred to as the founder of the Gravely family in Henry County, was born in England, in 1744. He settled in Henry County before the Revolutionary War, and was the owner of extensive lands. His home was distinguished as the one having the first brick chimney built in that section.

Mr. Gravely was a noted patriot and rendered his country splendid service in not only joining the ranks to assist General Greene at Guilford Court House, but gave of his means also, contributing both means and service in establishing American independence.

He married Eleanor, daughter of Lieutenant Francis Cox, September 1, 1775. Their children, eight sons and two daughters, were as follows: Jabez, Frank, Joseph Jefferson, George, Edmund, Lewis, Peyton, Willis, Eleanor and Mary (Polly).

Frank Gravely, son of Joseph Gravely, was one of Henry County's patriotic sons. He fought in the War of 1812, a member of the famous Staples Rifles, the men whose skill in marksmanship was marvelous. The test of a rifleman's skill was the ability to knock out the eye of a squirrel in the tallest tree without mutilating the body in any way. Mr. Gravely was killed in the celebrated Battle of Craney Island—the battle in which the Americans won a signal victory over an overwhelming British force.

Joseph Jefferson Gravely married a Miss King. Eleanor married Major Arnold Walker. A son, Logan, was the father of Major J. A. Walker, and Betsy, who married a Philpott.

George, 1788, married Mary Hughes. Their children were Letitia, who married George D. Gravely, and Mary, who married Dr. Henry D. Peters, of Leatherwood. Nancy married William Dickerson. Eleanor, unmarried.

Lillian and May Bud, children of the second wife, Elizabeth Jones, were not married.

Edmund Gravely, twin brother of George, married Susan Robinson. Their children were: Mary Jane, who married Elijah Richardson, Joe

PEYTON GRAVELY

From a portrait

Morton, unmarried. Eliza married Joseph Richardson. George and William, unmarried. Jabez (Jabe) married Anna Towler. Susan married John Belcher. Judith Elizabeth, the youngest child, married Captain John Cox, of the Virginia Militia. Only one child was born to them, Joanna, who married Gustave A. Giles.

Jabez Gravely married Judith Wells. Their children are as follows: John W. married Frances Marshall; Joseph, Eliza Dickerson; Judith, Ephram Riddle; Eleanor, William Moore; Jabez Leftwich, Miss Hankins; Francis Cox, Sallie A. Holman; Benjamin Franklin, Julia C. Thomas.

Mary (Polly) Gravely, another daughter of Joseph senior, married Benjamin Dyer. Lewis Gravely married Martha Dyer. Peyton Gravely married Matilda Thomas, sister of C. Y. Thomas.

Willis Gravely, the youngest son of Joseph senior, was twice married. His first wife was a daughter of Captain Stone, of Henry County, the second wife was Anne Nancy Marshall Barrow, daughter of William Barrow and Susan Marshall Barrow. Susan Marshall Barrow was a granddaughter of Colonel Thomas of historic fame.

The children of Lewis Gravely and Martha Dyer Gravely were: Spottswood, who married Alice Williams; Joseph Jackson, who married Martha Marshall, daughter of Dennis Marshall.

Lewis Gravely, Jr., moved to Missouri before the Civil War. His wife was Sarah Sherill. Their children were as follows: Eugenia, who lived in Oklahoma; Martha married John F. Pedigo. Rachel married first, a Cheatham; second, John F. Pedigo. Mary married Patrick Martin; Frank, Sallie Hughes Dillard; Thomas, Georgia Stultz; George, Letitia Gravely.

The children of Willis Gravely: Susan Ellen married Abner McCabe; Peyton B., Mary Walters; William, Sarah Morrison; Julia Cassandra died in infancy and an infant son died. Francis Marshall, unmarried. Joseph Henry married first, Frances McCabe; second, Eliza Griggs; third, Miss Hendricks. Mary Elizabeth married Dr. W. A. Holman; Chester Bullard, Emma Eugenia Pedigo; William Lewis married first, Berta Treadway; second, Mrs. Mattie Smith Ivey. Martha Anna married Royal Washington Morrison. The other members of the family are Matilda J. Gravely, Edna Bonner and Edd Gravely. Eleanor married Thomas Donnegan.

There was one daughter born to Willis Gravely and his first wife. Eliza Ann Gravely, who married Captain Rice and they were survived by one daughter, Sallie Anna Rice, who married John Gravely, father of John W. Gravely, of Washington, D. C.

JABEZ MARRIED JUDITH WELLS

JABEZ LEFTWICH
CHILDREN
J. M. (FIRST)
FRANCIS COX
BENJAMIN FRANKLIN
JOSEPH
JUDITH
ELEANOR

FRANK (UNMARRIED)
JOSEPH JEFFERSON
CHILDREN
JOHN
POLLY
NELLIE
PATSY

GEORGE
CHILDREN
NANCY
LETITIA
MARY
ELEANOR
LILLIAN
MAY

EDMUND GRAVELY

CHILDREN
MARY (POLLY)
ELIZA
JOSEPH MORTON
JABEZ
SUSAN
BETTIE
GEORGE
WILLIAM

PEYTON GRAVELY
NO CHILDREN
LEWIS GRAVELY
CHILDREN
JOSEPH JACKSON
LEWIS, JR.
MARY
MARTHA
RACHAEL
FRANK
THOMAS
GEORGE D.
ELEANOR

WILLIS GRAVELY
CHILDREN
SUSAN
PEYTON
WILLIAM
MARSHALL
JOE HENRY
ELIZABETH
CHESTER
WILLIS
ANNA
EDMUND
MATILDA

ELEANOR GRAVELY
MAR. A WALKER
ONE SON, LOGAN
MARY G. (SEE DYER)
BENJAMIN M.
ELEANOR M.

JOSEPH JACKSON
CHILDREN
BENJAMIN   PATTIE
NANNIE   ELLA
JACKSON   MINNIE
JOSEPH W.   LUTIE

LEWIS, JR.
DAUGHTER
EUGENIA
(OKLA)

MARY (SEE MARTIN)

FRANK

THOMAS

JABEZ LEFTWICH
CHILDREN
FOUNTAIN
WILLIAM
SUSAN
SALLIE
MARTHA

FRANCIS COX GRAVELY
CHILDREN
ALICE
BELLE
ROSA
BENJAMIN J.
WILLIAM (HART)
MORTON H.

JOHN W. GRAVELY
CHILDREN
JOHN W., JR.
MARSHALL
ELIZABETH
JUDITH
HARRIET (MRS. FINNEY)

JOSEPH (JABEZ' SON)
CHILDREN
GEORGE J.
JOSEPH BENJAMIN
ELLA
SALLIE

B. F. GRAVELY (JABEZ'
SON)
CHILDREN
NANNIE W.
BERTA
HENRY CLAY (HARRY)
JOHN THOMAS

KATE GRAVELY
(MAR. JOHN HUNDLEY)

GEORGE D. GRAVELY OF HENRY COUNTY

George D. Gravely, son of Lewis Gravely, occupied a position in his community attained by few men. He was a lawyer of splendid ability, fine judgment and was noted for his candor. He was one of the real builders of Martinsville and lived to see it grow into a substantial town. He served as county clerk for two terms and filled other positions of honor and trust. The county has never produced a man who was held in higher esteem by all who came in contact with him, knowing that, in all business transactions, fairness and justice would be his first consideration. He lived through the terrible period of the Civil War, opposing secession and always hoping that the Union would be preserved.

Mr. Gravely died in 1904 being survived by his wife, three sons and one daughter.

George L. Gravely, son of George D. and Letitia Gravely, practiced law with great success as a partner of his father for several years. After his father's death he continued his practice alone, holding a high place in the profession. His unusual talents and strict integrity, coupled with splendid business methods, won the confidence and esteem of all with whom he came in contact.

He married Mrs. Minnie Walker Gregory whose brightness and charm made her a popular member of Martinsville society. She passed away in 1930.

William H. Gravely practiced law in Martinsville for several years, being associated with Judge N. H. Hairston for a while. He was elected as a member of the Virginia House of Delegates. He married Caroline Anson, daughter of Rev. Alfred W. Anson. A son and daughter were born to them, William and Georgina, both of whom are engaged in educational work.

Mary Hughes (Mollie) Gravely makes her home in Martinsville. She is a bright and active member of the community and a member of the Methodist Church.

ALBERT S. GRAVELY OF HENRY COUNTY, VIRGINIA

Albert S. Gravely, youngest son of George D. Gravely and Letitia Gravely, after graduating from Ruffner Institute, and taking a business course in Poughkeepsie, New York, studied law and became proficient but his literary taste led him to enter the newspaper field and he soon became the successful editor of *The Henry Bulletin* and held that position for many years. Mr. Gravely retired from the newspaper field a few years since and was elected city clerk, which position he now holds.

Mrs. Gravely was Alice Kennon Williams, daughter of the late H. S. Williams and Mrs. Sue Dabney Williams and granddaughter of Colonel R. E. Withers, United States Senator. She occupies a prominent place in social circles, and has taken an active part as a member of the D. A. R., being now the Regent of The Patrick Henry Chapter.

The loyalty and devotion of the family of Mr. and Mrs. H. S. Williams to the Episcopal Church are proverbial. Mrs. Gravely and Mrs. Virginia Williams Brown have been leading members of the choir of Christ Church, in Martinsville, since girlhood.

The Gravely family has representatives in almost every state in the union, and wherever known, occupy prominent positions in the business and social world.

William G. Gravely, of Monroe, North Carolina, is a descendant of Joseph Gravely, of Leatherwood. The family owned land and lived near Martinsville, Virginia. Mr. Gravely's wife was a Miss Shelor, of Floyd County, Virginia.

MEMBERS OF THE GRAVELY FAMILY DISTINGUISHED
IN THE SERVICE OF THEIR COUNTRY

Peyton B. Gravely enlisted in the Confederate Army in the Danville Artillery, April 9, 1861, and later became Captain of Company F, 42d Regiment, and served through the War.

Joseph H. H. Gravely enlisted in the same regiment, became orderly sergeant and fought in many battles.

Marshall Francis Gravely was a member of the Danville Grays, entering the Army in 1862, and was in the First Battle of Manassas. He died in the service. William Armistead Gravely entered the Southern Army in 1862 from Henry County, was in the 24th Regiment of Volunteers and died in the service.

Chester Bullard Gravely was in the 10th Virginia Cavalry, went in before he was of legal age and served until the surrender.

Major Thomas M. Gravely enlisted in the Confederate Army and fought through the War. He became a major and was distinguished for bravery and daring. He was with Colonel George C. Cabell.

HENRY CLAY GRAVELY OF HENRY COUNTY, VIRGINIA

Henry Clay Gravely, son of Benjamin F. and Julia Thomas Gravely, was born in Henry County, at the Leatherwood home, and received his education in the rural schools and at Roanoke College, Salem, Virginia. He became one of the firm of B. F. Gravely & Sons, very prominent and successful tobacco manufacturers of Henry County. He succeeded his father as head of the firm, and like many other manufacturers sold the business to the American Tobacco Company.

Mr. Gravely moved to Martinsville, Virginia, and, while not actively engaged in business, has large interests which occupy his time and attention. He is one of the leading citizens of the town.

He married Hope, daughter of Honorable C. Y. and Mary Reamey Thomas. Four sons and one daughter complete the family circle. Richard P. married Sadie, daughter of H. G. and Whitten McCabe Mullins. Hope married Merrill Lea, of Richmond, Virginia. The other sons are: Benjamin, Paul and Harold, all of Martinsville, Virginia.

MR. J. O. W. GRAVELY OF ROCKY MOUNT, NORTH CAROLINA

Mr. J. O. W. Gravely, son of Mrs. N. O. Gravely, formerly of Henry County, Virginia, popularly known as "Captain Jack," was one of the pioneer tobacco men of eastern North Carolina and has long been a leader in that industry. He was one of the founders of the local tobacco market, having come to Rocky Mount in 1890. He first entered the warehouse business, but for more than thirty-five years he has been identified with the drying and resales industry. Through his business foresight and acumen, he was the founder of the China-American Tobacco Company of which he was the president at the time of his death.

Captain Gravely had long been identified with the social, industrial and religious life of his community. He was a senior member of the First Methodist Church, a former member of the board of stewards and a controlling factor in that congregation. He was an outstanding Mason in the Blue Lodge and the higher degrees, being a Thirty-Second Degree Mason and a Knight Templar.

Mr. and Mrs. Gravely are the parents of a daughter, Mrs. Kenly McGee, of Rocky Mount, North Carolina, and three sons, State Senator L. L. Gravely, P. K. Gravely and J. O. W. Gravely, of Richmond, Virginia.

Joseph King Gravely and Parmelia Stultz Gravely's heirs are as follows: Eleanor Parmelia Gravely (mother of T. E. Gravely, of Martinsville, Virginia) had six brothers:

Frank	married	Lizzie Haines
John W.	married	Nannie Oglesby Haines
Joseph	married	Bettie Wade
Jabe	married	Sallie Wingfield
William Goggin	married	Emily Thomas
Peyton	married	Anna Wingfield

The children of John W. and Nannie Haines Gravely are: John O. Winston Gravely, who married Lula Keene and reared the following children: Honorable Lee L. Gravely, legislator and ex-mayor of Rocky Mount, North Carolina; Paige K. Gravely, lawyer, who married Elizabeth Haines; J. O. W. Gravely, Jr.; Lula Gravely, who married Kenly McGee.

J. O. W. Gravely, Sr., had the following brothers and sisters: Stephin Ashford, King M., Peyton, Benjamin Franklin, Elisha, Bettie Anne and Ellie.

Benjamin Franklin Gravely and Mary J. Steagall Gravely's heirs are as follows:

NAME	TO WHOM MARRIED
Berta	Napoleon Gravely
Benjamin F., Jr.	Bess Downey, of Pomeroy, Ohio
Herbert Grayson	Willa Eve Graves, of West Virginia
Archie Henry	Helen Schaum, of Charleston, West Virginia
Lilly M.	Chesley Gordon Barker
Loula Nebletts	Professor John Thomas Erwin, of the George Washington University, Washington, D. C.
Cassie Bonner	Thomas Eleanor Gravely

B. F. Gravely, Jr., had the following heirs: Alexander Downey, Charles Benjamin, Mary Louise, Virginia and Thelma.

Archie H. Gravely's children were: Archie H., Jr., William Schaum, Margaretta and Ruth.

Herbert Gravely left no heirs.

Berta Gravely's children are: Benjamin F., Jr., Janie Franklin, Annette and Marjory.

Lilly Gravely Barker's children are: Vivian L., Grayson Adair, Mary Chesley, Garnett, Lizzie Moss and Lavillon.

Lula Erwin had no children.

Thomas Eleanor Gravely was the son and only child of John William Gravely and Eleanor Parmelia Gravely. His father was the son of William Leftwich Gravely and Patsy Hankins Gravely. His mother was the only daughter of Joseph King Gravely and Parmelia Stultz Gravely.

Thomas Eleanor Gravely married Cassie Bonner Gravely, daughter of Benjamin Franklin Gravely and Mary Steagall Gravely, their family included the following children: Berlynne Fremont (died in infancy); Willie Eleanor, married Dr. Tyree Dodson; Thomas Eleanor (died at the age of five years); Mary Parmelia; Cassie Edith; Nannie, married George Benjamin Clanton; Lula Neblett.

JAMES C. GREER OF MARTINSVILLE, VIRGINIA

James C. Greer, one of Martinsville's most popular and highly esteemed citizens, is a native of Franklin County, Virginia. He came to Martinsville when quite a young man, having accepted a position in the Farmers' National Bank which later became The First National Bank.

Mr. Greer's talent for the work and close application to business entitled him to promotion and he is now president of The First National Bank, of Martinsville.

No man in the community has had to handle more difficult business situations than Mr. Greer, and he has done so with consummate tact and ability, avoiding as far as possible distress and loss for others.

In addition to the business of the bank, Mr. Greer was made executor of a large estate left by an uncle of his wife, in Oklahoma, and was made guardian of one of the heirs living in that state.

Mrs. Greer, before her marriage, was Miss Goss, of Missouri, a woman of many accomplishments, the family circle consists of Mr. and Mrs. Greer and one daughter, Martha Conway.

THE GRIGGS FAMILY

Among the earliest emigrants to this country were the four Griggs brothers, one came to Boston, Massachusetts, one to New York, and later to New Jersey, and there formed the nucleus of the large Griggs family of that section. The other two, Michael and Robert, came to Virginia and settled in Lancaster County.

The Virginia branch as well as the northern was well represented in the Revolutionary War. From Virginia appeared the names of George, Peter, Philip, William, Lewis and Lee.

The Henry County branch of the family descended from Michael Griggs. Three brothers, Jeremiah Michael, Peter and John, came to Henry County just after the Revolutionary War. Peter Griggs spent his life in Henry County, near Preston.

Jeremiah Michael Griggs married first a Miss Minter, there were two children, Jeremiah and Mariah. His second wife was a Stultz and there were five children: Wesley, Peter, Franklin, George, Ira and Susan. His last marriage was to a Miss Pedigo and there were three children, Brice, Lewis and John.

Jeremiah Griggs, son of Jeremiah Michael and his first wife, was one of Henry County's leading citizens. He served in the Civil War and was in the Battle of Gettysburg. William, son of George Griggs, was also in that battle.

George King Griggs, son of Wesley and Susan King Griggs, enlisted in June, 1861, and participated in nearly all of the battles fought by the armies of northern Virginia. He was wounded several times, severely at Gettysburg. He rose rapidly from Captain to Colonel of the 38th Regiment of Infantry, and surrendered at Appomattox in charge of the Brigade.

Greenberry Thornton Griggs, son of Franklin Griggs, was only sixteen years of age when the war broke out, and served as Captain of Company H, 47th Virginia Regiment in Kemper's Brigade, Longstreet's Corps. He was captured before Appomattox and held a prisoner in Johnson's Island from which place he was paroled.

Samuel J. Griggs was elected to the Legislature in 1882–83. His wife was Ella Martin Dillard, daughter of Overton and Sallie Martin Dillard. Their children were Elizabeth, Frank, Cecil and Samuel. One little daughter died in infancy. Mrs. Griggs later married R. E. Lee, who died several years since. All members of that family have passed away.

Greenberry Griggs was untiring in his efforts to establish public schools. In collaboration with Dr. William Ruffner, when the system was adopted in 1871, he canvassed the state in behalf of the institution. He was the first county superintendent of schools in Henry County. As a result of his efforts, Henry County had one of the first high schools in the state and was named in honor of Dr. Ruffner.

His wife was Annie Griggs, daughter of Jeremiah Griggs, and their children were: Lila (Mrs. Pitzer, of Roanoke), Allie (Mrs. J. R. Bell), Louise, Bess, Mary, Rives and John D.

George Griggs, brother of Jeremiah and son of Jeremiah, Sr., and his second wife, settled near Ridgeway. He was born in 1816 and married Frances Wells. Their children were: William, Jerry M., Frances, Susan and George Ira.

Jerry W. Griggs (1844) married Emeline King. One son, George K., and an adopted daughter, Lena, compose the family.

Susan Griggs married Sol Franklin, of Irisburg. He died after a few years and was survived by his wife and the following children: Joe, Sol, George, Ben, John, Clay, Rose and Kate.

George I. Griggs was born in 1846. He married Susan Churchill and they made their home in Ridgeway. He conducted a general merchandise business for a long period of time. The firm of Jones & Griggs was the oldest business in the county. He died in 1912, and was survived by his wife and the following children: Kate, Susan, Maybird and George I., named for her father. One daughter, Margie, died in infancy.

THE HAIRSTON FAMILY OF VIRGINIA

From the earliest settlement of Henry County the Hairston family has ranked as one of the most important of the leading families.

The name has a most interesting origin, being derived from the old Scotch word "Hairst" meaning harvest and the second syllable "one" signifies one born in or near harvest time. The name was originally "Hairstone" and said to have been pronounced in Scotland "Herston."

The Hairstones were staunch royalists and owing to political disturbances moved from Scotland to England, thence to Wales, over into Ireland and back to Scotland.

When James VI, of Scotland, ascended the throne of England as James I, the name appears among those of the officers of his retinue. It was after the disastrous "Field of Culloden" that Peter Hairston gathered his children together and came to America. It is supposed that his wife, who is only mentioned as an "Irish lady of rank," died before he left Scotland. He brought with him to Virginia four sons and one daughter; one daughter,

Agnes, having died during the voyage and was buried at sea. The other daughter married a young man named Seldon, a member of whose family was afterward Governor Seldon of Kentucky.

The four sons of Peter Hairston were: Sam, Robert, Peter and Andrew. Peter was captain of a company of Virginia troops and served in North Carolina during the Revolution. He was a bachelor and his will was recorded in Bedford County in 1780. Samuel was a lieutenant of militia in Bedford County, and served as a member of the House of Burgesses several terms. Robert married, in 1749, Ruth Stovall, daughter of George Stovall, Clerk of the House of Burgesses (record at Beaver Creek), and Captain in the Revolutionary War. (Auditor's account, Library, Richmond, Virginia.) He settled in what is now Campbell County and served as captain in the war with the Indians. He also served one term in the House of Burgesses. He left three sons, George, Peter and Sam, and seven daughters. He died in 1793. Wife died, 1808.

Andrew, fourth son of Peter I, married in or near Manchester, Virginia, and left a large estate to his wife and three daughters, having provided for his two sons, Peter and Hugh.

Robert Hairston married Ruth Stovall and was the progenitor of the branch of the family of Henry County (Military and Public Service Recorded in Historical Magazine and Magazine of History and Biography, Vol. 9 and 10). He was Commissioner of Peace, took the oath of allegiance in 1776 and procured his commission from Governor Nelson appointing him high sheriff of Henry County. He established the first Hairston home in Henry County, "Marrowbone" about 1775–76, and later gave it to his son, George, who married Elizabeth Perkins, and he (George) built the Beaver Creek home, where he resided until his death. He and his wife are buried there.

Marrowbone descended from father to son to the fifth generation, all Georges but one. Judge N. H. Hairston, who fell heir to it at the death of his father, Dr. George Hairston.

Following the calamities of the War Between the States, this splendid property passed out of the hands of the former owners and has been allowed to deteriorate beyond recognition.

George Hairston, who inherited Marrowbone from his father, Robert, was a man of great firmness of character combined with elegance of manner and appearance. He was married in 1781 to Elizabeth Perkins, daughter of Nicholas and Bethenia Harden Perkins (see Note), widow of Captain William Letcher, his friend, who was shot through a window in the presence

COLONEL GEORGE HAIRSTON
OF
Hordsville, Henry County, Virginia
1784—1863

of his wife and infant daughter, by a band of tories. Hairston gathered a band of loyal men, caught the tories and tried and convicted them before a drumhead court martial and hanged them. This place in Patrick County is still called Drumhead.

The infant daughter of the Letchers grew up in the Hairston home as an own daughter. She married William Pannill, had a daughter, Elizabeth, who married Archibald Stuart and they were the parents of General J. E. B. Stuart of the Confederate Army.

George Hairston, first child of Robert and Ruth Stovall, was Captain in Colonel Penn's Regiment in 1781. From the Historical Magazine— "George Hairston, Captain in Colonel Penn's Regiment, April, 1781. The Commonwealth of Virginia to George Hairston, Greeting, Know you that from the special trust and confidence which is reposed in your fidelity, courage, activity and good conduct, our Governor, upon the recommendation of the Court of Henry County, doth appoint you County Lieutenant of said County to take rank as such the 11th day of February, 1790. Signed Beverly Randolph, Governor of Virginia. Registered, Samuel Coleman."

Colonel George Hairston donated fifty acres of land as a site for the court house and public halls of Henry County. He commanded the Third, Fourth, Fifth and Sixth Virginia and Thirty-Sixth North Carolina Regiments and was acting Brigadier General in the War of 1812. The following is copied from Acts of Assembly "Lieutenant Colonel George Hairston has arrived and will take command of the Brigade. By command of Bankhead, Adjutant-General." Also, Lieutenant Colonel George Hairston, Fifth Regiment, Virginia Militia Borough, of Norfolk, Virginia, March 11, 1814.

After the above date Colonel Hairston and his wife, Elizabeth Perkins Letcher Hairston, resided at Beaver Creek until they died, Mrs. Hairston in 1818 and Colonel Hairston in 1827.

Note—Colonel George Hairston and Elizabeth Letcher Hairston were married in 1781. They had twelve children as follows:

Robert..............................married.................Ruth Wilson
George..............................married.................Louisa Hardyman
Harden..............................married.................Sarah Staples
Sam..................................married.................Agnes J. P. Wilson
Nickolas............................unmarried
Henry................................married.................Mary Ewell
Peter and Constantine................unmarried   (Continued on next page)

John Adams..........................married.................Malinda Corn
America.............................married.................John Calloway
Marshall............................married.................Ann Hairston
Ruth...............................married.................Peter Hairston
of Franklin County.

Colonel George Hairston died in 1827, his wife died in 1818. Robert, the first son, settled at Berry Hill. He commanded a company in Scott's Army in the invasion of Canada. He served one term in the Virginia Legislature, before moving to Lownes County, Mississippi, and died in 1852. There were no children.

George Hairston, born 1784, graduated at Princeton University in 1805. In 1811 he married Louisa Hardyman, at Greenway, the home of Governor Tyler of Virginia, who was a kinsman of Miss Hardyman. He represented his native county in the House of Delegates and Senate longer than any member before or since. He was invincible as long as he would accept the nomination for either body. He was a zealous advocate of internal improvements and largely owing to his patriotism the Richmond and Danville Railroad received the aid which secured its completion. He was appointed State proxy.

Colonel Hairston was indefatigable in his energy and industry.

The children of George Hairston and Louisa Hardyman Hairston were as follows: John Tyler married Pocahontas Cabell and settled at Red Plains, Henry County. The children of John Tyler and Pocahontas Cabell Hairston, eight in number were:

Louisa.............................married...................Virginius Williams
Elizabeth..........................married...................Livingston Claiborn
Sallie Eppes.......................married...................John S. Redd
George Cabell......................married...................Ann Powell Lash
John Tyler.........................married...................Bettie Brown Dillard
Hardyman and Powhatan were unmarried.

Colonel Tyler Hairston was a lawyer of brilliant intellect. He died in early life.

Harden, third son of George and Elizabeth Perkins Letcher Hairston, born in 1786, was master of transportation in the Southern Division of the Army in 1812. He married Sallie Staples and moved to Lownes County, Mississippi, in 1842. Died in 1862.

Samuel, fourth son of Colonel George and Elizabeth Perkins Letcher Hairston, married his cousin, Agnes Wilson, and lived at Oak Hill, Pittsylvania County, Virginia. He served under General Scott in 1812 as Lieutenant. Nicholas died unmarried.

Henry, born 1793, married Mary Ewell, a relative of General Ewell C. S. A., and settled at Yallabusha, Mississippi. There were three children and they and their parents are all dead.

Peter died unmarried. Constantine, also died unmarried, he was a man of unusual personality, attractive in person and possessing literary taste.

John Adams Hairston, ninth son, born 1779, married Malinda Corn, whose ancestry dates to John Hancock, a vestryman in Lyne Haven Parish, Prince William County, and through this line to Nathaniel Hancock, who came to America. Died 1652. They moved to Yallabusha.

America, tenth child, born 1801, married John Calloway. Had two children, George and Ruth.

Marshall, the eleventh child, born 1802, married his cousin, Ann Hairston, and lived at Beaver Creek. Had only one son, John, who was killed in the Battle of Williamsburg, 1862. There were three daughters.

Ruth Stovall, twelfth child, born 1804, married her cousin, Peter Hairston, son of Samuel and Judith Saunders Hairston, of Franklin County, Virginia.

Robert Hairston, as noted before, had no children, but his wife, by a former marriage to Peter Wilson, had one child, Agnes Wilson, who married Sam Hairston, her stepfather's youngest brother. They had six children: Peter married first, Columbia Stuart, sister of General J. E. B. Stuart; second, Fannie Caldwell, daughter of Judge Caldwell, of North Carolina.

George married Elizabeth Lash. Henry and Robert died unmarried. Ruth married Sam Wilson, of Pittsylvania County. Alcie married her cousin, Samuel Harden Hairston.

John Adams Hairston and Malinda Hairston had five children. George, the first child, after completing his university education, was touring Europe. He hurried home to volunteer for service when the War Between the States broke out. He served under Albert Sydney Johnston and was killed in the Battle of Shiloh.

Marshall, the next child, joined the army when a youth and served through the War on General Walthall's staff. He married Mary Wendell, of Mississippi. Elizabeth married Dr. Lewis Jones, of Grenada, Mississippi. Susan married Captain Rowland Jones, of Yallabusha, Mississippi.

America Hairston Calloway died early. She was survived by two children, George and Ruth. George was never married and Ruth married George Pannill.

Children of Marshall Hairston and Elizabeth Perkins Hairston: Elizabeth Perkins Hairston married her cousin, J. T. W. Hairston. Ann Marshall died unmarried. Ruth Stovall, her twin sister, married Robert Wilson, of Dan Hill, Pittsylvania.

The only son of Marshall Hairston, John, was killed at Williamsburg.

The children of Ruth Stovall and Peter Hairston, of Franklin County, were four. Samuel married Henrietta Jones, of Appomattox County, Virginia; Peter married Lou Jones, of Appomattox, Virginia. George, another brother of Colonel Peter, married Pattie Smith, of Henry County, Virginia. Elizabeth married first, Dr. Peter Dillard. They had two sons. Her second marriage was to John Reamy, and four children were born to them, Sam, Overton, Sue Starling and Pattie.

George Stovall, the second son of George and Louisa Hardyman Hairston, graduated in medicine at the University of Pennsylvania. He married Matilda Martin, daughter of Colonel Hughes and Sallie Martin. Their home was Greenwood, Henry County, Virginia. They were the parents of eight children: Sallie Louisa married Colonel Fleming Saunders; Susan Jane married John Draper, of Pulaski; Elizabeth McLemore married first, Major Samuel Hale; second, Captain C. H. Ingles; George Stovall married Nannie Wilson Watkins; Matilda Martin, Robert C. Tate, of Wythe County; Nicholas Hardyman married Elizabeth Seawell Hairston.

Elizabeth Hairston, third child of Colonel George and Louisa Hardyman Hairston, married John T. Seawell, of Gloucester County. There were two children.

Susan Maria, fourth child, married William Martin, son of Colonel Joseph and Sallie Hughes Martin.

Nicholas Hardyman Hairston married Sarah Hughes Dillard. All children died leaving no descendants.

Louisa Hardyman Hairston married Peter Wilson Watkins. Peter Wilson Watkins was a descendant of the Wilsons who were in Virginia in 1720, and of Bartholomew Dupuy, who belonged to the army of Louis XIV, of France. He married the Countess Susanne Lavilon, was forced by the Edict of Nantes to take refuge in Germany. Later, with 170 other Huguenots, came on the ship "Peter and Anthony." Landed at Jamestown, September 20, 1700.

Robert Henry Hairston, son of George and Louisa Hardyman Hairston, married Elizabeth Saunders, daughter of Sam and Mary Saunders, of

Franklin County, a lineal descendant of Mary Ingles Draper of Trans-Allegheny Pioneers fame.

There were two daughters, Mary Louisa, who married Harry M. Darnall, and Lizzie Lee, who married William S. Gravely.

Samuel Hairston married Eliza Penn, of Patrick County. Their children are: Mrs. N. H. Hairston, of Roanoke, Virginia; Mrs. E. P. Zentmeyer, of Patrick County; George (deceased) and John Tyler, who married Nannie Watkins. He was survived by his wife and three children, Eliza (Lila), Nannie and Watt, the latter married Lelia Price. He died several years since and is survived by his wife and four children.

COLONEL PETER HAIRSTON

Colonel Peter Hairston is said to have been the first Henry County man to volunteer service to the Confederacy. He was educated at West Point and served first with General Early then with Beauregard. He is reported in Confederate Military Records as handling his regiment with coolness and skill, and commended in General Orders for fidelity and bravery. He was in the Virginia Senate in 1875, member of the V. M. I. Board and of the Board of Visitors to West Point in 1895.

Colonel Hairston's wife was Miss Lou Jones, of Appomattox, Virginia, and they lived at Irvin, a beautiful estate near the banks of Smith River.

The only sister of Colonel Hairston, Elizabeth, married first, Dr. Peter Dillard, there were two sons born to them. The second marriage was to John Reamy, and there were four children of this marriage.

Colonel and Mrs. Peter Hairston adopted their niece, Callie Hairston, daughter of Sam Hairston. She married T. A. Ranson, a merchant of Martinsville, formerly of Farmville, Virginia.

George married Elizabeth Lash and they were the parents of Sam, who inherited Oak Hill. Nicholas, Peter and Constantine died unmarried. Henry and John went to Mississippi and had large families. Marshall, the youngest, lived and died at Beaver Creek. He had one son, Jack, who was killed in the Battle of Williamsburg.

Ruth married Robert Wilson, of Pittsylvania County. Elizabeth Perkins married J. W. T. Hairston, of Mississippi, but later lived at Beaver Creek. Ann Marshall Hairston died unmarried.

GEORGE HAIRSTON'S SISTERS

America married Jack Calloway. One son, George, died unmarried. Ruth married George Pannill, their children were: America, who married

William Campbell; Mary married John Davis; Edmund married Eliza, daughter of Dr. Peter Reamy; William was said to have been the first Henry County boy to be killed in the Civil War. (See Pannill family.)

Laura Hughes Hairston (Mrs. Edwin G. Penn) was a daughter of William Lash Hairston and Elizabeth Dobson Hairston. William Lash Hairston was a son of George and Anne Elizabeth Lash Hairston. George Hairston was a son of Samuel Hairston, of Oak Ridge, Pittsylvania County, Virginia.

Laura Hughes Hairston Penn is a woman of unusual attainments. She received her education at Salem College, Winston-Salem, North Carolina, being placed in that school when a very young girl. Her taste for educational work has led her to continue teaching and she is now principal of one of the leading schools of Martinsville.

Mrs. Penn takes an active part in the work of the patriotic societies, as well as of social activities.

The other daughter of William Lash Hairston, Elizabeth (Bessie), married Pride Hunt, of Pittsylvania County. She passed away several years since.

Samuel Harden, born in Patrick County in 1822, graduated at William and Mary College, studied law, was county judge and served with the rank of major on the staff of J. E. B. Stuart in the Confederate Army. He was a member of the legislature and was killed in the Richmond Capitol disaster. His wife was Alcie Hairston, daughter of Samuel Hairston, of Oak Hill. He was survived by his wife and three children, Harden, Ruth and Sallie.

Ruth Stovall Hairston married Alfred Varley Sims, brother of Admiral Sims, U. S. A. The children of Mr. and Mrs. Sims are: Elsie Hairston, who married Frederick Q. Rickard; Ruth Stovall, Harold Churchill Norton; Adelaide Varleta, Charles Marshall Davidson, and one son, Alfred William.

Sarah Hairston married James Dodge Glenn, who was prominent in state affairs of North Carolina. He was a brother of Governor Glenn of that state and served several terms in the upper and lower branches of the House of Representatives of North Carolina. He was also Colonel of Militia and Adjutant General.

One daughter was born to them and after the death of General Glenn, Mrs. Glenn with her daughter, Alcie Hairston, returned to Virginia and have since made their home in Martinsville.

Alcie Hairston Glenn married William Murray Whittle, son of Judge Stafford G. Whittle.

Harden Hairston, son of Samuel and Alcie Hairston, spent his life in Henry County. He managed the extensive estate, Chatmoss, which he inherited. This estate is a few miles east of Martinsville and for generations was known as one of Virginia's most hospitable homes. Mr. Hairston was a country gentleman of the finest type. His hospitality, loyalty to friends and generosity were well known and appreciated by all who came in contact with him.

His wife was Delphine E. Hall, of Winston-Salem, North Carolina. Both Mr. and Mrs. Hairston passed away a few years since, within a few months of each other.

JUDGE NICHOLAS HARDYMAN HAIRSTON

Nicholas Hardyman Hairston was born at his ancestral home "Marrowbone," Henry County, Virginia. He chose law as his profession and after completing his law course and being admitted to the bar, practiced in Henry County, Virginia, and was for several years judge of the county court.

In 1903 he moved to Roanoke, Virginia, and continued his practice there until his death in 1927.

Judge Hairston was a man of splendid personality and his genial manner won many friends.

His wife who was, before her marriage, Elizabeth Seawell Hairston, with four children, survive him. Mrs. Hairston is a true type of Virginia gentlewoman.

Both of the sons of Judge and Mrs. Hairston, George and Samuel, inherited and developed a talent for legal work. Both graduated in law at Washington and Lee University. Samuel, the younger son, has the distinction of graduating and passing his bar examination before he was twenty-one years of age. He is the author of a book, "Answers to Virginia Bar Examination Questions."

Both daughters are married and live in Roanoke. Elizabeth married William Nelson Hobbie. Mary Martin married Dr. Walter Maynard Otey.

HORDSVILLE

A recent visit to Hordsville, one of the colonial homes of the Hairston family, was an event of great pleasure and interest. Approaching the house one passes along a walk bordered with English boxwood eight or ten feet in height. Being graciously received by the present owners of their ancestral home, Mr. Peter Hairston and his sister, Miss Mattie Hairston, one enters a veritable treasure house—furniture, china and silver centuries old, handed down from one generation to another, wise enough to appreciate and preserve what is really genuine and beautiful in antiques.

Guns, hundreds of years old, are still kept on brackets above the doors. The large rooms with wide fireplaces are a delight to behold, and the spacious hall contains a circular stairway extending through to the attic.

This brother and sister, living on their fine estate and keeping up the traditions of real Virginia hospitality, belong to a family that has been known from the first settlement of Virginia as the real aristocrats of this country.

Dr. George Hairston was an eminent physician and lived at Marrowbone farm, his father's old home. He married Matilda Martin. Their children were: George, who died at Hordsville, leaving three children, George, Peter and Mattie.

Robert, brother of George, married his cousin, Ruth Stovall Wilson, and established the home "Berry Hill" in Pittsylvania County, Virginia.

Harden married Sallie Staples and lived at the Old Fort in Patrick County.

Peter, brother of George, married Alcie Perkins (niece of Elizabeth mentioned above), and built a home at Sauratown, North Carolina.

Samuel married Judith Saunders, of Franklin County, Virginia. Their daughter, Ruth, was the mother of General Jubal Early.

One daughter, sister of George, married Alexander Hunter of the Hunters of Beaver Island to one of whom there is a monument at Guilford Court House.

Elizabeth, the first daughter, married a lawyer, John Seawell, of Gloucester County.

Susan married Colonel William Martin and Louisa married Peter Watkins, of Shawnee Farm.

Marshall Hairston's daughter, Ruth Stovall, left a daughter, Ann Marshall, who married Rorer James.

Elizabeth, daughter of Robert and Ruth Stovall Hairston, married Michale Rowland (1778). There was one daughter, Elizabeth Hampton. Sara, another daughter of Robert and Ruth Stovall Hairston, married Baldwin Rowland (1782). There was one daughter, Martha, who married a Bailey and from this line came the Traylors.

From Elizabeth Hairston Rowland are descended Dunbar Rowland, the historian, and Kate Mason Rowland, authoress, of Williamsburg, Virginia.

Among the members of the Hairston family who have gone to other states: Dr. Peter Hairston, son of Harden Hairston and Sallie Staples Hairston, born at "The Old Fort" in 1823, graduated in medicine and moved to Lownes County, Mississippi, married W. Virginia Moseley and reared a large family.

Nicholas Edward graduated from Harvard College and married Kesiah, daughter of Colonel Samuel and Lucinda Penn Staples, moved to Mississippi.

Robert Hairston took his A. M. degree at Chapel Hill, North Carolina, married Mary Hayes, of Alabama, and lived there.

J. T. W. Hairston, before mentioned, was born at "The Old Fort" in Patrick County, graduated at V. M. I. and was a major in the Confederate Army. The two sons of Major and Elizabeth Perkins Hairston died, Marshall, the elder, when quite young and Watt after reaching manhood.

There were two sisters of J. T. W. Hairston, Elizabeth Perkins and Sara Alcie. The former married her cousin, Sam Hairston, son of Sam and Judith Saunders Hairston, of Franklin County. The latter married T. B. Brooks, of Mississippi.

_____

THE HARBOUR FAMILY OF PATRICK COUNTY, VIRGINIA

Thomas Harbour was a native of the rugged country of Wales, and responding to the call of opportunities offered in the New World which were unknown in the old, made his way to Virginia, and settled on land lying on Mayo River near the state line in Lunenburg, now Patrick County. This settlement was made about 1740.

David Harbour, born in 1769, was a grandson of Thomas Harbour. By his superior intelligence and natural ability he was far in advance of his time, and, like all leaders, suffered some of the consequences of leadership. It was said of him in after life that he favored the mother country as against the colonies, and seeing that he was only seventeen years old at the beginning of the Revolutionary War, and that he was charged with the care of his father's family, it is not strange that he was in favor of order as opposed to violence. The British Government had never oppressed him or any one else so far as his knowledge extended. This shadow followed him through life, preventing all public preference, but in the light of our wider vision it is doubtful whether he made or lost by its existence.

David Harbour's eldest son, Abner, married a Thornhill and acquired land in the northwest part of Henry County, now Patrick County, on the

waters of Irwin's, now Smith, River. He was compelled to leave this land
on account of an Indian raid from Chillicothe, and he never returned to his
domain as he died soon afterwards.

The members of the Harbour family of whom we have a record are:
David Harbour, Moses Harbour and Thomas Harbour, the latter lived in
Henry County.

The children of David Harbour were: Mary, who married Abram
Reynolds; Sarah, Lewis Pedigo; Jennie, who married a Knowles and lived
on the Meadows of Dan, in Patrick County; Joyce Harbour was the wife of
Daniel Ross and lived in Patrick County; Richard Harbour married Judith
Nowlin and lived near Elamsville; Naeman Harbour lived and died near
Buffalo Ridge, Patrick County, Virginia; Ben Harbour and Jarrett Harbour
moved to Ohio; Abram Harbour moved to Illinois.

The children of Richard Harbour and Judith Nowlin Harbour are as
follows: Witt Harbour; Charles (killed in the Civil War); Richard Harbour
lived and died in Patrick County; Lucinda Harbour married Albert Pedigo;
Esther Cronk Harbour married Samuel Ross; Sallie Harbour married a
Rorer; Judith Virginia Harbour married W. H. Thomas; Mary married a
Burnette (died in Kansas).

The sons of Thomas Harbour: Green Harbour, Primitive Baptist
preacher (died while preaching in Surry County, North Carolina); James
Harbour, son of Thomas Harbour, lived near Stuart, Virginia. The children
of James Harbour were: Ewell Harbour, Tyler (killed in the Civil War),
Cain Harbour (wounded and died in the Civil War), Elishabe Harbour Ross,
Ruth Harbour Spencer, Evelyn Harbour Ross and Bettie Harbour Pilson.

Naeman Harbour's children (Buffalo Ridge): Chapman Johnson
Harbour lived and died near Buffalo Ridge; Mary Ella (Bird) Harbour
married a Terry, and James Abner (Zack) Harbour.

Thomas Harbour, a bachelor, lived in Henry County. He was a large
slave owner and owned large boundaries of land. His mother was Joyce
Ross. Mary Harbour, niece of Thomas Harbour, married Elie Watkins,
son of Ned Watkins. Their son, Peter D. Watkins, married Sarah Amos.
Tilla Joyce Watkins, daughter of Joyce Watkins, married Andrew J. Gann
and lives in Augusta County, Virginia. Beatrice Gann McAuley, daughter

of Andrew J. Gann and Tilla J. Watkins Gann, has lived in Winston-Salem, North Carolina, for a number of years.

PATRICK HENRY

Although there are volumes and more volumes extant written upon the life of Patrick Henry, this history would be incomplete without having some space devoted to the man in honor of whom the counties were named, who made his home for some years in Henry County, and whose constructive statesmanship as well as his leadership during the Revolutionary War were of superlative importance to the country.

Whatever may be said of his early youth he had the highest claim to an inheritance of brains through the lineage of both parents. His father was John Henry, of Aberdeen Scotland, and his mother was Sarah Winston Syme, of Welsh descent. The family home was in Hanover County where Patrick Henry was born May 29, 1746.

The system of education prevailing in Virginia at that time was extremely simple; it consisted of almost an entire lack of public schools mitigated by the sporadic and irregular exercise of domestic tuition. Those who could afford to import instruction into their homes had it if they desired, those who could not generally went without.

As to the youthful Patrick he and the kind of education thus provided never took kindly to each other. At that time he gave no token by work or act of the possession of any intellectual gifts that could make him rise above mediocrity or up to it.

During the first ten years of his life, he seems to have made some small and reluctant progress into the mysteries of reading, writing and arithmetic, whereupon his father took personal charge of the matter and conducted his further education at home along with that of other children, being aided in the task by the very competent help of a brother, the Rev. Patrick Henry, Rector of St. Paul's Parish in Hanover, and apparently a good Scotch classicist. In this way our Patrick acquired some knowledge of Latin and Greek and rather more knowledge of mathematics, the latter being the only branch of "book learning" for which he showed the least liking. In that very year, 1759, Thomas Jefferson, then a lad of sixteen and on his way to the College of William and Mary, happened to spend the Christmas holidays at the house of Colonel Nathan Dandridge, in Hanover, and there met Patrick Henry.

Long afterwards, in recalling these days, Jefferson furnished this picture of him " Mr. Henry had, a little before, broken up his store or rather it had broken him up, but his misfortunes were not to be traced either in his countenance or in his conduct.

"During the festivities of the season, I met him every day and we became well acquainted although I was much his junior. His manner had something of coarseness in it. His passion was music, dancing and pleasantry. He excelled in the last and it attracted every one to him."

Shortly afterwards Jefferson left these hilarious scenes for the somewhat more restrained festivities of the little college at Williamsburg, and Patrick succeeded in settling in his own mind what he was going to do next. He could not dig, so it seemed, neither could he traffic, but perhaps he could talk. Why not get a living by his tongue? Why not be a lawyer? His brilliant career following his decision is too well known and repetition of what occurred, beginning with his success in the Parsons case, is not necessary.

In this volume we wish to give an account of his constructive statesmanship with reference to Henry and Patrick Counties. Having bought 10,000 acres of land lying in the eastern and northeastern part of the county, he built his house on a ridge a few miles east of Henry Court House and began the practice of law.

The people of Henry County were proud to choose him as their representative in the General Assembly which met in May, 1780. From the moment of his arrival in the House of Delegates every kind of responsibility and honor was laid upon him. This was his first appearance in such an assembly since the Proclamation of Independence, and the prestige attaching to his name as well as his own undimmed genius for leadership made him not only the most conspicuous person in the House, but the nearly absolute director of its business in every detail of opinion and of procedure in which he should choose to express himself, his only rival in any particular being Richard Henry Lee.

It helps one now to understand the real reputation he had amongst his contemporaries for practical ability, and for not shrinking from any of the commonplace drudgeries of legislative work.

During the first few days after his accession to the House he was placed on the Committee of Ways and Means; on a committee to inquire into the present state of the account of the commonwealth against the United States, and the most speedy and effective method of finally settling the same; on a committee to prepare a bill for repeal of a part of the Act, "for sequestering British property, enabling those indebted to British subjects to pay off such debts and directing the proceedings in which such subjects are parties; on those several committees respecting the powers and duties of high sheriffs and of grand juries, and finally, on a committee to notify Jefferson of his election as Governor and to report his answer to the House."

On the seventh of June, however, after a service of little more than two weeks, his failing health forced him to ask leave to withdraw from the House for the remainder of the session.

At the autumn session of the Legislature he was once more in his place. On the sixth of November, the day on which the House was organized, he was made Chairman of the Committee on Privileges and Elections, and also of a committee for the better defense of the southern frontier, and was likewise placed on the Committee on Propositions and Grievances as well as on the Committee on Courts of Justice.

On the following day he was made a member of a committee on the defense of the eastern frontier. On the tenth of November he was placed on a committee to bring in a bill relating to the enlistment of Virginia troops and to the redemption of the state bill of credit, then in circulation, and the emission of new bills. On the twenty-second of November he was made a member of a committee to which was referred the account between the State and the United States. On the ninth of December he was made chairman of a committee to draw up bills for the organization and maintenance of a navy for the State, and the protection of navigation and commerce upon its waters.

On the fourteenth of December he was made chairman of a committee to draw up a bill for the better regulation and discipline of the militia, and of still another committee to prepare a bill for supplying the army with clothes and provisions. On the twenty-eighth of December, the House having the knowledge of the arrival in town of poor General Gates, then drooping under the burden of those southern willows which he had so plentifully gathered at Camden, Patrick Henry introduced the following resolution: "That a committee of four be appointed to wait upon Major General Gates and assure him of the high regard and esteem of the House, that the remembrance of his former glorious services cannot be obliterated by any reverses of fortune, but that this House, ever mindful of his great merit, will omit no opportunity of testifying to the world the gratitude which as a member of the American Union this country owes to him in his military character."

On the twenty-second day of June, 1781, the last day of the session, the House adopted, on Patrick Henry's motion, a resolution authorizing the Governor to convene the meeting of the Legislature at some other place than Richmond, in case its assembling in that city should be inconvenient by the operations of an invading enemy. A resolution reflecting their sense of peril then hanging over the State.

Before the Legislature could again meet events proved that it was no imaginary danger against which Patrick Henry's resolution had been intended to provide. On the second of January, 1781, the very day on which the Legislature had adjourned, a hostile fleet conveyed into James River a force of about eight hundred men under command of Benedict Arnold, whose eagerness to ravage Virginia was still further facilitated by the arrival on the twenty-sixth of March of 2,000 men under General Philips. Moreover, Lord Cornwallis having beaten General Greene at Guilford Court House, North Carolina, on the fifteenth of March, seemed to be gathering force for a speedy advance into Virginia.

The roar of his guns would soon be heard in the outskirts of their capital, was what all Virginians then felt to be inevitable. Richmond was captured and the country ravaged.

SUMMARY

I. Member of historic meeting of former burgesses in the Raleigh Tavern as a result of which came the first Revolutionary Convention of Virginia, August, 1774. He was chosen by that body a delegate to the First Continental Congress.

II. Member of provincial convention of March, 1775, in which he introduced resolutions to organize the militia and put the colony in an attitude of defense.

III. He was appointed commander of all the forces to be raised by a committee of public safety.

IV. Took an active part in the Continental Congress, May, 1776. Was chosen one of the committee who prepared the first Constitution of the Commonwealth of Virginia. In that year he was chosen by the convention which then exercised the power of election (later exercised by the assembly) to be Governor of Virginia, and was reëlected until 1779, when he became ineligible.

V. He returned to the Legislature in which he served until 1784, and was once more chosen governor, serving until 1784, when he finally resigned.

VI. In 1788 he was a member of the convention which ratified for Virginia the Federal Constitution which instrument he vigorously opposed chiefly on the grounds that it failed to protect the rights of states and individuals against the extreme centralization of power in the Federal Government.

VII. In 1794 he declined a seat in the United States Senate and in 1795 Washington offered him the position of Secretary of State, but he declined. He also declined the office of Chief Justice of the United States Supreme Court, and President Adams' offer of a special mission to France as well as an election to governor in 1796.

VIII. He was elected to the House of Delegates in 1799, but did not live to take his seat.

Patrick Henry was deeply religious—a member of the Episcopal Church and opposed to strong drink.

He moved to Charlotte County where he had a beautiful home and there he died, June 6, 1799. He left a large family and a still larger estate and his descendants number hundreds scattered throughout the United States. His fame as an orator is world wide and his name is among the immortals.

PATRICK HENRY'S FINANCIAL SUGGESTIONS

I. That ample and certain funds ought to be established for sinking the quota of the continental debt due from this State in fifteen years.

II. That certain funds ought to be established for furnishing to the continent the quota of this State for the support of the War for the current year.

III. That a specific tax ought to be laid for the use of the continent in full proportion to the abilities of the people.

1770-1780

Within a few days after the close of his term, Mr. Henry left Richmond with his family for Henry County where he took up his residence upon his Leatherwood estate. He found the land largely in the occupation of squatters, who were removed only after much trouble. He carried with him and settled on a part of his estate his son-in-law, Mr. Fontaine, who with his family became permanent residents of the county.

Mr. Henry's residence was about seven miles from the court house on the road leading to Danville. It is described as "situated on the waters of the famous Leatherwood Creek, surrounded on several sides by beautiful hill views with the creek twisting its way through them, and high mountains in the distance."

His object in making his home so far in the interior and among people so lacking in the culture of the capital seems to have been twofold; to place his family in a country which would be free from British raids and to get into a climate free from malarial fevers. He had a severe attack of sickness soon after reaching his new home, however, which was doubtless the further development of the disease from which he had been suffering at Williamsburg.

SUMMARY

Elected by Assembly (declined).

Committee to prepare bill for more diffusion of knowledge.

Chairman of Committee of Ways and Means.

Committee to settle accounts of the State with United States.

Committee on bill to repeal Sequestration Act.

Committee on the Duties of High Sheriffs and Grand Juries.

Within twenty days arms were sent to North Carolina to furnish her troops.

Governor empowered to impress horses upon which to mount the Maryland troops sent to South Carolina, and wagons to transport baggage.

A large body of militia ordered to South Carolina.

A company of 5,000 men ordered prepared to aid southern states and protect Virginia.

Governor empowered to take charge of the boundary at Westham on James River, also to appoint commissioners to examine into amount of provisions in each county and impress surplus for government.

Public arms ordered repaired and made fit for use and provision made for workmen needed.

Congress advised on subject of war being transferred to south (informed of exertions being put forth by Virginia to defend self and sister states south).

Urged to send promptly strong continental forces south to aid Virginia in arming North Carolina.

THE HILL FAMILY OF HENRY COUNTY, VIRGINIA

The founder of this family in Virginia was I. Y. Hill, of Amherst County, Virginia. His wife was Sarah Judith Bailey, daughter of Samuel and Augusta Parks Bailey. Two sons, Samuel C. and William, were with the troops sent to join General Greene at Guilford Court House, and afterwards settled in Henry County.

Samuel C. Hill settled near the present village of Preston about 1801. He married Lucy Mitchell. Their children were: Katherine Ann, Judith Parks, Matilda Winston, John Parks and Sallie.

William Hill, brother of Samuel, came to Henry County about 1793, his wife was Elizabeth Saunders and they established their home on Horsepasture Creek. The children of this family were: Thomas, John Waddy, David, Sallie Parks and Elizabeth Saunders.

Catherine Ann Hill married William A. Taylor; Judith Parks, her cousin, John Waddy Hill, the children of this family were: Samuel Robert, William Wirt, John Waddy, Jr., David Parks, Hester Ann, Elizabeth Saunders and Catherine Matilda.

Matilda Winston Hill married Henry G. Mullins; John Parks, Eliza Morris. He served in the War of 1812.

William Wirt Hill, a prominent Methodist minister, married Catherine Ann Bassett and they reared a large family, viz.: Judith Parks America, Mary Catherine, Martha Woodson, Elizabeth Saunders, Lucy Matilda, John Waddy III, Eliza James, Sarah Alexander, Samuel Robert, Frances Ruth and William Wirt.

Mary Catherine Hill married M. M. Koger; Martha Woodson married first, S. H. Lavinder, second, C. A. Hamilton; Eliza James, O. R. Gregory; Samuel Robert married first, Loula Craghead; second, Sallie Bryant; William Wirt married Grace Fish.

The children of Samuel R. Hill and Loula Craghead Hill are: Samuel Robert, William Wirt, Lucy M., Loula C., Thomas L., Mary C., Ruth Angeline and Overton Gregory.

The children of Samuel R. Hill and Sallie Bryant Hill are: Joseph Wilson, Edith Parks and Frances.

WILLIAM WIRT HILL OF NEWARK, NEW JERSEY

William Wirt Hill, youngest son of Rev. W. W. Hill, of Henry County, received his education at The Hall School near Mt. Bethel Church. Desiring to seek wider fields of endeavor than Henry County afforded at that time he attended the Business College at Poughkeepsie, New York.

After occupying several minor clerical positions, he accepted a position with the Metropolitan Life Insurance Company, of New York, which he has held for many years, being at present manager of one of the departments.

Mr. Hill married Grace Fish, of Newark, New Jersey, and the family circle consists of Mr. and Mrs. Hill and one son, William Nathan.

(See History of Henry County by Judith P. A. Hill.)

JAMES D. HODGES OF HENRY COUNTY

James D. Hodges, son of Hiram Hodges, of Henry County, after attending the public schools of the community in which he lived, went to Martinsville, Virginia, and accepted a position as salesman in the store of a local merchant. Later he was a member of a local firm. After several years in the mercantile business, Mr. Hodges opened a real estate and insurance office and has met with much success.

His first wife was Bettie Jamison. Three sons and one daughter were born to them, Julian, Jack, Mamie and James.

Mrs. Bettie Jamison Hodges passed away in 1926, and several years later Mr. Hodges married Mrs. Daisy Reamey Morris, daughter of D. W. and Elizabeth R. Dillard Reamey.

THE HOOKER FAMILY OF PATRICK COUNTY, VIRGINIA

The family of John W. Hooker owned and lived upon an estate near Elamsville, Patrick County, Virginia. The family included eight sons and three daughters, viz.: J. Murray Hooker (see sketch), of Stuart, Virginia; J. A. Hooker, Nokesville, Virginia; I. L., R. E., and Dr. G. W. Hooker, all of Roanoke, Virginia; S. H. Hooker, of Axton, Virginia; C. P. Hooker, of Palm Beach, Florida; H. L. Hooker, of Richmond, Virginia; Mesdames Nannie Turner and Ida Ross, of Roanoke, Virginia, and Jessie Hooker Nolen, of Elamsville, Virginia.

HONORABLE J. MURRAY HOOKER OF PATRICK COUNTY, VIRGINIA

J. Murray Hooker is a native of Patrick County, Virginia, and has practiced law there and in the surrounding counties and cities for a number of years.

He graduated in law at Washington and Lee University under the tutelage of J. Randolph Tucker and Charles A. Graves. He went to the Constitutional Convention of 1902, as a representative from his native county, and for several years served his people most acceptably as Commonwealth's Attorney.

Mr. Hooker succeeded the late R. A. James in Congress from the Fifth Virginia District and served therein for two terms.

For the past several years he has been Chairman of the Democratic Party in Virginia, and stands high in the councils of that party.

Mrs. Hooker was Annie R. Dillard, daughter of the late Dr. John Redd Dillard and Mrs. Adele Lee Dillard, of Henry County. Mr. Hooker's family circle consists of Mr. and Mrs. Hooker, a son, John Dillard, and a daughter, Annie Murray. Their elder daughter, Margaret Hooker McNiel, passed away in 1931. She was the wife of George Saunders McNiel, of Stuart, Virginia.

THE HUGHES FAMILY OF PATRICK COUNTY, VIRGINIA

Orlando, Leander and William Hughes came from Wales to Virginia about 1700.

Mrs. Harriet D. Pitman, in her work entitled "Americans of Gentle Birth and their Descendants," says that the Hughes family of Virginia descend from Roderick the Great.

The Welsh are among the proudest people on earth, even the humblest Welshman loves to trace his lineage and it has become a proverb, "His lineage is as long as that of a Welshman."

Orlando and Leander Hughes had land grants in Powhatan and Goochland Counties, near Richmond, Virginia. Mrs. Pitman speaks of Colonel Archelaus Hughes, of the Revolution, as belonging to an old Virginia family and that his father's name was Leander.

Orlando Hughes, the immigrant, died in 1768. His sons were: Anthony, Josiah and Leander. This son, Leander, died in 1775. His sons were: Powell, Stephen, John and Archelaus. The county records show that Colonel Archelaus Hughes, of Revolutionary fame, was of the third generation in America.

The name Hughes is sometimes spelled Hewes. The mother of Mary Ball, grandmother of George Washington, was Mrs. Mary Hewes. Their descent from the Princes of Wales is many times reiterated by geneologists.

Archelaus Hughes was born in Goochland County, in 1747. When quite young he went to Pittsylvania County to live. He was married to Mary Dalton, daughter of Samuel Dalton. After his marriage he lived in what is now Patrick County. His home was first in Pittsylvania County, in the part that was made Henry County in 1776. When Henry was divided into two counties in 1791, the western portion being made into a separate county, Patrick, Colonel Hughes' home was then in Patrick County, so "believe it or not" the Hughes' home occupied the same location, but was in three counties.

The home was called Hughesville, and was the first frame house built in what is now Patrick County. In calling their home Hughesville they were following an old Saxon custom—a single farmhouse in Scotland is still called a town or tun, meaning a fence or hedge, because they were surrounded by a rampart of earth set with a thick hedge.

Colonel Archelaus Hughes had large estates, but he seemed to like to add to his income through merchandise. He operated seven stores in different localities. Hughesville, a house of ten rooms, still stands. All of the children of Colonel Hughes and Mary Dalton Hughes were born there.

On the twenty-seventh day of September, 1775, Archelaus Hughes was appointed, by the Committee of Safety, captain of a company of militia, in Pittsylvania. Later he was made colonel of a Virginia regiment.

The children of Colonel Hughes and Mary Dalton Hughes are as follows: Leander, unmarried; Archelaus, Nancy Martin, daughter of Captain and Rev. William and Rachel Dalton Martin; William married first, a Miss Moore, second, Alice Carr, of North Carolina; Jeancy, Colonel John Fulkerson, of Lee County, Virginia; John, Lily Martin, daughter of Captain William Martin; Samuel, unmarried, served in the Virginia Senate; Reuben; Nancy, Brett Stovall; Madison Redd Hughes was thrice married, first, ... Moore, second, ... Matthews, third, Sally Dillard; Sally Hughes married Colonel John Dillard, son of Captain John Dillard of the Revolution.

Greenwood was built about 1810, it was near Belmont, the home of General Martin, which had been purchased from General Harrison. Also near the Leatherwood home of Patrick Henry.

THE HUNDLEY FAMILY OF HENRY COUNTY, VIRGINIA

H. B. Hundley, one of Martinsville's well known business men, was the son of Captain H. B. and Martha Hundley, of Henry County. Mr. Hundley was interested in fine horses and was owner of a livery stable and also a hardware establishment which he managed with great success. His interest extended to all activities that promoted the advancement of the town. He served as mayor two terms and was a member of the County School Board, as he greatly favored popular education.

Mr. Hundley married Ella, daughter of James B. and Lucy Holt Dyer. They were the parents of three children, one died in infancy and two daughters reaching maturity. Mamie developed an aptitude for business and for several years taught in the county schools and also held a position as business woman.

Mattie married I. M. Groves, Jr., of Martinsville, and they have a very attractive home in Martinsville (see Groves family).

The other members of Captain H. B. Hundley's family were: Mary who married a Burge; Roxy, C. C. Bassett; Pocahontas, J. D. Bassett; Frances, a Burchfield; Willis, Sallie Carter; Melissa and Jim.

THE JAMISON FAMILY OF HENRY COUNTY, VIRGINIA

John Hairston Jamison married Jane Spencer. They were the parents of seven children, four sons and three daughters. The sons were: James, George, Tom and John William (Dick). The daughters were: Sallie, who married Nick Finley (see sketch of George M. Finley); Fannie married G. W. Trent; Elizabeth married J. W. Tyree.

John Hairston Jamison and his wife, Jane Spencer Jamison, were prominent citizens of Henry County, and their descendants are well and favorably known in the social, business and professional life in Henry County and other sections in which they live.

George H. Jamison, a son of Thomas Jamison and grandson of John H. Jamison, after graduating from West Point, joined the American Army where he made an honorable name for himself, becoming, during the World War, a Brigadier General. He is another Henry County boy who is a credit to his country, and to the State of Virginia.

THE JONES FAMILY

There are three families by the same name, but are separate families. They are the families of Benjamin, Charles and Ambrose Jones.

David Jones (1679) came from Wales and entered land where the City of Baltimore now stands. His grandson, Joshua Jones, lived in Culpeper, Virginia, and married Isabel Norman. Their children were: Benjamin, John, James and Thomas.

John reared two sons, John and Masten, and a daughter, Sallie, who married a Houston, General Sam Houston was a descendant. James went to Tennessee and Thomas located in Georgia.

Benjamin Jones married (1752) Elizabeth de Remi (1776), and settled on Jones' Creek near Martinsville, Virginia. They reared the following children: Thomas, Sanford, Gabriel Remi, Bartlett, George Washington, Pamela, Benjamin Churchill and Elizabeth.

Children of Benjamin Jones, son of Joshua Jones: Thomas, married Elizabeth Lyell, Pittsylvania County, Virginia; their children were: Benjamin, Bartlett, Mary Decatur, Elizabeth and Martha. Sanford married a Miss Hodges and lived in Pittsylvania County; Gabriel Remi married Mary Bryant, and reared two children, viz.: Mary Elizabeth, who married Moses Carper, of Franklin County; a son, Beverly. Dr. Bartlett Jones married Eliza Dunlap and settled in South Carolina. Their children are: Benjamin Rush, Constantine, Mary, Theresa and Virginia. George Washington Jones married Salina Dunlap, of South Carolina, and settled at Leaksville, North Carolina, where he practiced medicine for many years. There were two sons, Erasmus Dowen and Adolphus Dorsett. Pamela married John Menzies and settled in Tennessee. There were two children, Mary and Remi. Dr. Benjamin Churchill Jones located in Lancaster, South Carolina. He married a daughter of General Davis, United States Minister to France. Elizabeth Jones married James Kyle, and settled in Georgia. There was one son, Colonel Robert Kyle.

Benjamin Jones' daughter, Nannie, married John Anthony, of Axton, Virginia. Decatur, Harriet Keane, and lived at Bachelors Hall, Virginia. They reared the following children, viz.: Araminter, who married John Holcomb, of Danville, Virginia; Maria Louisa married H. B. Haase; William Henry, Elizabeth Keane; Bettie, M. C. Cunningham, of Greensboro, North Carolina; Nannie Witcher, Victor McAdoo; second, R. R. King; Emma Jones, unmarried; John Kean Jones married Mary Wilkinson, of Maryland; Thomas D. married Mattie Southgate, of Durham, North Carolina; Kate Jones married Joseph Morehead, of Greensboro, North Carolina; Charles, unmarried; Dorsey married Mary Glenn, Halifax, Virginia.

Bartlett Jones, of Pittsylvania, married Miss Kern. Their children are: Witcher Jones, of California; Kean Jones; Elisha Jones, of Danville, married Annie Robinson; Annie M. Jones married Dr. John James, of Danville, Virginia, and they were the parents of Lieutenant Jules James, U. S. N.

Mary married James O. Martin, of Pittsylvania County; Martha, unmarried.

Children of Dr. Bartlett Jones: Benjamin Rush practiced medicine in Alabama; Mary married Judge James Witherspoon, of South Carolina; Theresa married Dr. J. Martin Simms, famous New York surgeon and physician to Empress Eugenia, of Paris; Virginia married Mr. William Hooper, son of William Hooper. Her daughter married Governor Joseph Johnston, of Alabama.

Children of Gabriel Remi Jones: Jane Elizabeth married Moses Carper. Robert Beverly went west at the close of the Civil War. The other children were: James Jones and Mary Wilson, Mary J. and Lily Turnbull. Mary J. Wilson and Emma are the only living children of Moses Carper.

Dr. Beverly Jones, son of Gabriel Remi Jones, 1811, studied medicine, graduated at Jefferson Medical College, Philadelphia, and began his practice in Germantown, North Carolina. In 1848, he married Julia Conrad, a great granddaughter of Jacob Leosch, one of the founders of the Moravian colony of Wachovia and long connected with the government. Dr. Jones moved to Oak Grove, 1848, where he practiced medicine for fifty years. The children of this union are: Abram Gabriel, James Benjamin, Alexander Conrad, Robert Henry, Erasmus Beverly, Ella Mary, Virginia E., Julia, Kate and Lucien.

Dr. Abram Jones (1843) married Nannie Dalton. He is a practicing physician at Walnut Cove, North Carolina.

James B. Jones was a minister of the Christian Church. He married Mary Frances Rogers first, then Carrie Anderson. He was president of William Woods College, Fulton, Missouri, for fifteen years. Both he and Dr. Abram Jones saw service in the Civil War. Two daughters survive him, Eleanor Conrad and Frances Adair.

Alexander C. Jones was a military cadet, Horner Institute, died 1865.

Robert Henry Jones practiced dentistry in Martinsville, Virginia, a number of years. He moved to Winston-Salem, 1890. His first wife was Sallie Wayt, whose mother was a member of the prominent Redd family of Virginia. His second wife was Amelia Holland.

Erasmus Beverly Jones married first, Ida Matthewson; second, Sue

Barbour, a member of a prominent Kentucky family. Judge Jones was a prominent lawyer and politician. He was elected to the House and Senate of North Carolina several times and for seven years he was Judge of the Superior Court, taking rank with the eminent jurists of the state. He died in 1922, and is survived by his wife, Mrs. Sue Barbour Jones, and a daughter, Louise.

Virginia E. Jones married H. L. Sullivan, and died in 1893, leaving one son, Beverly N. Sullivan. Ella, Kate, Julia and Lucien live at the old home, Oak Grove.

Descendants of Dr. Benjamin Jones living in Henry County: James O. Martin, Jr., a great grandson of the founder of the family was born in 1851, and came back to this county when a boy. He married Ella Turner and they reared the following children: Lucy, who married Dr. Fagg, of Axton; Mary Martin married A. J. Lester, of Martinsville (see Lester family); Susan Martin married Dr. J. P. McCabe, for many years the popular pastor of the First Baptist Church, of Martinsville, Virginia. Rorer James Martin married Margaret Slawron.

CHARLES JONES FAMILY

The family is of Welch descent but by marriage claim direct descent from Lord Baltimore of England. This family can be traced to the first settlers of Virginia.

Charles Jones was born in Grayson County in 1768, and came to Henry after the Revolutionary War, settling just south of Ridgeway. He acquired a large boundary of land and in 1790 married Polly King, sister of George King. Their children were: Betsy, Polly, Jane, another daughter who married an Allen and went to Missouri to live, and George King.

George King Jones (b 1803–1881) married Ann, daughter of Honorable John King, of Henry County, and settled at Ridgeway, where he reared his family. He was a farmer on a large scale, and for a long time magistrate.

Nancy Jones married Robert Anderson. Their children were: King, Charles, Seward, Betsy Anne. Jane Jones married John Ziggler. Their children were: Charles, Eliza, Mary. Betsy Jones married Sill Webb. Polly Jones married William Dalton, of Rockingham, North Carolina, and their children are as follows: William Robert, who died in early life; John, who died in the Confederate Army; Rufus, killed in the same conflict; Lou, who married Robert B. Price; Susan married Larkin DeShazo; Jane married Sheriff Walter Smith; Mary married Valentine Hylton; Sarah,

Edd Foster; Puss, Francis Stone; Elizabeth, Edward Matthews, and Charlotte married Dave Matthews. The other member of the family was Walter.

Children of Charles and Polly Jones: Benjamin Seward married first, Mary DeShazo; second, Nannie Price. The children of the first union were: Sallie, Ann, George King, Nathaniel L., William, Lelia, Mary Bennie, Henrietta and Robert L., who died in 1917.

John C. Jones, 1830, married Ann Coan, of South Carolina, and settled in Ridgeway where he was a farmer and supervisor for a long term of years. He was the first postmaster of Ridgeway when the office was established in 1852, and was also in the mercantile business with Smith and Hairston in the brick store built by this firm. He died in 1819. Their children are: Anna, Mollie, John William, Estelle and Charlie Coan.

Mary Ann Jones married John O. Coan, of South Carolina, who had a mercantile business in Ridgeway, besides being a farmer. He was a popular teacher and was chosen the first mayor of Ridgeway, being reëlected several times. He died in 1809. The children of this family are: Bettie, Loula, George William, Posey, Bird and John O., Jr.

George Osborne Jones (1846–1922) married Mary Churchill. Their children are: Annie, George Byron, John Brengle, Thomas King, James Benjamin, Mary Churchill, Daisy Gertrude and Paul, who died in infancy.

Third. Children of Benjamin S. Jones: Sallie married William H. Norman; Ann, Robert Hall, of Reidsville, North Carolina; George King Jones, unmarried. He was a very successful business man and was engaged in selling manufactured tobacco. Nathaniel Jones married Anna Perry; Lelia, Thomas J. Garrett, of Rockingham, North Carolina; Mary Bennie, Hylton Clanton, of Spencer, Virginia; William B. Jones married Bettie Rachael Garrett; he was a popular merchant of Ridgeway. The children of this family are: Dr. W. Clyde Jones, of Salem, Virginia; Mayor Ben S. Jones, of Leaksville, North Carolina; Thomas G. Jones; Mrs. T. D. DeShazo; Mrs. Jesse Hall, of Mebane, North Carolina; Mrs. Alphus Jones, of the Valley of Virginia.

Henrietta Jones married George W. DeShazo, of Rockingham, North Carolina; Robert L. Jones married Bettie Meadows.

Of the children of John C. Jones, Anna married William D. Mitchell, of Franklin County; Mollie, Dr. Dorsey B. Downey, of Frederick, Maryland. There were two children: Mary and Dorsey.

John William Jones married Loula Grogan, of Rockingham, North

Carolina; Estelle Jones, unmarried; Charlie Coan Jones married Bessie Strother, of Culpeper, Virginia. He was a fine business man of Ridgeway, and met a tragic death while on the way to the funeral of his brother-in-law, Dr. Downey. He was struck by an automobile. He was survived by his wife and one child, John C.

The children of John O. Jones and Mary Churchill Jones are: Annie, who married Dr. J. B. DeShazo, a prominent physician of Ridgeway; George Byron, unmarried; Thomas King Jones, a merchant of Ridgeway, married Ethel Grogan, of North Carolina; James Benjamin, Lina Griggs; Mary Churchill, William D. Mitchell, merchant of Ridgeway; Daisy King, Dr. Andrew F. Tuttle, of Spray, North Carolina; Gertrude, C. S. Oakley.

AMBROSE JEFFERSON JONES

This family is of Welch descent, although it comes through England, with Lord Baltimore in their line.

Ambrose Jones settled on Beaver Creek about 1790. His wife was Mary Le Seau, a descendant of French nobility and he reared a large family. The children were: Joseph Moseby, William, Green, Jackson, Mary, Dolly, Pitsy and Winnie.

Mary Jones married Thomas West; Dolly, Leftridge Baker; Pitsy, Seth Barber; Martha, John Burgess; Winnie, Carter Barber.

William Jones married Elizabeth Hardy. Their children: Mary married Silas N. Self; Abram died during the War Between the States; William married Elizabeth Jones, and John Green, Nannie Wells.

Jackson Jones married Nellie Barber. Their children are: James, Charles and Ruth, who married George Dyer.

Joseph Moseby Jones married Margaret C. Davis, daughter of Peter Davis, a descendant of Lord Baltimore. They made their home on Reed Creek, where they reared a large family. Their children were: Charles W., Benjamin Tazewell, Alonzo Thomas, Lucy Ann, Sallie, Margaret Elizabeth, Joseph and Mary Lou.

Charles W. and Alonzo T. were never married. Mary Lou married John P. Lavinder; Margaret Elizabeth, William J. Jones; Lucy Ann, Pinckney Davis; Benjamin Tazewell, Sallie Lewis Pedigo, daughter of John H. Pedigo.

Joseph P. Jones was killed in the Civil War at Drury's Bluff.

Charles W. Jones was a soldier in the Civil War, having joined the Twenty-Fourth Virginia Cavalry. He was captured with his cousin, William

J. Jones, and taken to Point Lookout, Maryland. His terrible experiences there, like those of thousands of others, are told by him in his "In Prison at Point Lookout." He was public-spirited and popular, serving as Postmaster of Martinsville several terms, and was nominated for Congress once but declined to enter the political field, preferring to give his time to his business activities. He died in 1919.

Benjamin Tazewell Jones spent most of his life in Martinsville. He held the office of Commissioner of Revenue for some time and was also Circuit Clerk. He was much interested in all that pertained to politics. The children of Benjamin T. Jones and Sallie Lewis Jones are as follows: William Clark, who died in infancy; Elizabeth Gray married Earl M. Shultz, of Augusta County, Virginia; C. C. Jones married H. M. Watts, of Missouri. Ruth Tazewell and Mary Baldwin, after teaching school for a short while, decided upon business careers. Ruth accepted a position with an abstract and insurance firm and now has charge of an office as manager for an insurance company, in Jefferson City, Missouri. Mary B. has held a position as secretary to the State Auditor for several years, in Jefferson City, Missouri.

DR. BENJAMIN JONES

Dr. Benjamin Jones, great grandson of David Jones, the first actual settler of Baltimore, was a very remarkable man and deserves special mention in the history of Henry County. He was born April 25, 1752, in Culpeper County, Virginia. When he was nine years of age his father died, and soon much responsibility of the family fell upon him, which probably developed the manly qualities which distinguished him in after years.

In July, 1776, he enlisted as a Culpeper Minute man. His first service was on the Potomac with troops of the third regiment under Colonel Taylor, "To watch movement of British fleet under Lord Dunmore" (Howe's History of Virginia, Page 443). The War Department record reads, "Soldier in continental establishment Benjamin Jones (Infantry) received pay December 21, 1776." He assisted Dr. White, a surgeon, during the War and by close observation and practical experience laid the foundation for the practice of medicine and became a fine physician and surgeon.

He married Elizabeth de Remi, September, 1776, in Prince William County. They were Episcopalians and were married by Devereau Jarrett. She was a great granddaughter of a Huguenot refugee, Jean de Remi, who came to Charleston, 1690, his son, Pierre, later moving to Virginia.

After living two years in Rockingham County, North Carolina, rebuilding the forge and operating "Troublesome Iron Works" for a company, he moved to Henry County, 1792, where his wife's brothers, Daniel and Samuel de Remi, had located. As there were few roads and no bridges, the trip was made on pack horses. Mrs. Jones carried her baby in her arms and guided her horse.

He purchased a large tract of land from Mr. Whitesides and lodged his family in a cabin north of Martinsville on Jones' Creek. He later built one of the first weatherboarded, papered and painted houses in the county. In a park he kept over a hundred deer to amuse his children and grandchildren. A little bell he used on a pet deer is owned by one of his descendants.

He was active in politics and several times represented Henry County in the State Legislature. He was a friend of the poor and needy and the suffering in every walk of life. A high-toned Virginia gentleman, a true patriot proved on the field of battle and an honor to Henry County. He died in 1843, aged ninety-one. His remains, with those of his wife, rest in Oaklawn cemetery in Martinsville, Virginia.

Elizabeth de Remi Jones was a woman of unusual mind and wonderful constitution. In 1846, aged ninety years, she told her grandson, Beverly Jones, of General Washington taking breakfast with them at "Troublesome Iron Works." She said, "In company with General Washington was one Jackson detestable to all for his pride." The family tradition was corroborated in 1921, by publication of Washington's diary (Page 9), "In this tour I was accompanied by Major Jackson (Page 44)." "We breakfasted at 'Troublesome Iron Works'." Soon after this Mrs. Jones named her infant George Washington. She reared six sons and two daughters, lived to see numerous descendants and enjoyed perfect health through her entire life. She passed away in 1856, having lived two months over a century. On her last day on earth "she but wrapped the drapery of her couch about her and lay down to pleasant dreams."

THE KEARFOTT FAMILY OF MARTINSVILLE, VIRGINIA

The town of Martinsville has never known a more enterprising citizen than Dr. Clarence P. Kearfott, or one who has done more for the progress of the town.

He was born in St. Joseph, Missouri, and grew up in Martinsburg, West Virginia, to which place his parents moved. He received a liberal education and was graduated in pharmacy from the National College of Pharmacy.

He began business in Martinsville under the firm name of Kearfott, Haile & Company, later buying the interests of the other members of the firm. His son, J. Conrad Kearfott, became a partner and the firm since has been C. P. Kearfott & Son.

The contributions of Dr. Kearfott to the progress of Martinsville cannot be over-estimated. He was the first to begin the use of the telephone, a room in his store being used as an office. He was a leading member of the Baptist Church, that organization in Martinsville began with meetings in his home. For a long term of years he was president of the Peoples National Bank and under his management the institution grew in importance and held high rank. His high place in his profession was attested by his appointment as a member of the Pharmacy Board of Virginia. He held this position longer than any other druggist in the state.

Dr. Kearfott's wife was Rebecca Grats, of West Virginia, a woman of unusual intellectual attainments and culture. Their children are: Clarence B., J. Conrad, Robert Ryland, Mary Lucretia, Rebecca and Hugh Smith.

J. Conrad married Margaret Rives; Mary Lucretia, Dr. Harry B. Stone; Rebecca, Jefferson D. Sparrow; Hugh, Margaret Barr, of Washington, D. C.; Clarence married Mae Hunter; Robert married Mrs. Barron.

MR. CHARLES BLACKWELL KEESEE

Mr. Charles B. Keesee has for many years occupied a prominent position in the business affairs of Martinsville. He was for some time promoter and large stockholder in the noted granite quarries of Mt. Airy, North Carolina.

After retiring from that business he made his home in Martinsville, where he held the position as president of a local bank.

Mr. and Mrs. Keesee have traveled extensively, both in this country and abroad. They are loyal and devoted members of the Baptist Church.

MRS. CHARLES BLACKWELL KEESEE

Mrs. Charles Blackwell Keesee occupies a position of prominence not only in the community in which she lives, but in the State of Virginia as well.

Before her marriage she was Olivia Helm Simmons, of Floyd County, daughter of Roley Madison Simmons. Upon her maternal side she was descended from Nancy Helm, daughter of Colonel John Webb Helm, of Burks Fork, Floyd County, Virginia.

Since her residence in Martinsville, Virginia, Mrs. Keesee has contributed largely to society in many ways. As a member of the Daughters of the American Revolution she has had conferred upon her high honors. She was vice regent, then regent, of the Patrick Henry Chapter for several years and is now State Regent of Virginia.

Mrs. Keesee is also a member of the Pocahontas Society of American Colonists, deriving her eligibility from Thomas Carter (1634–1705). She takes an active interest in the work of the United Daughters of the Confederacy and of the Baptist Church, of which she is a devoted member, her contributions being real personal service as well as of things material, and a charming personality and gracious manner have given Mrs. Keesee the popularity and appreciation she so well deserves.

THE KING FAMILY OF HENRY COUNTY

The King family, of Henry County, is very prominent and widely known as there are representatives of that family not only throughout that county and others in Virginia, but in other states as well.

One of the Henry County pioneers was George King (1734), who came from Brunswick County, Virginia, and settled in the Leatherwood community. He was a soldier in the Revolutionary War. His wife's name was Mary Niblet and they reared a large family.

The eldest son, George W., married Susan, daughter of General Joseph Martin. He went out with his father-in-law to fight the Indians and died while on one of these raids. He was a landowner on a large scale.

There were eight children of this family: Susan, Lewis, Graves, Elizabeth, Thomas, Sallie, William and George W.

Thomas, the next son, married Charity Stockton. He was a prominent farmer and was killed by a neighbor in a quarrel. Their children were: Camillus, Columbus, Cephas, Martha and Elizabeth.

John King, the youngest son, also lived on Leatherwood where he accumulated much property. His wife was Mary Love, of Pittsylvania County,

MRS. CHARLES BLACKWELL KEESEE

and their children's names are as follows: Thomas, George, William, John, Sallie, Frances, Columbus, Jane and Jacob Love.

Jane King married William DeShazo (see DeShazo family). Frances married James McCullock; Thenia and Susan married men of the same name, Wills; Mary married Charles Jones; Tabby married John de Graffenried.

II. Of the children of George W. King and Susan Martin King, Susan married Wesley Griggs; Lewis Graves, Elizabeth King; his home was on Leatherwood. He served as a soldier in the Confederate Army, Forty-Second Virginia Regiment, was wounded and died at Fortress Monroe, Virginia. His children were: George W., Emmeline, John M. and Lewis Graves, Jr.

Neither Elizabeth, William, Nancy or George King married; Sallie King married Ira Griggs; Thomas married Mary Jane Cahill.

III. Thomas King's children were: Camillus (1811-80), who married Sallie Jane Hylton. There were three children, Nannie, Jeremiah and Thomas.

Columbus King, second son, married Marie Cahill, his second wife was Sallie Stockton, their children were: Susan, who married George Hylton; Sallie, Jesse Clanton; Cephas King settled in Missouri; Martha King married (1812), William Barrow; Elizabeth married a Cabiness.

Children of John and Mary Love King: Thomas (1790) married Mary Cahill and moved to Missouri; George King married Mary Smith and settled in Kentucky; William King married a Miss Stockton and moved to Missouri, he was a Baptist minister; Columbus King lived in Missouri; Jacob King married Jane Thornton; Jane King married Daniel Pace; Frances King married John Finney; Sallie, William Cooper; Katherine Oglesby married John Price; T. B. King, of Marion, Virginia, married Margaret Painter; Sallie R. King married W. H. Wheelwright, of Richmond, Virginia; Helen King married Harvey H. Price, of Martinsville, Virginia.

John C. King married Abba Farmer, of Missouri, where they make their home.

Columbus King and his second wife were the parents of the following children: Susan E., who married George W. Hylton; Sallie, Jesse Clanton; his first wife's only son was John C. King.

Mary Elizabeth King, only daughter of Jacob King, married Major William Parker Terry, a great grandson of Sir William Parker Terry, Admiral of the British Navy. Ten children were born to them, namely: William, Benjamin, Lou, Jacob, Annie Scales, Mary, Edward, Starling, James W. Corinne and Thornton.

III. Children of Lewis Graves King: George W., a Confederate soldier; John W. died in early life; Emmeline married Jerre Griggs, and lived at Ridgeway, Virginia. Both died there and were survived by one son, George K. Lewis Graves King, Jr., married Lucy K. Gibboney, of Wytheville, Virginia. There were two daughters, Lucy Elizabeth and Estelle.

Children of Camillus King, Jr.: Thomas J. King married Alice Martin, he was a prominent farmer, was public-spirited and served as Commissioner of the Revenue for Henry County; Nannie H. King, only daughter, married Jesse R. Clanton; Jeremiah C. King married Eliza Rangeley; Dr. John C. King, of Radford, married Fannie Price; Clare L. King, of the First National Bank, Pearisburg, married Katherine Oglesby; Nannie married John W. Price, a merchant of Price, North Carolina; T. B. King, vice president and cashier of the Marion National Bank, married Margaret Painter; Sallie R. King married J. D. Miller, a merchant of Newport News. He died in 1921.

SECOND LINE

Another Henry County pioneer, brother of George King who died in 1728, John King, was a soldier in the Revolutionary War. Mary, his only daughter, married Henry Koger and lived in the western part of Henry County.

REV. JOHN KING FAMILY

Rev. John King and his wife, Mary Seward King, of Brunswick County, Virginia, came to Henry County about 1780. He was known as a man of strong convictions and preached "as one having authority." In early life he had the misfortune to lose one of his legs. The children of this family were: Benjamin, John and Joseph Seward.

Benjamin, the eldest son, was born about 1785. He was a member of the Virginia Legislature, 1817–18. John (Jack) King, 1778, married Polly Wells. They lived on Leatherwood where they reared a large family. He also represented Henry County in the House of Delegates, 1842–43. Their children were: Benjamin S., John O., Joe, Dolly, Ann and Elizabeth.

Joseph Seward King, son of Rev. John King (1794), also settled on Leatherwood. He married first, Sallie Clanton, and they were parents of the following children: Martha, Betsy, Susan and John Seward. The children of his second wife, who was Mary Lester, were: Jesse, Benjamin S., William, Joseph Bouldin, John Tyler and Dr. Franklin. Seven sons served in the Civil War; three, Jesse O., William and Benjamin Seward, were killed.

Joseph Seward King was the third of the King brothers to serve as a member of the House of Delegates.

Annie King married George King Jones; Dolly, James Trent; children: William, John Tyler, King, Benjamin, George, Mary, Martha and Roxy.

Elizabeth married Lewis Graves King, four children were born to them, George W., Emmaline, John M. and Lewis Graves, Jr.

Benjamin Seward King was born in this county in 1812. He married Mary Jones of the Ambrose Jones line. Their children were as follows: George Shelton, William, John, Benjamin Seward, Jr., Ruth, Sallie and Bettie.

John O. King (1834) married a Miss Alexander, of Charlotte, North Carolina. The following children were born to them, of the first marriage, Joseph. His second wife was a Booker.

Joseph B. King was born in 1837. He was a Confederate soldier in the Tenth Virginia Cavalry. He was never married and died at the Soldiers' Home in Richmond.

Martha King, daughter of John Seward King, born in 1820, married Daniel Taylor; Betsy married Joseph Bason; Susan married John Francis Gregory; John Seward married Sallie Ivey. Three children were born to them: Joseph W. King, who married Roxy Stultz; Elizabeth married George Penny, of Georgia, and Mary married D. M. Moore.

William King, one of the second wife's children, married Maggie Moore, of South Carolina. There was one son, Herman, who was killed in the Civil War.

Captain John O. King was a soldier in the Confederate Army and was never married. Joseph Bouldin King was a Confederate soldier and served four years. He was a prominent planter and later moved to Leaksville, North Carolina.

John Tyler King, a younger brother, married Eliza Whitlock. Their children were: William King, who married Mattie Grogan; Frank, Melissa Aaron; Herman, Sallie Grogan; Robert L., Ida King; Mollie, William Grogan; Mattie, Jack Stultz; Joseph, Alice Grogan.

Dr. Franklin King married Eliza Dyer. He was a lieutenant in the Confederate Army and belonged to the Forty-Second Virginia Regiment. The children of this marriage were: Irene, who married Jesse Ben Taylor; Lottie, Rev. J. B. Beeker; Daisy married a Mr. Hayes, of Leaksville, North Carolina; Myrtle, J. Platt Turner, of Leaksville-Spray; Mary Lilly, Lester J. Martin, of North Carolina; Frank married Anna Adele Neal, of Reidsville, North Carolina.

Children of Benjamin, Sr.: William E. married Lelia Seymore; Ernest, Laura Robertson; Annie Adele married first, M. Thrasher; second, Jesse Carter, of Stoneville, North Carolina.

George Shelton King married Eliza Jane Matthews. Their children were: Beulah, Sarah, Anna, James, George, Caleb, Charles and Frank.

Benjamin King lived in Patrick County. He married Laura Smith. The names of their children follow: Minnie; George, who married Dorothy Bondurant, of South Boston; Edna, W. B. Hundley, of Draper, North Carolina; Caleb King, of Florida, married Harriet Bondurant. He was manager for years of the Associated Press. Annie Ruth married F. J. Dovell, of Virginia, later of Lake City, South Carolina, where he practiced law.

THE KOGER FAMILY OF HENRY COUNTY, VIRGINIA

The history of the Koger family is one of unusual interest. They left their native land of the Palitinate upon the Rhine and came to seek homes in which to rear their families in the New World. They took the oath of allegiance to Great Britain (George II). There were four brothers, Jacob, Nicholas, Joseph and Peter.

Jacob Koger, one of the four brothers, settled first in Pennsylvania, next he located in Augusta County, Virginia, where he accumulated much property. In 1762 he had settled in Henry County about twenty miles west of Martinsville. The land was hilly and well adapted to the growing of tobacco. The danger from Indian raids was great at that time and the family took refuge at times in the fort which was built three miles from his home.

In 1782 he gave his son, Henry, the tract of land lying on both sides of Stone Creek. He died in 1783.

Henry Koger was born in 1742, and was twice married. His second wife was Mary King and their children were: John, Catherine, Betsy, Polly, Sallie, Joseph, Henry, Abraham, Jacob and Billy. The following went to the west to make their homes: Jacob, Billy, Abraham, Betsy and Sallie.

John Koger, son of Henry and Mary King Koger, married Gillie C. Napier about 1819. Their children were: Susan, Woodson, Bettie, Moses, Marion, John, Jr., Kittie, Emily, Gillie, Lute, Hill, Victoria and George.

Joseph Koger, brother of John Koger, married a Miss Slaughter. Their children were: John S. William married a Miss Ingram; Mary married an

Ingram; Joe Henry married Mary Turner; Daniel King and James were killed in the Civil War. Kitty married James Via, and died in 1919.

Henry Koger, Jr., was born in 1792. He married Lucinda Thomas, died in 1868. Their children were: Thomas, who married a Webb; Middleton married a Mills, he served in the Civil War and died in 1912; Mary married William Corn; Perry, Emily Burgess; Lee and Edd were both killed in the Civil War; Susan married a Shelton; Lucinda and Caroline were unmarried; Emily married John Zeigler; Pink, Emma Ford; Mary Koger, daughter of Henry Koger, married A. H. Bassett. Children of this union were: Martha A. Woodson, John Harden, Eliza and Mary Catherine.

Katie Koger married James Baker. Their children were: Ruth, who married J. P. H. Taylor; Lucinda, Ludowick Craghead; Polly, a Mr. Via; John married in Georgia; James was twice married, first, to a Miss Ingram; second, Fannie Kelly, who had one daughter, Minnie.

Leftridge Baker had one son born of his first marriage. His second wife was Dolly Burgess. Their children were: Lucy, Henry Clay and Daniel Webster.

Moses Marion Koger, son of John and Gillie Koger, married Mary Catherine, daughter of William W. Hill. Their children were: Kora, Minor Botts, Mary C., Marion, Gillie, Judith, Emma and Woodson Hill.

Emma married John Lewis, of Ohio; Minor Botts married Virginia Morris and they reared a large family, namely: William Morris, Mary Annie, John M., Kit Carson, Kate, Benny, Bland Schoolfield, Martha and Minor Botts, Jr. John M. served through the World War, and was in the occupation forces left in Germany for a while. Mary C. Koger, daughter of Moses Marion Koger, married James W. Matthews. Their children were: Mary, Sadie, Robert, Warren, Botts, Celia and Catherine.

THE LAVINDER FAMILY OF HENRY COUNTY, VIRGINIA

The Lavinder family is of French origin the name originally being de la Vinder. They were Huguenots and escaped from France on account of persecution.

The Lavinders, of Virginia, are descendants of two brothers, Richard and William, who came to America after the close of the Revolutionary War.

John Lavinder settled in Franklin County, and owned a large planta-
tion and numerous slaves. His wife was Mary Deppity and their children,
Thornton, William, James, Joseph Chilton, John, Mary, Frances, Nancy,
Emily and Jesse.

Jesse married Jane Hickey Davis and they moved from Reed Creek
to Martinsville (1874). The members of this family were: Mary, Letitia,
John Peter, Sam Henry, Emma Jane, Margaret Alzira and Jesse Ben.

Mary Letitia married . . . . . . Hurd and moved to Missouri; Emma
Jane, Frank M. Wells; Jane Hickey, Anthony Hundley; Sam Henry, M.
Woodson Hill; Margaret Alzira, Joseph C. Ford; Jesse Ben, Alice, daughter
of Dr. H. D. Peters. Mr. Lavinder died . . . . being survived by his
wife and three children, Henry George, Mary Peters and Grayson. He was
a successful merchant of Martinsville and a loyal member of the Methodist
Church. Of this family Henry, after graduating in law from the University
of Virginia, went to Bristol, Tennessee, and joined his uncle, H. G. Peters,
in a partnership for the practice of law. He married Katherine Haynes, of
Bristol.

Mary Peters married Richard B. Semple, who was a tobacco manufacturer of Martinsville. Grayson married D. H. Pannill. (See Pannill family.)

John Peter Lavinder married first, Mary Louisa Jones; second, Annie
Fleming. He was a popular business man of Martinsville, and was one of
the first to erect a commodious business building in the town.

Both John Peter, and Jesse Ben Lavinder deserve a place of honor in
the history of Henry County. They were soldiers who served their country
throughout the War Between the States as members of the Forty-Second
Regiment in Joseph Hereford's "Fencibles." They were with Jackson at
Chancellorsville, when Jackson was brought into camp mortally wounded.

THE LYBROOK FAMILY OF PATRICK COUNTY, VIRGINIA

Judge Andrew Murray Lybrook was a native of Giles County, Virginia.
When a young man he located at Stuart, Patrick County, Virginia, and
practiced law in the courts of Patrick and other counties. On May 24, 1861,
as captain, he lead Company I, Twenty-Fourth Virginia Regiment, Confederate States Army from Stuart. He also served his county as judge
of the county court, 1880–1881.

JUDGE ANDREW MURRAY LYBROOK
OF
Patrick County, Virginia

Judge Lybrook married Mary Reynolds, eldest daughter of Harden W. Reynolds, a woman whose intelligence, fine traits of character, lovely personality and kindness of heart made her one of the best beloved women of her community.

The Lybrook home, situated on a plateau or sort of table land, was noted for some of its novel features, as well as beauty. A lovely fountain of pure spring water brought down from the mountain side, flowers and shrubbery ornamented the large lawn which sloped down towards the river valley altogether making a place of rare beauty.

Mrs. Lybrook passed away in 1885, being survived by her husband and eight children. Judge Lybrook married a second time but his wife, who was Miss Bettie Forkner, lived only a few years.

After the death of Judge Lybrook the children made their home in Winston-Salem with members of their mother's family.

Harden Philip, eldest son of Judge and Mrs. Mary Reynolds Lybrook, after completing his education received the appointment as postmaster in Winston-Salem and filled that position for several years. He passed away while still a very young man. Richard J., another son of Judge and Mrs. Lybrook, a splendid young man, died just as he reached life's threshold with every promise of happiness and success in the future.

Samuel Murray Lybrook lived in Patrick County for a number of years after the other members of the family moved to other places. He and William Lybrook own and live upon large ranches in New Mexico. William married Miss Lightle, of Oklahoma, who died a few years since. Her husband and three sons survive her.

Johnson, the youngest son of Judge and Mrs. Lybrook, has a beautiful estate in Davie County. He farms on an extensive scale. His wife was Muriel Piper, a very bright and attractive young woman. The family includes three sons: David, William and Murray, and two daughters, Mary Martha now Mrs. Charles Neal and Elizabeth. David married Bettie Blood, a charming young girl, who died a few months after their marriage.

Nancy Margaret Lybrook, eldest daughter of Captain and Mrs. A. M. Lybrook, married R. E. Lasater, who is now one of the officials of the R. J. Reynolds Tobacco Company. Mrs. Lasater presides over her magnificent home with charming grace. The estate "Forest Hills" is one of the outstanding places in this part of the country. Beautifully situated, it commands a fine view of the Yadkin River. The grounds are extensive, with lovely gardens and miles of beautiful driveways. Mr. and Mrs. Lasater are the parents of four daughters, the eldest, Nancy Margaret, passed away in infancy. Mary Lybrook married J. T. Barnes and Virginia married George Lee Irving. Both young men are engaged in business and have established homes in the City of Winston-Salem. The youngest daughter, Mildred (Bob Edd), is just growing into womanhood.

Lucy married Porter H. Stedman, a prominent business man connected with the R. J. Reynolds Tobacco Company. Mrs. Stedman, like her mother, Mary Reynolds Lybrook, is much beloved for many lovely qualities. Mr. and Mrs. Stedman spend much time in Florida.

Mary Lybrook received a liberal education in the schools of this country and abroad. She has a decided taste for literature and has traveled extensively. Her winters are spent in her beautiful Florida home.

THE BIG FOUR

In the winter of 1881-2 an interesting and epoch-making Legislature was in session in Richmond. This body was elected at the end of the most strenuous and violent campaign that had occurred in Virginia since the Civil War. The Readjusters, Coalitionists or Mahonites, as they were variously called, had carried the state with a majority of fourteen in the House of Delegates and of six in the Senate.

General Mahone came to Richmond from his seat in the United States Senate to take charge of the situation and engineer certain ambitious schemes of his through the Legislature. At this juncture he made his first great political mistake. He and his associates offered to reëlect "Parson" Massey to the office of Auditor of Public Accounts if he would sign a pledge to abide by the decrees of the Readjuster Caucus. This Massey refused to do. Four Readjuster Senators had been elected who had refused to sign a pledge to be governed by the caucus. They resented the treatment of "Parson" Massey, who had been supplanted by Brown Allen. Furthermore, they objected to Mahone's schemes to get more and more appointing power in his own hands so as to become an absolute dictator in Virginia public life.

These four men worked together, possibly were organized. They were not only free and independent but they also had the balance of power in their own hands—a dangerous weapon unless wisely and conscientiously used. These four became known as The Big Four. They were: A. M. Lybrook, of Patrick County, Samuel H. Newberry, of Bland County, Peyton G. Hall, of Grayson County, and B. F. Williams, of Nottoway.

Judge Lybrook was recognized far and wide as the brains of The Big Four, and the others instinctively looked to him as their leader. Mahone had made the reputation of being the ablest politician the state had produced since the Civil War, indeed his friends and followers had begun to allude to him as the "Napoleon of Virginia politics." If this grandiloquent comparison might be carried a step further I might suggest that he met his Talleyrand in the person of A. M. Lybrook. The subtlety of his methods, the masterly handling of The Big Four, his clear insight into the machinations of his antagonists together with the splendid moral courage and the incorruptible honesty of these four notable men placed an obstacle in the path of General Mahone which he could never overcome. All the cajolery, the threats, the bullying, the political inducements offered were as futile as a bombardment of the Himalayas with popguns.

Any reasonable and impartial man who will make a study of this crisis in Virginia history and will make special note of the measures Mahone had formulated and passed through the Readjuster Caucus which were defeated by The Big Four will agree that this was the beginning of the end of Mahone's leadership and influence in Virginia politics.

JUDGE A. M. LYBROOK'S SERVICES TO HIS STATE

This vital bit of Virginia history so closely associated with Patrick County, as Captain Lybrook was one of the most important leaders, would be incomplete without recalling something of William Mahone who was a remarkable character and brought about the political upheaval in which The Big Four figured.

William Mahone, soldier and legislator, was born in 1826 in Southampton County, Virginia, graduated from the Virginia Military Institute in 1847 and became a civil engineer.

Upon the outbreak of the Civil War he joined the Confederate Army and assisted in the capture of the Norfolk Navy Yard. He participated in most of the battles of the Peninsula and Rappahannock campaigns, was distinguished for bravery at Petersburg, where he earned the title of Hero of the Crater, became Major General and commanded a division.

After the War he became president of the Virginia and Tennessee Railroad, took an active interest in politics and was an unsuccessful candidate for the Democratic nomination for the Governorship of Virginia in 1878. He became the recognized leader of the Readjusters, a Democratic faction which favored a partial or conditional repudiation of the state debt, and in

1880 was elected largely by this faction to the United States Senate. He took the unexpected course of allying himself with the Republicans, and thus brought about a tie in place of the slight Democratic majority which had been anticipated. He further alienated his constituents by his use of federal patronage, in Virginia, which had been assigned to him by President Arthur and, at the expiration of his term in 1887, he failed to secure a reëlection. He died in 1895.

The important part played by The Big Four in the political history of Virginia has not been fully appreciated. Such history indeed has been written from opposite and extreme points of view. When a reader has completed his perusal of this period of our history he comes away from it in the full belief in the favorite aphorism of Sydney Smith, that "in all the world there is nothing more unreliable than *facts* except possibly *figures*." A careful and impartial reader, however, may glean a few actual facts upon which all intelligent and observant contemporaries of Judge Lybrook would agree.

THE CAUCUS

A bill was introduced by the caucus providing for the removal of a great many of the petty officers of the state, such as notaries public, public school trustees and commissioners in chancery, in order to create vacancies for Mahone's followers. The appointment of many of these was to be made, in Richmond, in order to bring them under Mahone's central control.

There was an attempt to gerrymander the congressional district in such a manner as to increase the number of representatives in the black counties, which supported Mahone and the Republican Party. Mahone's paper, *The Richmond Whig*, openly asserted that should the bill which had already passed the House by a large majority be accepted by the Senate, Virginia would send eight instead of two administration representatives to Washington. The Whig regretted that still more could not be sent, and added, "But it is the best that can be done and we are content."

Another caucus bill provided for the creation of a Board of Railroad Commissioners to be chosen by the Governor. The Board was to have complete supervisory control of the railroads and could dismiss employees at its pleasure. The purpose of this was to bring the railroad system of the State with their numerous employees under Mahone's control.

Another caucus measure provided that judicial sales should be made only through a commissioner of sales appointed in each county by the Governor. Commissioners of sales had always been appointed by the court as occasion demanded, and no fault had been found with that custom. Furthermore, a bill was introduced which provided that the commissioners thus chosen should select a newspaper in each of their respective counties and cities which should have the exclusive right to publish their official notices. In this way Mahone could secure both an agent and a subsidized newspaper in each county. These and similar bills designed to further Mahone's interests were introduced into the Legislature by the Readjuster Caucus and failed to pass only through the aid of The Big Four, whom Mahone tried in vain to reduce.

Mahone's position in the Senate, however, gave him prestige and complete control over Federal appointments in Virginia. He was now also in a position to obtain campaign funds in the North. He used his increased prestige and power to strengthen his party and his position in it. The Readjuster party was rapidly changing into Mahone's party. By working quietly through his confederates, Mahone laid his plans to further increase his power. In the fall of 1881 he had the following pledge sent to each of the candidates for the Legislature for his signature: "I hereby pledge myself to stand by the Readjuster party and platform and to go into caucus with the Readjuster members of the Legislature and to vote for all measures and candidates to be elected by the Legislature that meets in Richmond as the caucus may agree upon. Given under my hand and seal, ... day of September, A. D. ...... 188..."

THE MARTIN FAMILY OF HENRY COUNTY, VIRGINIA

MOTTO: "Sure and Steadfast."

Two kinsmen, first cousins, came from Great Britain and settled in Caroline County, Virginia, in the early years of the Eighteenth Century. The first generation in America included Joseph Martin; the second included General Joseph Martin (1740–1808); Captain William Martin (1742); Captain Jack Martin, of Rock House, North Carolina; Captain Brice Martin and several daughters.

Joseph Martin, son of Joseph Martin and Susanna Childs Martin, was born in Albemarle County, Virginia, and died in Henry County, Virginia, 1808. He was one of three men who attempted to settle Powell's Valley, which included Cumberland Gap. The settlement was abandoned on account of the hostility of the Indians. A second attempt was made by Joseph Martin, this time with sixteen others from Henry County, in 1774. Richard Henderson tells of his memorable trip from the Holston to the Kentucky River after his treaty with the Indians and the Transylvania Purchase. He arrived on the thirtieth day of May, 1775, at Captain Martin's in Powell's Valley (Powell's Valley was included in the Transylvania Purchase), and Joseph Martin was made attorney and entry taker for this division of the purchase. Martin's chief merit lay in Indian diplomacy.

After coming to Henry County he built a commodious house on Leatherwood Creek, where he spent his declining years with his second wife, Susanna Graves. He left a large family and an extensive estate.

Joseph Martin, son of General Joseph and Susanna Graves Martin, was born in Henry County at Belmont. He married Sallie Hughes, daughter of Colonel Archelaus, of Patrick County. His home was "Greenwood" and he owned large landed estates and many negroes. He served many years in the House of Delegates and eight years in the Senate of Virginia. He was presidential elector three times successively, once for Monroe, and twice for Jackson, each time on a successful ticket. He did much to promote free schools in Virginia.

Joseph Martin, son of Joseph, Jr., was educated at Lexington, Virginia, and took his law course at Harvard. He practiced in Pittsylvania County, Virginia. His wife was Susan Pannill, a cousin of J. E. B. Stuart, who was present at the wedding, coming from West Point and wearing "regimentals." There was one son born to them, Joseph H. Martin, who inherited Greenwood and spent his life there.

In the old Martin cemetery at Belmont, overlooking Leatherwood Creek, there are four Joseph Martins side by side. General Joseph, Colonel Joseph, his son and grandson.

The children of Colonel Joseph Martin and his wife, Sallie Hughes, were: Susan married Robert Cook, of Pittsylvania County; Mary, John Staples, of Patrick County; Colonel William, Susan Hairston, of Henry County; Jane, John D. Watkins; Archelaus Hughes died in childhood. Ann married Judge John Dillard, of the Supreme Court of North Carolina; Captain Thomas, a Miss Pannell, of Pittsylvania County, he was killed at Malvern Hill; Matilda married George Stovall Hairston, of Henry County. They were parents of Judge Nicholas Hardyman Hairston and Mrs. Bettie Ingles.

Elizabeth married Captain Robert Williams, of Danville, Virginia; Sallie, Colonel Overton Dillard, of Henry County; Ella married Dr. John Robertson, of Pittsylvania County.

One daughter of John D. Watkins married William Wirt Werth. The children of Mary Martin and Colonel John Staples are as follows: William married Anne Penn; Abram, ...Penn; Susan married Colonel Steadman; Lucinda, a Mr. Peeler. The others were: Martin, John, Joseph and Samuel.

COLONEL WILLIAM MARTIN OF HENRY COUNTY, VIRGINIA

William Martin, son of Colonel Joseph and Sallie Hughes Martin, was born at Greenwood, 1814. He was educated at the University of Virginia. As an orator, lawyer and statesman, he was regarded as the peer of any man in Virginia. He was prominent in politics and was a member of the Constitutional Convention of 1850–51. He served as Colonel of a Confederate regiment. After his brother was killed at Malvern Hill, he returned home and served as commonwealth's attorney for some time. His death occurred in 1888.

The children of Colonel William and Susan Hairston Martin are as follows: Sallie Elizabeth married Dr. William Brengle, of Ridgeway, Virginia; Louise Hardeman, Samuel Sheffield, merchant of Martinsville; Jane, Samuel Watkins, of Henry County, Virginia; Susan, William H. West; Matilda, George Hairston, who represented his district in Congress for a number of years. He was the largest land and slave owner in this part of Virginia.

The other sons of William and Susan Hairston Martin were: Samuel Hughes, George and Joseph.

COLONEL JOSEPH MARTIN

Colonel Joseph Martin during a long life received the most flattering evidences of the public confidence and regard. At one time he was the commandant of the regiment of this county. For many years he represented with marked ability the county and senatorial district in the General Assembly of Virginia.

At a later period he was chosen to deliberate with the illustrious men called, in 1829, to revise the Constitution of the State, and for more than a quarter of a century was presiding or associate justice of the court, and in every position he was fully equal to the performance of the duties imposed. In military tactics he was a great disciplinarian, in the deliberative assembly a sagacious and faithful representative and on the bench a sound and impartial judge. The various public stations which he filled and his long continuance in them is the best evidence of the high estimate which was placed on his services.

He was uniformly courteous and commanded respect in return. Diligent and prudent in the management of his private affairs he acquired large boundaries of land in Patrick and Henry Counties, with hundreds of slaves and other personal property which placed him as one of the wealthiest men of the time.

Sallie Martin, daughter of Colonel Joseph and Sallie Hughes Martin, married Colonel Overton Dillard, of Henry County. Their children are as follows: Sallie Hughes married Frank Gravely, of Danville, Virginia; Elizabeth Redd, D. W. Reamey; Susan Jane, Samuel Ford; Anne Marshall .... Arrington; Ella Martin, Samuel Griggs; second, R. E. Lee.

MARTIN FAMILY (NOTES)

ORIGIN OF MARTIN

Eleanor Lexington, in the *Nashville American*, tells us that the first Baron of Cemmeas was Martin de Tours. More than one knight of that connection are recorded on the Roll of Battle Abbey.

William Martin is a name still honored in Europe. When Germany and the Allied Powers signed the Treaty of Peace, June 28, 1919, at Versailles, France, William Martin was the master of ceremonies.

In the early years of the Eighteenth Century, two kinsmen, Colonel John Martin and Joseph Martin came from Great Britain to live in Caroline County, Virginia. The fathers of these two men were brothers. Colonel John Martin was a member of the House of Burgesses from Caroline County, 1738–1740. He married Malinda Burwell, kinswoman of the Page family.

Children of General Joseph Martin and his first wife, Susan Lucas:

Susanna Martin married Jacob Burnes; Colonel William Martin, 1765–1846; Elizabeth Martin married Carr Waller; Brice Martin, 1770–1846, married Malinda Perkins. Children of the second wife: Susanna Graves Martin; Colonel Joseph Martin, of Henry County, Virginia. Jesse Martin married Annie Armistead, one son was born to them. His second wife was Cecilia Reid, and they were parents of eight sons and a daughter.

Thomas W. Martin married a Miss Carr, of North Carolina, and went to Tennessee to live. Lewis Martin also went to Tennessee.

Alexander Martin married a Miss Carr and went to Missouri to live.

THE MARTIN FAMILY OF HENRY COUNTY

The Martin family is one of the most distinguished of the early settlers of Henry County. There were two brothers, who came to the county and bought land, Brice Martin, on the south side of Smith's River, and Joseph Martin, on the north side, his estate being known as Scuffle Hill. Joseph Martin and his wife came from Orange County. She died in 1782, and was survived by her husband and seven children.

William Martin (1765–1846) was born in Orange County, Virginia. He was a man of great patriotism, going on an expedition against the Indians in 1781, and was in Powell's Valley two years. His wife was Franky Farris and they moved to South Carolina in 1791. He served in the War of 1812, also against the Creeks, and took command after General Pillow was wounded.

The other children of General Joseph Martin were: Susanna, who married Jacob Burrus; Elizabeth, Carr Waller; Brice, Jr., Matilda Perkins; Polly, Daniel Hammock; Martha, William Cleveland; Nancy, Archelaus Hughes.

General Martin married Susanna Graves (1784). Their children were: Joseph, known as Colonel Joseph Martin (1785), married Sallie Hughes. He was a member of the Virginia Legislature, 1809, and of the Constitutional Convention, 1820–1830. His family consisted of eight daughters and four sons.

Jesse Martin was in the War of 1812. He married first, Annie Armistead; second, Cecelia Read. She left one child, Captain Thomas King Martin, of Reed Creek. Polly Martin married Reuben Hughes. Patrick Henry Martin was taken to Tennessee by his half brothers, Brice and William, Jr., and educated. He studied law and began practicing about 1812, served in Jackson's Army and died after returning from New Orleans in 1814.

William Martin's children were: Sallie, Matilda, Susan, Ella, Ann, Eliza, Jane, William, Archie, Sam, Tom and Joseph. Sallie Martin married O. R. Dillard; Matilda, Dr. George Hairston, of Marrowbone; Susan, Robert Cook; Ella, Dr. John Robertson; Anne, John H. Dillard; Eliza, Samuel Williams, of Wytheville; Jane, a Mr. McCabe; Colonel William, Susan Hairston, daughter of "Old Rusty"; Archie and Sam were not married; Tom married Susan Pannill and was killed at Malvern Hill, 1862; Joseph married Susan Pannill.

Greenwood, the home of this family, was noted for its splendid hospitality and luxury.

Colonel William Martin was one of Henry County's gifted sons. He was an orator of great ability and was a man of great culture and elegance of manner. He represented the county in the Legislature before he was twenty years of age. It is said that when the other members of the House learned that he was so young, his eligibility was questioned, but upon hearing his speeches he was allowed to take his seat without further objections. He was several times elected commonwealth's attorney for Henry County.

The children of this family were: Joseph, Samuel, Loula and Bettie Martin.

Loula Martin married Samuel G. Sheffield; Bettie Martin, Dr. W. D. Brengle, of Ridgeway. Two daughters, Maizie and Bettie Martin, survive them.

Four generations of Joseph Martins are buried at Belle Monte, the ancestral home of the Martin family.

THE MATTHEWS FAMILY OF HENRY COUNTY, VIRGINIA

The Matthews family is of Welsh descent. Three brothers came to this country and one, called Tandy, settled in North Carolina near Germantown (1773). He married Betsy Hill and they reared the following children: Robert, William, James, Tandy, Caleb, Eliza, Patsy and Calvin. His second wife was Pink Coffer, and one child was born to them, Marcella. He was the owner of 2,000 acres of land and 150 slaves. He died in 1855.

Robert, the eldest of the family, was born about 1797. He married Mary Critz, and reared one child, William.

William Matthews married Mary Staples, a sister of Colonel George Staples, of Henry County.

James Matthews was born about 1799 and married Eliza Allen, daughter of Robert Allen and lived at the old Allen home, Lewiston, near Ridgeway, after the Allens moved to Mississippi. There were the following children: Robert Edward, Mary, William, Celia, David, Caleb and Eliza Jane. Tandy Matthews, Jr., and Eliza remained unmarried. Patsy married Colonel Bitting, of North Carolina. Caleb was a lawyer and located in Germanton, North Carolina. Calvin married Lucy Mullins, of Henry County, and reared two sons, John Hill and Calvin, the latter never married.

II. Robert Matthews, son of James Matthews and Eliza Allen Matthews, married Sarah Abingdon, and reared the following children: James, who married Mollie Koger; Bettie and John unmarried; Celia, married

William Marshall, and reared the following sons: George married Miss Purdy, and William was never married.

Edmund Matthews married Elizabeth Dalton, their children were: Eliza, who married first, William King; second Hannibal Simpson. Mary married Thomas Seamore, of Virginia; Ginnie married a Heggie; Thomas married Sallie Adams. He was killed in the Civil War. William married Sallie Stuart and Mary married a Dalton.

William Matthews married Mrs. Antoinette Conrad. Their children were Sallie and Frank.

David Matthews married Charlotte Dalton, of Stoneville, North Carolina. Their children were: Robert; Caleb, who married Sarah E. King; Leonard, Elizabeth Price; Waller, Nannie Davenport, and John unmarried.

Celia married Zachary Wall, their children were as follows: James, Walter, Mollie, Nannie, Charles, Granville, John, Hunter, Muncie and Catrina.

Eliza Jane Matthews married George Shelton King, of Patrick County (1868), and reared a large family, namely: Beulah, who married John Smith; Sarah Elizabeth, Caleb Matthews; Anne, Mat Holland; James King, Mattie Holland; George, Mamie Pulliam, of North Carolina; Caleb, Fannie Hunter, of Kernersville, North Carolina; Charles, Lilly Pratt; Frank, Mamie Taylor, of Stoneville.

Sallie Matthews, only daughter of William Matthews and Antoinette Conrad Matthews, married William Glenn, nephew of Governor Glenn, of North Carolina.

JOHN HILL MATTHEWS OF HENRY COUNTY, VIRGINIA

John Hill Matthews, one of Henry County's outstanding citizens and popular officeholders, was the son of Calvin and Lucy Mullins Matthews. Their home was in the western part of the county and after his father's death, which occurred when he was about seven years of age, he spent most of his time at the home of his grandfather, Henry G. Mullins. He received his high school education at Germanton, North Carolina, and after reaching maturity returned to his home in Henry County.

During the Civil War he was awarded a contract to carry the mail and was assigned the duty of transferring troops between Martinsville and Danville. His official career began as deputy sheriff which office he held for five years, he then served as commissioner of the revenue for a term. In May, 1875, he was elected clerk of the county court, and held that office for the almost unprecedented period of thirty-six years. His genial manner, friendliness, and kindness of heart won for him popularity enjoyed by few men in public life.

Mr. Matthews was married three times, his first wife was Annie Morris; his second wife was Sallie Craghead, and the children of this union were: Lucy, who married Thomas P. Parish, of Smithfield, Virginia; Minnie married George Akers Brown; Annie, Dr. R. R. Lee; Thomas Calvin, Ida Coleman.

Mr. Matthews died in 1912 and his son, Thomas C. Matthews, was elected to fill his place, and his efficiency and popularity compare most favorably with that of his father. Always "on the job," but never too busy to give attention to those who apply to him for assistance and information concerning affairs with which Mr. Matthews is familiar. Few men possess more sincere friends and earnest supporters than "Tom" Matthews.

THE MITCHELL FAMILY

There were two distinct families in Henry County by the name of Mitchell, distant cousins.

William Mitchell married Mary Bondurant and they reared the following children: Benjamin Franklin, Thomas Bondurant, William, Eliza, Sarah and Edwin.

Thomas B. Mitchell (1829–1914) married Katherine Price, of Ridgeway. He was a member of the Tenth Virginia Cavalry and fought through the War. After the War he returned and became a successful farmer. The children of this family were: William D., Anna, Belva and Edwin who died in early life.

Benjamin Franklin Mitchell married Nannie Abbingdon and lived near Mt. Bethel Church. Of that family Bettie and Virginia died in infancy; Annie married a Canaday; Ella, a Craig; Richard, a Mitchell; William married Mary Price, and they reared the following children: William, Fletcher, Robert, Mollie, Laura and Kittie; Eliza married James W. Trent and moved to Tennessee; Sarah married Robert Trent and moved to Tennessee, also.

III. William D. Mitchell married Anna Jones, daughter of John C. Jones, of Ridgeway. He was in the mercantile business for many years. His second marriage was to Mrs. Jennie Sparrow McKiver. The children of the first marriage were William and Bessie.

Anna Mitchell married James P. Garrett, of Ridgeway. They were parents of the following children: Alma, Kate, Paul, Annie, May, Peter G., Rachael, William and Ruth.

Belva Mitchell married J. D. Sparrow, of Martinsville, Virginia. She died many years ago being survived by her husband and two daughters, Kathleen, who married Alex Mahood, of Bluefield, West Virginia, and Rose, who passed away a few years since.

William Mitchell, of the Mt. Bethel section of Henry County, married Lucy Trotter and reared the following children: Joseph T., Edward B. and Elizabeth. He married a second time, Annie Haygood. The children of this marriage were: Mary Frances, Sallie Ann and George.

Joseph T. Mitchell married Sallie Stovall and reared the following children: Willie and Jubal unmarried; Edd died young; Joseph married Mrs. Loula Lester Hurd; Landis married Mary Garnett and Nannie, George D. Craig.

Edward R. Mitchell married Martha Schoolfield. He was a soldier in the War Between the States, took part in the Gettysburg Battle, and spent some time in a Federal prison.

Elizabeth Mitchell married John W. Morris. Of the second family of Mitchells, Mary Frances married Jack Dillon. Their children were: Joe, Lizzie, Jesse Davis and Annie.

Sallie Ann Mitchell was not married. Wade died in the Civil War. George married Florence Stovall. Their children were: Dora, Annie, Elizabeth, Harry, James, Hughes and Wade.

THE MOIR FAMILY OF PATRICK COUNTY, VIRGINIA

The Moir family is descended from the distinguished Scotch family of Stonywood Castle. The first member of the family of whom we have a record was Alexander Moir, of Torres, Scotland.

The members of the Moir family of Patrick County, were: Lucy, Ann Elizabeth (Mrs. Henry Tuggle), Margaret (Mrs. James Norman), Cybella (Mrs. W. T. Noel), Susan, James Moir, John, Alexander, Robert T. and W. W. Moir.

The children of W. W. and Caroline V. Moir are the late Judge Percy McPherson Moir, a very prominent attorney of Roanoke, he was a graduate of V. P. I. and received his degree from Washington and Lee University. He was a native of Patrick County, Virginia.

Judge Moir joined Company D, Second Virginia Volunteers and was appointed to Civil Service in the Philippine Islands in 1901, and served there as District Attorney, District Judge and Associate Justice of the Supreme Court of the Philippines until 1920, when he resigned. His wife was Miss Maude Kirkland, of Washington.

There are four other sons and two daughters of W. W. and Caroline V. Moir, viz.: H. M. Moir, Stuart, Virginia; V. P. Moir, Winston-Salem, North Carolina; W. W. Moir and C. R. Moir, of Roanoke; Mrs. J. J. Norman, of Winston-Salem, and Mrs. M. M. Bouldin, of Roanoke.

THE MORRIS FAMILY OF HENRY COUNTY, VIRGINIA

Samuel Coleman Morris and his wife, who was a Miss Wade, came from Goochland to Henry County, about 1776. There were four sons and two daughters of that family, viz.: William, Ben, John, Joseph, Nancy and Rebecca.

William Morris married Tabitha Cheatham and their children were: William, Ben, Tabitha, Susan, Booker, Eliza, Patsy and Eleanor.

Ben Morris married Nancy Haygood. The following were their children: William Wade, Gregory, Eliza and Virginia.

John Morris, another brother, married Reamy Pharis. Their children were: William, James Madison, John Wesley, Dandridge Wade and Logan.

No record of Joseph, the fourth son, is available; Nancy married a Brewer; Rebecca, a Bradley.

Ben Morris, son of Captain William and Tabitha Morris, was a Colonel in the Confederate Army. His home was in Alabama. William Morris died in the Civil War. Tabitha married Andrew Jackson Smith; Booker, ... Finney; Patsy, Daniel Pace; Eleanor Morris married a Cheatham and moved to Mississippi.

Dr. William W. Morris, son of Ben and Nancy Haygood Morris, married Emmeline Schoolfield. Dr. Morris was a man of such unusual personality that his very presence in a sick room inspired hope and confidence for the patients. He had a happy disposition, and was a physician of ability. He was born in 1836, and was reared in the Mt. Bethel neighborhood. Having chosen medicine as his profession, he attended the Jefferson Medical College and began his practice about the beginning of the War Between the States. He joined the army and was captain of the second company that volunteered from Henry County. He served his country faithfully, and was severely wounded at Kearnstown and was slightly lame from the effects of the wound the rest of his life.

After the close of the War, Dr. Morris resumed the practice of medicine, giving much of his time to attending the poor and needy without expectation of remuneration. He left his country home, and continued his practice in Martinsville, Virginia, for a few years but returned and spent the rest of his life amongst the people who were his loyal and devoted friends. Up to the last years of his life he was a loyal Veteran and enjoyed the reunions, even going to distant states to attend them. He died in................aged .... His wife passed away a few years earlier.

The children of Dr. and Emmeline Schoolfield Morris are as follows: Ben, William, Addison, Virginia and Annie.

Virginia Morris married Minor Botts Koger and reared a large family in the neighborhood of her birth.

Annie married first, Vincent Smith and she and the following children survived him, viz.: Emily, Martha and Vincent. Later she married .... Graham and they occupy a beautiful home in Danville, Virginia.

Robert Sanders Morris, a brother of John T. Morris, married Mary Campbell Mason. Their children were: Samuel Madison, Martha Louisa, Thomas Hill, Robert Ernest, Ann Eliza, Bessie Haymaker and Henry Sanders.

Samuel Anderson Morris married N. E. Forbes. Their children are as follows: Melissa, Mary Emma, Georgia, John William, Kelly Reed, Mattie, Rosa, Brooksie and Edgar.

V. Samuel Madison Morris married ....Philpott. Their children are: Martha Louisa, John Thomas Hill, Henry Sanders and Bernard.

John Thomas Hill Morris married Annie Lou Vaughn. Their children are: Robert Vaughn, George Emerson, Mary Evelyn, Katherine Leak and Thomas Hill.

Ann Eliza Morris married James R. Wray; Robert Ernest Morris, Ruth Dillard Donevant; Bessie Haymaker Morris married C. M. Stone; Henry Sanders Morris, Nannie Elizabeth Craig.

James Walter Morris married Sallie Elizabeth Bouldin.

Ann Elizabeth Morris married Pinckney Cox; Pocahontas, Elijah Richard Nelson; Mamie, Robert B. Winn; Lucy Matt, Jess Thomas Byrd; Ellen Morton, John William Wingfield; Maggie, Watt Wade Smith, and Emma Hairston, John Harrison Frye.

William F. Morris, son of John and Reamy Pharis Morris, never married. James Wesley married Elizabeth Mitchell; Dandridge Wade married Ann Waller. Neither of the above mentioned left descendants. James Madison Morris married Mary Hill, daughter of Thomas S. Hill. Their children were: Ann Eliza, Mary, John T., William W., Samuel A., James M., Robert S., David, Sarah, Walter and Virginia Dare.

IV. Ann Eliza Morris married John Hill Matthews; Richard Hairston Morris married Emma Lou Coleman, 1874. Their children were: Maggie, Ellen Morton, Emma Hairston, James Harrison, Dewy and Grace.

Virginia Dare Morris, daughter of James Madison and Mary Hill Morris, married B. D. Grogan. John T. Morris married a Miles and their children were: Hairston, who was a merchant in Martinsville for a number of years, and married Daisy Reamey, daughter of the late D. W. and Elizabeth Dillard Reamey. One daughter, Mildred, was born to them. Thomas Morris married first, Helen, daughter of Dr. John R. Dillard, and died after a few years being survived by one son, John Dillard. Thomas Morris was married the second time to Elizabeth Smithson. William Morris married Virginia Wells, and moved to Martinsville, Virginia, some years since, where they reared a large family. Edgar died in early youth.

LINEAGE OF THE MULLINS FAMILY

The Irish ancestors of the Mullins family settled in Goochland County, Virginia.

David Mullins, Revolutionary soldier under General Greene, married Susan Herndon.

Henry Greene Mullins named for General Greene.

Celia, sister of Henry Greene married David Allen. Maternal ancestry.

General Samuel Bailey, wounded in the French and Indian War, married Augusta Parks.

Parks Bailey married Mary Cabaniss.

Sarah Judith Bailey married I. Y. Hill, their son, Samuel Hill, married Lucy Mitchell. Children, Matilda and Judith.

Matilda Hill married Henry Greene Mullins. Children of H. G. and Matilda Mullins. Lucy married Calvin Matthews. Their son was John H. Matthews. Celia married Robert Traylor; Susan, Pink Hay; Matilda, John Hardie; Augusta, James Penn; Hill, Virginia Wood; Patrick, Mary Wood; Samuel Jesse married first, Sarah Athey; second, Minnie Martin.

Children of S. J. Mullins and Sarah Athey Mullins. Henry G. married Whitten McCabe; Peter H., Annie Lee Stiggleman; Sallie.

Children of S. J. Mullins and Minnie Martin Mullins. Allie married Ashby Edwards; Hattie married John W. Gravely. Their only child, Virginia. James Alexander married first, Aurora Black. Children, Creston and Jay. His second marriage was to Agnes Brennan.

Children of Henry G. and Whitten McCabe Mullins: Annie Green married Clifton Huff, is survived by one son. Nellie married Colonel Stearns Dodson; children, Julia, Richard and Elinor. Henry married Lelia Nelson; children, Henry Green and Anne. Peter, Frances Dodson; children, Peter and Robert. Sadie married Richard P. Gravely; children, Richard, Nancy, Harry Reginald, Sadie Hay, Frank, Virginia, Bobbie and Betsey.

Creston B. Mullins, son of James Alexander Mullins, married Reva Lemmons.

Daughter of Peter and Annie Stiggleman Mullins, Elinor, married Thomas Risco. Children, Elinor, Thomas and Samuel Jesse (nicknamed Con).

1700

Samuel Bailey came from Ireland and lived in Richmond County, Virginia. He was "Gentleman Justice" under the King of England. His son, Samuel Bailey, married Sarah Lewis, and their son, General Samuel Bailey, served in the French and Indian War, and later in the Revolutionary War (Eleventh Virginia Regiment). He married Augusta Parks, their daughter, Sarah Judith Bailey, married I. Y. Hill, whose son, Samuel C. Hill, married Lucy Mitchell, whose daughter, Matilda Winston Hill, married Henry Greene Mullins, son of David Mullins, a Revolutionary soldier, at one time on General Greene's staff.

MULLINS ANCESTRY

Patrick Mullins came from Ireland, 1727, and took up a grant of land, 3,000 acres, in Goochland County, Virginia. His son, Henry Mullins, was born in Goochland County, Virginia, whose son, David Mullins, was born in Goochland County, Virginia, and was a Revolutionary soldier under General Greene (on General Greene's staff). He lived and died in Henry County.

His son, Henry Greene Mullins, married Matilda W. Hill, and their sons were: Hill, Patrick and Samuel Jesse Mullins.

Samuel Jesse's sons, Henry G., Peter H. and J. Alexander. Henry's sons, Henry and Peter. Peter's son, Samuel Jesse (Con). J. Alexander's sons, Creston and Jay.

Henry's son, Henry Greene Mullins.

Peter's sons, Peter and Robert.

THE MULLINS FAMILY OF HENRY COUNTY, VIRGINIA

The Mullins trace their lineage to the Duke of Connaught in Ireland. The first of the family on record is David Mullins born in 1770. He married Susannah Herndon and they made their home in Henry County, Virginia. There were three children, Celia, John and Henry Greene. Burwell and Nathaniel were children of the second wife.

David Mullins was a soldier in the Revolutionary War, serving with General Greene in many campaigns. Henry Greene was named in honor of the General.

Celia Mullins of the next generation married Robert Allen; John lived in Fayette, North Carolina. Henry Greene married Matilda Winston Hill. Burwell moved to Indiana; Nathaniel married Nancy Watkins.

The children of Henry Greene Mullins: Lucy Catherine Mullins married Calvin Matthews, who died, being survived by his wife and two children, John Hill and Calvin. Mrs. Matthews married, the second time, Robert Walker, who died leaving three daughters, Susan Matilda, Alice, who married a Dean and another daughter who married a Nelson.

David Hill Mullins married Virginia Wood, of Georgia. He died and was survived by his wife and five children, Anna, Henry Hill, William, Winston and Jack.

Susan Mullins married Tandy Matthews and after his death she married Pinkney Hayes.

Patrick Henry Mullins married Mary Wood, of Georgia. They had two daughters and a son.

Celia Mullins married Robert Traylor. Their children were: John H. and Matilda Traylor, who married a Mr. Wright. Another son, Hill Mullins Traylor, was killed in the Battle of Chancellorsville.

SAMUEL JESSE MULLINS

Samuel Jesse Mullins, one of Henry County's prominent citizens, was born in 1831. He was one of the patriotic young men of his time and organized a company to join the Confederate forces. As captain of the company he served for some time but resigned to accept a seat in the Legislature of Virginia. His popularity was further attested by his appointment as Judge of the Henry County Court, which office he held for a number of years.

Judge Mullins' first wife was Sarah Hay Athey, and their three children were: Henry Greene, Peter Hill and Sallie.

Henry Greene Mullins married Annie Whitten McCabe, daughter of Mrs. Susan Gravely McCabe. The children of this union were: Annie Greene, who married Clifton P. Huff, of Roanoke, Virginia. She passed away after a few years, being survived by her husband and one son.

Sadie Mullins married Richard P. Gravely. (See Gravely family.) Nellie married Lieutenant Stearns Dodson of the United States Army.

Marion, the youngest daughter, makes her home in Martinsville, Virginia, where she takes a great interest in social and literary activities.

Peter Hill Mullins graduated at the Virginia Medical College and located at Floyd Court House for the practice of his profession. He married Annie Steigleman, daughter of a prominent physician of that place. He and his wife both passed away a few years since and were survived by a daughter and a son.

Sallie Mullins, only daughter of this union, died in early life.

MRS. MINNIE MARTIN MULLINS

Mrs. Minnie Martin Mullins, second wife of Judge Samuel J. Mullins, has for many years occupied a prominent position in the social, literary and religious activities of Martinsville, Virginia.

Her education and culture created a taste for literary pursuits which found expression in imparting knowledge to others. While living in her country home near Mayo, Virginia, after her marriage to Judge Mullins, she taught school, exerting an uplifting influence upon the people of the community which is incalculable.

Judge Mullins moved with his family to Martinsville and, even in her comfortable and attractive home, Mrs. Mullins would take time from her many duties to give instruction to a limited number of pupils, who were glad to go to her for the privilege of being taught.

Mrs. Mullins is a notable leader in the society of the Daughters of the American Revolution, having held the office of secretary for many years, the duties of which she has performed admirably. She is also a leader in the United Daughters of the Confederacy and is an active member of the Baptist Church, always ready to answer a call for service.

A few years past, when the country homes were the social centers, a strong and lasting friendship existed amongst three of Henry County's prominent women, the subject of this sketch, Mrs. Mullins, Mrs. Adele Lee Dillard, wife of Dr. John R. Dillard, and Mrs. John H. Schoolfield. They were about the same age, were married about the same time and lived only a few miles apart. Mrs. Mullins in the Mayo community, Mrs. Dillard near Spencer and Mrs. Schoolfield at Horsepasture. This intimate friendship existed until death claimed two of them, Mrs. Mullins being the only one now living.

The children of Judge Samuel J. Mullins and Mrs. Minnie Martin Mullins were: Jessie, who died just as she reached womanhood; Alice (Allie), who married Ashly Edwards, of Floyd County, and after his death returned to Martinsville to make her home with her mother. Harriet married John W. Gravely, a successful business man, of Washington, District of Columbia. Mr. Gravely was formerly interested in the manufacture of tobacco and they made their home for a number of years in Danville, Virginia. Their only child, a lovely little daughter, Virginia, died in childhood; James Alexander married first, Aurora Black; second, Agnes Brennan.

DR. J. P. McCABE OF MARTINSVILLE, VIRGINIA

A very few months since, an anniversary celebration which created widespread interest was held in Martinsville, Virginia, in honor of Rev. J. P. McCabe, a well-beloved pastor who completed the twenty-fifth year of his pastorate of the First Baptist Church.

After many years in the Broad Street Church, the congregation decided to build a more commodious edifice and a beautiful new church stands on the corner of Church and Broad Streets.

While the building was in progress Dr. McCabe might be seen, any day, coat off, trowel or hammer in hand, and with beaming face, taking a delight in doing a little for the pure pleasure of it, while watching the building grow in strength and beauty.

MRS. MINNIE MARTIN MULLINS
WIFE OF
Colonel Samuel Jesse Mullins

An attractive and comfortable pastorium has been built close by the church and over this home Mrs. McCabe, who was, before her marriage, Miss Sue Martin, presides with dignity and efficiency.

THE NOWLIN FAMILY OF PATRICK COUNTY, VIRGINIA

The name was originally O'Naullain, the O in Gaelic signifying son of. This was corrupted to O'Nolan, O'Nowlan, then Nowlan and in Virginia it became Nowlin.

Three brothers, whose names were James, John and William Nowlan, came to Virginia from Ireland about 1700. James remained in Virginia, the others moving to other states.

At that time the Old Dominion was but sparsely settled. Wild beasts roamed the forests, the red man was the worst menace of all, his cunning and craftiness to be most dreaded, yet all these did not daunt the Irish immigrant. His mother country was the scene of devastation at this period of time. They are a people who do not let adverse circumstances discourage them, but only serve to buoy them on to greater effort.

The family of John Nowlin, of Patrick County, Virginia, included the following children: Charles, Judith Nowlin Harbour, Lucinda Nowlin Rakes, Pleasant, Witt and Alice.

The children of Charles Nowlin are: John A., Alexander, Charles, George, Lillie A. Nowlin Agee, Mary Nowlin Adams, Ocie Nowlin Akers, Martha Nowlin Rakes, Adaline Nowlin Turner.

THE PANNILL FAMILY OF HENRY COUNTY, VIRGINIA

The Pannills are of English descent. From an article in the William and Mary *Quarterly*, published in 1898 by David H. Pannill, volume now in New York City Library, comes, under the head of J. E. B. Stuart ancestry, "On Battle Roll of Battle Abbey will be found the name Painell and from him are supposed to be descended the Pannells of England and Ireland. Those of England were Churchmen and Royalists, those of Ireland, Catholics."

Upon the accession of Cromwell the three English Pannells emigrated to America, one to Maryland, one to Norfolk, Virginia, and the third to Rappahannock, Virginia. The orthography of the Rappahannock branch was changed from Pannell to Pannill. The other branches kept the first form. General J. E. B. Stuart was descended from the Rappahannock Branch.

Thomas Pannill settled in Virginia, on the Rappahannock, his son, William, when he became of age, sold his property and moved to Richmond County, Virginia. He married Frances Mills. His son, William II, married Sarah Bailey, of Middlesex County, Virginia. William III, son of William II, and Sarah Bailey, married Ann Morton. There were three children, Morton, David and Samuel. Samuel died unmarried. Morton married Mary Johns, of Lynchburg. Their children were: George, Joseph, William, Ann and Morton.

George Pannill, son of Morton and Mary Johns Pannill, married Bethenia Ruth Calloway, daughter of John and America Hairston Pannill. Their home, Claremont, was one of Henry County's attractive estates.

Mr. and Mrs. Pannill were the parents of the following children: George, Jack, America Hairston, William Hairstin, Mary, Bethenia Ruth, Loula, Harden, Edmond, John, S. Ann Katherine. George, Jack, William, Harden and Loula died unmarried. William belonged to Captain Graham's Company K, Tenth Virginia Cavalry, and was killed near Ream's Station, August 25, 1864.

America Hairston Pannill married William Campbell. They were parents of the following children: Bethenia, William Pannill and Ruth Janet.

Mary Pannill married John Henry Davis. They lived at Rocky Hill, the ancestral home of the Calloways, in Henry County. They were parents of five children: George Evans, John H., Elizabeth Ruth, Edmond Pannill and Ernest.

Bethenia Ruth Pannill married Martin Penn. Two sons were born to them (see Penn family). Katherine Pannill married Dr. William T. Woodley, of Charlotte, North Carolina.

Edmond J. Pannill married Eliza Reamy, daughter of Dr. Peter R. Reamy and Sallie Waller Reamy. Mr. and Mrs. Pannill's family included seven daughters and two sons, all born at the ancestral home of the Pannills. After the death of Mr. Pannill the family moved to Martinsville, Virginia. Sallie Reamy, the eldest daughter, married John Redd Smith (see Smith family). Maria Waller married W. Brumfield Read (see sketch of Brumfield

Read). Katherine Langhorn, Bethenia Letcher and America Hairston are at the present time engaged in educational work. Katherine possesses a talent for art and, after making splendid preparation for teaching, is an instructor in a large school in Winchester, Virginia.

Ruth Calloway chose nursing as her profession, for which she is eminently fitted, nature having bestowed upon her a high order of intelligence, a deep, sympathetic understanding of human nature and a charming personality. Mary Elizabeth, after finishing high school and attending Chatham Episcopal Institute, lives with her mother at the family home in Martinsville, where she takes a lively interest in all social and other activities of interest to young people.

"WHAT MAN HATH GREATER LOVE THAN THIS"

George Edmond and J. E. B. Stuart Pannill, young sons of Mrs. Eliza Reamy Pannill and the late Edmond J. Pannill, went bravely forth and voluntarily faced the horrors of modern warfare from a high sense of duty, and for the sake of helping to secure protection for their own country against the menace of war. In the veins of these young men flowed the blood of generations of brave soldiers—the blood of the Stuarts, Wallers and many others. Although under the required age, when they felt that their country needed them, they were ready. Nothing could exceed the brave sacrifice of these young men, except that of the mother, who, with splendid Spartan courage, let them go.

Both enlisted in Second Division, Company K, Ninth Infantry, A. E. F. George was killed in action, July 18, 1918, in Chateau-Thierry. Stuart was wounded about that time and died August 4th.

MRS. FAITH THOMAS PARROTT, OF MARTINSVILLE, VIRGINIA

Faith Thomas Parrott, second daughter of the late Honorable C. Y. Thomas and Mrs. Mary Reamy Thomas, was one of Martinsville's brightest and most patriotic women, always taking a leading part in the activities in which she participated.

After her marriage to Mr. Parrott, she assisted him in conducting a select school in Martinsville for several years. She possessed musical talent and was organist and musical director in the Episcopal Church for many years.

Mrs. Parrott was one of the founders of the Patrick Henry Chapter, D. A. R., June 15, 1905, and for twenty-three years was the faithful regent. Her enthusiasm and devotion to the work of the organization were proverbial. When anything was undertaken by the society, Mrs. Parrott was never known to falter in her determination to reach the goal. During her regency a handsome monument was erected in memory of Patrick Henry, on land formerly owned by him, donated by the present owner, Mr. Samuel Hooker; Mrs. Charles B. Keesee donating the imposing granite shaft. A large number of people gathered to witness and take part in the ceremonies of unveiling the monument, which was done by Master Madison Fontaine, son of William H. Fontaine, a descendant of Patrick Henry.

A splendid and expensive oil portrait was placed in Continental Hall in Washington, District of Columbia, the presentation ceremonies being conducted by Mrs. Parrott.

Patriotism and temperance formed a large part of her life work. She was president of the W. C. T. U. in Martinsville for many years, and took an active interest in the patriotic work in the public schools, instilling in the minds of the students the importance of Good Citizenship by offering rewards for the best essays on the subject, thereby making deep impressions on those who could be induced to give thought and time to the work.

In appreciation of the life work of Mrs. Parrott, who passed away in 1928, the members of the chapter give each year a gold medal, known as the Faith Thomas Parrott medal, to the member of the graduating class of the high school ranking highest in Good Citizenship.

During her life a chair was placed in Continental Hall in her honor.

THOMAS STARLING PAYNE

A Henry County soldier of the Civil War.

Old letters reveal thrilling experiences of a soldier of the Civil War and he graphically describes many of the battles in which he was engaged.

Thomas Starling Payne was born January 28, 1830. He was the son of William and Letitia Bouldin Payne, of Horsepasture, Henry County, Virginia. He left Henry County with the Henry Guards, June 3, 1861, and joined Company H, Twenty-Fourth Virginia Regiment.

After the War, in 1867, he went to Kentucky and lived there until his death in 1929. He married Addie Willis and is survived by two children.

His early letters show the spirit of youth going to battle—we might well say the spirit of deluded youth. He stated, "We are all in fine spirits and nothing on earth would do us more good than to get into a fight. We would not go home for anything in the world."

His letters lead on through many battles, victories, hardships, hunger, and a long period of suffering in hospitals from a severely wounded leg.

In a letter dated four years later than the first, he says, "Our patience is worn out waiting for peace. We don't get anything like enough to eat. There is a great deal of desertion but I will never leave until peace is made. I can stay as long as anybody else."

THE FOUNDERS OF THE PEDIGO (PEREGOY) FAMILY OF VIRGINIA

THE PEDIGO FAMILY

The name Perigord from which Peregoy and afterwards Pedigo are derived is an extremely ancient and illustrious name in France. One of the most distinguished and interesting representatives of that family was the great father of diplomacy, Charles Maurice Talleyrand du Perigord.

The first of the family of whom we have a record are Edward or Edwin and Robert or Robin Perigord, who settled a little farther east than the location chosen by his brother, which was in Franklin County. Edward married Mary Elkin and Robert, Hannah Elkin, sisters.

Edward's family consisted of fourteen children: Joseph was the eldest and he and his second wife moved to Kentucky. Later Edward and some of his younger sons and daughters went out there and stayed. He died in 1832, and his descendants stated that he was 103 years of age. Some of his descendants have his knife and whetstone that he used while in the Revolutionary War.

We have always been told that "Grandfather Ned" came here when about fourteen years of age (information secured in Washington). Several of the children married and remained in Patrick. Edward's son was Abel Pedigo; his brother, Elijah, with his wife and baby, were drowned in Smith's River. One daughter married a Cochran, one a Snead, and one a Clark.

CAPTAIN JOHN FOUNTAIN PEDIGO OF HENRY COUNTY, VIRGINIA

Captain John F. Pedigo was a descendant of Robert or Robin Pedigo, one of the brothers who came to this county from Maryland, formerly from

France. Captain Pedigo's father and grandfather both bore the name of Henry.

The family home was upon an estate in the Leatherwood community, in Henry County. Captain Pedigo was a merchant as well as a planter and was one of Henry County's prominent citizens, taking a great interest in political as well as business affairs.

During the War Between the States he was elected sheriff of Henry County, and was distributor of supplies to widows and orphans of the men who had served in the War. Captain Pedigo was Referee in Bankruptcy for the Fifth District of Virginia.

The first wife of Captain Pedigo was Martha Gravely. Their children were: Emma Eugenie and Lewis Gravely. His second wife was Mrs. Rachael Gravely Cheatham, sister of his first wife. J. Edward Pedigo is their only son.

Emma Eugenie Pedigo married Chester Bullard Gravely (see Gravely family). Lewis Gravely Pedigo married Caroline Martin. J. Edward Pedigo married Lilly Turner (see sketches).

DR. LEWIS GRAVELY PEDIGO

Should anyone in several counties of Southern Virginia ask to have pointed out the man holding the highest rank as a diagnostician, specialist in many lines of medical practice and one having a thorough understanding of his profession, the honor would no doubt be accorded Dr. Lewis Gravely Pedigo, of Roanoke, Virginia.

The subject of this sketch is the elder son of Captain John F. Pedigo and Martha Gravely Pedigo, of Leatherwood, Henry County, Virginia. Manifesting a decided inclination for literary pursuits at an early age, he was sent to Salem College, entering that institution at the age of fourteen years, and graduating at eighteen, with an A. B. degree and after four years received his A. M. degree.

Deciding upon the practice of medicine as his life work, he entered the University of Virginia, received a certificate of distinction from the University and practiced as an undergraduate for twelve months, then entered the University of New York and secured his M. D. degree in six months. In a class of two hundred he was outranked by only three.

Dr. Pedigo practiced for some time in Henry County, making his headquarters in Martinsville and at Leatherwood. Desiring a broader field, he located in Roanoke but the failing health of his father made it imperative

DR. LEWIS GRAVELY PEDIGO

for him to return to Henry County and give his father the care that could not otherwise be obtained.

Some time after his father's death, although his practice in Henry County had been well established, he returned to Roanoke and resumed his practice there, also taking a leading part in other activities. He was at the head of the Board of Charities for a number of years, and has been much sought as a lecturer and teacher of Bible classes. He is a leading member of the Presbyterian church.

Dr. Pedigo married Miss Caroline Martin, of Franklin County, who had been an instructor in the high schools of Roanoke for some time. She now has charge of a department in the Salem, Virginia, High School, and is a most efficient and popular teacher of English.

Their library, containing an extensive collection of rare books, is a prominent feature of the home and affords great pleasure to both, especially to the doctor, whose health at present renders it necessary for him to give up some of his usual activities and confine his practice for the most part to his office, which he maintains in his home.

J. EDWARD PEDIGO, OF HENRY COUNTY, VIRGINIA

J. Edward Pedigo, younger son of Captain John F. Pedigo and Rachael Gravely Pedigo, received his education in the local schools of Leatherwood, Ruffner Institute, in Martinsville, and Blacksburg College. His inclination was for a life of activity, the professional fields did not appeal to him.

For some time he served as mail clerk on the Danville and Western Railroad, running from Danville, Virginia, to Stuart, Patrick County. Later he became connected with the United States Tobacco Company and was very successful, being promoted to department manager of a large territory, superintending a number of salesmen.

Mr. Pedigo's wife was Lilly Turner, daughter of Captain Murray Turner, of Stuart, Virginia. On her maternal side she was descended from the prominent Rangeley family.

The family of Mr. and Mrs. Pedigo included one daughter and two sons, namely: Lois, Weir Rangeley and Aubrey Turner.

Lois possesses the beauty and vivacity which bespeak her French ancestry. She married Dr. R. J. Ford, of Charleston, West Virginia. The two sons, Weir and Aubrey, developed into brave and patriotic men, both serving in the World War, on the soil once trodden by their French ancestors.

They returned in safety after the close of the war and are engaged in business, Weir in Birmingham, Alabama, and Aubrey in Charleston, West Virginia.

Weir married Eva Hester, of Georgia, and Aubrey married Ruth Street, of Alabama.

J. Edward Pedigo, after many years of residence in West Virginia and New York City, returned to his native county where he has hosts of friends and for the present makes his home in Ridgeway, near Martinsville, Virginia.

THE PEDIGO FAMILY OF PATRICK AND HENRY COUNTIES, VIRGINIA

There are two branches of the Pedigo family, one, the descendants of Robert Pedigo and the other the descendants of Edward Pedigo, the two brothers who came to Virginia from Maryland, formerly from France.

Abel Pedigo, descendant of Edward Pedigo, born 1770. He married Susannah Ray, born 1774. Their children were: Lewis, Daniel, Elijah, Churchill, Mary Elizabeth and Docia.

Lewis Pedigo was born in Patrick County, Virginia, near Elamsville, 1794, but later moved to the section known as "The Hollow," from the fact that a large expanse of land is in a bowl shape, enclosed by broken hills and mountains. Like many of the people of the earlier times, Lewis Pedigo married young. His wife, too, Sarah Harbour, was very young, being scarcely sixteen years of age at the time of their marriage. They lived on a farm and reared a large family. The names of the children are as follows: Henry Clay, Albert Gallatin, John Harden, Ira Pulaski, David Floyd, Abram L., Joseph Read, Norborne Elijah, Mack Robert, Benjamin Franklin died in infancy. The daughters were: Caroline Matilda, Susan Joyce, Louisa Elizabeth and Mary Bethenia.

Henry Clay Pedigo became a distinguished jurist in Harden County, Texas. He married there, but there were no children born of this union. Ira P. spent many years of his life in Texas. He married Mrs. Ann Smith, and one son, Bruce, was born to them. They returned to Virginia and spent the last years of their lives in Henry County, Virginia. D. Floyd Pedigo was a physician and practiced medicine both in Ohio and Henry and Patrick Counties, Virginia. He married Miss Sallie May, of North Carolina, and, after spending many years in Ohio, came back to his old home in Patrick County, with his children, his wife having passed away. The children were: Elizabeth, who married Walter Taylor, and have, for many years, made their home in California. Manie married Joseph H. Bondurant and lives in Patrick County, where Mr. Bondurant owns large tracts of land. Mack

Robert Pedigo made his home in Patrick, where he passed away a few years since. Joseph R. and the three sisters were unmarried, living on a large farm and taking much interest in reading and all the affairs of the day. All of that generation have passed away.

JOHN HARDEN PEDIGO

John Harden Pedigo, descendant of an old and historic French family, was born in Patrick County, Virginia, November 13, 1823. He spent most of his life in Henry County, his home being for many years near Spencer, Virginia, where he owned large tracts of land. He moved to Martinsville, in 1892, where he spent the remainder of his life. He was married to Miss Eleanor Cornelia Davison, in 1855, and they reared a large family, nine reaching maturity. One little daughter passed away when eleven months old.

Mr. Pedigo mastered civil engineering and law, and until the waning strength of greatly advanced years forced him to give up active work, he gave much time to surveying and the settling up of large estates.

By reason of his strong native qualities, his broad intelligence, and an excellent English education, as well as the uprightness of his character, he was always a man of prominence and influence in the affairs of the county. With his rare sense of humor and keen discernment of the foibles, as well as the good qualities of others, he loved a jest at the expense of his fellows, but those who knew him well realized the depth of kindness in his heart and the real charity of his judgment in the appraisement of his fellow men.

His strict sense of integrity and high sense of honor, his independence and strength of character, were among the qualities which earned and held for him the respect and esteem of those who knew him.

Mr. Pedigo died at his home in Martinsville, Virginia, September 30, 1920, and was survived by four daughters and three sons, Mrs. John W. Edwards, Oklahoma City; Mrs. F. B. Norfleet, Washington, District of Columbia; Mrs. W. H. Shultz and Miss Virginia Pedigo, of Martinsville; Messrs. R. E. and M. H. Pedigo, of West Virginia, and John H. Pedigo, of Walla Walla, Washington. Mrs. Pedigo passed away eight years before and a daughter, Mrs. B. T. Jones, and N. E. Pedigo, a son, passed away a short while before Mr. Pedigo's death.

Of the children of this family, Eleanor Conway married John W. Edwards, of Jefferson City, Missouri, later of Oklahoma City (see sketch). Anne Maury married Frederick B. Norfleet, of Washington, District of Columbia, a daughter and son were born to them, Cornelia and Maury F.

Jessie Davison married Warwick H. Shultz, of Augusta County, Virginia, now connected with the Norfolk and Western Railway with headquarters in Winston-Salem, North Carolina, where they make their home. They have one son, John Warwick. Sallie Lewis married Benjamin T. Jones, of Martinsville, Virginia (see Jones family). Virginia G. Pedigo, now of Winston-Salem, has spent much time in educational work in Missouri and in Virginia. R. E. Pedigo was engaged in mining in West Virginia for some time and M. H. Pedigo was an architect and builder, also for some time has been an insurance adjuster with a business covering a large territory. He married Virginia Marshall, of Henry County, and they have reared a family of two sons and two daughters, viz.: Ethel, who married first, Johnson Wootton, of Farmville, Virginia, who passed away several years ago. Her second marriage was to Jesse Lewis, of Bluefield, West Virginia. William B. married Eva Tinsley. He is a dentist and located at Pearisburg, West Virginia. Horace, the younger son, is an expert accountant and lives in Bluefield. Anne, the younger daughter, married Thomas Bryan and they make their home in Greensboro, North Carolina.

HONORABLE ABRAM L. PEDIGO

Honorable Abram L. Pedigo was one of Henry County's most distinguished citizens. He was a man of brilliant mind, strong convictions and irreproachable character. He was a strong Union man and when Virginia seceded, not being in sympathy with the movement, he went to Ohio and located at Hillsville, where his marked ability and faculty for making friends won the confidence of the people and he was elected mayor. After the War he returned to Henry County, Virginia.

He was a Republican, and was probably the only man who had a part in the making of two Virginia Constitutions. When the first was made, Honorable C. Y. Thomas, of Martinsville, member of Congress, was a member of the convention and took an important part in drafting the instrument. He and Mr. Pedigo were close friends and he frequently consulted him, and when the Constitution was completed, not a small part of it was due to the wise judgment of Mr. Pedigo.

He was a member of the General Assembly from Henry County in the '80s. He received the nomination for the State Senate but the election was carried by the Democratic Party and the late H. G. Peters, then of Henry County, later of Bristol, Tennessee, was declared elected.

When the time came to elect a member of the Constitutional Con-

HONORABLE ABRAM L. PEDIGO
OF
Henry County, Virginia

vention in 1898 to represent Henry County, the choice fell upon Mr. Pedigo, his ability was recognized by Democrats as well as members of his own party, and he was placed on some of the most important committees. He occupied a prominent position in the convention being the leader of the minority. He died at his home in Martinsville in 1908 at the age of seventy years.

JOHN HARDEN PEDIGO, OF WALLA WALLA, WASHINGTON

Upon reaching manhood, John H. Pedigo, Jr., son of John H. and Eleanor C. Davison Pedigo, decided upon law as his profession and realizing that, although "there is always room at the top," the rungs of the ladder in old Henry County were filled with climbers and newer fields would offer better opportunities for a successful ascent.

Mr. Pedigo joined an uncle, W. S. Davison, his mother's brother, who had gone to the beautiful City of Walla Walla, Washington, and established a law practice. After completing his law course, Mr. Pedigo was admitted to the bar in 1895, and practiced as a member of the law firm of Pedigo and Watson. Since then he has filled various offices amongst them, Vice President and General Attorney for the Walla Walla Valley Railroad; the Northern Pacific Railway Company; Attorney for the First National Bank of Walla Walla.

Mr. Pedigo married Miss Clara Harris, of Ogden, Utah, and they occupied a very attractive home in Walla Walla. Mrs. Pedigo died in 1920, being survived by her husband and several brothers and sisters.

MRS. ELEANOR C. PEDIGO EDWARDS

(From an Oklahoma Daily Newspaper)

Better romances than have ever been written rub elbows in the family portfolio of a prominent woman of Oklahoma City. Mrs. Edwards is a descendant of Alfred the Great of England, and of the French Louis. "I never say which Louis" she said, "because some of them were such scoundrels." Mrs. Edwards' mother was a descendant of the Madison family, and can be traced back to the senior Mrs. Madison. The name Eleanor was given to the eldest daughter in each family after the time of "Nellie Madison," the president's sister, who married Major Isaac Hite. Eleanor or Nellie Hite married Cornelius Baldwin; then in direct line there were Eleanor Davison, Eleanor Pedigo, the subject of this sketch, Eleanor Edwards and Eleanor Moerchel.

Mrs. Edwards has a relic among many others that would delight the heart of an antique collector—two frames, with glass to protect the fabric, hold pieces of hand embroidery that formed the dress Nellie Madison wore to the inauguration of her brother as President. The fabric is covered with elaborate eyelet work all handmade, and they say that the little lady danced the minuet with exactly nine petticoats swirling around her ankles.

The subject of this sketch is the eldest daughter of the late John H. and Eleanor C. Pedigo. She was born in Martinsville, Virginia, and was educated in the private select school of the late Miss Mary Wade, in Martinsville. Her parents having moved to the country, she spent several years at the country home, and taught several terms in the public schools. She was married to Mr. John W. Edwards, of Jefferson City, Missouri. Later the family moved to Oklahoma City, at which place Mr. Edwards was engaged in business and where Mrs. Edwards is now making her home. Mr. Edwards passed away in 1916, and was survived by four sons, children of his first wife, who was Miss Clay Lockett, and one daughter and two sons, children of the second marriage. The stepsons of Mrs. Edwards have been a source of great pride to her. George Lockett is a prominent lawyer in Kansas City, Missouri. Edward became a successful business man in Louisiana. Arthur is an attorney at law in Oregon, and Warren and the sons, John and Maury, and daughter, Mrs. H. H. Moerchel, of Mrs. Edwards make their homes in Oklahoma City. One little daughter, Mabel, died before the family left Jefferson City.

THE PEDIGO FAMILY

Albert Gallatin Pedigo, second son of Lewis and Sarah Harbour Pedigo, was born in Patrick County, Virginia, in 1821. He married Lucinda Harbour and they reared the following children, viz.: Rufus C., Benjamin F., A. Lincoln, Cordelia, Rosa, Pensie and Laura. The family moved from Patrick County to Floyd many years since, and later to Vinton, Virginia.

Benjamin F. has been a successful attorney at law, remaining at Floyd Court House for the practice of his profession. His first wife was Lelia Kirby. Two daughters were born to them. His second wife was Pattie Ross, a very popular teacher of Patrick County.

A. Lincoln married Daisy Tucker, and one son was born to them, Kenneth. Mr. Pedigo was a druggist in Vinton, Virginia, for many years, but later has engaged in contracting and building.

Rosa died in early youth and Laura married William M. Brown. Her death occurred a good many years ago. She was survived by her husband and an infant daughter. Pensie died in early life.

JOHN HARDIN PEDIGO
OF
Walla Walla, Washington

The family of Albert Gallatin Pedigo and Lucinda R. Pedigo are as follows: Rufus Clay married Ruth Pamelia Ross; Cordelia H., Thomas Martin; Benjamin first, Lelia Kirby, second; Pattie Ross; A. Lincoln, Daisy Tucker; Laura, William M. Brown; Theodora V.; Millard Filmore; Penciannah.

Rufus Pedigo and Ruth Ross Pedigo are the parents of three children: Josephine, who married Orren Clay Harper; Edgar, Della Floyd; Harry, Clara Stanley.

Benjamin S. Pedigo and Lelia Kirby Pedigo were the parents of two daughters: Elizabeth and Josephine. A. Lincoln and Daisy Tucker Pedigo have one son, Kenneth Styne.

CORDELIA PEDIGO MARTIN

The history of few women of this age can compare with that of Cordelia Pedigo Martin for true, unselfish devotion to duty, industry and energy. At an early day she taught school in rural districts in Floyd and Patrick Counties, and in North Carolina, always ready to assist in the upbringing and education of her younger sisters. She married H. C. Martin, of Sandy Ridge, North Carolina, and continued her work of teaching as well as keeping house and making a home for her husband. Upon the death of her sister, Laura, she took the infant daughter, Pearl, and cared for her as only a mother could. In the meantime, Mr. Martin died and Cordelia's father also, so with her adopted daughter this brave woman went to Vinton to live with and care for her aged mother. Pearl grew to womanhood, a beautiful girl, and married Ross McGhee. After a short while Mrs. McGhee died leaving an infant daughter. Cordelia Pedigo Martin again opened her arms and received the little orphan, giving her a mother's care until the little girl was ten or twelve years of age when her father, having married a second time, provided a home for her. Mrs. Martin's mother, Mrs. Lucinda Pedigo, having died at the advanced age of ninety-eight, and she, having suffered a paralytic stroke which renders her unable to continue an active life, sits at home usually with some relative as a companion and in her bright, cheerful way takes a lively interest in reading, keeping up with the current events of the day and enjoying the many friends who take great pleasure in visiting her.

THE PEDIGO FAMILY

Daniel Pedigo, son of Abel Pedigo and Susannah Ray Pedigo, was born in Patrick County in 1798. His son, James Selden Pedigo, was born in 1828.

Daniel Thomas Pedigo was born in Surry County, North Carolina, in 1871, his one brother, now dead, was named Jimmie. His sisters, Pocahontas and Phoebe, are living, one in Bluefield, West Virginia, and the other in Pulaski.

Daniel Thomas Pedigo reared six children, three daughters and three sons. Two of the daughters, Louise and Lennie, have clerical positions in a government office in Washington, District of Columbia.

The other children of Daniel Pedigo were: Barber and Charles, and the twin sisters were Polly and Melissa.

THE PEDIGO FAMILY OF PATRICK COUNTY, VIRGINIA

Abel Pedigo born 1770, Susannah Ray Pedigo, 1774. Their children were: Lewis (1794), Daniel (1798), Elijah (1800), Churchill (1802), Mary (1806), Elizabeth (1808), Docia (1811).

Elijah Bluford, son of Daniel Pedigo, had a son, Elijah Bluford, and his children were: James Henry, Melissa Elizabeth, William Abram, Charles Selden, Benjamin Barber, Emily Agnes, Sarah Ann, Amanda Perkins and Robert Lovelace.

WILLIAM ABRAM PEDIGO

William Abram Pedigo was born in Patrick County where his boyhood was spent. He later moved to Franklin, then to Roanoke, Virginia, in which place he served as postmaster for several years, then engaged in the real estate business, which was quite profitable at that time as the city was growing rapidly. Mr. Pedigo was genial and popular and had many loyal friends in his community. His wife was, before her marriage, Julia Ann Moore, and they were the parents of the following children, viz.: Alice Moore, Lucy Katherine, Walter Raleigh, Edmund Stewart, William Bluford and John Alvin.

Alice Moore married Elias M. Herringdon, a prominent business man, of Roanoke, Virginia, who on his maternal side was connected with the Ball family of which Mary Ball Washington was a member.

Mr. and Mrs. Herringdon are the parents of two daughters: Mary, who married Henry G. Sites, son of D. P. Sites, a prominent wholesale merchant and stationer, of Roanoke; Julia Herringdon, the younger daughter, a beautiful and charming young girl, met a tragic death in an automobile accident.

Walter Raleigh Pedigo, eldest son of W. A. and Julia Moore Pedigo, after receiving his education in the schools of Roanoke, was appointed Secretary to General Fitzhugh Lee and served with him through the Spanish-American War.

Lucy Katherine married Percy G. Camden, a business man of Roanoke. Both Mr. and Mrs. Camden are ardent nature lovers, and are developing a country place a few miles from the city where they cultivate a variety of flowers, fruits, etc. Mrs. Camden has decided literary tastes and takes an active interest in clubs. William B. married Attaway Francis, of Roanoke, and Edmund S., Mamie Hicks, of North Carolina.

DESCENDANTS OF DANIEL PEDIGO OF PATRICK COUNTY, VIRGINIA

The sons of Daniel Pedigo were: James Selden, Abel, Barber and Charles. His daughters were Mary (Polly) and Melissa. The family were landowners and lived near Elamsville.

Daniel Thomas Pedigo, son of Selden Pedigo, and his brother, James (deceased), were born in Surry County, North Carolina, but the family returned to Patrick. Selden Pedigo's daughters were Pocahontas and Phoebe.

THE PENN FAMILY

(Data copied from the New York National Historical and Genealogical Society)

The Penn family is of English origin, the chief sources of the name being from "Inar a Fold." Another theory is that the name came from (originally) the Altic topographical word "pen," signifying a conical top, generally along with hills, as penchride—pen and "skel fill pen."

From the English, Burke County, Penn, spelled Penne (in the Thirteenth Century), situated on an eminence from which can be obtained views of many countries, was derived indirectly the first part of the name Pennsylvania, named after William Penn, the Quaker, whose family originally came from that parish.

On the Hundred Rolls of the Thirteenth Century list appear the names William de la Penne, of County Norfolk, John de la Penne, of Burkshire, and Adam de la Penne, of County Oxford. Families bearing this name are found in Counties Gloucester, Wills, Sommersetshire and Dorset.

Since the arrival of the Penn family in America, various of its members have married into families of distinction and honor. One who bore marked distinction was William Penn, founder of the province of Pennsylvania. He

was born at Tower Hill, London, October 16, 1644, son of Admiral William
Penn, 1629–70, and grandson of Captain Giles Penn (of English Navy), of
a Gloucestershire family.

The earliest mention of the Penn family in Virginia is found in Clement's
"Penn Family in Virginia," where the following items occur: 1621, Robert
Penn, age twenty-two years, passenger on the Abigail, to Captain Matthews'
plantation, James City County. 1635, William Penn, age twenty-six, passenger on "Merchant's Hope" to Virginia. We find William Penn first in old
Rappahannock, in that part which later became Westmoreland and Essex,
and in order to identify its members in later years, it is necessary to know
something of the formation of the counties. Caroline County was a part of
King and Queen in 1727, when Drysdale Parish, in which the lands of the
Penn family were situated, fell to the newly formed county. Formerly Caroline was also a part of Essex and King William Counties and before King
William County was taken from King and Queen, 1704, King and Queen
bordered on Essex County, the latter having been created from Old Rappahannock.

Westmoreland County is just opposite and across the Rappahannock
River from Caroline, and it was nothing unusual for grandsons of William
Penn to have crossed into King and Queen County, where records show
that John and George Penn lived.

William Penn, the Quaker, was twice married and had several children,
but from none of these can be traced the Penns of Virginia. The William
Penn, who is believed to be the American ancestor, is first on record as a
co-patentee of John Walker of a tract of land lying on Corotoman Creek.

THE PENN FAMILY

The Penn family, from the earliest times of the settlement of Patrick
and Henry Counties, occupied a prominent place as patriotic citizens.

The first to come to this state was Moses Penn, who settled in Caroline
County. His wife was Catherine Taylor, and they were the parents of the
following children: Frances, George, Philip, Gabriel, Abram, William
and Moses.

Frances Penn married a Rucker, and spent her life in Patrick County.
No children survived. Philip Penn had several daughters, who married
into the Lee, Pendleton and Cabell families.

Gabriel Penn was a soldier in the Revolutionary War, and was promoted
to Colonel of the Amherst Militia, serving until the surrender at Yorktown.

Colonel Abram Penn married Ruth Stovall (see sketch). Their children were: George, Lucinda, Gabriel, Horatio, Polly, Greenville, Thomas, Abram, Jr., James, Luvenia, Edmund and Philip.

The home of Colonel Abram Penn was three miles north of Martinsville. George Penn (1770), married a Miss Gordon, of Manchester, and moved to Louisiana. Lucinda Penn married Samuel Staples. Gabriel Penn married Ginsey Clark, of Patrick County. Horatio Penn married Nancy Parr, and moved to Mississippi.

Polly Penn married Charles Foster. Their home was in Patrick County, where their lives were spent. Greenville Penn married Anna Leath, of Manchester. One son, Gabriel, was born to them. His second wife was Martha Read, of Bedford. They reared several children.

Thomas G. Penn (1781) married Frances Leath, of Manchester. His second wife was Christine Kennerly, of Amherst County. During the War of 1812 he was Captain of the Minute Men.

Abram Penn, Jr., married Sallie Critz and moved to Tennessee. James Penn (1785) married a Miss Leath, of Manchester. His second wife was Polly Shelton, of Henry County. Their home was in Patrick County. Luvenia Penn died in childhood. Edmund Penn married Polly Ferris and moved to Kentucky. Philip Penn (1792) married Louise Briscoe, of Bedford County.

III. Gabriel Penn, son of Greenville Penn (1814), married Susan L. Franz. Two sons were born to them, William Leath and John Edmund.

Joseph G. Penn (1831), son of Thomas Penn, of Patrick County, who lived at Poplar Camp, original home of Abram Penn, who was a soldier in the Civil War. He was captain in 1865, and was taken to Point Lookout where the men suffered terribly. After his release he returned to Henry County. He engaged in the manufacture of tobacco very successfully and spent the rest of his life there. His wife was Ruth Shelton, daughter of Peter Shelton, prominent citizen of Henry County. Their children are: John T., Magdalen, Annie, Edwin G. and Sallie. Sallie Penn married H. D. Vickers, prominent citizen of Roanoke. They are parents of one son, Penn Vickers.

John T. Penn married Anna Bowe, of Richmond, Virginia, and they have made Martinsville their home. Mr. Penn was for many years engaged in manufacturing tobacco. Mrs. Penn has taken a leading part in social activities and is a member of the patriotic societies. The family is composed of Mr. and Mrs. Penn and three daughters. Natalie, who married Claybrook

Lester, son of Mr. and Mrs. A. J. Lester, of Martinsville. Bowe and Anne belong to the younger social set and take a lively interest in its activities.

Annie Penn, daughter of Joseph G. Penn, married White Blair, a successful business man of Martinsville. After her death he married Mrs. Magdalen Penn Dillard, sister of his first wife. They later moved to Texas where they still reside.

Edwin G. Penn married Laura Hughes Hairston (see sketch of Mrs. Penn). One son, Edwin, Jr., is their only child.

William Leath Penn, son of Gabriel Penn, was born in 1834. His wife was Priscilla J. Tatum, granddaughter of General Joseph Martin. They moved to Roanoke in 1898. The members of this family are: William F., Hugh C., Ernest G., John Harrison, Hattie M., Mary Tatum, Susan Letitia and Robert Leath. Robert Leath Penn married Margaret Moore, of North Carolina; Hugh C., Jennie Carson; Ernest G., Annie Penn; Hattie M., Peter L. Zentmeyer.

COLONEL ABRAM PENN

Abram Penn was born in Amherst County, in 1743. He was a nephew of John Penn, a signer of the Declaration of Independence.

He was in the campaign against the Shawnee Indians and was in command of a company at the Battle of Point Pleasant, in which the Indians were defeated, October 10, 1774.

Three years later he enlisted as a captain in the Continental Army from Amherst County. In 1779, after two years of distinguished service, he was promoted to colonel. Soon after this he was granted a furlough and moved to Henry County, settling on Beaver Creek, three miles north of Martinsville's present site, which was his home thereafter.

On his return to the army he was commissioned a colonel of militia, and sent back to organize a regiment in this sparsely settled region out of which all of Patrick and Henry and a part of Franklin Counties were carved.

During the winter of 1780 and 1781, he organized the first and only organized body of troops that went from this and the adjoining counties. He was in charge of this regiment when it marched to General Greene's assistance, and took part in the battles of Guilford Court House and Eutaw Springs, and finally, after being in other battles, was at the surrender of Cornwallis at Yorktown, in October, 1781.

Colonel Penn was a man of resolute purpose, magnetic, with a vigorous intellect and a commanding presence. When one considers how he gathered up men from this section, drilled them into soldiers and fought them like veterans against the British, he is in a class by himself and should be forever honored as the highest type of patriot in the wilds of the forest primeval.

He died in 1801, and was buried at Poplar Grove, in Patrick County. To his descendants he left his sword, brought back from Yorktown, a muster roll, and a name that will be cherished by his countrymen throughout the ages.

COLONEL GEORGE PENN

Colonel George Penn, of Revolutionary fame, son of Colonel Abram Penn, for several years represented the senatorial district in the General Assembly of Virginia of which Patrick County formed a part. He was a member of the Senate when the celebrated resolutions of 1798 and 1799, which formed the basis upon which the platform of principles that bore the Republican Party, under the leadership of Mr. Jefferson, into power was erected, were passed. Mr. Penn took a leading part in their discussion and in their final passage.

He was among the few men who had the honor of receiving the unanimous vote in his district during a canvass of no ordinary activity and excitement.

He was one of nine brothers, all men who were highly respected, seven of whom filled the office of Justice of the Peace during that period of Virginia history when the magistracy was graced by the finest gentlemen of the land, a class of men who had no superiors in their day and generation; they filled an office which Mr. Madison and Mr. Monroe, after their retirement from the presidency, did not feel it beneath their dignity to accept and hold until the days of their death.

THE PENN FAMILY OF HENRY COUNTY

Greenville Penn, was a son of Colonel Abram Penn. His son, Peter Philip, was the father of Rufus G. Penn, who married Elizabeth Spencer, daughter of J. Harrison Spencer. He was United States Consul to Vancouver during Cleveland's administration, and died while serving in that capacity.

The following are the names of the children of this family: Walter Lee, Arthur, Wade, H. Carter, William Spencer, Birdie, Annie, Champe, Lucy Dillard, Hartley and Mary Dillard.

Walter Lee Penn spent the early years of his life in business with his uncle, D. W. Spencer, of Spencer, Virginia. He later moved to Martinsville, Virginia, where he engaged in the mercantile business with L. C. Claybrook. Later he became associated with the Pannill Textile Mills.

Mrs. Penn, before her marriage, was Caroline Lightfoot Lee Dillard, daughter of Dr. John R. Dillard and Mrs. Adele Lee Dillard. She possesses the charming, gracious manner inherited from generations of cultured people and the home of Mr. and Mrs. Penn is one of the most hospitable in the community. The family circle consists of Mr. and Mrs. Penn and two sons, Walter Lee and John Redd, two of Martinsville's young business men.

Mrs. Penn's first marriage was to Mr. Charles Wilmut, of Dallas, Texas, who died a few years after their marriage.

Birdie Penn married first, Dr. William Pendleton, of Floyd County. Three children were born to them. Hailes Janney, who died in early youth; Elizabeth married Andrew Lewis Micou, direct descendant of General Andrew Lewis. Mr. and Mrs. Micou make their home in Radford, Virginia. Mary Spencer Pendleton married Luther Hunt Davis, of Oxford, North Carolina. Mr. Davis is a descendant of John Penn, signer of the Declaration of Independence.

Some years after the death of Dr. Pendleton, Mrs. Pendleton married Richard Watson Lindsay. Mr. Lindsay died a few years since.

THE PENN FAMILY OF PENN STORE

The Penn Store community, which developed into an important village with the tobacco factories, stores, etc., owned exclusively by the Penn family, was close to the Henry County line. Mr. Thomas Jefferson Penn, son of James Penn, was the principal founder. His sons, who had large interests in the tobacco and mercantile business, built attractive homes and Penn's Store or "Pennville" became a beautiful and important village. The sons of Jefferson Penn and Lucinda Catherine Penn were: Frank, who married Annie Spencer, daughter of Harrison Spencer, prominent manufacturer, of Spencer, Virginia; Greenville married Kate Rucker, of Lynchburg, Virginia; James married first, Sallie Pemberton, of Richmond, Virginia; second, Sallie Johnson, of Alabama; John Penn married Annie Bethel, of Danville; Samuel, Birdie Watt, of Reidsville; George, Stella Gilmer, of Abingdon; Thomas (unmarried); Jennie married Peter Penn; Pattie, Thales Penn; Lillie, John Rison, of Danville, Virginia; Kate, Robert Bass; Annie died in early life.

In order to expand the already prosperous and extensive business, the members of the Penn family moved to larger cities. The larger places offering better facilities.

Frank Penn moved to Reidsville, North Carolina, where he established a lucrative business and a handsome home. The family circle included the following children: Kitty May, Daisy, Pearle, Harrison, Jefferson, Charles, Anita, Frank, Jr., Jennie Lind and Mattie Irving.

Of the surviving children of Frank Penn and Annie Spencer Penn, two sons, Jefferson and the late Charles became very prominent business men of Reidsville, North Carolina. Charles married Miss Edrington; Jefferson married Miss Schoellkopf, of Buffalo, New York. Mr. and Mrs. Penn have developed a fine estate a few miles from Reidsville, with a house that is most attractive and unique. The name given this unusual place is "Chinquepenn Lodge," and Mr. and Mrs. Penn dispense hospitality to a large circle of friends including many from other states, as well as North Carolina.

THE PERKINS FAMILY OF PATRICK COUNTY, VIRGINIA

Joseph Franklin Perkins was born in Surry County, North Carolina, and at the age of twenty-one years moved to Stuart, Patrick County, Virginia, where he spent the remainder of his life.

He took much interest in public and civic affairs. He died at the age of fifty-nine years (1913). His wife was Minnie Morton Cheatham, daughter of William Cheatham, of Lynchburg, Virginia, and Mildred Bishop Cheatham, formerly of Charlottesville, Virginia. Mrs. Perkins died at the early age of thirty-three. Her family was of English descent.

There were four children of this union, viz.: Katherine Mildred, now Mrs. Henry Marley, of Greensboro, North Carolina; Lillian Adair, wife of Judge A. G. Lively, of Lebanon, Virginia; Jean Morton, who married Dr. R. S. Martin, of Stuart, Virginia; Mrs. Martin died at the age of thirty-three; Edna, another daughter, died at an early age.

John Russell Perkins was graduated from the Medical College of Virginia, 1904, and after internship in the City Hospital, of Richmond, Virginia, located at Spencer, Henry County, Virginia, where he practiced medicine (as a general practitioner) for nine years. After this he took special work in New York City and was appointed resident physician of the Baltimore Eye, Ear, Nose and Throat Hospital, of Baltimore, Maryland. At the expiration of his term there he located in Winston-Salem, North Carolina (1915), where he has practiced as a specialist in diseases of the eye, ear, nose and throat. From the first, Dr. Perkins gained the confidence and esteem of the public and has been one of the most successful professional men of the community.

Mrs. Perkins before her marriage was Miss Juliette M. Miles, daughter of Dr. James Henry Miles, of St. Mary's City, Maryland. Mrs. Perkins possesses musical talent and an unusual voice.

Two daughters, Anne Worthington Lilburne and Jean Miles, complete the family circle of Dr. and Mrs. Perkins.

THE RANGELEY FAMILY

Patrick and Henry Counties have in many instances been honored by being chosen as the homes of some of Europe's leading families. Descendants of royalty and of the important families of the Old World have settled in these counties and their descendants still live here.

Rangeley, about six miles southwest of Martinsville, in Henry County, was settled by James Rangeley in 1841. He bought large landed estates in Maine and moved there. This section is still known as the Rangeley Region in his honor as were the Rangeley Lakes.

Being of a restless disposition Mr. Rangeley, after living in Maine a few years, left the village of Rangeley and moved to Portland where Mrs. Rangeley's brother, William Newbold, had given her a beautiful home but the climate was too severe, and thus the Henry County estate was chosen for a home.

The children of James Rangeley and Mary Newbold Rangeley were: Henry, James, John, Hannah, Mary and Sarah.

Henry was adopted by his uncle, William Newbold, and remained in England, paying only one visit to America. He reared one son, William.

Hannah married Reid Ayres; Mary married Dr. Noel. There were no children born to either of them.

John married a Miss Webster, a lineal descendant of Daniel Webster, of Ipswich, Massachusetts. Children of this union were: John, Susan Webster, Eliza Caroline and William H. Rangeley.

Two of Mr. Rangeley's sons, John and James, came south before the family did and bought a home together near Stuart, Patrick County, and accumulated much property. They conducted a tannery, a sawmill and store successfully.

James Rangeley III married Miss Weir, of Bangor, Maine. Their children are: James, Joseph, William, Sarah and Anna.

James Rangeley IV married Alice Via. The children of this union are: Dr. Walter, Fred, John, Frank, Clarence, Hattie, Maggie, Lilly, Annie and Carrie.

William married in Texas and reared a large family; Sarah married Murray Turner. Their children were: Lilly, Noel, Harry, Nellie and Edward.

John, the eldest son of John Rangeley, died in the Civil War; Susan Webster married Dr. Robert B. Dandridge. (See Dandridge family.) Eliza Caroline Rangeley married J. C. King. (See King family.)

W. H. Rangeley married Nannie Clanton. The children of this family are: Raynie, John, Annie, George, Alice, Emily, Eliza, William and Nannie.

DR. ROBERT A. READ, OF HENRY COUNTY, VIRGINIA

In the light of present-day conditions it is difficult to understand why such outstanding men of the medical profession such as Dr. Read, Dr. John Dillard, and others would have confined their practice to rural districts unless we recall that in their time the day of "specialists" had not reached its height and the people of culture and means lived in the country where the large estates were in cultivation and the tobacco factories formed the nucleus of villages of considerable size and importance. Such a community was Spencer near which the Read home was located, surrounded by many acres of good farm land.

Dr. Read's practice extended over two or more counties and, good roads being practically unknown, made his rounds on horseback, carrying peculiarly constructed saddle bags containing rows of mysterious looking vials and measures as the doctors not only wrote prescriptions, but filled them from those queer-looking saddle bags.

With a big, kind heart and deep human sympathy, often concealed under a gruff exterior, Dr. Read's life was one of true service.

His wife was Miss Frances Pendleton, of Richmond, Virginia, a woman of rare culture and refinement and a homemaker of the finest type, she and her sister, Miss Charlotte Pendleton, who made her home with her, were known far and wide for their splendid hospitality.

A family of eight children were reared in this home, one of whom was Dr. Manson Read, who married Frances Pendleton and moved to Missouri.

John Read engaged in the mercantile business in Halifax County, but later moved to Martinsville where he spent the rest of his life. His wife was Josephine Withers, daughter of United States Senator Withers, of Wytheville, Virginia. Two sons were born to them.

Charlotte Read married Rev. R. A. Haymore, a Missionary Baptist minister, and survived him for several years. Mr. and Mrs. Haymore were the parents of two sons, Robert and Nathan. Virginia Dare Read married a Mr. Thurman; Janet Read, Reed Taylor; Frances, a Morefield; Louisa Read owns and lives at the Read homestead, Taylor P. Read also makes his home there, he married Lizzie Boyd and during her life was engaged in business in Halifax County; later he returned to Henry County and married Lizzie Royall. Of the first union two sons were born, Austin and Pendleton. Five daughters and two sons compose the family of Mr. Read and his second wife, viz.: Mary, Frances, Mattie Lee, Josephine, William Brumfield, Holcolm and Lucile.

WILLIAM BRUMFIELD READ

William Brumfield Read, son of Taylor P. and Lizzie Royall Read, is one of Henry County's young men of whom the community may well be proud. When the World War demanded the service of many young Americans, Brumfield joined the forces and served with honor and faithfulness through the terrible scenes of horror.

Before joining the army, Mr. Read had been engaged in railroad and telegraphic work but after the close of the war and his return he accepted a responsible position in the First National Bank, of Martinsville, Virginia, and has since made his home there.

He married Maria Pannill, daughter of the late E. J. Pannill and Eliza Reamey Pannill. Mrs. Read is a young woman whose sterling qualities of character, vivacity and charm have won for her a large circle of friends.

THE REAMEY FAMILY OF HENRY COUNTY, VIRGINIA

The Reameys, of Henry County, Virginia, are descendants of the de Remis, of Picardy, France. The first to come to America of which there is any record available was Abram de Remi, descendant of Count Ravul de Remi. He settled near Richmond, Virginia, and reared one son of whom no definite record is available.

Daniel "Remie" was a Revolutionary soldier and served with General Washington at Valley Forge. He belonged to the Augusta County Militia and was promoted to colonel. Two sons, John and Daniel, and a daughter, Elizabeth, survived him. Elizabeth Reamey married Benjamin Jones and they spent their lives in Henry County. John Reamey married a Miss Pace, and their home was near Irisburg, Henry County.

Daniel Reamey II married Susan Starling, a granddaughter of Major John Redd. They taught school in Henry County and as there were few schools at that time—the public schools not having been established, Mr. and Mrs. Reamey were highly appreciated as educators.

They were parents of five sons and three daughters, Mary Ann, who married Honorable C. Y. Thomas (see sketches); Peter R. Reamey, a distinguished physician, scholar and soldier; Kate, who married Dr. James Semple; Overton Redd Reamey married .... Smith; Henry Clay died in the Civil War; Lucy married James Smith, of Ohio; John, Elizabeth Hairston; Daniel Webster, Elizabeth Redd Dillard, daughter of Colonel Overton R. Dillard.

Daniel Webster Reamey was a patriot and a soldier, he was a member of the Tenth Virginia Cavalry and fought in the Confederate Army under General William Henry Lee.

Daniel W. Reamey married Elizabeth Redd Dillard and their children are as follows: Overton, James, Frank, Daisy, who married first, Hairston Morris; second, James D. Hodges; Annie married Wilcox Brightwell; Lyne married Thomas Scott.

Lucy Reamey, after acquiring a good education and fitting herself to teach, was an instructor in the Martinsville schools, then she accepted a position in the schools of Newbern, North Carolina, where her ability was recognized and she was soon promoted to the principalship of the high school of that place. She married Colonel........Thompson, and after his death she decided to become a nurse and took thorough training to fit herself for that work. Mrs. Thompson is now the head of a staff of nurses and instructor in a hospital in Lynchburg, Virginia.

PETER R. REAMEY, OF HENRY COUNTY

Peter R. Reamey, as a child, showed the most marvelous aptitude for mastering studies far beyond the ability of even the brightest pupils of his age. When twelve years old he had finished the Greek and Latin courses offered in the colleges. After that he was a student at Sullivan's College at

Columbus, Ohio. Choosing medicine as his profession he entered the Virginia Medical College, and graduated in 1850, after which he began the practice of medicine in Henry County.

When the Civil War broke out he joined the Confederate Army and trained the first company, The Henry Guards, that went from the county in 1861. This company, with Captain Reamey leading, was assigned to the Twenty-Fourth Virginia Regiment under General Jubal Early, and fought in the battles of Bull Run, Manassas and many others.

After peace was declared he returned to Martinsville, Virginia, and resumed his practice.

Dr. Reamey's first wife was Sallie Waller and their children, Starling, Jack, George, Florence, Henry, Eliza and Sallie. His second wife was Bettie Keesee and three children were born to them, Walter, Mattie and Jasper.

THE FAMILY OF DR. PETER R. REAMEY

The children of Dr. Peter R. Reamey are: Eliza, who married Edmund Pannill (see Pannill family); Henry, who married Elsie Gravely, and for many years they have made their home in Danville, Virginia; Sallie, who has been a popular teacher for a number of years; Florence, Jack, Starling and George.

George Reamey married Julia McLennan and reared three daughters, Grace L. Reamey, one of the Henry County girls whose talents and the ability to use them have made her work a marked success. She entered upon a business career in Roanoke, Virginia, later accepting a clerical position in one of the government departments in Washington, D. C., which she fills with great success. Lizzie Reamey married .... Pollard; Mary Ryland Reamey married Howard S. Holland. They are the parents of three children, Jack, George and Allen.

THE REDD FAMILY OF HENRY COUNTY, VIRGINIA

Major John Redd came to Henry County from Albemarle. The home of the family was Belleview in the Marrowbone Valley. He was born in 1755, and came to this county about the time of the Revolutionary War. His wife was Mary, daughter of Colonel George Waller, and their children, Annie, James Madison, Elizabeth, Martha, Waller, Edmund Burwell, Polly, Lucy Dabney, Dr. John Giles, Overton and Carr.

Annie Redd married Thomas Starling; James Madison, Ruth Penn Staples; Elizabeth, Peter Dillard; Martha Redd married first, a Clark, then James M. Smith; Waller Redd married Keziah Staples, he was the second county clerk after the Revolution; Polly Redd married Jack Fontaine; Lucy Dabney Redd married first, John Taylor Wootton, second, William Bullard; Dr. John Giles Redd married Apphia Carter; Overton Redd married Martha Fontaine. Edmund Burwell Redd was born about 1795 and married Sarah Ann Fontaine, their children were: Martha, who married John Francis Wootton; Mary, Dr. John Wayt; Celestia, Samuel Caldwell; Nannie, Patrick Fontaine; Ella, John Wattlington; Dr. John Giles, Marion Fontaine; William Spottswood, Mary Taylor Wootton; James S. Redd, Sallie Hairston, daughter of Tyler Hairston, of Red Plains; Edmund Madison Redd married Annie Richardson.

James S. and Spottswood Redd were soldiers in the Civil War and both rose to the rank of captain.

The children of W. Spottswood and Taylor Wootton Redd were: Lucy, Edmund, Pattie and Ella.

THE REYNOLDS FAMILY OF PATRICK COUNTY, VIRGINIA

Among the many distinguished families of Virginia a prominent place is accorded the family of Harden W. Reynolds, whose ancestors for several generations were natives of Virginia, having acquired and owned large tracts of land in Patrick County, Virginia, and in Stokes County, North Carolina.

Harden W. Reynolds was the son of Abram D. and Mary Harbour Reynolds; his only brother, David, died in early life, unmarried.

The family of this prominent couple consisted of five sons and three daughters who reached maturity, although one daughter, Katherine, died soon after being graduated from a college in Danville, Virginia. Several other children died in early childhood.

The Reynolds home, beautiful and spacious, attractively situated near the mountains, surrounded by lovely lawns and gardens, was a fitting background for a happy and prosperous family.

Besides being the owner of a large estate, Captain Reynolds was a successful tobacco manufacturer and was in every way a notable figure in his community. His sociability, kindness of heart and hospitality, were known not only in Patrick County but throughout a large section of the country as well. He was a leading member of the Methodist Church, and his religion was a part of the web of his daily life. Most people close the day with prayer, when they pray at all, but in the Reynolds home the day's activities were ushered in with prayer and thanksgiving.

Of the cardinal virtues it is said "The greatest of these is charity." Many who were poor and in trouble were ever ready to testify that they had never gone empty-handed from his door.

After a long and useful life, Harden W. Reynolds passed away at the age of seventy-one and was laid to rest in the family cemetery, close by the home he loved.

He was survived by his wife and seven children, Major A. D. Reynolds, of Bristol, Tennessee; R. J. Reynolds, William N. Reynolds and Walter R. Reynolds, of Winston-Salem, North Carolina; H. H. Reynolds, of Patrick County, Virginia; Mrs. A. M. Lybrook, of Stuart, Virginia, and Mrs. Robert C. Critz, of Winston-Salem, North Carolina.

Major Abram D. Reynolds, eldest son of Harden W. and Nancy Cox Reynolds, was born in Patrick County, Virginia. (See sketch.) After the close of the Civil War, he joined his father in the tobacco manufacturing business in which they were very successful. After five years he decided to locate in Bristol, Tennessee, at which place the rest of his life was spent.

Major Reynolds was widely known as a man of the finest type, splendid and dignified in appearance, and deeply religious, he was one of the supporters of the Methodist Church, which has since been named in his honor. He was very successful in business and was a blessing to the community in which he lived. He died at his home in Bristol in 1926 and only two weeks later his wife who, before her marriage, was Miss Senah Hoge, of Giles County, Virginia, followed him to the grave. Thus they were "united in death as in life."

The account of the services rendered his home and country by Major Reynolds is given in this volume and is of especial interest and value as the writer had the inestimable privilege of receiving the manuscript from Major Reynolds shortly before his death. The closing paragraph of his will is quoted here as it is a keynote to his character:

"With implicit faith in God who rules over nations and individuals, and whom I have tried to serve, I commit my children to his care. It has been my policy to treat my Creator as my partner in all my business affairs, and it is my desire that my children will not dissolve this partnership that

CAPTAIN HARDIN W. REYNOLDS
OF
Patrick County, Virginia

I entered into with Him in 1875, and which partnership has been so satisfactory to me all along through these many years, and I pray that they will
acknowledge His leadership and follow the teachings of His spirit and that
they will use the small inheritance which I have been able to provide for
them under His leadership, without abusing the trust.

"All I have is His and I simply commit a part of it to my dear children
to use for their comfort and His glory and for the upbuilding of His kingdom,
asking Him to help them, multiply and increase their faith and to supply
His grace that they may meet me in Heaven."

Major and Mrs. A. D. Reynolds were the parents of eight children,
one daughter and seven sons, Harden William, who married Ethel Romfh;
Joseph Hoge, Scottie Brown; Abram David, Grace Smith; Richard S.,
Louise Parham; William Walter, Myrtle Anderson; Clarence Kelly, Edna
Dalrymple; John Harbour died in infancy; Sue Sayers married Dr. T. F.
Staley, a prominent physician of Bristol, Tennessee. Mrs. Staley received a
liberal education and has done much in the way of literary work. She is
the author of "Soul Savers," a very interesting and instructive work composed of sketches of great religious leaders. Mrs. Staley has traveled extensively and is a leader in social and literary circles in her community.

The only child of Dr. and Mrs. Staley is their son, T. F. Staley, Jr.,
who is a young man of fine business ability, now holding a position with the
Reynolds Metals Company, of New York. He married Miss Shirley Hanes,
a popular and accomplished young woman of Bristol.

RICHARD JOSHUA REYNOLDS, OF WINSTON-SALEM, NORTH CAROLINA

Richard J. Reynolds, second son of Harden W. and Nancy Cox Reynolds,
spent his early years in the home of his parents in Patrick County, Virginia.
His father's large estate and successful tobacco manufacturing business
and the distribution of the manufactured products furnished ample opportunities for a liberal business education.

Private schools were available for members of the family, and as they
reached the proper age they were sent to the best colleges to continue their
studies. Notwithstanding the fact that R. J. Reynolds had no particular
taste for books, after attending the neighborhood schools he entered Emory
and Henry College and spent some time as a student in that institution.
He is said to have been a marvelous mathematician and worked out a
system that enabled him to make calculations with amazing accuracy.

For several years Mr. Reynolds traveled in the interest of his father's business. In those days distributors did not speed from one point to another in automobiles, stopping over night at the best hotels, but traveled in well-loaded wagons drawn by stout horses or mules, often over rocky or muddy roads and camped when it was not convenient to find a lodging place in which to spend the night. There was time, however, for thinking and studying human nature and working out problems with intelligence and originality.

After reaching the age of twenty-five Mr. Reynolds' wonderful genius began to be recognized. He having sought new fields for the expansion of business, decided upon Winston, now Winston-Salem, as a desirable location and in 1876, the R. J. Reynolds Tobacco Company was organized.

Mr. Reynolds was a man of such impressive personality that once having met him he would not be forgotten, tall, dark, with keenly discerning eyes, his marvelous executive ability was apparent to anyone spending a few minutes with him in his place of business. Orders or instructions were given clearly and tersely and no doubt were seldom misunderstood or disobeyed.

Mr. Reynolds was married to Katherine Smith, of Mt. Airy, North Carolina, a woman of great charm, intelligence and ability. They occupied a palatial home in the city for a number of years, after which a large estate was purchased about four miles northwest of the city and under the direction of Mrs. Reynolds, a beautiful and very spacious home of the English type was built. Extensive grounds, with acres of woodland carpeted with grass and flowers and a succession of gardens, present vistas of beauty to the visitor. A large lake and swimming pool are additional attractions. The name, "Reynolda," was given the estate and is preëminently appropriate and euphonious.

A village of considerable proportions was added, an attractive church (Presbyterian) was built, also a manse for the minister stationed there, a good school building, shops and cottages for employees. Farming, dairying, stock raising and horticulture, superintended by experts, make "Reynolda" one of the finest estates in North Carolina.

Mr. Reynolds died in 1916 and was survived by his wife and four children, two sons and two daughters, Richard J., Jr., Z. Smith, Mary Catherine and Nancy.

The elder son, Richard J., has given a great deal of time and attention to aviation and is interested in the development of aviation fields. He has traveled in foreign countries extensively.

Z. Smith Reynolds is also interested in aviation, and has made a record as one of the youngest aviators on long-distance flights. Mary

Katherine married Charles Babcock and they make their home in New York. Nancy married Henry Walker Bagley and also lives in New York. Many features of the city of Winston-Salem are monuments to the splendid public spirit of Mr. and Mrs. R. J. Reynolds. Not only the great business, furnishing opportunities for employment to thousands and fortune-building to many, but gifts to the city are memorials which will stand for the benefit of future generations.

Several years after the death of Mr. Reynolds, Mrs. Reynolds married J. Edward Johnston. She passed away in 1924, being survived by Mr. Johnston and an infant son.

HARDEN HARBOUR REYNOLDS, OF PATRICK COUNTY, VIRGINIA

Harden Harbour Reynolds, after engaging in the tobacco manufacturing business in Winston, North Carolina, for a few years, decided, after the death of his father, to return to the home in Patrick County, Virginia, and manage the large estate, no other member of the family remaining there. He married Annie Dobyns, of Patrick County, and with a family of four children, a lovely, spacious home and congenial friends, life reached the fullest satisfaction for one of his optimistic temperament, jovial disposition and the capacity for the enjoyment of rural life.

The death of his eldest daughter, in childhood, brought deep sorrow to the family.

The elder son, Harden, lives in Winston-Salem, and has a position with the R. J. Reynolds Tobacco Company. He married Katherine Dobyns and they have an attractive home in the city.

The younger son, William, makes his home in Patrick County, with his mother.

Lucy, the daughter who was just reaching womanhood, passed away in 1929, after a brief illness.

Harbour Reynolds died in 1927, after an illness of several months, mourned by a large circle of relatives and friends.

WILLIAM N. REYNOLDS, OF WINSTON-SALEM, NORTH CAROLINA

William N. Reynolds, one of Winston-Salem's most distinguished and popular citizens, was born in Patrick County, Virginia, and spent his boyhood in the home of his parents, Captain and Mrs. Harden W. Reynolds. He attended the schools in that locality until he entered Trinity College. After his graduation he joined his brother, R. J. Reynolds, whose tobacco manufacturing business was established in Winston, and by his talents and close application to business as a member of the firm, while still a young man became a leader in the management of the colossal manufacturing business, being elected president upon the death of his brother, R. J. Reynolds. He filled that position for a number of years and when he decided to resign was made Chairman of the Board of Directors.

Mr. Reynolds is widely known in this country and abroad and is admired and esteemed for his many splendid qualities of mind and heart. If the story of what Mr. Reynolds has done for them could be told by employees and many others, it would fill volumes.

The advancement of popular education has claimed his interest, and he has given largely to the Cox School in Stokes County, North Carolina, established as a memorial to his mother, and the Harden Reynolds school in Patrick County as a memorial to his father. Through his munificence the latter school has been enabled to enter the list of accredited high schools.

Mrs. W. N. Reynolds, who was Miss Kate Bitting, member of one of Winston's most prominent families, is possessed of a wonderful personality and perpetual vivacity. She is a leader in social circles, very prominent as a leader in the society of the Daughters of the American Revolution and many other activities. She is the donor of a magnificent organ to Colonial Hall in Washington, D. C., a splendid dormitory to Salem College, this city, in memory of her mother, Mrs. Louise Bitting, and Sunday school building, a memorial to her father, to the First Presbyterian Church, of which both she and Mr. Reynolds are leading members.

Mr. and Mrs. Reynolds occupied a handsome home in the city for a number of years but "Tanglewood," a magnificent estate several miles from the city near the Yadkin River, is a favorite place of residence. There Mr. Reynolds' fine horses, splendidly cultivated land, the home in an ideal location, surrounded with wonderful gardens and magnificent trees, some of them centuries old, and where unstinted and gracious hospitality is dispensed, make it one of the outstanding places in the state.

Mr. and Mrs. Reynolds also have a winter home in Orlando, Florida, where they spend a portion of each year.

WALTER ROBERT REYNOLDS, OF WINSTON-SALEM, NORTH CAROLINA

In the very prime of life Walter R. Reynolds passed away at his home in Winston-Salem in the year 1921. Beloved by hosts of friends and

WILLIAM N. REYNOLDS
Winston-Salem, North Carolina

relatives, with large financial interests, life seemed to have reached its fullness when his death came as a great blow to the community and deep sorrow to relatives and friends. He was the youngest son of Harden W. and Nancy Cox Reynolds. His early years were spent in Patrick County, where he attended school until he entered college.

After finishing college Mr. Reynolds engaged in business with his father and when his father's death made it unnecessary to continue the business in Patrick County, he went to Bristol, Tennessee, with other members of the family and became interested in the business established by his brother, Major A. D. Reynolds. Later he decided to join R. J. Reynolds in the manufacturing of tobacco in Winston, North Carolina, in which he was very successful, but his fortune, like that of the other members of that noted family, did not "just happen," but was accumulated by industry, close application to business and vision in the investment and care of means acquired.

Walter R. Reynolds had the faculty in an unusual degree of making lifelong friends. In one instance, especially, his friendship for and constant association with Robert L. Williamson, a prominent tobacco manufacturer of this city, has been likened to that of David and Jonathan or Roland and Oliver. He took a deep and abiding interest in "just folks," often making inquiries about people one would have supposed he had forgotten.

THE ROSS FAMILY OF PATRICK COUNTY, VIRGINIA

The Ross family is of Scotch origin as the name clearly indicates. Three brothers came from Ross Shire, Scotland, and settled in Albemarle County, near Charlottesville, later one came to Patrick County. The names of the early settlers were: David, Daniel and Charles.

David Ross lived and died near Elamsville, Virginia. His children were as follows: Peyton Ross, whose home was about five miles east of Elamsville, Robert, Lewis, Joseph, Wiley, Nathaniel, Ben, James, Jefferson and Samuel. Samuel Ross married Esther Harbour and lived near Elamsville.

The daughters were: Jane Ross Loudy; Polly Ross Anderson, who went to Grayson County to live; another daughter, Docia, died young.

Peyton Ross's children (first marriage) were: Ruth Ross Pedigo, wife of Rufus Pedigo, Draper, Virginia; Delancy Ross McGhee, first wife of Green McGhee, Center, Virginia, Pencie Ross McGhee, second wife of Green McGhee; Annie Ross Wright, wife of Washington Wright, Vinton, Virginia; Augusta Ross Nowlin, wife of Joseph Nowlin, Franklin County, Virginia; and Joseph Ross.

Second marriage: Lizzie Ross, Vinton, Virginia; Ada Ross Cox, Dodson, Virginia; Pattie Ross Turner, deceased; and Ben P. Ross, Draper, Virginia.

Hardin Ross lived and died five miles east of Elamsville. His wife was a Miss Coward.

William Ross's children were: Abe and Tom Ross. Children of Hardin Ross were: Mrs. Ella Ross Rakes, deceased; Mrs. Alice Ross Hooker, wife of W. C. Hooker, Elamsville, Virginia; William T. Ross, M. D.; C. H. Ross, M. D., died at Bassett, Virginia; Jefferson D. Ross, Elamsville, Virginia; Creed Ross, deceased; Burwell Ross, Tennessee.

Children of Daniel Ross are as follows (first marriage): Susan Ross Turner, wife of Crawford Turner, Buffalo Ridge, Patrick County, Virginia; Augusta Ross Jefferson, wife of Ed. Jefferson, Charity, Virginia; Kizzie Ross Connor, Onie Ross Connor, Dicie Ross Prillaman, Franklin County, Virginia; Martha Ross Kenley, Tennessee; Burwell Ross married Miss Lester; Buck Ross married Helen Burnette; Charles Ross married Miss Foster.

Second marriage, Joyce Harbour. D. Lee Ross married Bettie Jamerson; Mack D. Ross married Letitia Harbour; Bettie Ross married Dr. George Clark and lived near Stuart, Virginia.

Children of Charles Ross (first): Charlie Ross married . . . . Jamison and lived near Ferrum, Franklin County; John Abe Ross married Ida Hooker and lived at Woolwine, Patrick County, Virginia; Pattie Ross Nowlin, wife of J. A. Nowlin, Woolwine, Virginia; Fannie Ross Akers, wife of Samuel R. Akers, Woolwine, Virginia. Buck Ross went to California. George Ross also went to California. The two last mentioned accumulated considerable wealth. Neither married.

NOTE—When Daniel Ross came to Patrick from Franklin County, and settled at what is known as the Mack Ross place, four miles from Elamsville, the settlements were so sparse that he never saw a single living person, except his wife, for six weeks after moving there.

WILLIAM MIRANDA—SARAH ANNE (HARREL) SCHOOLFIELD

ISSUE

1. Martha Anne, b. 1836; d. 1861....married..............Edward Mitchell
2. John Harrel, b. Feb. 13, 1838; d...married, Oct. 17, 1860...Susan Barbara France
3. Mary Emeline, b. Jan. 29, 1841;
     d. Jan. 27, 1916............married, June 10, 1860..Dr. William Wade Morris
4. Laura Virginia.................married......................................
5. Sarah Elizabeth, b. Mar. 27, 1843..married..............1 James Penn France
                                                           2 James H. Carter
6. William Henry, b. April 5, 1848...married..............Elizabeth Palmer
7. James Edward, b. Sept. 18, 1850;
     d. Aug. 6, 1902............married, Jan. 22, 1873..Lucy Dillard France
8. Robert Addison, b. May 7, 1853;
     d........ 1931..........married..............1 Annie Redd France
                                                   2 Belle Vass
                                                   3 Sadie Vass Van Wagnen

William Miranda Schoolfield was born June 6, 1804, in Lynchburg, Virginia. He died June 12, 1855, in Henry County, Virginia, and is buried at the old homestead, near Mt. Bethel, Virginia. His father was John Schoolfield, son of Samuel David and Rachel (Greaves) Schoolfield. His mother was Sarah Thurman. On December 11, 1834, he was married to Sarah Anne Harrel, born March 15, 1812, in Bertie County, North Carolina. His brothers were: Henry Ormond and James Lorenzo. His sisters were: Emeline; Anne; Martha, who married George W. Humphreys, and Betsy.

THE SCHOOLFIELD FAMILY

The first of the Schoolfield family to settle in Henry County were: David and Rachel Schoolfield. There were eight children of this family, Samuel, John, Enoch, Benjamin, Sydney, Jane, David and Aaron.

John, the second son, was born 1765. He married Sarah Thurman. Their children were: Henry Esmond, James Lorenzo, Emmeline Ann, Martha and William Miranda. Martha married Geo. W. Humphries. One son was born to them.

William Miranda married Sarah Ann Harrell, of North Carolina. Joining the conference soon after his marriage, he was sent to the Henry Circuit. He was one of that group whose mission it was to foster the seeds of Methodism sown by Francis Asbury. When his services were over he settled permanently in the western part of the county near Mt. Bethel Church, where he preached once a month during the remainder of his life.

The children of this family were: Martha Ann, John Harrell, Mary Emmeline, Sarah Elizabeth, Laura Virginia, William Henry, James Edward and Robert Addison.

John Harrell Schoolfield was widely known and highly esteemed throughout the community in which he lived. He was the owner of a tobacco manufacturing plant, with a good store, carrying general merchandise, and the usual adjuncts of a village, shops, etc., which spring up where there is a tobacco factory as a nucleus. The Schoolfield home was situated a short distance from the business buildings, in a level plat of several acres. The country roads, converging, formed the lines of a triangle. The lawn was ornamented with English boxwood, other shrubbery and large shade trees, making the place very attractive.

Mrs. Schoolfield was Susan France, daughter of Captain Carter France, a prominent citizen of the county. The Schoolfield family occupied a prominent place in business, social and church circles. John H. Schoolfield, with his brother, R. Addison, his partner in business, moved to Danville, Virginia, and established an extensive textile industry. The village that sprang up was called "Schoolfield."

Robert Addison Schoolfield married first, Annie France, daughter of Captain Carter France, second, Belle Vass, and later he married Mrs. Saidie Vass Van Wagnen.

Mary Emmeline married Dr. W. W. Morris, a popular physician and Confederate soldier (see Morris family).

Martha Ann married E. R. Mitchell; Sarah Elizabeth married first, James France, second, James Carter; Laura Virginia was not married; James Edward married Lucy France, he was a successful business man, but joined the ministry and became a noted evangelist.

The children of John Harrell Schoolfield and Susan France Schoolfield are as follows: Eugene (unmarried) died when a young man; Kate married Dr. Tillett, a Methodist minister; Annie May married Dr. R. Bruce James; Hughes, Tina Cleveland; Henry, Sue Bethel; Daisy, Archie Keene; John, Miss Frank Hanes.

Robert Addison Schoolfield and Annie France Schoolfield were the parents of one daughter, Bland, who married Howard Church, of Pennsylvania.

The children of William Henry Schoolfield and Mary Elizabeth Palmer Schoolfield are as follows: Pettis married Martha Gardner; Sallie Annie, Jesse C. Roberts; Lelia Mae, James Dudley Glass; Pauline Josephine, Ford H. Wheatly; Stella, J. Nathan Gardner; Emma Susan, W. Lawrence Clark.

JAMES EDWARD SCHOOLFIELD—LUCY DILLARD (FRANCE) SCHOOLFIELD

ISSUE

1. Orin Cottrell, b. Aug. 15, 1875; d. April 10, 1900. . married. . .Annie Bloomfield Gamble
2. Lilly, died in infancy
3. Sue France
4. James Edwin
5. Harrison Carter, b. June 4, 1884; d. Dec. 12, 1918
6. John Hannon, b. Nov. 4, 1887. . . . . .married. . .Rose Briscoe
7. Samuel Addison, b. Feb. 11, 1889; d. Feb. 4, 1930
8. William Lovick, b. Sept., 1891; d. Jan. 28, 1922
9. Lucille Dillard

James Edward Schoolfield was the son of Rev. William Maranda and Sara Anne (Harrel) Schoolfield. He was born in Henry County, Virginia, September 18, 1850, and died in Danville, Virginia, August 6, 1902. He married Lucy Dillard France, January 22, 1872, the daughter of Captain Harrison Carter and Katherine (Penn) France. At an early age he went to Lynchburg, the city of his forbears, to live with his uncle, Henry Ormond Schoolfield, whose home stood on the site now occupied by the Young Men's Christian Association. His youth and early manhood were spent there. In 1871, he went to Richmond to live, where he was connected with the firm of Watkins and Cottrell. Later he moved to Danville, Virginia, to engage in business for himself, which city he made his home.

J. E. S.

The tobacconists in Danville were using colored labor almost exclusively in their factories. The white people were staggering under the poverty caused by the Civil War. T. B. Fitzgerald and J. E. Schoolfield conceived the idea of utilizing the water power of the Dan River to establish a cotton mill, to give employment to the white people in that section.

With this idea in mind, in 1882 a historic meeting was arranged, to be held in the home of J. E. Schoolfield, to which the following named gentlemen were invited: J. H. Schoolfield, B. F. Jefferson, R. A. Schoolfield and H. W. Cole. Plans were discussed and a stock company was formed. The Riverside Cotton Mills came into existence, a company which, in time, was to develop into one of the largest and most prosperous plants in the new industrial south. T. B. Fitzgerald was its first president. James Schoolfield was a director and a stockholder as long as he lived, and very active in shaping the policies of the mills in the last century, a service for which he was well equipped, due to his wide business experience. It was while surveying and planning the site for the Dan River Plant that he contracted typhoid fever, his last illness.

The town of Schoolfield was named for him and his brothers, J. H. Schoolfield and R. A. Schoolfield, who became vice president and president of the company in the course of their careers.

He served a term in the Legislature of Virginia, declining reëlection.

In association with the late Major W. T. Sutherlin he took an active part in the building, and was an able director of the Danville and New River Railway, now a part of the Southern, which opened up the Counties of Patrick and Henry to further development.

An enthusiastic Mason, he was one of those responsible for the erection of a new Masonic Temple in 1902.

J. E. Schoolfield and his wife were known for their social and civic activities and their philanthropies, which were as varied as they were numerous. Their spacious home, which is now occupied by the Young Women's Christian Association, was "open house," to all who knew them. It was rare indeed when there were no guests within its hospitable walls.

The Danville Register, August, 1902, says of him: "He was a man of varied and vigorous powers. Built in a large mould, his was a commanding figure and an influential personality. Truly, he was one of our leading citizens, a man whom all honored and delighted to follow. In all his enterprises he achieved a gratifying success."

His life was beyond reproach, and when he gave up a successful business to become a lay minister, it was because he loved God and loved people. The spiritual and the personal meant more to him than the material. He loved mankind. Among his last papers were found these words: "Say to all the world, I love them."

> *"And yet, for us all man could give*
> *He gave, with that which never dies,*
> *The gift through which great nations live,*
> *The lifelong gift of sacrifice."*

Mrs. Lucy Dillard France Schoolfield was born in Henry County, December 6, 1850; married James Edward Schoolfield in January, 1872. Although Mr. and Mrs. Schoolfield had a large family of children, because of their love and sympathy for people, for years they shared the comforts and luxuries of their beautiful home with ten other people. Mrs. Schoolfield was the architect of her beautiful home and garden, and when she and Mr. Schoolfield moved into their new home, it was dedicated to God. When the children were grown up and left the parental home, Mrs. Schoolfield could no longer have the care of such a large, expensive place and the home was sold to the Young Women's Christian Association. It is always a source of joy and comfort to Mrs. Schoolfield that her beautiful, dear old home is still being used for the cause of Christ and so well cared for. It is her sincere prayer that it may continually be used for this glorious cause, until the second coming of the Lord Jesus. According to prophecy this great and all-important event is now 2,000 years on the way. Many prophecies lead us to believe that the second coming of Christ is right at the door. For many years Mrs. Schoolfield was president of a Gospel mission, and services were held almost nightly and very often a noonday service. Many weary travelers professed conversion and were refreshed by hearing the ever-lasting words of eternal life, from the Book of Books, the Holy Bible. Mrs. Lucy France Schoolfield bought a beautiful house and lot on Grove Street, Danville, Virginia, and set aside a sum of money for the purpose of establishing a Bible School (undenominational), but was so hindered this was not successful. She was for years president of a rescue home and two day nurseries, has been active in D. A. R. work, U. D. C., and is a member of the Woman's Christian Temperance Union and Young Women's Christian Association. Mrs. Schoolfield is near eighty-two years old, and has been studying a correspondence Bible course for some time.

THE SCHOTTLAND FAMILY

Among the prominent men who have come to Martinsville and established a successful business enterprise are M. H. and N. H. Schottland, of New York.

Their mirror factory has added greatly to the list of manufactured products of which Martinsville is a center.

Mr. M. H. Schottland married Purnell, daughter of C. D. and Lucy Brown English, and they have a beautiful and commodious home on Starling Avenue. This interesting family circle includes five charming daughters.

N. H. Schottland married May, daughter of George M. and May Brown Finley. They have a lovely home also on Starling Avenue and two children complete the family circle.

THE SHACKELFORD FAMILY OF VIRGINIA

The Shackelford family records go back to Baron Jacques Laforte, a nobleman of Normandy, who came to England, in 1066, as an officer in the army of William the Conqueror. From this ancestor sprang the English and Virginia Shackelfords.

Francis and Sarah Shackelford were of the Virginia family and the family Bible of their son, John, is still in possession of the descendants.

A prominent member of this distinguished family is Dr. Jesse Martin Shackelford, of Martinsville, Virginia, who for many years has practiced medicine in Martinsville and the surrounding counties, giving hope, relief and cheer to the sick and comfort and tenderness to the dying.

Dr. Shackelford and his son, Dr. John A. Shackelford, have established a hospital in Martinsville, which is an outstanding institution in the town and is patronized to its full capacity, not only by local people but by many from other localities.

Dr. Shackelford married Miss Frances Armstrong, a woman of high intelligence and attractive personality. She is the daughter of the late John Armstrong, of Henry County.

Dr. John A. Shackelford, only son of Dr. J. M. and Frances Armstrong Shackelford, is one of Henry County's most prominent young men. His connection with his father in the hospital at Martinsville has given to that institution two of the ablest surgeons of the state.

After his graduation from the Martinsville High School and College, he spent some time in Johns Hopkins Hospital in Baltimore. He married Margaret Spencer, daughter of the late J. Harrison Spencer and Mrs. Blanche Williamson Spencer.

THE SHACKELFORD FAMILY ASSOCIATION

Due to the long and honored connection of the Shackelford family with this section of Virginia, many descendants here will be interested in the Shackelford Family Association, which was organized at Pintlala, Montgomery County, Alabama, on July 4, 1931, by descendants of George Shackelford (1770–1852) and his wife, Annette Jeter. The purpose of the association is to collect all data possible on the Shackelfords or Shacklefords for the purpose of putting it into permanent form. All descendants are to be included.

The first Shackelford came from England about 1659. There are

Shackelfords in Surry County, England, to-day, in King and Queen County, Virginia, in Missouri, in Texas and Florida.

The association holds reunions annually at Pintlala, on July 4th. All descendants are invited to attend the reunions.

THE SHEFFIELD FAMILY OF HENRY COUNTY, VIRGINIA

Sheffield is distinctly an English name, and the family is of aristocratic lineage, being descendants of a Duke of Sheffield, whose statue stands in Westminster Abbey.

Jesse Sheffield, son of one of three brothers, who came from England, was born in Nottoway County, in 1746, and came to Henry County when a young man. He married Susan Cheatham and their children were: Leonard, Susan, Joseph, Nancy, Nicholas and John.

I. Leonard Sheffield, the eldest, was born in 1779, his wife was Lucy Wootton. He served in the War of 1812 with distinction. The children of this family were as follows: Jesse, Martha Ann, William, Henry, Thomas, James M., John A., Frances Jane, America W., Lucy, Susan, Samuel and Leonard.

Jesse Sheffield was born in 1810. He served in the Civil War. James M. Sheffield was engaged in the historic battle between the Monitor and Merrimac and never fully recovered from wounds received in that battle. Thomas Sheffield settled in Oklahoma. Samuel G. Sheffield, born in 1836, was a lieutenant in the Civil War. He was engaged in the mercantile business in Ridgeway for a number of years, then moved to Martinsville where he continued in business successfully. He married Loula Martin, daughter of Colonel William Martin, of Magna Vista.

Leonard, the youngest of the family, left a son, Leonard III. He has served as postmaster at Spray, North Carolina, and as the popular deputy sheriff of Rockingham, North Carolina.

William A. Sheffield was a large landowner and successful business man. He was a colonel in the Sixty-Fourth Regiment, Twelfth Brigade, First Division of the Virginia Riflemen in the Confederacy.

His home, noted for hospitality, was on Marrowbone Creek and he left his children a heritage of rich lands.

The children of Colonel and Mrs. Sheffield were: Judith Parks, who married B. F. Barrow; Elizabeth, Lyne Starling Thomas; Leonard, Bettie Coan.

John Waddy Sheffield inherited the home of his father which he managed with great success. He died at an early age.

One of his sons was a World War veteran.

THE SHELTON FAMILY OF HENRY COUNTY, VIRGINIA

William Shelton, the founder of the Shelton family, of Henry County, came from Goochland County. His wife was Peonia Critz. Three sons were born to them, William, James and Nathan.

James was born in 1750, his wife was Fannie Allen, daughter of William Allen, of Henry County. Their family included the following children: Pines Henderson, Nancy, Polly and James. Mr. Shelton had the unusual distinction of fighting in the Revolutionary War and the War of 1812. He rose to the rank of captain in the War of 1812, and died in Norfolk.

William married Pattie Dillard, daughter of Colonel John Dillard, of Henry County. Their children were: Peter, John, George, Ruth, Polly and Susan.

Nathan Shelton married Mary Hatcher, and their family included four children: Alfred, Joseph, Judith and James.

Peter Shelton was born in Henry County in 1798. He lived upon a large farm in the Spencer community. His wife was Magdalene Dupuy Watkins, daughter of John Watkins and Wilson Watkins. This large family included six sons and six daughters. Their names are as follows:

William Henderson	married	Nancy Jane Hylton
Sarah Martin	married	Joseph Pannill
John Watkins	married	Road E. Howard
Annie Wilson	married	James S. Martin
Virginia Magdalene	married	Dr. R. R. Robinson
Peter Fowler	married	Laura Howard
Mary Elizabeth		
Ruth Stovall	married	Joseph G. Penn
Susan Louisa	married	John Hill Matthews
Thomas Meade	married	Fannie Clopton
George Hunt	married	
James Buchanan	married	Price

THE SIMMONS FAMILY OF HENRY COUNTY, VIRGINIA

The Simmons family is of English origin, being descended from the Booths and Howards, families of note in England. Their Virginia ancestry includes the Coxes, Webbs, Presleys, McGeorges and Carters, of Henrico County, who are not only distinguished, but are especially noted for patriotism, six of them serving in the Revolutionary War, and fourteen in the War Between the States.

Four members of this family have made their homes in Martinsville, Virginia, having come to this county from Floyd County: Dr. Thomas Simmons located in Martinsville for the practice of medicine; he established a good practice and made many warm friends, but passed away after a few years; Dr. John W. Simmons, one of Martinsville's leading physicians; Mrs. Charles B. Keesee and Mrs. James D. Martin, whose husband died several years since, being survived by Mrs. Martin and two sons, James D. and Simmons. The untimely death of Simmons Martin occurred while he, following the traditions of his ancestors, was in training to serve his country in the World War.

DR. JOHN W. SIMMONS

Dr. John W. Simmons, one of the popular physicians of Martinsville, has a large practice not only in Martinsville, but in the surrounding country. In addition to his skill as a physician, his genial manner and kindly sympathy for the sick and suffering, in every walk of life, has made him respected and beloved by those with whom he comes in contact.

Mrs. Simmons was Elizabeth Morgan, daughter of Captain W. H. Morgan, C. S. A., Floyd Court House. Two sons, Morgan and John, and three daughters, Nancy Lee, Anna and Alice, complete the family circle.

Morgan W. Simmons, a prosperous young business man, of Martinsville, married Miss Margaret Sydnor, of Mt. Airy, North Carolina; Nancy Lee married Leet O'Brien, of Winston-Salem, North Carolina.

THE SMITH FAMILY OF HENRY COUNTY

The Smith family, of Henry County, have for generations occupied a very prominent place in the professional, business and social life of the community.

The founder of the family, Mr. James Moss Smith, was of English descent, and spent a long and useful life in Martinsville. He owned large tracts of land cultivated by slaves in the early times. He was also a merchant and good business man.

His beautiful colonial home, now owned and occupied by his grandson, John Redd Smith, is a landmark of great beauty and distinction. The house, a brick structure, still preserving the perfect colonial type, is surrounded by a spacious lawn with walks bordered by a wealth of the finest English boxwood.

Mr. Smith was born in Halifax County, February 8, 1798. He married Mrs. Martha Redd Clark, daughter of Major John Redd, in 1828. He was opposed to secession, but followed his state. When the Federals were stationed at Martinsville during the Civil War, the Smith home was used as a hospital.

Mr. Smith was commissioner in chancery for many years and settled up more estates in the county than any man before or after him. In one instance a loving cup was presented to him in appreciation of his eminently satisfactory work in settling up an estate and the cup is a valued souvenir greatly prized by his descendants. His ability and fair dealing won for him the respect and confidence of his business associates.

He was an official of the Methodist Church, and so have his descendants been, their combined services being over a hundred years in one organization. He died December 17, 1883.

The children of this union were as follows: John Redd, James Moss, Pattie, Elizabeth and Electa.

John Redd Smith was educated as a lawyer, was admitted to the Henry bar, but both he and his wife, who was Letitia Claiborne, died young. There were no surviving children.

Dr. James Moss Smith was born in Martinsville, in 1830. He attended Jefferson Medical College, in Philadelphia, and graduated in 1854, after which he practiced medicine for many years. He was surgeon in Stonewall Jackson's Army and participated in his wonderful evolutions in the Valley of Virginia. He served as Mayor of Martinsville, and was one of the town's most efficient officers.

Dr. Smith did great service, while Supervisor from the Martinsville District, in securing improved roads. He secured for the making of roads the services of the state convicts, and with the coöperation of the people a new era in road building began and continues to this day. Dr. Smith died

JOHN REDD SMITH
OF
Martinsville, Henry County, Virginia

May 19, 1919, and was survived by his wife and the following children: Charles P., John Redd, Electra and Elizabeth.

Mrs. Smith, who, before her marriage, was Miss Corinna Smith, possessed qualities of mind and heart that in all ages command admiration and respect. Loyal and devoted to her family and friends, she was greatly beloved by the people of the community in which she had spent a long and active life. Her home, before her marriage, was in Petersburg, Virginia.

Pattie Smith, the only daughter of James M. Smith, Sr., married George Isham Hairston, who went into the mercantile business at Ridgeway with John C. Jones and Dr. John Smith. The lands of the three cornered at a point and on this their brick store was built, and is still standing. He owned much land and did extensive farming. Both he and his wife died in early life and were buried at Belleview, the ancestral home of the family.

Charles Purnell Smith received his education, and has practiced medicine in Martinsville and the surrounding country for a number of years. He has taken an interest in political affairs and was appointed postmaster for Martinsville, and served a number of years. He married Nannie J. Brown, daughter of the late Honorable J. R. Brown, and they have reared two sons, John B. and Charles Purnell. John is engaged in mercantile pursuits and Charles is postmaster in Martinsville, Virginia, his home town.

James Moss Smith, son of Dr. James M. Smith, married Mattie Gravely, daughter of the late Frank Gravely, of Danville, Virginia. He passed away several years since, being survived by his wife and three children, two daughters and one son. The elder daughter, Dillard, married Edgar Boatright, of Roxboro, North Carolina. The younger, Mattie Rogers, married Dr. Sydnor, of Farmville, Virginia.

The son, James M. IV, died in early manhood.

Pattie Hairston Smith, daughter of Dr. J. M. Smith, married John Andrew Brown, son of the late J. R. Brown (see Brown family). Her second husband was E. M. Dickinson.

Electra Smith married Herbert G. Peters. Elizabeth Smith married T. N. Barbour, a successful hardware merchant, of Martinsville.

JOHN REDD SMITH

John Redd Smith, son of Dr. J. M. Smith, is a man whose talents and rare gift of oratory made law his logical profession. After finishing the courses given in the public schools of Martinsville, Mr. Smith attended....

He has practiced his profession successfully in Martinsville, and is constantly in demand as a speaker for almost all important occasions, and responds to such requests graciously. His ready wit, gracious manner and unusual versatility afford great pleasure to an audience. Mr. Smith is also a writer of much ability and his articles, some of which are included in this volume, will be of much interest to our readers.

Mrs. Smith was before her marriage, Miss Sallie Reamy Pannill, daughter of Mrs. Eliza Reamy and the late Edmund J. Pannill. They occupy the charming colonial home inherited by Mr. Smith from his father. The home is in a very attractive part of the town and Mr. and Mrs. Smith see to it that the type which is true colonial is preserved in every detail. A son and two daughters complete the family circle in this ancestral home.

William Smith died when quite a young man.

THE SPARROW FAMILY OF MARTINSVILLE, VIRGINIA

Jefferson D. Sparrow, member of the tobacco manufacturing firm of Sparrow & Gravely, was for many years a leading business man of Martinsville, and enjoyed decided popularity in civic and social life. He served as a member of the city council for a number of terms.

His first wife was Belva Mitchell, and three children were born to them, one son, who died in early childhood, and two daughters, Kathleen, who married Alex Mahood, of Bluefield, West Virginia, and Rose, who died after reaching young womanhood. Mr. Sparrow's second wife was Rebecca Kearfott, daughter of Dr. C. P. Kearfott, who survives him. Mrs. Mahood, his daughter, also survives him.

John B. Sparrow has also made his home in Martinsville for a number of years, and has been actively engaged in business. His wife was Gertrude Brown, and their family circle was composed of Mr. and Mrs. Sparrow, two sons, John B. and Kavanaugh, and one daughter, Pamela, who married Spencer Williamson, of Danville, Virginia.

THE SPENCER FAMILY OF HENRY COUNTY, VIRGINIA

The Spencer family was established by an early settler, William Spencer, whose wife was Sallie Parks Hill, daughter of William and Elizabeth

Saunders Hill. There were three children, America, Sallie Ann and David Harrison.

America married Greenberry Nichols, son of Thomas and Sarah Lane Nichols, the latter of a Maryland family; David Harrison Spencer married Mary Waller Dillard, daughter of Colonel Peter Dillard and Elizabeth Redd Dillard; Sallie Ann Spencer married David Allen, of Mississippi.

David Harrison Spencer was one of Henry County's most prominent citizens. He was a large landowner and manufacturer of tobacco, employing hundreds of the colored population, both young and old, in the different departments of the factory with capable white men to direct the work. On his extensive farms, the work was done by negro laborers supervised by overseers. The Spencer factory formed a nucleus for a village as in other localities villages were formed. A store carrying general merchandise was a necessity, not only for the numerous employees, but was patronized by the people of the community. A post office, blacksmith shop, etc., followed.

The eldest son, David William, upon reaching maturity, became his father's partner and the firm, D. W. Spencer & Son, became well known in many states.

After the advent of the railroad, with a station at Spencer, quite an impetus was given to the expansion of the village. A hotel was built, an office for a resident physician, and a number of good homes were built close by. A few hundred yards from the village, the Spencer home "The Homestead," one of Virginia's real colonial homes is situated. The extensive grounds, in a grove of magnificent oaks, centuries old, walks forming a semicircle on either side of the walk leading to the house, all bordered with genuine English boxwood planted ages ago, make this home one of the most attractive in the county.

Besides David William, there were five sons and six daughters of this family, all reaching maturity, namely: Peter Dillard, George Overton, John Dillard, James Harrison, Robert Lee, Elizabeth Annie, Lucy, Mary America, Mattie and Margaret.

Peter Spencer was engaged in manufacturing tobacco in Martinsville for several years. He died there after a few years of successful business. George O. spent his time looking after the farms which he managed successfully. Neither he nor Peter Spencer married. George O. died in his lifelong home a few years ago.

John D. Spencer engaged in business in Danville, Virginia. He married

Annie Clark, daughter of Major William Clark, a prominent citizen of Danville.

James Harrison Spencer engaged in the manufacture of tobacco in Martinsville. He married Miss Blanche Williamson, whose family was very prominent in the business and social life of Burlington, North Carolina, her father being owner of large textile mills in that section. Mr. and Mrs. Spencer established a home in Martinsville, where Mrs. Spencer soon became a social leader and a popular hostess.

The children of this family reaching maturity are: Margaret, Mary Holt, Blanche and James, the only son, who, on the very threshold of manhood, passed away.

Margaret Spencer married Dr. John A. Shackelford, of Martinsville; Mary Holt married Kennon C. Whittle (see Whittle and Shackelford families); Blanche Williamson Spencer married Julian Robertson, of Salisbury, North Carolina, a prominent young business man of that town.

Elizabeth Redd Spencer, daughter of D. H. Spencer, married Rufus G. Penn; Annie married Frank Penn (see Penn family); Lucy Williams married first, Judge John Dillard; second, C. S. Bill, of Snowville, Virginia; Mary America Spencer married H. C. Buchannan, of Alabama. After the death of her husband, Mrs. Buchannan returned to Spencer, her former home, and since the death of her parents has presided over "Homestead," the beautiful colonial home which she inherited. She takes great interest in the affairs of her community, and has been a potent factor in the upbuilding of the school and church.

Mattie Spencer married W. G. Lee, of South Carolina; Maggie married Haile Janney, of Alabama.

John D. Spencer married Annie Carr Clark, daughter of Captain William Clark, of Danville, Virginia.

THE STANLEY FAMILY

One of the best known members of the Stanley family, in Henry County, was Crockett Stanley, who was a highly respected citizen. He served his country as a soldier in the War Between the States, being a member of Company H, Twenty-Fourth Virginia Regiment and served throughout the war. Always interested in public affairs, he was commissioner of revenue for a number of years, and was also a successful farmer.

Mrs. Stanley was Susan Matilda Walker, and the following children were born to them: Robert Hillie, Lucy Matthews, Jessie Roberta, John Walker, Samuel William, Berta Anna and Thomas Bohnson. Robert Hillie, Berta Anna and Lucy Matthews all died before reaching maturity. Samuel William died in 1906. Jessie Roberta married John Reid Aaron; John Walker married Addie Vaughn.

Thomas Bohnson Stanley, while still a young man, has become a prominent citizen of the county. He began his business career as a cashier in the First National Bank of Martinsville, later he accepted a position with the Bassett Furniture Company, of Bassett, Virginia. Continuing in the furniture business with marked success, he built a separate plant near Bassett and with the homes necessary for the workers, shops, etc., a village soon sprang up and the name "Stanleytown" was assumed.

Mr. Stanley married Ann Pocahontas Bassett, daughter of J. D. Bassett. A large and handsome home, upon a beautiful estate, is being developed by Mr. and Mrs. Stanley, near the highway, between Martinsville and Bassett. Mr. Stanley was elected a member of the House of Delegates in 1929.

JUDGE WALLER REDD STAPLES

Honorable Waller Redd Staples was born in Patrick County, Virginia, February 24, 1826. He attended the local schools of that county, and his academic studies were completed at the University of North Carolina and William and Mary College, graduating from the latter with honors.

In 1848, he began the practice of law in Montgomery County, as the junior associate of the Honorable William Ballard Preston, a kinsman. Mr. Preston was soon afterwards chosen by President Taylor, as one of his cabinet advisers, and his necessary absence forced his young associate to assume the heavy responsibilities of the extensive law practice of Mr. Preston.

Mr. Staples was a man possessing a brilliant intellect, was energetic and well equipped for the practice of his profession, so while still a young man he attained a position before the courts and in the community that few men can hope to reach before the meridian of life.

In addition to his close application to the professional duties, he found time for the advancement of his political opinions, and became a recognized leader of the Whig Party. He was elected a member of the House of Delegates from Montgomery County for the session of 1853–54, and although less than thirty years of age, became a leader, his rare gift as a public speaker and debater made him a formidable force in the political canvasses of the state and, in 1856 and 1860, he was a candidate for presidential elector.

After the election, in 1860, he sympathized fully with the great body of southern people who deprecated the transfer of the government of the United States to Republican administration, and shared their apprehension of coming trouble. He was opposed to immediate secession, hoping that the destruction of the Union might be averted, however, when Virginia adopted the ordinance of secession, he was loyal to the state and to the Confederate cause. He was elected by the convention, as one of the four representatives of Virginia, in the provisional Congress of the Confederate States, his three associates being William C. Rives, R. M. T. Hunter and John W. Brockenbrough, and after the adoption of the Constitution of the Confederate States he was, during the continuance of that government, a member of the House of Representatives.

Judge Staples resumed the practice of law after the close of the war, holding his former leading position as a member of the bar. Upon the recovery of the control of the state government, the people of Virginia chose him Judge of the Court of Appeals, and he served through the term of twelve years with distinguished ability.

When his term of office expired, through constitutional limitation, Judge Staples resumed his practice as a private member of the bar and while he made his old county, Montgomery, his home, he was practically a resident member of the bar of Richmond, Virginia, until his death. "He was an enthusiast in his love of his profession."

During the year of 1893-94, he was president of the State Bar Association. The last great public service he rendered was in conjunction with Honorable E. C. Burks and Honorable John W. Riely, as revisors of the Code. The result of their labors was the Code of 1887, and the satisfactory manner in which this duty was performed has been gratefully recognized by the bar and the public of Virginia, and many of his opinions handed down while serving as Judge of the Supreme Court of Virginia have a place in the legal literature of the State.

Judge Staples died on the twenty-first day of August, 1897.

THE AMERICAN OR KNOW NOTHING PARTY

"About 1852-1856, a new party was organized, called by its members the American Party but generally known as the Know Nothing Party.

This name arose from the fact that in the earlier days of the organization it was a secret order and its members when asked any questions about it always answered 'I don't know.' As the name 'American' indicated it was opposed to everything foreign, its watchword being 'America for Americans.' The large increase in the number of immigrants and the looseness with which the naturalization laws were carried out made the restriction of suffrage to native Americans and to those who had resided for a long period in the United States a cardinal doctrine of the Americans. To this was added, at first, opposition to the alleged political influence of the Catholic Church.

"This party grew rapidly and at one time it seemed likely to become a rival to the Democrats; but, dodging the question of slavery, it tried to make nativism a national issue. Where so many voters were themselves immigrants, it was natural that the attempt failed. The party disappeared after the election of 1856."

JUDGE WALLER STAPLES' SPEECH IN THE LYNCHBURG CONVENTION, 1855

After the deliberations of the day were over the Convention adjourned to Friends' warehouse, to listen to the patriotic appeals of distinguished orators. Mr. Thomas Stanhope Flournoy discoursed the audience for about three hours upon the so-called principles of the American Party. Mr. A. Judson Crane, of the Richmond Congressional District, was then loudly called for, but excused himself on account of indisposition, then came Mr. John D. Imboden, of Augusta. Mr. Nathaniel C. Claiborn, of Franklin, was then called for, he appeared, and in his peculiar way, amused the audience for a little while. Then appeared the eloquent, but totally unprepared and off-hand orator, Mr. Waller Staples, of Montgomery. We have read the Honorable Jere Clemens' eulogy upon Henry Clay, likewise the eulogy of the Honorable John C. Breckenridge, also William Wirt's upon Thomas Jefferson and John Adams, but Mr. Staples' off-hand speech before that Convention surpassed and totally eclipsed anything that we, in the most extravagant mood of imagination, could possibly conceive of. If the Know Nothing Party had not just abolished their ceremonies of initiation, etc., we should have looked out for a council as soon as the oration was over.

It is said that John Hampden Pleasants attempted to take down in shorthand the speech of John Randolph, of Roanoke, in the delivery of his eloquent philipic against the administration of John Q. Adams, but the eloquence, pathos and satire of the orator completely entranced him. It was so on this occasion. A reporter from the New York Herald was present, but after hearing a few sentences from the gentleman from Montgomery and seeing his anatomical mien, he threw himself back and appeared, as did the whole audience, perfectly enraptured and bewildered. Virginia has had her Henrys, her Randolphs, her Morrisses, and gave birth to a Clay, but still she has her Staples.

THE STAPLES FAMILY OF PATRICK COUNTY, VIRGINIA

Judge Samuel Staples, of Patrick County, Virginia, was one of the most prominent men of his time. He was a brother of Judge Waller Staples, of Montgomery County, who was preëminent in the legal profession.

The sons and daughters of Judge Samuel Staples were as follows: Abram P. Staples, a distinguished lawyer of Roanoke. Later he occupied the chair of commercial law in Washington and Lee University. His death occurred .... His wife was Sallie Hunt.

Waller Staples, another son of Judge Samuel Staples, studied civil engineering but later decided upon law as his profession, he, too, having made his home in Roanoke. He was elected Judge of the Hustings Court but after some time resigned to resume regular practice of law. He was special counsel for the Norfolk and Western Railway, and was most efficient in cases involving engineering.

He married Miss Trout, of Staunton, Virginia.

Hulda Staples married Edd Moir.

Callie Staples married Joel Daniel and for some time they made their home in Martinsville, Virginia.

COLONEL SAMUEL STAPLES OF PATRICK COUNTY, VIRGINIA

In the early years of the eighteenth century two brothers, Samuel and John Staples, immigrated to this country from England, the former settling in one of the northern states and the latter in Buckingham County, Virginia, where Colonel Samuel Staples, the subject of this sketch, was born in the year 1762.

In the spring of 1781, when barely nineteen years of age, he succeeded in raising a volunteer company in his native county, which was assigned to that division of the army under General Wayne.

He took an active part in the attack made by Wayne, aided by the French under Lafayette, upon Cornwallis on the ninth of July, at old Jamestown, by which a severe blow was inflicted and by which the British commander suffered a great loss. He continued in active service until the termination of the battle of Yorktown, was present at the surrender of Cornwallis and was promoted to the rank of major for gallantry on that memorable day.

Upon the declaration of peace, Colonel Staples moved to Henry and was soon appointed by Major John Redd, then high sheriff of the county, as one of his deputies and was assigned to that portion of the county now Patrick, as his field of operations.

In 1791, an act was passed by the legislature forming a new county out of that portion of the county of Henry, now embraced in Patrick, the new county containing about 500 square miles. The country was very rough and broken, so the duties of the sheriff were laborious and not very profitable.

The site of the present town of Stuart had been selected as the county seat, but not a house had been built and when the court convened for the purpose of electing a clerk, constable and other county officers and recommending a sheriff to be commissioned by the Governor, that august tribunal selected a stout log under a large walnut tree, as a county court bench. The election resulted in the unanimous choice of Colonel Samuel Staples, as clerk of the county court.

The records of the first superior court of Patrick County, October 6, 1809, show that Colonel Samuel Staples was appointed its first clerk, the clerks of both county and superior courts being appointed for life or "during good behavior." Colonel Staples discharged the duties of the two offices continuously, to the entire satisfaction of both bar and county, until May, 1826, when a severe attack of paralysis incapacitated him, forcing him to resign. He died three years later.

Although he was no politician in the broader sense of that term, he usually felt and expressed a deep interest in the political questions of the day, and was a decided Republican of the Jeffersonian School.

In person, he was of full medium height, being near six feet tall, a form erect and commanding, a full forehead with all the marks of a superior intellect. He had received no training but what his own observation of men and things had produced, but for reflection and strong reasoning power he was superior to most men of his community.

He was united in marriage to Lucinda Penn, a lady of rare personal attractions, a daughter of Colonel Abram Penn.

The children of Colonel Samuel and Lucinda Penn Staples were: Abram Staples (see sketch); Colonel John C. Staples; Ruth, who married James M. Redd, of Henry County (one of whose granddaughters was the wife of Judge Stafford G. Whittle).

Colonel Samuel Staples was a man of note in his day, of great personal popularity, scrupulously honest in all his dealings, possessing a sound mind and discriminating judgment. By industry and perseverance, he amassed a large fortune for that day. He was a great sportsman, fond of fishing and hunting, but indulged in those pastimes only when business occupations permitted. His skill as a marksman with his old-fashioned rifle was the subject of wonder and astonishment to the hunters of his day.

Lucinda Staples married Colonel Ballard Preston.

COLONEL ABRAM STAPLES

Colonel Abram Staples, son of Colonel Samuel and Lucinda Penn Staples, was born near the present town of Stuart, March 9, 1793. During his boyhood he attended what is known as the old field schools of Virginia, at the same time assisting his father, who was then clerk of the court, in the discharge of the duties of his office.

At the age of seventeen he was sent to Chapel Hill, the University of North Carolina. While there the War of 1812 broke out between the United States and Great Britain and, fired by patriotism, in the spring of 1812 he returned home and raised a volunteer rifle company and, in the summer of that year, marched to Norfolk and joined the American forces assembled there under the command of General Robert B. Taylor. His company was stationed on Craney Island, a low, flat and bare island at the mouth of Elizabeth River, about five miles below Norfolk, commanding the inward approach from Hampton Roads and on its successful defense depended the safety of the borough, as well as of Portsmouth and the surrounding country.

While there he assisted in that noble and gallant repulse of the British, under the command of the notorious and infamous Admiral Cockburn, whose mission (as he declared) was to lay waste the country, burn, pillage and destroy property, both public and private, and whose boast was that he intended to chastise the Americans into submission. On the twenty-second day of January, 1813, he entered Hampton Roads with an imposing and formidable array of about twenty vessels, consisting of fourteen frigates and transports and with an armed force of four thousand men. The American army consisted of four hundred militia, one company of light infantry and a detachment of thirty men sent from Norfolk by General Taylor. While attempting to go up to that city, he landed about twenty-six hundred men on the island and made an attack on the Americans under the immediate command of Major Faulkner, a gallant and meritorious officer, and was signally repulsed with a loss of four hundred men, killed and wounded, while the loss of the Americans did not exceed thirty.

The writer of this article read some years later a letter, addressed by General Taylor to Mr. Staples, complimenting him and speaking in high terms of the gallantry his company displayed on that occasion. This company, a rifle company, consisting of sixty men, rank and file, was composed of brave, hardy mountaineers such as they were in those days, inured to hardships and privations and accustomed to the use of the old-fashioned, long-bored rifle, with which they were armed. The only uniform in which they were clad was the hunting shirt, made of blue domestic jeans with a frill around the edges, and pants of the same color and material.

Upon the declaration of peace Captain Staples returned to his native county, and soon after was elected a member of the General Assembly, and was reëlected every successive year for a period of eight years. He was appointed on a committee to invite General Lafayette to a dinner tendered by the legislature in the winter of 1824, during his memorable visit to the United States, the first he made after the close of the Revolutionary War.

During his protracted legislative career he took a prominent part in the proceedings and debates of that body and was uniformly appointed on its most important standing committees.

His father having died in March, 1825, and a vacancy existing in both the offices of the county and superior courts, he was elected, by the justices of county court, its clerk, and at the May term of the circuit superior court he was appointed by Judge Fleming Saunders, clerk of that court. Having determined to accept these offices he resigned his seat in the General Assembly.

Few men who ever lived in that portion of Virginia of which Patrick County forms a part ever filled a larger place in public life than Colonel Abram Staples.

By economy, sound practical sense and judgment, he amassed a large fortune. He conformed to the old adage, take care of the small sums and the large sums will take care of themselves, yet he was liberal and very charitable when occasion required. He was fond of reading and during his legislative career collected a good library.

In person he was tall and commanding, with a stout, muscular frame, form and features indicating manly firmness and intellectual vigor. In the spring of 1853, he was suddenly prostrated by an attack of paralysis from which he never recovered and passed away on the twenty-sixth of April, 1853.

THE STARLING FAMILY OF HENRY COUNTY

Thomas Starling came to Henry County as the adopted son of his uncle, Henry Lyne, when sixteen years of age. He was fond of reading and continued his education in that way. He married Annie, the daughter of Major John Redd, in 1903, and maintained a hospitable home. He died in 1852. The children of this family were: Susanna, William, Overton, John R., Elizabeth, Jane C., Lyne and Edmund Thomas.

Edmund Thomas Starling married Mary Anderson, of Prince William County, a sister of the Rev. Robert Anderson, and settled in the southern part of Henry County, on Smith's River. There were four children: Leonard, Annie, Thomas and Ballard.

Leonard Starling was born in 1846, and married Marie Ralls. There was only one child born to them, Leonard, who married Floria Anderson.

Annie Redd Starling married Rex Cabiness. Eight children were born to them: Jack, Roy, Isabel, Annie Redd, Elizabeth Starling and Mary.

Thomas Starling married Permelia Daniel, and reared a large family. Robert, who married Josie Lee Lightsey; Sallie Miller; Elizabeth married James Dabney Estes; Annie Maria, Thomas; Mary Anderson married Dr. Madison Drewry; Alvis Daniel married Mary Withers; Jervis Daniel; and Edmund Thomas married Virginia Robey.

Ballard Preston Starling married Agnes Deslin. Their children are: Edmund, Annie Preston, Hallie Brown and Pattie.

The Starlings trace their lineage to Sir William Starling, Lord Mayor of London. William Starling came to America in 1740, and settled in King William County. He married Jane Gordon. Both died young and were survived by three children: William, Roderick and Sallie.

THE STEPHENS FAMILY OF MARTINSVILLE, VIRGINIA

Samuel S. Stephens, a prominent business man of Martinsville, Virginia, was born in Montgomery County, Virginia. He came to Martinsville about 1896, and was connected with the Rucker & Witten Tobacco

Company. After a few years he returned to Montgomery County, but in 1907 came back to Martinsville to help in the organization of the American Furniture Company, organized by his brother-in-law, A. D. Witten, with which he has been associated since its founding, serving as the secretary and treasurer until 1927, when a merger with The American Dining Room Furniture Company was consummated. Mr. Stephens was then made vice president.

Under the management of Mr. A. D. Witten, Mr. Stephens and other business men of Martinsville, the furniture business has expanded until it has reached enormous proportions.

Mrs. Stephens was Miss Jessie Shanks, of Washington, D. C., and the family circle consists of Mr. and Mrs. Stephens, and two daughters, Juliet and Margaret.

Both Mr. and Mrs. Stephens are loyal and devoted members of the Anderson Memorial Presbyterian Church. Mrs. Stephens also takes a leading part in literary, patriotic societies, and in the social activities of the community.

THE STONE FAMILY OF HENRY COUNTY, VIRGINIA

The Stone family is of English and Danish origin. They are descendants of distinguished and noble ancestors with one grand history of philosophers, mathematicians, journalists, musicians, astronomers, naturalists and divines of England down to the Sixteenth Century. There are three distinct lines of the family in America, all related in some degree.

The family in Virginia, whose founder was George Stone, came to America about 1620. The Stone family, of Maryland, are descendants of Governor William Stone, who came to this country about 1640. Simon and Gregory Stone came about 1635 and located in Watertown, Connecticut. The original spelling of the name as far back as the Fifteenth Century was Stonne, then Stow, then Ston. Stone was adopted just before coming to America.

Clack Stone was the son of Edmund Stone, whose mother was Nancy Dickerson, daughter of a prominent Henry County Civil War officer. The wife of Clack Stone was Sallie Cassandra Barrow. Their children are as follows: Alvah, a prominent physician of Roanoke; he married Martha Norton; Orrin Watkins married Martha Bergher, of St. Louis, Missouri;

Nannie Dickerson, Edward T. Tyree; Edmund Crispen, Blanche Early; Anna Page, Richard Henry Jones; Susan and Thomas.

Dr. Harry B. Stone has become a distinguished oculist of Roanoke, his practice is extensive, many patients from other localities seeking the benefit of his skill.

Mrs. Stone was Mary Lou Kearfott, of Martinsville, Virginia, daughter of the late Dr. C. P. Kearfott.

THE STOVALL FAMILY

The Stovall family is of English descent. There are two families bearing that name, who came to Henry County from Goochland County, they are said to belong to distinct families.

"In the Henrico Records we find that Bartholomew Stovall married Anne Burton, in 1693. They had a son, George Stovall, who married Polly Cooper, a descendant of Sir Ashley Cooper, the first Earl of Shaftsbury. He was clerk of the first House of Burgesses, as late as 1688. Their daughter, Ruth, married Robert Hairston, a member of the Henry County family, in 1748. James Stovall, the eldest son of George, married Mollie Cooper, a relative of his mother. Their daughter, Ruth, married Colonel Abraham Penn, of Revolutionary fame, and settled on Beaver Creek, in 1778. The other children were: Joseph Stovall; Brett, who married Nancy Hughes and her descendants lived in Patrick County; James Stovall married and settled in Georgia; Thomas Stovall married Elizabeth Cooper, and a descendant, Honorable Pleasant A. Stovall, was Minister to Switzerland; Sallie Stovall married a Mr. Farris and went to Tennessee to live; Elizabeth Stovall married a France and also moved to Tennessee; Martha Stovall married John Staples and they were the parents of the distinguished Colonel John and Samuel Staples.

THE STOVALL FAMILY

Dr. Stovall came from Goochland County, with his wife, about the end of the Eighteenth Century and settled at Hordsville, in Henry County. Their children were: Joseph, Albert, Dr. Read, George and Dr. Quince. Dr. Quince was born about 1820, and married Mary Watson, of Danville, Virginia. Their children were: Annie, who married a Garland; Bonnie and Jack. Dr. Stovall practiced in the southern part of the county for many years.

Dr. Read Stovall practiced medicine in the Ridgeway and Smith's River Districts for many years. The children of that family were: James and Alexander (Tony). The second wife was Miss Wingfield and the children of this marriage were: Sallie, who married Dick Jamison; Bettie, who married first, John Davis; second, Edd Philpott; John and Christopher were unmarried; Jennie married Frank Wells.

Joseph Stovall, the eldest son of Landis, married Nancy Grayer Mitchell and they spent their lives in Henry County. Their children were as follows: Landis, Tom, William Francis, Mary, Sallie, Florence Quince and James Read.

Landis Stovall married Virginia Watson, of Danville, Virginia. Callie died in infancy. Melvina married Frederick William Townes, of Danville, Virginia. Frances married Joseph Mitchell (see Mitchell family).

Sallie Stovall married John Jarrett. Florence married George Mitchell. James Read married Manassa Holt, daughter of John W. and Mary Powers Holt. The father of Manassa Holt Stovall was killed in the Battle of Manassas, and her mother, Mrs. Mary Powers Holt, was a woman of gentle manners, well educated and a teacher of ability. The children of the late James Read and Manassa Stovall are: William Morris, of Roanoke; Mary and Lucy F.

THE STUART FAMILY OF VIRGINIA

Archibald Stuart, a man of substance and a Presbyterian of the great clan in the lowlands of Scotland, landed in Pennsylvania, in 1746, the mercurial and stubborn Stuart blood having involved him in the political troubles of the period. Avoiding Scotland, he had refugeed briefly in Londonderry, Ireland, and thence come with many others to Pennsylvania, where he lived obscurely for seven years. After that things were calmer and he was able to send back for his family, but the Stuarts in common with numerous families of Scotch-Irishry found neither Pennsylvania nor its placid citizens congenial. The Scotch-Irish are a clannish lot and live by preference in the shadow of the hills with a line of retreat always open.

There was a steady draft of them from Pennsylvania, south, across the Potomac and up the Valley of the Shenandoah, and in 1738, Archibald Stuart established his family in what is now Augusta County, Virginia. He reared four children and acquired large lands.

His second son was Alexander Stuart, who came to manhood with the Revolutionary War, and was Major in Colonel Samuel McDowell's regiment at the battle of Guilford Court House. He commanded the regiment, had two horses killed under him and took a heavy wound. He was captured and was admired of his enemies, for when he was exchanged, the British returned his sword to him and it is treasured in this family to this day with certain other blades that are bright with honor.

Major Stuart was an able man. He advanced the fortunes of his family and took a leading part in the affairs of his generation. He was one of the founders of Washington College, in Lexington, now Washington and Lee. He lived ninety years.

The youngest son of Major Stuart, called Alexander after him, was the first Stuart to see the West and to serve the Federal Government. He was United States Judge in Illinois and in Missouri, Speaker of the Missouri Legislature and member of the Executive Council in Virginia. He died in 1832, full of honors.

Archibald Stuart, his eldest son, served in the army in the War of 1812, and followed the profession of law. He went to the Virginia Legislature from Campbell County, and later from Patrick. He was heard in the Constitutional Convention of 1829 and 1850, and represented the Patrick District in Federal Congress.

His portrait shows a handsome face, high-bred, genial and ruddy with a bright eye and certain weakness about the mouth. He was a notable orator, famous on the hustings, admired in legislative halls and exceedingly convivial.

Old men relate that no gathering of gentle folk in his section was complete without Arch Stuart, to tell the liveliest tales and trill songs in his golden voice, when the cloth was drawn and the bottle passed.

But under him the family affairs did not prosper. Young James was born on the farm, called Laurel Hill, which Elizabeth Letcher Stuart inherited from the Letchers and it is further related that when Archibald Stuart was defeated for Congress by the Honorable A. T. Averett, the victor's first official act was to give Arch Stuart's son, James, an appointment to the United States Military Academy.

JAMES EWELL BROWN STUART

*"Take him for all in all
We ne'er shall look upon his like again."*

James Ewell Brown Stuart was born in Patrick County, Virginia, on the sixth day of February, 1833. He was the youngest son of Archibald Stuart and Elizabeth, his wife, and whether or not our democratic simplicity attaches any significance to his alleged descent from the royal line of Scotland's kings, we, who know this true son of Virginia, make bold to declare that no prince of the blood ever did more honor to an illustrious ancestry. Strong in mind and body, educated in the three cardinal virtues of Virginia youth, he grew up to manhood, a splendid specimen of the hardy young mountaineer and fresh from the meadows and pinnacles of Dan, he took his place among the boys at West Point and there learned the science that "teacheth the hands to war and the fingers to fight." Noted in his famous school as the most daring and skillful horseman among all his fellows, he sought and obtained active duty as a lieutenant in the second United States Cavalry, then engaged in an arduous expedition against the Indians of the southwest.

In close encounter with this subtle enemy, he received a severe wound, the only injury he ever suffered until his fatal wounding in his last battle. Soon recovering, he was sent to the plains of Kansas where his command vainly strove to keep the peace between the warring factions of Northern and Southern settlers, the first mutterings of the storm which soon broke upon our country in the whirlwind of Civil War.

In October, 1859, as aide-de-camp to Colonel Robert E. Lee at Harper's Ferry, he bore the summons to John Brown to surrender himself and his fanatic followers to the authority of the United States and to Virginia, whose peace and dignity they had criminally violated. With grim humor old Ossawattomie Brown told the young man how easily he could have taken his life, as he felt tempted to do when Lieutenant Stuart approached the engine house door and demanded his surrender.

Stuart did as much toward saving the Battle of First Manassas as any subordinate who participated in it. To Stuart belongs the credit of having brought to perfection a use of the cavalry arm which had been foreshadowed by the dragoons of Marlborough's epoch, but which had not been seen during the intervening great wars of Europe, nor has it ever yet been successfully imitated. In the bold combination of fire and shock at the right moment Stuart's Cavalry stands preëminent among the nations of the world.

In official orders announcing his death to the army, May 20, 1864, General Lee said, "Among the gallant soldiers who have fallen in this war, General Stuart was second to none in valor, in zeal and in unflinching devotion to his country. His achievements form a conspicuous part of the history of this army, with which his name and services will be forever associated. To military capacity of a high order and to the nobler virtues of the soldier, he added the brighter graces of a pure life guided and sustained by the Christian's faith and hope. The mysterious hand of an all-wise God has removed him from the scene of his usefulness and fame."

And he added these words, carved upon this monument and graven in our hearts: "His grateful countrymen will mourn his loss and cherish his memory. To his comrades in arms, he has left the proud recollection of his deeds and inspiring influence of his example."

Theodore S. Garnett, an English military critic, has recently recorded this opinion: "Without the help which Stuart was able to give, the flank march around Pope's army by Jackson's corps, and the concentration of the two Confederate wings on the battlefield the victory of Manassas would not have been possible, 'Crisis of the Confederacy'."

STUART'S MONUMENT

(East side)

MAJOR GENERAL J. E. B. STUART
*Commanding Cavalry Corps, Army
of Northern Virginia*
THIS STATUE ERECTED BY HIS COMRADES
AND THE CITY OF RICHMOND
A. D. 1907

(West side)

*Born in Patrick County, Virginia, February 6, 1833
Died in Richmond, Virginia, May 11, 1864
Aged 31 years*
MORTALLY WOUNDED IN THE BATTLE OF YELLOW TAVERN
May 11, 1864
"He gave his life for his country and saved this
city from capture."

(South side)

"Tell General Stuart to act on his own judgment, and do what he thinks best. I have implicit confidence in him." General T. J. (Stonewall) Jackson on turning over the command of his troops to Stuart after being wounded at Chancellorsville.
May 2, 1863

(North side)

"His grateful countrymen will mourn his loss and cherish his memory. To his comrades in arms he has left the proud recollection of his deeds and inspiring influence of his example."

General R. E. Lee announcing the death of General Stuart to his army, May 20, 1864.

THE STULTZ FAMILY OF HENRY COUNTY

Miss Anna Stultz is known, by a large circle of acquaintances, as a woman of unusual ability. She, assisted by her sister, Alice, is manager of the domestic department of the Fieldale Club, owned by officers of the Marshall Field Textile Company.

The clubhouse with its surroundings is one of the most picturesque places in the country. It occupies the crest of a high hill with a winding driveway as an approach. The building is large and constructed of native stone making a massive and handsome structure. The grounds and gardens are very attractive, and the view from the clubhouse is fine, showing miles of Smith's River Valley.

Miss Stultz was born at Ridgeway and was educated in the schools of that vicinity. She is a daughter of the late Brice Stultz, a business man of that town.

Henry Stultz, one of Winston-Salem's prosperous business men, came from Ridgeway, Henry County, Virginia, when a youth and secured employment in the tobacco factory of R. J. Reynolds.

By industry, close attention to duty and business ability, Mr. Stultz won the confidence of his employers and received promotions until he became manager of a department in the manufacturing plant. He married Myrtle Dean of this city, an honor graduate of Salem College and an accomplished musician. The family is composed of Mr. and Mrs. Stultz and one son, Henry, Jr., who after graduating from the high schools of this city, and taking both collegiate and business courses, is filling a position with the R. J. Reynolds Tobacco Company.

Zephaniah Stultz, son of Brice Stultz, of Ridgeway, spent many years of his life in Martinsville, Virginia. He was claim adjuster for the Norfolk and Western Railway for a long period of time. His wife was Adeline Griggs, daughter of Franklin Griggs, and they reared a large family, two daughters and six sons. The family moved to Roanoke, Virginia, their present home.

Hattie, the elder daughter, married E. W. Hawks; Josephine married first, Mr. Henderson, and a few years after his death married George A. Garber.

Fred B. and Edd, two brave and fine young men, faced the horrors of the World War. Fred losing his life in battle. Edd, who was one of the first volunteers, returned after the close of the war, and upon the retirement of his father was appointed to fill his position with the Norfolk and Western Railway. He married Louise Mosely, of Roanoke.

If the God of Hosts would only,

> "*Let those who make the quarrels*
> *Be the only ones to fight.*"

THE STULTZ FAMILY OF HENRY COUNTY

The Stultz family is one of the county's best known and widely connected families. Many of them deserving special mention in the records of the county.

The first who came to this county was Adam Stultz (born about 1750), who settled on Leatherwood Creek before the Revolutionary War. He married Mary Gravely, an aunt of Peyton Gravely.

FAMILY RECORD

Adam Stultz (1750).................................Mary Gravely
    Abner, Joe, Katy and Polly.

II. Abner Stultz (1770)................................Nancy Eggleston
    Thomas J., Adam, Joe, Cynthia, Patsy, Nancy, Nellie and Betsy.

Joe Stultz (1773)...................................Amy Withers
    Anderson, Zephania, Brice, Amelia, Thenia, Lucinda and Sarena.

Katy Stultz..Michael Griggs
    Wesley, Peter Franklin, Ira, George, Joe and Maria.

Polly Stultz.......................................Tom Haley
    Jeff, Jim, John, Polly and Leanna.

III. Thomas J. Stultz..................................Susan Minter
    Cassandra, Nancy, William Davis, Delilah, Orthniel, Joe A., Martha Ann, Johnson W., George H., Achilles M. and Thomas Leftwich.

Adam Stultz.......................................Betsy Taylor
    Martha Jane, Peyton M. and Sallie.

Joe Stultz...Lucy Eggleston
    Ben, Saunders, Tyler, Letha, Clarissa, Julia, Judith and Louisa.

Cynthia Stultz.....................................Anderson Purdy
    Jim, George and Chester.

Nancy Stultz.......................................Silas Minter
    Richard, Joe, Jim, William, Silas, John, Betty, Cynthia M., Nancy, Martha and Susan.

Nellie Stultz.......................................Tom Hicks
    William, Tom, John, Nancy, Betsy, Lucy, Nellie and Melinda.

Betsy Stultz..John Richardson
  Abner, George, Nelly, Nancy, Lucinda, Frank, John, Eliza and Joe.
Anderson Stultz....................................Polly Lester
  George, Brice, Melinda, Frances, Eliza.
....Jane Wingfield
  Edd, John, Ben, Calvin, Joe, Amy and Sallie.
Zephania Stultz....................................Sarah Virginia Stockton
  Georgia, Alice, Millard Filmore, Rufus Janifer, Jubal Early, and a daughter
  named "Zeph."
Brice Stultz.......................................Tamsy Wells
  Zephania, Brice, Henry, Anna, Alice. Four sons, Frank, John W., Daniel and
  Ben passed away.
Pamelia Stultz.....................................Joe K. Gravely
  Frank, John W., Joe, Goggin, Jabe and Eleanor.
Thenia Stultz......................................Jeff Lyle
  Joe Henry, Bartlett and Ruth Anna.
Lucinda Stultz.....................................John Atkins
  William Stultz, John Francis, Lucinda and Lizzie.
Sarina Stultz......................................Daniel Pace
  William, Sally, Ann, Henry, Mary Tabitha Julia, Jimmie, Ballard P. and Pace.

IV.   CHILDREN OF THOMAS J. STULTZ

Cassandra Stultz...................................Gideon Clark
  Tom, Letitia, Sarah, Nathaniel, William, Patty, Joe and Cernetta.
Nancy Stultz.......................................John Beal
  Eliza, Tom and Julia.
William Davis Stultz...............................Francis Harper Marshall
  Ruben Nance, Sam Johnson, Susan Frances, Abner D., William Marshall, Thomas
  Benjamin, Nancy Missouri, Jesse Davis, Sallie Malissa, James Achilles and
  Peter Hairston.
Delilah Stultz.....................................Nat Eggleston
  William S., Peyton W., John H., Eliza and Nathaniel.
Orthniel Stultz....................................Sallie Griggs
  Ida, Henry, Frank, Tom, Will, Anna, Bob, Jack, Lula, Betty, Janie, Mattie,
  Katie, Jim and Julia.
Joe Abner Stultz...................................Mary Wingfield
  Virginia, Achilles, Joe King, Mary Lou and Nancy.
Johnson W. Stultz..................................Mary Burch
  Isabella, Girard, Nellie, Mary, Johnson, Davis, Lou, Shields, Walter and George H.
  Achilles and Thomas were Civil War veterans and were unmarried.
George H. Stultz...................................Polly Glass
  Achilles, Eliza Ann, Beachy, Emma and Betty.

THE TAYLOR FAMILY OF PATRICK AND HENRY COUNTIES, VIRGINIA

The first of this family of whom we have a record was George Taylor, who came from Wales, and in 1774 obtained a grant of land on North Mayo River in the southwestern part of Henry County, and added to his property until he was one of the large landowners. His wife was Elizabeth Anyon, who came with him from their native country.

They were survived by the following children: James, Blagrove, George, John, Josiah, William A. and Reuben. Three of the sons, James, Blagrove and George served in the War of 1812. The first two lost their lives, and George returned and went to Tennessee to make his home. John Taylor moved to Kentucky. Josiah settled in Stokes County, North Carolina. William A. was a prominent Henry County citizen, who lived to a great age. His wife was Kitty Ann Hill. The children of William Taylor and Kitty Ann Taylor were: Spottswood, Samuel, Jack, William F. B., Kitty Ann Hill, Judith and Lucy Elizabeth, who married James Baker Pace. Spottswood Taylor and three sisters live in Danville, Virginia.

Reuben Taylor, youngest son of George, Sr., was born in 1815, and married Nancy Gray, of Patrick County. He was a large landowner. There were five sons in this family, Daniel G., George W., James, Josiah and Samuel.

In 1844 he donated the land upon which a Missionary Baptist Church was built. The first services were conducted by elder John Lee, and elder John Robertson, of Leaksville, North Carolina.

The daughters of Reuben Taylor were: Mary, Lucy, Adeline, Sarah and Nancy.

Spottswood Taylor, son of William A. Taylor, lived at Danbury, North Carolina. Samuel Taylor lived at Mt. Airy, North Carolina, where he served as sheriff of Surry County. Jack Taylor remained at the family home. His wife was Ruth Baker, their children were: J. W. B., John L. and Kitty. J. W. B. married Ann Forbes. She was survived by her husband and two children, Kate and Botts, the latter married Lucy Wells. John L. lives in Danville, Virginia, and was city treasurer. William F. B. Taylor, the youngest son, was a physician. He married Fannie Bishop and located at Elamsville, Patrick County. He served in the legislature. His son, John S. Taylor, married Ruth Davis. He represented Patrick County in the legislature and later was elected clerk of the Patrick County Court.

Reuben Taylor's sons, John L., George W., Josiah, Samuel, and a son-in-law, J. F. Lancaster, a minister, served in the Confederate Army.

Daniel G. Taylor was a minister of the Missionary Baptist Church and preached at Mayo Church throughout the war period.

Samuel C. Taylor, the youngest son of Reuben Taylor, was twice married, his first wife was Sallie Atkins. His second wife was Lucy Shelton, their children are: Joseph, Thomas, Samuel, Lily, Nannie, Henry, Mollie, Jessie, Maggie, Ella and Lucy. Mr. Taylor was a man of prominence in his community, he served as magistrate, church trustee and Sunday school superintendent.

Joseph R. Taylor has practiced law and served as commonwealth's attorney in Martinsville, Virginia, for a number of years and his popularity and ability were attested by the length of time that he remained in office. His wife was Miss Florence Trogdin.

John L. Taylor was a local minister for many years, and also served his community as magistrate. Reed Taylor was a minister. He married Janet Read, daughter of Dr. R. A. Read, of Spencer, Henry County.

Sam Frank Taylor located in Missouri. He was a prominent minister and for ten years was president of Stephens College, in Columbia, Missouri. Judson Taylor was a very distinguished man. He was a minister, president of Georgetown College, in Kentucky, and preached in a number of cities.

Dr. Tom G. Taylor and J. B. Taylor are successful business men of Leaksville, North Carolina.

Seven grandsons of Reuben Taylor were ministers.

SILAS WRIGHT TERRY

Admiral Silas Wright Terry, of the United States Navy, descendant of a Henry County family, was born on December 28, 1841, in the little village of Wallonia, Trigg County, Kentucky. His father was Abner R. Terry, a highly educated Virginia gentleman, who moved with his family to Kentucky, in 1829, and engaged in the mercantile business at Wallonia until 1844, when he moved to Cadiz and continued successfully in business until his death in 1848. His mother was a Miss Dyer, of an old and representative family of Henry County, Virginia.

Admiral Terry received his education in Cadiz, partly under the instruction of a noted teacher, Quint M. Tyler, of Tennessee.

In September, 1858, he was appointed acting midshipman. He passed a highly creditable examination and was admitted to the United States Naval Academy at Annapolis, Maryland, where he pursued his studies until April, 1861. At this time the War Between the States having broken out, all the students were removed to Newport, Rhode Island, and he, with the others of his class, was assigned to duty on ships then engaged in blockading the southern ports. He continued in this service until the latter part of 1862, when he was graduated.

In 1863 he was transferred to the warship, Black Hawk, of the Mississippi squadron, under the command of Admiral D. D. Porter, and was sent on several important expeditions.

In the Admiral's special report to the Secretary of the Navy, dated May 4, 1864, he said, "I endeavor to do justice to all officers under my command, but have to mention the gallant conduct of Ensign S. W. Terry on the expedition of Red River."

At the close of the war he was placed in command of the Iowa, at that time the most formidable fighting machine in the American Navy, which he took around the Pacific. Later he was promoted to Rear Admiral and given command of the Washington Navy Yard.

Admiral Terry's wife was Lou Mason, daughter of Judge John Thomas Mason, member of Congress from Annapolis district for several years. Their home was in Annapolis.

Admiral Terry was a martinet in discipline and organization. He was chosen to take charge of the McKinley funeral which was the finest pageant ever seen on such an occasion.

He was the highest authority on hydrography and was further honored by being placed in charge of the receiving ship, Norfolk, to train recruits for the Spanish-American War.

Admiral Terry's eldest daughter, Eleanor, married Count Comperio, an officer of the Royal Navy, of Italy. This marriage might be considered unique in the annals of international marriages. The Count was both wealthy and of noble birth and Miss Terry was not an heiress.

HONORABLE C. Y. THOMAS

The late Honorable C. Y. Thomas was a member of the Virginia Senate at the time of the secession convention. At this time he was a most intimate friend and advisor of his brother-in-law, Peyton Gravely, representative of

Henry County, in that historic body. Like all others elected in a representative capacity from Henry County, on the issues of that time, he was strongly in favor of the preservation of the Union, and bent all his energies and his influence toward that consummation. Unlike many others, he continued openly, but quietly, to avow his sympathy for the Union cause, through all the stirring scenes of that eventful time and through the epoch which followed. In spite of this fact he held the office of Commonwealth's Attorney in Henry County through the period of the war, and was designated by the Confederate government to have charge of the distribution of supplies to needy families of Confederate soldiers.

After the war was over and the period of reconstruction had begun, he was appointed Military Governor of Virginia, but this he declined. With the strict construction views he always held on questions of conscience, he did not feel that he could conscientiously take the iron-clad oath. The fact that he had distributed supplies to the needy families of Confederate soldiers, who at the time were in the firing lines, he construed as giving aid and comfort to the enemy. Not only this, but he remembered that many of his own private benefactions had been directed to the same end. After the war he was the representative of Henry County in the convention which framed the Constitution of Virginia, and for all the defects of that historic document, real and imagined, and in spite of the bitter criticisms directed against it, and the convention which enacted it, the fact remains that it continued to be the organic law of Virginia for more than thirty-three years. Whatever praise or blame may attach to the adoption of the old Constitution, those who are familiar with the inside history of the time, know that C. Y. Thomas was the most potent and influential agency in shaping its provisions. To him more than to any other man belongs the unquestionable credit for having fixed in that constitution, as a prerequisite for re-admission of Virginia to the Union, a public school system. Not only this, but one further point in connection should be recorded. Mr. Thomas at this time was a thorough and accomplished lawyer, with a genius for details—attention to details and notwithstanding the parties, an application at this time of the word "Radical" to men of his party, he was a born conservative, and in his characteristic, calm and unshakable manner took his stand against the destructive influence of the negro and carpet-bag elements.

In this way and by the use of his unbounded influence with the administration in Washington, the people of Virginia will never know how deeply they are indebted to this man for tempering the rigors of reconstruction in this state, and rendering her post-bellum history different from that of states farther south.

He was an intimate friend of President Grant, and in an important way he was the most trusted man by the administration in the State of Virginia. In all the professional and public career of C. Y. Thomas two traits stand out prominently above the surface, one intellectual and one temperamental. He had that infinite capacity for taking pains which Carlyle used as the definition of genius.

It is significant of this capacity for details that he was the one treasurer of his county, for a period of many years, whose business was kept right up to date and who did not fail financially. The other trait which is worth recording was his imperturbable coolness. No circumstances, no emergency could excite him. A mob could not disturb him and a violent wave of public sentiment seemed to have no influence over him. No man was ever more aloof in his individual opinions, consequently, he was capable of a certain farsightedness. This generation, for example, should thank him for embodying in our statute law a conservative provision to the effect that a majority of freeholders is required to vote an issue of bonds. This statute of which he was the author stands to-day despite the spasmodic assaults of dangerous demagogues, as the protection for our municipalities against plundering by floating, irresponsible voters. Without this bulwark the present high credit of our cities and towns could not exist.

In war time when other men were impressed by current reports of victories and consequent enthusiasm for the Confederate arms, he would coolly call attention to the fact that, "with all your glorious victories the territory you control seems to be steadily narrowing." Under whatever surrounding excitement he had the gift of seeing the end from the beginning, a faculty which is sometimes depressing in the reflex influence and almost never popular.

His public career covered a long period of time. A very old man might recall that he was the intimate friend of Henry A. Wise, and served on the commission to define the boundary between Virginia and Tennessee before the Civil War, and a comparatively young one will remember when he represented the Fifth District of Virginia in the National Congress.

MRS. MARY A. REAMEY THOMAS

The subject of this sketch, Mrs. Mary A. Reamey Thomas, was born June 15, 1834, and was therefore seventy-six years old at the time of her death. She was a daughter of Colonel Daniel Reamey and Mrs. Susanna Starling Reamey, of Henry County. Through the maternal side of the family she was a great granddaughter of Major John Redd, of the Colonial and Revolutionary period. The Reameys were an old French Huguenot family and trace their origin through the Reameys of Champaigne and Lorraine, to the locality of the forests of Domreamey. They are descendants from collateral relatives of Jean D'Arc. As a family they are characterized by exceptional brilliancy of intellect and the name has been borne by men of distinction on both sides of the water.

Mrs. Mary Reamey Thomas was educated at the old Greensboro Female College, under the presidency of the then distinguished educator, Dr. Charles F. Deems, afterwards founder and pastor of the world famous Church of the Stranger, in New York City. As a student she was exceptionally precocious, and was a constant surprise to her friends, by the ease with which she mastered subjects and the tenacity with which she remembered everything she read.

The writer remembers to have met Dr. Deems, in New York, twenty-five years ago, and to have casually asked him if he remembered a school girl by the name of Mary Reamey. He answered with enthusiasm, "I will never forget her as long as I live. She was the most brilliant and satisfactory student I have ever had the pleasure of teaching."

Only one slight irregularity is charged up to her account in the college tradition of her time, and that is characteristic of her intellectual superiority, and the tendency of her immediate associates at all periods of her life to depend upon her. She was suspected of being the author of every essay read by the graduating class on commencement day. Dr. Deems believed in the truth of the rumor and Mrs. Thomas could never be induced to discuss it.

In endeavoring to make an estimate of the intellectual life of this exceptional woman, two or three striking mental traits and items of early training should be noticed. To start with, she had a prodigious memory so that, notwithstanding the vast breadth of her course of reading and the rapidity with which she read and mastered a book, she never seemed to forget. For example, she read "The Country Doctor," by Balzac, when it was first translated into English. Thirty-five years later, without having reviewed it, she told a friend the whole story with all its complexity of plot and all its wealth of detail in such a thrilling and interesting fashion, that it took the novelty out of the book when afterwards he attempted to read it. This illustration, striking as it is, is not exceptional in her case. In the stress and haste of our modern life and in the consequent perversion of our latter-day training of boys and girls, there are two lost arts, one is correspondence and the other is conversation. Mrs. Thomas was thoroughly accomplished in both these fields of endeavor. In contrast with the hastily, slavishly written letters of to-day between friends, we find that she kept up a regular correspondence with one of her classmates from the time of her graduation to the inception of her final illness, and the interest was sustained to the last. Her personal correspondence, collected, would fill volumes, and would cover a wide and interesting variety of subjects. As a conversationalist she was easy, unaffected and always spontaneous. There was no effort and no posing. The strongest impression that one could get by talking with her and hearing her talk, was a certain sense of her reserve force. You would have a comfortable feeling that there was no danger of exhausting her stock of knowledge. The ideal thing in the enjoyment of literature is not merely to read a book, but for two persons to have read the same book and then to discuss it. In a conversation of this kind she was particularly happy, because of her excellent memory, her exceptionally strong grasp of the plot of a story and her appreciation of its finest points. Not only this, but she was uncommonly flexible and adaptable to the demands of the occasion. Therefore, as many grateful persons have reason to remember, her conversation in the sick room not only never disturbed, but was always soothing to the mind of the patient and her presence a benediction and a blessing.

In making an estimate of the life and character of a deceased person, I do not believe in the extravagant use of superlatives, but I do wish to record here the opinion which I expressed many times without reserve while she lived, that Mrs. Mary Thomas was altogether the most intellectual woman I have ever known. Not only this, but she was gently and tenderly feminine in every fiber of her being, and embodied and represented, to all who knew her, that old-fashioned type of Virginia woman.

She kept abreast of the times and with her active and versatile mind, even in advancing age, continued to take an interest in current affairs. It was characteristic of her last illness when she awoke one day from a refreshing sleep, not to say something about slavery or old times or introduce some reminiscence of ante bellum days, but to ask the sudden and surprising question, "How is Mr. Taft coming on with his Canadian reciprocity scheme?"

As the wife of a public man in a historic era the life of such a woman could easily be inferred. She was ever the appreciative sharer of his councils and felt an abiding interest in his work.

In the times that tried the souls of men and women alike, through a social strife that divided families and alienated friends, she was the intelligent and sympathetic partner of his trials and triumphs and defeats. Through it all she carried herself with that womanly strength and dignity which won the respect of people of all shades of opinion.

As an illustration of another side of her nature, in the long course of her last illness it was a revelation how many of the poor and lowly, from huts and hovels she had visited, without the knowledge of her family, would come in with their clumsily arranged bouquets and stammering speeches of sympathy. She had preserved through the stress that had hardened many hearts the charity "that suffereth long and is kind," and realized in the end Max Ehrman's prayer, "May the evening's twilight find me gentle still."

                                                              L. G. P.

The children of Honorable C. Y. Thomas and Mary A. Reamey Thomas were: Hope (Mrs. H. C. Gravely), Faith (Mrs. Parrott), sketch page . . . . . Jane, Susan (deceased) and Katherine, who occupies the family home in Martinsville.

L. Starling, the elder son, prepared for the practice of law, but his taste for literary pursuits led to an intense interest in the educational affairs of his community, and he gave much time and effort in the encouragement of higher standards for the public schools.

He married Elizabeth Sheffield, daughter of Colonel William Sheffield, of Henry County, and their family circle included two daughters: Mary Reamey and Katherine, and a son, Archie.

Mary Reamey, the elder daughter, was one of Martinsville's most brilliant young women, her intellectual attainments being of a high order. Prior to her marriage she studied and traveled extensively. She married Dr. William P. Few, Professor in Trinity College, now Duke University, Durham, North Carolina. Dr. Few has been president of the latter institution since its establishment, a position of great distinction.

Katherine, the second daughter, married Mr. Ross-Duggan and has spent many years abroad.

Archie Thomas grew to manhood in Martinsville, Virginia, but has made his home in other states.

Frank Thomas, son of Honorable C. Y. Thomas and Mary Reamey Thomas, has for many years made his home in Topeka, Kansas, where he has been engaged in business. He married Miss Bessie Carson, of Salem, Virginia. John Y. Thomas died in early life.

THE THOMAS FAMILY OF PATRICK COUNTY, VIRGINIA

The pedigree of the Thomas family can be historically traced for twelve centuries. Sir Rhysap Thomas, in the reign of Henry VIII, created Knight of the Garter in 1507, was one of the four knights who accompanied the king to the field of the Cloth of Gold, and was the ancestor of numerous branches bearing his name in both England and America at the present time. He was descended from Urien Rhaged, a British prince, who lived in the early part of the sixth century, and tradition in regard to the family goes farther back than that, writers on the history of Wales and genealogy holding that its records are distinguishable in the early centuries of the Christian era. There are many branches of the Thomas family in the United States. Several pioneers came from the Old World to the New during the early years of migration in the seventeenth century, and established themselves in different parts of the country. Their representatives have become distinguished in every walk of life. Several of the name settled at an early date in New England, where their descendants have been numerous and influential. Other representatives of the family settled in South Carolina and the south, Rev. Samuel Thomas having been sent by the Church of England, in seventeen hundred, to establish a church in South Carolina.

Philip Thomas came to the province of Maryland, 1651, with his wife, Sarah Harrison and three children. Their descendants are numerous.

Nathaniel Thomas, the earliest emigrant ancestor of the family, came to Virginia on the ship "Temperance" in 1621. Robert and William came to the same state in 1636.

Charles Thomas first came to Patrick County early in life. His wife was Judith Ripley. He was a great hunter and was interested in keeping a record of the wild animals he killed. The list included three hundred deer, sixty-five bears and forty-four panthers.

Homes were then seven and eight miles apart, schools were crude, houses were built of logs and, for admitting light, greased paper was used in windows.

FAMILY RECORD

Charles Thomas............................Judith Patterson Thomas
Children were as follows: Joab, Cornelius, Richard, John, Pleasant, Nick, Susan Jordan, Mary Nolen, Charles.

Tyler L. Thomas.........................Malinda Prillaman Thomas
    Children: Mary E. Short, Martha E. Rakes, George Lee Thomas,
Victoria E. Turner, Susan A. Turner, John W. Thomas, Daniel L. Thomas,
Nannie B. Houchins, Thomas R. Thomas, Henderson S. Thomas.

SECOND GENERATION

Richard Thomas............................Elizabeth Ferrell Thomas
    Children: Charles Thomas (moved to Missouri); Carroll, Alfred, Lucy
Turner (moved to Kentucky); Sallie Johnson, Mary Booth (went to Kentucky); Roxie Foley, Judith Foley (went to West Virginia).

Richard Thomas (second wife).................Martha Turner Thomas
    Children: Willington, Walter Henry, Tyler L. Tazewell, James Mar-
shall, Andrew Jackson.

    Carroll Thomas, son of Richard Thomas and Elizabeth Ferrell Thomas,
married Rebecca De Hart. Their children are: Richard Thomas III,
Tyler, Mary Griffith (moved to West Virginia), Malinda and Aaron.

    Walter Henry Thomas, son of Richard Thomas and Martha Turner
Thomas, married Judith Virginia Harbour. Their children are as follows:
Flora A. Turner, Mary E. Anglin, James W. Thomas, Martha A. Lester,
Lina, Nannie P. Elgin, Richard F. Thomas, Dr. Charles Walter Thomas
and Abram L. Thomas. Dr. Charles Walter Thomas has practiced medicine
in Patrick and Henry Counties with great success for several years.

    Richard L. Thomas III. Children: John, James H., Eliza M., Charles
H., Walter, Alice, Grace Thomas Bailey, Reuben and Andrew Jackson.

    James W. Thomas. Children: Myrtle, Pearle, Beulah and Walter Henry.

    Tazewell L. Thomas married Letitia Laskey. Children: John Tyler,
James M., Elizabeth Rorer, Lora Witt, Richard, Andrew Jackson and
William Green.

    Richard Thomas, born August 3, 1773, died September 18, 1852.
Elizabeth Ferrell Thomas, his first wife, born October 5, 1776, died April
13, 1823. Their children were: Sallie Thomas, born March 5, 1796, married
a Johnson; Judith Thomas, born February 26, 1799, married a Foley;
Maxie Mille Thomas, born September 6, 1801, married a Foley; Charles
Thomas, born November 27, 1803, married ....; Lucy Thomas,
born June 16, 1806, married a Turner; Polly (Mary) Thomas, born March
21, 1809, married a Boothe; John Alfred Thomas, born April 5, 1814, died
young; Richard Carroll Thomas, born October 25, 1816, married Rebecca
DeHart.

November 24, 1826, the first named, Richard Thomas, married his second wife, Martha Turner Thomas, born May 22, 1801, died October 19, 1875. Their children were: Wellington Thomas, born November 25, 1827, died January 27, 1894, he married Martha V. Hall; Walter Henry Thomas, born April 29, 1829, died May 8, 1919, he married Judith Virginia Harbour, living December 5, 1927; Tyler Thomas, born September 2, 1830, died June 28, 1914, he married Malinda Prillaman; Tazewell Thomas, born July 12, 1832, died December 22, 1916, he married Letitia Lackey; James Marshall Thomas, born March 18, 1834, died January 5, 1863, while serving in the war, single; Jackson Thomas, born November 7, 1835, died June 6, 1863, while serving in the war, married Sallie Terry.

THE TOWNES FAMILY

The Townes family are of English descent. The first of the family to settle in Henry County was Edward Townes, who came from Pittsylvania County. His wife was Harriet Gravely, and their children were: George, Jabe, John S., Daniel Marshall, Edward, Thomas J., Mary, Frances, Kate, Sallie and Nettie Willia.

Mr. Townes was for many years manager of the large estate of the late Marshall Hairston.

George Townes married Martha Jane Davis. Their children were: Florence, Ben Marshall, George Edward, Ida May, James, Stobey, Lucy Ellen, John Willie and Charlie Davis.

Florence Ann Townes was married first, to John O. King; second, Michael Richard Hennessey; third, to William J. Beard.

Ben M. Townes married Zela Davis; George Edward, Pattie Hundley; Frank D., Helen Dietrick; Ida May, Charles W. Davis; James Stobey went to Baltimore to live. He married Mary Warren. Lucy Ellen married Charles M. Hart; Charles Davis Townes graduated in dentistry and located in Waverly, West Virginia. His wife was Mary Chamberlain.

THE TUDOR FAMILY

George C. Tudor, prominent business man of Winston-Salem, North Carolina, is a native of Patrick County, Virginia. His paternal grandfather was John A. Tudor and his maternal grandfather was John W. Lee. His grandmother was a member of the France family, well known in Patrick County.

Mr. Tudor is a son of William A. and Martha Jane Lee Tudor, whose family includes nine children, viz.:

John A. Tudor.....................................Roanoke, Virginia
Robert L. Tudor, Commissioner, Department of Corrections.New York City
George C. Tudor..................................Winston-Salem, North Carolina
Nannie Tudor Joyce..............................Mayodan, North Carolina
Ernest Cabel Tudor..............................Roanoke, Virginia
Ella Tudor Corbin................................Roanoke, Virginia
Walter P. Tudor..................................Danville, Virginia
William Hardin Tudor............................Roanoke, Virginia
Dock C. Tudor....................................New York City

George C. Tudor married Bessie Hanes, March 21, 1900. Four children were born to them, viz.: George C., who married Elizabeth Hobbs, of Edenton, North Carolina; Bynum E., who married Ruth Heath, of Martinsville, Virginia, William Drew and Shirley Anne.

Mr. Tudor left Patrick County in 1891, and was with the Wm. M. Semple Tobacco Company, Martinsville, Virginia, until 1897, when he came to Winston-Salem and became connected with the P. H. Hanes Tobacco Company, continuing in that business for five years. Since that time he has been connected with the Mutual Benefit Insurance Company, from 1903 to 1916 as district manager, then promoted to general agent, his territory consisting of forty-seven North Carolina and Virginia counties.

Mr. Tudor was director of a North Carolina railroad for eight years, director of Farmers National Bank and Trust Company ten years, chairman executive committee ten years. In 1931 he was made vice president and chairman of the board of directors, also director and vice president of the First Industrial Bank of Winston-Salem for three years. President of Insurance Federation of North Carolina, director of Winston-Salem Chamber of Commerce, and Winston-Salem Automobile Club, and secretary and treasurer of Planters' Warehouse Company, Inc.

THE TUGGLE FAMILY OF PATRICK AND HENRY COUNTIES, VIRGINIA

The Tuggle family has for many years occupied a prominent place in the community, having moved to Henry from Patrick, where they owned and occupied the former home of the Stuarts, the birthplace of J. E. B. Stuart.

Of English descent, this family is traced in unbroken line back to one, William Tuggle, who was born in Exeter, England, June 5, 1699, and came to the colonies in 1734. The name Tuggle is listed in an old biographical dictionary, only three of which are now extant.

From early records we find the Tuggles first emigrated to the colonies in 1614, antedating the Mayflower by about six years. Old records at Saluda, Middlesex County, show that they kept coming until about 1740, when they were listed under the various callings of lawyers, planters, teachers, churchmen, surveyors, adventurers, gentlemen.

The family name was given to a square in London, England, known as Tuggle Square.

Romance is said to have played a part in the emigration of the first of the family to come to America. The story is as follows: Two brothers, living in London, were enamored of the same girl, and when her choice was made the rejected lover left England, never to return, casting his lot with the people of the New World.

Henry Tuggle, descendant of the emigrant from England, married Lucy Anne Elizabeth Moir, of Patrick County. He served as clerk of the court of Patrick County for some time and after coming to Henry County, he was elected sheriff and filled that office for twelve years.

The family of Mr. and Mrs. Tuggle included the following children: James E. (died young), Henry Irvine, Thomas A., Mary E., John William, Lucy Emma, Robert Emmet, Walter Lee, Carrie M. and Nellie Noel.

Henry I. (Harry) Tuggle, was a man of fine literary ability. He taught school for a few years, but after coming to Martinsville to make his home, he was appointed postmaster and served under two presidential administrations. His strict integrity and conscientious attention to business won, and kept, for him the approval and friendship of the people of the community.

Mr. Tuggle's wife was Nora Clark, daughter of Dr. George R. Clark, of Patrick County. Their children are as follows: Lucy Annie, Aubrey, Harry Gordon, Elizabeth, Carolyn Clark, James E. (deceased) and Irvine. Lucy Annie and Carolyn Clark are residents of Oakland, California. The latter married Dr. A. M. Gall of that place. Aubrey married first, Addie W. Garrett. His second wife was Katherine Wheatly, of Danville, Virginia. They have a fine estate overlooking Smith's River Valley, a few miles from Martinsville. Harry Gordon married Toccoa Gray, of Laurence, South

Carolina. They make their home in Danville, Virginia. Irvine married Margaret Roper, of Sumter, South Carolina.

Elizabeth (Bessie) Tuggle, is one of Martinsville's most energetic, efficient and popular young women. She takes a leading part in social, patriotic and civic affairs, and with marvelous ability manages a flower shop where beautiful plants and cut flowers are always to be found, and she is interested in other business activities besides.

Mary E. Tuggle, daughter of Henry Tuggle and Mrs. Lucy Moir Tuggle, married Reverdy J. Scales, of Patrick County, Virginia, and later moved to Richmond, Virginia. Their children are: Jessie, who married S. A. Wood; Hattie; Maggie; Nellie N.; Thomas H., a prominent dentist, of Richmond; and Robert E., who married Pattie Taylor, of Richmond.

Lucy Emma Tuggle, since the death of her parents, has presided over the family home in Martinsville. Thomas E. Tuggle was for many years deputy sheriff and deputy treasurer of Henry County, and later was connected with the Westinghouse Electric Company. He died in Pittsburgh, Pennsylvania. Walter Tuggle served also as deputy sheriff and deputy treasurer.

John William Tuggle married Mary Putzel, daughter of Sigmund Putzel, one of the pioneers of Martinsville. They moved to Portsmouth, Virginia, where Mr. Tuggle engaged in business. Their children are: William Henry, John E., James Beverly and Mary.

Nellie Noel Tuggle married Charles J. Lightly, and since his death has made her home in Martinsville, where she has been for some time an instructor in music.

Carrie M. Tuggle married Mr. Hudspeth and he was survived by his wife and one daughter, Bessie, who married S. R. Pannill, a successful business man of Martinsville, Virginia. Their family circle consists of Mr. and Mrs. Pannill, a son, Robert, and a daughter, Lucy Moir.

Robert E. Tuggle has for many years held a prominent place in Martinsville, as the representative of the leading insurance companies. Among them are the Royal Insurance Company, of Liverpool; Continental, of New York; Fire and Marine, of Richmond (oldest fire insurance company); Fidelity and Casualty, Northwestern Mutual, etc.

Since the death of his parents Mr. Tuggle has taken the place as head of the household in an attractive Martinsville home.

A collateral branch of the Tuggle family is represented by James Tuggle, who went from Patrick County, to Cass County, Missouri, about 1835–40. His wife was a Miss Alexander.

Mr. M. L. Tuggle, of Fallon, Nevada, is also a connection of the Virginia family. His grandfather was named Henry and was clerk of the court in Harlan County, Kentucky, in 1834.

THE TURNER FAMILY

Among the prominent Roanoke people originally from Henry County are: Mrs. Morton W. Turner, daughter of Mr. and Mrs. Andrew E. Turner, of Henry County. Mr. Morton W. Turner was born in Franklin County, Virginia, and is one of the most prominent business men of Roanoke. He is chairman of the executive committee of the Colonial-American National Bank.

Mr. W. Cal Turner, of the firm Turner & Turner, real estate and general insurance, was born in Henry County, Virginia. His wife was Annie Lee, of Martinsville, Virginia.

J. A. Turner, of the same firm, was born in Henry County. He married Miss Lorena Tillman, of Roanoke.

A. L. Turner, president, W. G. Jones Candy Manufacturing Company, was a native of Henry County. His wife was Miss Elsie Lemon, of Roanoke, Virginia.

Miss Della Turner married W. L. Wilhelm.

THE WALLER FAMILY

The Waller family has been in the state for three centuries. The first of whom we have a record was Dr. John Waller, born in 1617. He married Mary Key and there were nine children of this union. Of these Colonel John Waller, who married Dorothy King, and his second son, William Waller, the progenitor of most of the Henry County branch of the family, were the most prominent.

The children of Colonel John Waller and Dorothy King Waller were: Mary, Edmund, Thomas, John, William and Benjamin.

Edmund married Mary Pendleton. Their children were: John, Mary, William Edmund, Benjamin, Leonard, James M. and Dorothy Jemima.

William Edmund married Mildred Smith. Their children were: Mary, Nancy, Stephen, Edmund, George, Richard and William.

George Waller, son of William Edmund and Mildred Smith Waller, was born in Henry County about 1773, and married Polly Staples, a daughter of John Staples of this county. He accumulated much property and many slaves and lived near Preston all his life. He was a surveyor and a good business man. After his death his widow moved to Mississippi where their descendants are to be found. Their children are: John, who married a Miss Walters, of Pittsylvania County; George married Laura Fontaine; Sallie married Elam Williams; Mary was unmarried.

William Waller, another son of William Edmund and Mary Smith Waller, was born in this county about 1775. He was highly educated and taught school. He married Mary Barksdale, daughter of John Barksdale of Revolutionary fame, who lived at the ford of the river of that name near Edgewood. He moved to his Clinch Valley (Tennessee) estate, given him by his father. His descendants live in that part of Tennessee.

FIRST GENERATION COLLATERAL BRANCH

John Waller, son of Colonel George and Ann W. Waller, was born in Spottsylvania County in 1765. He married Polly Cooper in 1790, and died in 1842 near Horsepasture, Henry County, Virginia, his old home. The father of Polly Cooper was Major Thomas Cooper of this county, who had been a member of the House of Burgesses, was captain of militia during the Revolution and along with the distinguished John Marr, of Henry County, was a member of the Virginia Convention of 1788, which adopted the Federal Constitution.

The children of this family were: Penelope, Sarah, Thomas, Mary, Margaret, William D., Patsy, Judith, George, Nancy, Elizabeth, Edmund, John, James Anthony and Winston.

George Waller, son of John and Polly Cooper Waller, was born in 1782. He married Eliza Finley Waller. The children of this union were: Maria, Sallie, Mary Eliza, John Stephens, George E., Samuel, Judith, William, Albert R. and Lewis S.

Elizabeth Waller, a sister of George Waller, was born about 1786 and married Jacob McCraw of this county and settled with her husband in Surry, North Carolina, then largely inhabited by Tories. Being loyal to America and being a soldier of the Revolutionary Army he had many personal conflicts and narrow escapes from the numerous bands of Tories.

Edmund Waller, a prominent Henry County citizen and brother of the two above mentioned, was born in 1777 and married Marie Duncan at

Kingston, Tennessee. He was a gallant soldier of the War of 1812, being a member of Colonel Edward Johnson's regiment and took part in all the important engagements of that command about Norfolk. He lived only a few years after his war career at his home, Waller's Ford, and died there in 1817. Their children were: Eliza Finley, who married George Waller; Ann Winston, who married Dandridge Morris; Narcissus Jane, who was not married, and Malinda, who married Burwell Bassett.

DR. GEORGE E. WALLER

Dr. George E. Waller, son of George and Eliza F. Waller, was born in 1838. He was a graduate of the Medical College of Virginia and practiced his profession in Martinsville, Virginia, for many years.

He was hospital steward in the Twenty-Fourth Virginia Infantry and was identified with Pickett's and Longstreet's Divisions in the Confederate Army until the disbanding April 8, 1865. His services were on the battlefields and once, in the battle of Fredericksburg, a ball passed through the hair of his head and a cannon ball passed between his legs, wounding a surgeon behind him.

Dr. Waller filled other prominent positions besides being a practitioner of medicine and health officer. He was elected councilman, mayor and magistrate of his town and in every position gained and held the confidence and respect of the people.

His wife was Sarah Louise Putzel, daughter of Sigmund and Mary Putzel, a woman of bright intellect, great energy and wonderful initiative. She was a charter member of the Mildred Lee Chapter, U. D. C., and, assisted at first by only seven members, undertook the building of a monument to the Confederate dead. The monument is now standing in the public square of the court house at Martinsville. The children of Dr. and Mrs. Sarah Putzel Waller are: William Lewis, Samuel Sigmund, Mary McCauley, Jean, George Crawford and Ed.

George Waller, son of Dr. George E. and Sarah L. Waller, makes his home in the South.

William Lewis Waller, another son of Dr. George E. and Sarah L. Waller, makes his home in the South.

Crawford C. Waller is a successful business man of Martinsville, Virginia, being connected with the furniture manufacturing industry.

Edward Waller graduated from the Virginia Polytechnic Institute, in 1900, and entered the employ of the General Electric Company, of

Schenectady, New York, where he is now manager of the transportation department of that company, and as such his duties are the supervision of sales of all general electrical products to steam and electric railways, ship lines and other transportation companies.

Mary McCauley Waller married G. F. Kuykendall, of Romney, W. Va., and since the death of her husband has made her home in Martinsville with her four children: two sons, David and Waller, and two daughters, Louise and Lyda Hopkins.

Jean Waller married George Clark, who had some time previously moved to California, and since their marriage have lived in that state.

Lewis S. Waller, son of George and Eliza F. Waller, married Katherine (Kate) Putzel, made their home in Martinsville, Virginia, for a number of years, then moved to Spray, North Carolina. Their family included four children: two sons, Lewis and Sigmund, and two daughters, Anne and Katherine.

THE WALLER FAMILY OF VIRGINIA

The lineage of the Waller family of Virginia is traced back in unbroken line to Allured de Waller, who died in 1183. There are many prominent names on this family chart, among them being Edmund Waller, Poet Laureate of England during the reign of King Charles II. Edmund was born in 1606 and died in 1687. In the first edition of his poems, published in 1705, there is a short sketch of the poet's life. The author, whose name is not known, says, "The antiquity of this family and the service they have rendered their country deservedly places it amongst the most honored in England." Another to stand out prominently is Sir Richard Waller, the hero of the Battle of Agincourt, in 1415.

The first of the Waller family to settle in Henry County, Virginia, was Colonel George Waller, who was born in Spottsylvania County, Virginia, in 1734, and died in Henry County, Virginia, in 1814. He married Anne Winston Carr, daughter of Captain William Carr, whose will was recorded in Spottsylvania County, in 1760.

As a major of militia, on the seventh day of March, 1781, under an order from his superior officer, Colonel Abram Penn, George Waller marched sixteen companies of militia from Henry County, Virginia, to join Colonel Adam Stevens, at Hillsboro, North Carolina, for service in the then impending battle of Guilford Court House, fought four days later. George Waller was afterwards promoted and commissioned colonel of militia.

The descendants of George Waller are numerous and they have emigrated from Henry County, Virginia, to many states throughout the union.

THE WATKINS FAMILY OF HENRY COUNTY, VIRGINIA

The Watkins family, originally from Prince Edward County, were quite prominent in Henry. Major Peter Watkins married a daughter of George Hairston II, at Hordsville (now owned by his grandson, Peter Watkins Hairston, and granddaughter, Mattie Hairston), and lived on a beautiful estate in the Marrowbone Valley called Shawnee. He was the father of the late Mrs. Nannie Hairston; Mrs. Tyler Hairston, of Roanoke, and Miss Lillie Watkins, of Richmond.

Dr. Richard Watkins married the daughter of the late General Dillard and lived and died at the old Dillard home on Leatherwood Creek in Henry County. This family was also connected with A. M. Dupuy, for many years clerk of the Henry County Court. Two of Mr. Dupuy's nieces, Misses Mary and Jennie Watkins, lived in Martinsville years ago and were highly regarded.

THE WHITTLE FAMILY OF HENRY COUNTY

Prominent among the men who came to Martinsville many years ago and cast their lot with our people was Stafford G. Whittle, then a young and promising lawyer. He was born at Woodstock, the country home of his father in Mecklenburg County, Virginia. His father was Captain W. C. Whittle, a brother of Bishop F. M. Whittle; he was an officer in the United States Navy until the outbreak of the War Between the States when he resigned to join the Confederate Navy. His mother was a daughter of Commodore Arthur Sinclair, of the United States Navy. He was a grandson of General Richard Kennon, prominent Virginian, who became the first Military Governor of Louisiana, after that territory was acquired by the United States.

Judge Whittle's education was obtained in the schools of Norfolk and in Mecklenburg County. For a while he attended Chatham Military Institute in Pittsylvania County, he also attended Washington and Lee University during the presidency of General Robert E. Lee, and later the

University of Virginia, from which he graduated in law, being admitted to the bar in 1871.

After practicing his profession for ten years in Martinsville, Virginia, he was appointed Judge of the Fourth Judicial Circuit to fill the unexpired term of Judge Berryman Green, resigned.

The Democratic Caucus of the General Assembly of 1882 nominated him to succeed himself, but he was defeated by the Readjuster element. In 1885, however, he was elected for an eight-year term.

After declining an invitation to become dean of the law school of Washington and Lee, following the death of Judge Randolph Tucker, Judge Whittle was elected to the Supreme Court of Appeals of Virginia, 1901, to succeed Judge John W. Riely, he was reëlected for subsequent terms serving until December 30, 1919, when he retired.

Judge Whittle was an able and fearless jurist although he was kind and considerate, always willing to temper justice with mercy, and was greatly beloved by his associates on the bench and by members of the bar.

In his private life Judge Whittle was considered exemplary. His loyalty to relatives and friends, generosity, hospitality and his steadfast religious faith, made his career an inspiration not only to members of the bar, but to all who knew him.

Judge Whittle's wife was Ruth Redd Drewry, daughter of the late Dr. Henry D. Drewry and Mrs. Flora Redd Drewry. Mrs. Whittle's loveliness and beauty of character made her one of the best beloved women of the community.

Five sons and three daughters of this family reached maturity, Henry Drewry, Stafford G., William Murray, Kennon C., Randolph, Flora, Elizabeth and Ruth.

Henry D. Whittle has followed civil engineering as an occupation. He married Flora Redd, daughter of the late John M. Redd and Mrs. Cora Barksdale Redd. They have an attractive home in Martinsville.

Stafford G. Whittle is a prominent attorney at law in Martinsville, being the senior member of the law firm of Whittle & Whittle.

William Murray Whittle rendered his country distinguished service in the World War, and his splendid personality, kindness and tact made him beloved and respected by the men under his authority. All honor is due the man who faced the horrors of war that justice might be done in the world, and our homeland made safe. Mr. Whittle married Alcie Hairston Glenn, daughter of the late J. D. Glenn and Sara Hairston Glenn. They make their home in Martinsville, Virginia.

JUDGE STAFFORD G. WHITTLE
OF
Martinsville, Henry County, Virginia

Kennon C. Whittle is an attorney at law, member of the law firm of Whittle & Whittle. He married Mary Holt Spencer, daughter of the late J. Harrison Spencer and Mrs. Blanche Williamson Spencer.

Randolph Whittle is also an attorney at law, practicing in Roanoke, and although still a young man, has been called upon to fill the place of Judge of the Juvenile Court. Mr. Whittle married Miss Josephine Parrott, of Roanoke.

Ruth Whittle married Robert Hubbard and they made their home in Fayetteville, West Virginia. She passed away a few years since being survived by her husband and four children.

Elizabeth Whittle married Colonel James D. Johnston a prominent attorney at law of Roanoke.

Flora Whittle has, since her mother's death, been the splendid and capable head of her father's household. She is a fine musician and is prominent in social, literary and musical circles.

From the remarks of Judge E. J. Harvey, on March 10, 1931, in presenting to the Supreme Court of Appeals of Virginia a portrait of Judge Stafford Gorman Whittle:

"It has been said that republics are ungrateful, but this cannot be said of our great American Republic or of its people. The memory of the deeds of our heroes in field and forum are not only cherished and abide in the hearts of the people, but we have reproduced and preserved their features in marble and in bronze.

"Virginia has given to our country many great jurists who have illuminated and adorned the pages of her history, and it is fitting that we should preserve the features of our great jurists not in marble or bronze, but in the finer and gentler art of oil and canvass.

"To-day as I look about me and behold the portraits of many of the distinguished sons of Virginia, whose services have enhanced the greatness of our state and nation, I am reminded that this gallery would be incomplete without the portrait of Judge Stafford G. Whittle, who for many years rendered such distinguished service as a member of this court."

In referring to the fact that Judge Whittle attended Washington and Lee University while General Lee was at the head of the law department, Judge Harvey says: "There is no doubt that he imbibed from that great patriot, and exponent of duty, many of the principles which characterized his course of life. Later he went to the University of Virginia where he studied law under that incomparable master, Professor John B. Minor.

"His numerous opinions as a member of this court constitute a memorial to the greatness of his mind and to his exalted sense of justice that will stand through the ages.

"On March 6, 1917, he was elected president of this court which position he filled with signal ability until the time of his resignation on December 31, 1919.

"On June 14th, his alma mater, Washington and Lee University, conferred upon him the degree of Doctor of Laws.

"It has been said of him by a distinguished lawyer, 'he is a man of sound judgment, of extensive legal learning and excellent abilities, a student, a hard worker, fearless and forceful. He has few equals and no superiors on the bench of our state.'

"In honoring him we honor ourselves. But time forbids that we multiply these deserved tributes to the greatness of his mind and character.

"It gives me pleasure to present to this court and to the people of Virginia this portrait of Judge Whittle."

E. L. WILLIAMSON, OF MARTINSVILLE, VIRGINIA

E. L. Williamson attained and held a position in the community in which he lived that has been reached by only a few men of his time, his talents and ability to use them carried him through various lines of work, success seeming to attend him in every line of endeavor.

In his early years he was a salesman for the Guggenheim mercantile establishment in Lynchburg, Virginia. Then he became a civil engineer and railway contractor.

After coming to Martinsville, he was engaged in the manufacture of building material, brick, etc., and later became president of the First National Bank, of Martinsville, a position which he held until his death in 1930.

Mr. Williamson was recognized as an authority on financial matters. He was a man of unblemished character—a loyal member of the Presbyterian Church and a citizen whom the people of the entire community held in the highest esteem.

Mrs. Williamson was Miss Nannie Anderson, daughter of Rev. Robert Anderson, the distinguished Presbyterian minister of Henry County.

A. S. Witten

A. D. WITTEN, OF MARTINSVILLE, VIRGINIA

Ancil D. Witten, one of Martinsville's leading business men, was a native of Tazewell County, son of the late James Richard Witten and lineal descendant of Thomas Witten, who was the first settler of Clinch Valley. When a very young man Mr. Witten began to carve out his future and made his business career eminently successful. About thirty-five years ago he located in Martinsville, Virginia, engaging in the manufacturing of tobacco under the firm name of Rucker & Witten. Later he engaged in the furniture manufacturing business which has been a marked success.

At the time of his death, in 1927, Mr. Witten was president of the American Furniture Company, American Dining Room Furniture Company, director in other furniture companies, several banks and other enterprises in the South.

Mr. Witten was an elder in the Presbyterian Church, and his contributions in devoted service, as well as financial aid, were incalculable in the upbuilding of the church.

Mrs. Witten was Bettie Montague Stephens, of Montgomery County. She has also been a leading member of the Presbyterian Church, and interested in the work of the Daughters of the American Revolution, and in other patriotic and social activities of the community.

The family circle consisted of Mr. and Mrs. Witten, a son and daughter, Laurence and Cecil.

Laurence Claiborne Witten, only son of Mr. and Mrs. Ancil D. Witten, after finishing grammar and high schools entered Washington and Lee University and graduated in law. After practicing that profession for one and a half years, he accepted a position with a Life Insurance Company in which business he has continued in the city of Cincinnati, Ohio, since 1915.

Mr. Witten married Julia McLaren, of Cincinnati, and the family circle consists of Mr. and Mrs. Witten and two sons.

Cecil, the only daughter of Mr. and Mrs. Ancil D. Witten, was born and reared in Martinsville, Virginia. She married Overton Dillard Ford (see Ford family). Her loveliness of character has made her a favorite in social circles and she also takes a leading part in church work, and in the activities of the patriotic societies.

THE ZENTMEYER FAMILY OF PATRICK COUNTY

The earliest known of this family was John Zentmeyer, who came from Germany to Maryland then to Cave Spring, Roanoke County.

John N. Zentmeyer was born at Cave Spring, and he was the progenitor of the Patrick County family by that name. He married Martha Penn and their sons are Edwin Penn and Peter Leath; daughters, Sarah Lou and Flora.

NAMES OF A FEW OF THE DISTINGUISHED MEN BORN IN PATRICK AND HENRY COUNTIES, VIRGINIA

David Patterson Dyer, Representative in Congress from Missouri, also Judge of the United States Court of Appeals, born in Henry County, Virginia, February 12, 1838.

Joseph J. Gravely, a Representative in Congress from Missouri and Governor of the State of Missouri, born in Henry County, Virginia, in 1828.

James Madison Gregg, a Representative from Indiana, born in Patrick County, June 26, 1808.

Alexander G. Penn, a Representative from Louisiana, born in Patrick County. First elected to the Thirty-First Congress then to several succeeding congresses.

SKETCHES

DOCTOR CLOPTON

I am tempted to cull one more illustration from unrecorded judicial history of Henry County. The incident I shall narrate here will necessitate one or two brief character "studies." Dr. Clopton was located on the Pittsylvania side of the line, but since at least half of his territory was in Henry County, he comes into this story. He was an uncommonly brilliant man, highly educated and well qualified for the practice of medicine, but he was an extremely eccentric man. From my childhood days I remember having seen him at old Mt. Vernon Church at Sunday morning service, dressed in a long, white, priestly looking gown.

Once when he had a rather flattering call to a consultation at Patrick Court House, he rode through Martinsville on a bitter snowy day dressed in a white linen duster, with trousers to match and a straw hat. An eyewitness told me that with this costume and his long white beard, his deliberate manner without a trace of self-consciousness, he made a striking picture, but he could not tell me how much heavy winter flannel the old gentleman had on beneath that linen duster. This was one of hundreds of his eccentric performances.

Such a man would make friends but likewise he would make enemies, but all alike, friends and enemies, agreed on one thing, they never doubted his ability. General B. F. Butler once said he had been called "names" all his life, but in looking over the record he had never seen where any man had ever called him a fool. Clopton was like that.

Once upon a time a man connected with Clopton by marriage was taken seriously ill. He and Clopton were not on speaking terms, so he employed another doctor, but as the case developed, he became so alarmed about his condition, that he dismissed his doctor and sent for Clopton in whose skill he had implicit confidence. The doctor came, took charge of the case, and attended upon it faithfully night and day. The patient recovered. The doctor sent in his bill with only one item in it worded like this—"To snatching self from the jaws of hell, $500.00."

The patient refused to pay it on the ground that the fee was exorbitant and Clopton sued. Judge Gilmer, in his instructions to the jury, used the following language in his most engaging manner, "chiseling" every syllable in his dainty and precise fashion: "Gentlemen of the jury, it is your province to determine whether a bill is reasonable or not, but the court will say this much, that if it appears from the evidence that the service specified on the bill was actually rendered, the court is under the impression that the fee is entirely reasonable."

A HENRY COUNTY HEROINE

IT seems to me that a true story of a heroine should be written and given a place in the annals of her native county. A story of her love, her sacrifice and her hardships witnessed by a near neighbor and kinsman who had every opportunity to see the heroic efforts she made to convince herself, her doubting relatives and the people at large that she had made no mistake when she chose for her life partner and the object of her affections as ugly and unattractive a man as could be well imagined.

Our heroine's name was Nellie, daughter of an aristocratic father and granddaughter of one of the Revolutionary heroes who fought and helped to defeat the British at Guilford Court House, which is said to have been the decisive battle of the Revolution. Her uncle also fought and was killed in Norfolk Harbor, in the Battle of El Caney, during the War of 1812. She was entitled to a membership in the D. A. R.'s and Colonial Dames.

She weighed about one hundred pounds, was a blond with a pleasing personality and more than average intelligence. At an early age she fell desperately in love with the man described above and in spite of the opposition of her parents and friends she married him. In addition to the man's lack of attractive personality he had no prospects of business success and but mediocre intelligence. Added to these handicaps, soon after the marriage he was stricken with inflammatory rheumatism from which he never recovered.

Within twelve years after this marriage six children were born, five sons and one daughter. Then it was that our heroine commenced her really strenuous work which never ceased for one hour until she died at the age of seventy-eight.

During all these years, due to her untiring energy, industry and splendid management, the family never lacked the necessities of life. She raised hogs, cattle, horses, sheep, chickens. She carded the wool with hand cards, wove and made the clothes her husband and children wore, always had Sunday suits for them and always had ten or twelve nicely pressed suits for her husband, and when he died at an old age she had laid a dozen new suits of home-made cloth away.

When her friends came to see her she showed that she was highly pleased to see them but never quit work to entertain them. In order not to hurt her feelings her best friends had to acknowledge that her husband was very handsome as she insisted upon them doing so. Sometimes she would ask her friends if they did not think he favored an uncle of hers who was acknowledged to be one of the handsomest men in Virginia.

OUR FAITHFUL COLORED PEOPLE

IN no community in the South or elsewhere was there a better class of colored people than those of Patrick and Henry Counties. In many other parts of the southland there were stories of crime, insolence and indolence engendered by the emancipation of slaves and the suddenness of the new freedom, but in these counties the colored people for the most part went on with their usual occupations.

Identities had to be established after freedom, and the colored people were allowed to choose names, most of them taking the family names of their former owners. Wages were fixed upon for house servants and day laborers and land rented on a crop-sharing basis to those who were to do the farming. Usually the landowner furnished the teams and seed and received a fourth of the crop.

Many instances of house servants and tenants spending practically a lifetime with the same people, sometimes former owners and sometimes those to whom they hired or from whom they rented land, and many instances of real devotion to former owners could be told. One especially worthy of note was that of "Aunt Kitty Reynolds," former slave of Captain Harden Reynolds. Aunt Kitty's story was, that she and a number of others were milking when the master, passing along, stopped within the enclosure and was attacked by a cow, thrown to the ground, and was in imminent danger of being gored to death. The other servants fled in terror but Aunt Kitty, seizing a stout stick, struck the animal such blows that she retreated and the master was assisted to a place of safety. The story was colorful and thinking that possibly imagination played a part, the writer asked a member of the family about it and found that it was true in every detail. It is also true that Aunt Kitty was well provided for during the rest of her life by the members of her master's family.

"Aunt Maria Walker," was another character well deserving mention. She was employed as cook in the writer's family a few years after the close of the Civil War and remained with them during a period of fifteen or twenty years. She was a real colored "mammy" to the large family of children and they all loved her. Brown in color, neat, and an excellent cook, she also possessed qualities that were unusual. She sang about her work in a rich contralto voice and was a wonderful mimic and story teller. She told Uncle

Remus' stories as I have never heard them told by any one else and Brer Rabbit, Brer Fox, Brer "Tarrapin" and the rest were such real people that the impression of their high order of intelligence cannot be entirely eradicated.

With her meager wages Aunt Maria bought a few acres of land on the side of the Chestnut Knob and there spent the last years of her life in comfort. She built a good house, with some assistance from her "white folks," and had some of her grandchildren live with her. Her fruit trees and garden were the best in the neighborhood and her simple home was surrounded with old-fashioned flowers. She passed away in 1926.

"UNCLE JIM"

One of the most unique characters that I have ever known was an old colored man, popularly known as "Uncle Jim," who for many years did gardening, lawn tending and errands about Martinsville. So shrewd was he that he "put one over" the white folk occasionally. He was very fond of his "dram" and managed to keep pretty well supplied with booze even after the prohibition law was passed. Uncle Jim ran a charge account with a grocer who was so accommodating as to furnish his customers with ardent spirits when they particularly requested it, and so much for "Mdse" was charged on the statements.

Uncle Jim's "code of ethics" did not include the payment of bills if he could get out of it, and, strange to say, he managed to run accounts possibly with those who did not know him very well—so in one instance when the account was growing too large, the merchant presented the bill, and Jim paying no attention to it, presented the bill to Jim's employer, a man of means and the strictest integrity, who accosted Jim thus, "Jim, why don't you pay your bill, and what is this charged on so many dates as 'mdse'?" "Mr.——I jes doan know whut he charge me fur, please, Sur, jes ax him to itemize dat bill." The employer took the bill to the storekeeper and it is said that the bill was torn to pieces and no more was said about collection.

The wife of Jim's employer, in order to get a reasonable amount of work done in a given time, had to superintend Jim's labors very closely, so when going out she would give Jim a list of things to be done in her absence. He was heard to grumble "Miss —— she give out a whole passel of wuk fer me to do while she gone ter town—den she go and come back more samer dan a race hoss and fuss kase de wuk ain't all done." "Well, Jim," some one asked, "what did you do while Mrs. —— was away?" "Jes sot down and went to sleep," replied Jim, as if it would have been quite unreasonable for anyone to expect anything else.

"AUNT EDIE," SERVANT FOR MANY YEARS IN THE GRAVELY FAMILY

A young negro girl, about sixteen years of age, was given as a present to Mrs. Lewis Gravely by her mother, Mrs. Rachael Dalton Dyer. This girl being possessed of rather unusual intelligence, Mrs. Gravely said, "I shall train Edie to be a cook, I don't mean just a cook but one who can cook and serve a meal satisfactorily." Thus Edie became a noted cook and five generations of the Gravely family ate of her cooking.

So devoted was she to the family that she was looked upon as a beloved "black mammy" and her pride in her "white folks' " children was evident in all she did throughout her long life of faithful service. She died at the age of ninety-five at the home of Mrs. Chester B. Gravely, in Salem, Virginia, granddaughter of Mrs. Lewis Gravely.

It is thought by some who knew this unusual colored woman that she had in her veins a mixture of East Indian blood and, after death, her features strongly indicated that fact.

HENRY COUNTY COMMONWEALTH'S GRANTS OR PATENTS

(*Copied Verbatim from the Land Books in the Land Office in Richmond, Virginia*)

BOOK A

	Page	Name	Date	Acres	Location
1	11	William Furgason........	20 Oct. 1779	427	On Nicholas's Creek, adjoining land of Alley.
2	13	John Doughton...........	" "	198	On the branches of Chestnut Creek.
3	14	Thomas Prenty..........	" "	354	On waters of Snow Crk., adjoining land of Jeremiah Morrow.
4	16	Peter Gruheart..........	" "	343	On the head of Hatchett Run and Pounding Mill Branch waters of Pigg River.
5	18	James Standefer, Sr......	" "	493	On Stony Creek, adjoining William Davis.
6	25	Henry Jones.............	" "	288	On Hatchett Run and branches of Pigg River.
7	33	John Robinson...........	26 "	78	On the waters of Pigg River, adjoining Callaway's land.
8	36	Peter Gilliam...........	20 "	112	On Blackwater River, adjoining Chirtwood's land.
9	46	Robert Mavity...........	" "	110	On Little Otter Creek, adjoining the land of Christopher Choat.
10	53	Shadrack Turner.........	" "	336	On the south side of Town Creek.
11	54	William Hurd............	2 Nov. "	335	On Indian Branch of Snow Creek, adjoining the lands of Randolph and Morrow.
12	55	Thomas and Swinkfield Hill, Executors and Legatees of Robert Hill, dec'd.	20 Oct. "	468	On Hatchett Run.
13	61	Owen Ruble.............	" "	100	On Turner's Creek of Pigg River.
14	65	Israel Standefer.........	" "	600	On Standefer's Branch.
15	65	Daniel Spangleg.........	" "	197	On the south side of Pigg River, adjoining William Cook.
16	91	John Kemp..............	" "	345	Beginning, etc., on Camp Branch of Blackwater, adjoining the land of Edmondson.
17	92	John Heard.............	" "	363	On the head of the Maple Branch and head of Roberson's Branch.
18	101	Thomas Hill............	" "	278	On the south side of Pigg River and adjoining Doughton's land.
19	115	John Willis.............	" "	174	On Hatchett Run, adjoining Henry Jones' land.
20	124	Josiah Carter...........	" "	200	On both sides of Blackwater River.
21	131	John Ramsey............	" "	346	On the branches of Chestnut Crk., adjoining Standefer's land.
22	135	John Willis.............	" "	384	On the waters of Hatchett Run, adjoining Turnpin's land.
23	136	James Cooly............	" "	154	On the north branches of the North Fork of Chestnut Creek.
24	141	David Prewit...........	" "	264	On Camp's Branch of Snow Creek, adjoining his own land.
25	147	Henry Willis............	" "	62	On a branch of Blackwater, adjoining Hilton's land.

HENRY COUNTY COMMONWEALTH'S GRANTS OR PATENTS—Continued

BOOK A

	Page	Name	Date	Acres	Location
26	164	William Mavity	20 Oct. 1779	366	On the north branches of Pigg River, adjoining the land of Hill, Jones, etc.
27	234	John Ferrill	1 May 1780	336	On the Great Sycamore Creek and adjoining the land of White.
28	258	William Akers	1 Feb, "	400	On Lazy Run of Blackwater River, adjoining Thomas Miller.
29	273	John Marr	4 May "	16,331	On Dan River, beginning Creek.
30	347	Bartley Foley	5 June "	171	On Sycamore Creek.
31	415	Aaron and Abraham Fountain, Legatees of Peter Fountain, dec'd.	7 "	2,000	On the County Line, Crooked Creek and Mayo River.
32	428	William Graves	4 "	201	On the waters of Smith's River and adjoining Randolph's land.
33	451	Stephen Heard	20 "	342	On Blackwater River, adjoining John Heard.
34	480	John Dickenson	26 "	466	On the Cool Branch of Blackwater River, adjoining land of Cowan.
35	489	Archelus Hughes	6 "	239	On the branches of the North Fork of Mayo's River, adjoining the land of Gray.
36	498	Isaac David	27 "	192	On the branches of Bull Run, adjoining Richard Walden's line.
37	540	Joshua Hudson	3 July "	82	On the branches of the Mayo River and Russell Creek.
38	545	John Tunley	4 "	145	On the branches of the Crabtree Fork of Snow Creek.
39	553	Garrot Birch	4 "	412	On the Dung Branch of Leatherwood Creek.
40	554	Robert Stockton	5 "	172	On the waters of Smith's River, adjoining his own land.
41	560	Reuben Nance	4 "	182	On the draughts of Leatherwood Creek, adjoining Terry's land.
42	563	Susanna Reynolds	5 "	38	On the north side of the South Branch of Mayo River.
43	571	Stephen Heard	" "	254	On the branches of Blackwater River, adjoining Ward's land.
44	595	Eliphaz Shelton	6 July "	846	On Bull Mountain Fork of Mayo River.
45	604	James Prenty	7 "	232	On the branches of Grass Fork of Snow Creek, adjoining Randolph's land, etc.
46	629	John Colliar	13 "	336	On the branches of Fishing Fork of Leatherwood Creek.
47	647	Augustine Brown	14 "	324	On the branches of Peter's Creek and Russell's Creek.
48	552	Edward Richards	15 "	230	On the North Fork of Chestnut Creek, adjoining Jas. Smith.
49	655	George Runnolds	" "	200	On the waters of the Muster Branch of Leatherwood Creek.
50	656	Michael Dunn	14 "	120	On the branches of Snow Creek, adjoining Richard Vamon.

HENRY COUNTY COMMONWEALTH'S GRANTS OR PATENTS—Continued

BOOK A

	Page	Name	Date	Acres	Location
51	668	Tully Choice	14 July 1780	147	On the Fork of Gullery Run, adjoining his own and the land of Heard.
52	669	Joseph Gravly	"	196	On the Grassy Fork of the Fishing Fork of Leatherwood Creek.
53	672	John Ellis	"	407	On the branches of Bull Run, Jack's Creek and Turkey Creek.
54	673	William Ryon	"	202	On the branches of the Grassy Fork of Snow Creek, adjoining Bradshaw's land.
55	675	John Hargar	"	152	On the waters of the North Fork of Chestnut Creek, adjoining Richards' land.
56	118	Robert Mason	20 Oct. 1779	236	On both sides of the Muddy Fork of Chestnut Creek, adjoining Frazer's land.

BOOK B

	Page	Name	Date	Acres	Location
57	1	Thomas and Swinkfield Hill, Executors and Legatees of Robert Hill, dec'd.	8 Nov. 1779	468	On the Meadow Branch, adjoining Hill's old Survey, etc.
58	3	Daniel Spangler	"	30	On Pigg River, adjoining his own land.
59	4	William Mavity	"	193	On the South Fork of Pigg River, adjoining Thomas Hutchings.
60	4	John Huff	"	82	On the South Fork of Pigg River, adjoining his own and James Rentfroe's land.
61	6	Thomas and Swinkfield Hill, Executors and Legatees of Robert Hill, dec'd.	10	378	On the Meadow Branch and McDowel's Branch.
62	6	William Menifee	"	212	On both sides of Pigg River, adjoining Callaway's land.
63	7	Thomas Hail	"	75	On both sides of Pigg River.
64	8	John Wilson	"	176	Adjoining his own land he now lives on, on the South Fork of Blackwater River.
65	8	Darby Ryon	"	162	On both sides of Otter Creek.
66	9	James Poteete	"	422	On the branches of Poplar Camp Creek, adjoining Rentfroe's land.
67	9	George Heard	"	250	On Simmon's Creek, adjoining his old lines.
68	10	Daniel Spangler	"	84	On the branches of Blackwater, adjoining Joseph Byrd and James Rentfroe.
69	11	John Kemp	"	172	On the south side of Blackwater River, adjoining Grier's land.

HENRY COUNTY COMMONWEALTH'S GRANTS OR PATENTS—Continued

BOOK B

	Page	Name	Date	Acres	Location
70	14	William Young	10 Nov. 1779	250	On Cole's Creek and Blackwater River.
71	15	John Ramsey	"	113	On Chestnut Creek.
72	17	Lewis Jinkings	"	335	On Turkey Creek a north branch of Pigg River.
73	17	David Prewitt	"	255	On both sides of Camp Branch of Snow Creek.
74	18	John Willis	"	391	On the waters of Hatchett Run.
75	20	Joseph Bowling	"	264	On the head of Chestnut Creek a branch of Town Creek.
76	21	John Dickenson	"	206	On both sides of Pigg River.
77	23	Thomas Hail	"	52	On a branch of Pigg River, adjoining the land he now lives on.
78	25	James Martin	"	375	On the branches of Chestnut Creek, adjoining David Haley.
79	28	Amose Richardson	12 "	292	On the Grassy Fork of Snow Creek and on both sides thereof.
80	29	John Dickenson	16 "	656	On the South Fork of Stony Creek, adjoining Luke Standifer.
81	31	Thomas Hickerson	"	342	On Mountain Creek of Pigg River.
82	35	James Turpin	2 "	100	On the branches of Blackwater and Pigg Rivers, adjoining his own and the land of Tolbot, etc.
83	37	Robert Pedigon	"	362	On the branches of Reed Creek, adjoining Inness, Copeland, etc.
84	44	Israel Standifer	10 "	280	On Standifer's Creek a branch of Blackwater River.
85	45	John Hartwell	"	209	On the north side of Pigg River on Robertson's Branch.
86	51	Swinkfield Hill	"	188	On Pigg River, adjoining Bates's land.
87	58	Owen Ruble	20 "	164	On the waters of Turner's Creek.
88	69	Thomas and Swinkfield Hill, Executors and Legatees of Robert Hill, dec'd.	"	371	On the south side of Pigg River, adjoining John Furgason.
89	70	Thomas and Swinkfield Hill, Executors and Legatees of Robert Hill, dec'd.	22 Nov. "	266	On the south side of Pigg River, adjoining Swinkfield Hill's line.
90	71	William McVeaty	"	140	On Pigg River, adjoining Thomas Jones.
91	137	Lamboth Dodson	1 Dec. "	200	On both sides of the South Fork of Mayo River.
92	194	James Strange	"	352	On both sides of Mullins's Fork of Bull Run and the head branches of Bull Run.
93	293	David Patterson	1 May 1780	186	On the head branches of Irven's River.
94	341	Peter Saunders	22 June "	156	On Orter Creek, adjoining Smith's land.
95	343	Luke Standifer	"	324	On Blackwater River, adjoining John Kemp's land.
96	349	Shadrack Woodson	"	79	Adjoining Stephen Lee's land on the waters of Blackwater River.

HENRY COUNTY COMMONWEALTH'S GRANTS OR PATENTS—Continued

BOOK B

	Page	Name	Date	Acres	Location
97	367	Shadrack Woodson	22 June 1780	154	On the waters of Blackwater River and adjoining Richard Doggatt.
98	372	John Dickinson	7 July "	308	On the branches of the North Fork of Leatherwood Creek.
99	392	William Ryon	13 "	242	On the Grassy Fork of Snow Creek.
100	412	Philip Hutchison	14 "	274	On Buck Branch of Snow Creek.
101	420	Stephen Sinter	" "	216	On the branches of Turkey Cock Creek.

BOOK C

	Page	Name	Date	Acres	Location
102	16	Jacob Stallings	1 Feb. 1781	204	On both sides of Ball's Creek of Smith's River, adjoining Merray Webb.
103	20	John Dickenson	" "	279	On the south side of Pigg River, adjoining Early and Callaway's land.
104	24	William Weaks	" "	447	On the North Fork of Story Creek, adjoining Renfroe, etc.
105	28	William Farguson	" "	169	On the branches of the South Fork of Pigg River, adjoining Robert Jones.
106	29	Charles Burnett	" "	188	On Mulberry Creek.
107	31	John Swilivant	" "	210	On the south side of Blackwater River, adjoining Jeremiah Sowsbury.
108	32	Philip Rayley	" "	212	On the branches of Bull Run.
109	33	William Hunter	" "	182	On the North Fork of Butramstown Creek, adjoining the land whereon he lives.
110	36	Daniel Goosby	" "	120	On both sides of Mayo River.
111	37	James Callaway	" "	707	On the branches of Chestnut Creek, adjoining Samuel Patterson.
112	121	George Carter	" "	127	On the Bull Mountain a fork of the Mayo River.
113	123	Luke Foley	" "	173	On the draughts of Goblingtown Creek.
114	131	Solomon Davis	" "	162	On both sides of Pigg River, adjoining Patterson's land.
115	193	John Salmon	" "	375	On Jourdans Creek, adjoining his own land.
116	197	Hugh Cambril	" "	281	On Turkey Pen Branch, adjoining John May.
117	207	Richard Adams	" "	377	On the branches of Green Creek, adjoining Archelous Hughes.
118	209	John Dickenson	" "	180	On the master branch of Leatherwood Creek.
119	213	William Amose	" "	299	On Sycamore Creek, adjoining Harbour's land.
120	219	William Wilson	" "	411	On both sides of Spoon Creek, adjoining Philip Buzzard.

HENRY COUNTY COMMONWEALTH'S GRANTS OR PATENTS—Continued

BOOK C

	Page	Name	Date	Acres	Location
121	223	Adam Lackley	1 Feb. 1781	70	On Rockcastle Creek, adjoining Walton's land.
122	224	John Salmon	"	363	On the Grassey Fork of Wharf Mountain, adjoining Jordan's line.
123	225	Richard Kerby	"	358	On Sycamore Creek, adjoining his own land.
124	227	Henry Barksdale	"	142	On branches of Reedy Creek and Rock Run.
125	228	John Cammeron	"	213	On the Nobusiness Fork of Mayo River and adjoining Runnold's land.
126	231	John Dickenson	"	219	On both sides of Pigg River, adjoining William Hodges' land.
127	233	William Hayes	"	112	In the fork between the North and South Mayo Rivers, adjoining the land of Lambert Dotson.
128	237	Zachariah Smith	"	261	On the waters of the Mayo River and adjoining Philip Angling.
129	239	Benjamin Handcock	"	206	On Sycamore Creek, adjoining Ward's land.
130	243	Archelaus Hughes	"	304	On Green Creek, adjoining Walton's line.
131	244	Samuel Johnston	"	350	On the Grassey Fork of the Fishing Fork of Leatherwood Creek.
132	260	Josiah Smith	"	302	On the branches of Stone's Creek, adjoining Jacob Cogar.
133	263	William Smith	"	353	On Russell's Branch and South Mayo River, adjoining James Mankin.
134	281	Dutton Layne	"	642	On Horse Pasture Creek, adjoining James East.
135	285	Jesse Atkerson	"	280	On the south side of Mayo River and adjoining his own land.
136	298	Samuel Johnston	"	410	On the branches of Leatherwood Creek.
137	305	William Hodges	"	93	On Pigg River, adjoining Patterson's land.
138	325	Josiah Smith	"	189	On the branches of Horse Pasture Creek, adjoining his own and the land of Randolph, etc.
139	361	Daniel Smith	1 Mar. "	232	On the Roundabout Branch of Butramstown Creek.
140	366	Abraham Penn	"	150	On both sides of Beaver Creek.
141	390	Paul Beck	"	459	Adjoining his own and Robert Jones' land.
142	403	John Polley	"	63	On the south side of the South Fork of the Mayo River.
143	407	John Kelly	"	88	On Smith's River.
144	411	Benjamin Bristo	"	104	On Goblingtown Creek.
145	414	Solomon Davis	"	202	On the south side of Pigg River, adjoining Smith's land.
146	418	George Taylor	"	254	On the south side of the North Mayo River, adjoining Bradley Smith.

HENRY COUNTY COMMONWEALTH'S GRANTS OR PATENTS—Continued

BOOK C

	Page	Name	Date	Acres	Location
147	445	William Young	1 Mar.1781	379	On the Fish Fork of Snow Creek.
148	455	William Read	"	53	On both sides of Blackberry Creek.
149	456	Henry Fee	"	152	On the north side of South Mayo River.
150	459	Andrew Rea	"	102	On the Grassy Fork of Smith's River, beginning at Jesse Willingham's corner.
151	462	Isham Hodges	"	193	On Chestnut Creek, adjoining Robert Grimmitt.
152	464	John Nevill	"	334	On Sycamore Creek, adjoining Thomas Morrison.
153	466	John Richardson	"	259	On the waters of Horse Pasture Creek, adjoining Randolph, etc.
154	467	Thomas Lockhart	"	453	On the branches of North Mayo River.
155	469	Miles Jennings	"	474	On the north side of Mayo River, adjoining Randolph and Jordan.
156	473	Garrat Moar	"	238	On the first bold branch of Leatherwood Creek, adjoining land of Walter Dunn.
157	486	James Manking	"	140	On Rossell's Creek.
158	491	James Melton	"	430	On the draughts of Leatherwood Creek, adjoining Lomax's land.
159	494	John Marr, George Hairston and Thomas Bedford	"	126	On the south side of Smith River.
160	495	Nicholas Darnel	"	204	On both sides of the South Fork of Sandy River.
161	498	Daniel McBride	"	278	On the waters of Leatherwood Creek, adjoining Lomax and Company.
162	507	John Dickenson	"	420	On Pigg River, adjoining Isham Hodges.
163	514	James Turpine	"	225	On the branches of Hatchett Run and Pigg River.
164	543	Henry Dillian	"	300	On Stroud's Creek, adjoining his own land.
165	450	William Young	"	330	On the waters of Snow Creek, adjoining James Keff.

BOOK D

	Page	Name	Date	Acres	Location
166	5	Thomas Flower	20 July 1780	327	On the head of Runnett Bag Creek, a branch of Ewin River.
167	8	Thomas Flower	"	930	On both sides of Flatt Creek of Smith's River.
168	29	John Ward	"	100	On the east side of Sycamore Creek.
169	38	John Ward	"	128	On the draughts of Rock Castle Creek.
170	40	John Ward	"	327	On Runnett Bag Creek.
171	42	John Ward	"	138	On the draughts of Wagion and Jointcrack Creek.

HENRY COUNTY COMMONWEALTH'S GRANTS OR PATENTS—Continued

BOOK D

	Page	Name	Date	Acres	Location
172	44	Jeremiah Early and James Callaway.	20 July 1780	40	It being More's Entry No. 66 by some called the Bald Knob.
173	47	John Ward.	"	278	On the head of the South Branch of the Middle Fork of Jack's Creek.
174	74	John Kickey.	1 Sept.	478	On the Grassy Fork of Butramstown Creek.
175	97	James Standeford.	"	224	On Story Creek.
176	97	William Davis.	"	327	On Story Creek, adjoining Dillingham's line.
177	100	Shadrack Turner.	"	306	Adjoining his own lines on the branches of Butramstown Creek.
178	114	Isham Talbot, Jr.	"	192	On both sides of Little Bull Run.
179	125	David Rogers.	"	154	On the North Fork of Russell's Creek, adjoining George Carter.
180	132	Michael Real.	"	178	On Nicholas's Creek, adjoining John Jones, etc.
181	133	Jacob Atkins.	"	404	On the South Branches of Pigg River near the head of the North Fork of Story Creek and a Nobb called Jones' Knobb.
182	150	Josiah Turner.	"	326	On Butramstown Creek, adjoining Shadrack Turner's land.
183	159	Stephen Heard.	"	170	On Blackwater River, adjoining William Heard.
184	160	Robert Pruntey.	"	76	On the waters of Pigg River.
185	161	John Forguson.	"	229	On both sides of Jumping Branch of Story Creek.
186	162	Abner Echolds.	"	177	On the North Fork of Goblingtown Creek, adjoining Callaway's land.
187	163	Abner Echolds.	"	160	On both sides of Goblingtown Creek.
188	165	Josiah Watkins.	"	411	On Savil Creek, adjoining Clay's land.
189	166	Francis Grimes.	"	272¾	On both sides of Goblingtown Creek, adjoining Tittle's land.
190	167	William Forguson.	"	93	On the South Fork of Pigg River, adjoining James Rentfroe.
191	170	John Forguson.	"	66	On Pigg River, adjoining Cole's land.
192	176	John Forguson.	"	275	On the branches of Pigg River, adjoining his own land.
193	187	Francis Cox.	"	278	On the branches of the Muster Branch of Leatherwood Creek.
194	246	John Ward.	"	277	On the waters of Jack's Creek.
195	286	William Haynes.	"	193	On the North Branches of Pigg River on a branch called Dinner Creek.
196	330	William Evans.	11 Dec.	130	On both sides of the North Fork of Chestnut Creek.
197	331	John Huff.	"	308	On the waters of Turner's Creek and branches of Pigg River.
198	333	Thomas Nelson.	"	164	On the draughts of Smith's River, adjoining Martin Webb.

HENRY COUNTY COMMONWEALTH'S GRANTS OR PATENTS—Continued

BOOK D

	Page	Name	Date	Acres	Location
199	334	John Farguson	11 Dec. 1780	230	On the south side of Pigg River, adjoining William Davis's land.
200	337	Darby Ryon	" "	370	On the branches of Pigg River, adjoining Thomas Jones.
201	339	Darby Ryon	" "	268	On Pigg River and branches thereof, adjoining Miller Doggett.
202	352	Isham Edwards	1 Sept. "	174	On the branches of Clout Creek, adjoining William James.
203	372	John Stuart	1 Feb. 1781	225	On Blackwater River, adjoining John Clay.
204	373	Walter Maxey	" "	228	On Smith's River, adjoining the land of John Rieve.
205	374	Isaac Cloud	" "	175	On both sides of Elk Creek.
206	375	William Mavity	" "	285	Adjoining William Weak and Philip Sheridan.
207	378	Sampson Stephens	" "	200	On the branches of the Muster Branch of Leatherwood Creek.
208	379	Robert Podigow	" "	395	On the branches of Leatherwood Creek, adjoining Daniel McBride, etc.
209	380	Henry Dillian	" "	535	On Stroud's Creek a fork of Wharf Mountain Creek, adjoining Jordan and Randolph's lines.
210	381	William Swanson	" "	309	On the branches of Bull Run.
211	382	Philip Sheridan	" "	362	On the North Fork of Story Creek.
212	385	James Ray	" "	194	On Little Marrowbone Creek.
213	386	Jonathan Hanbey	" "	36	On both sides of Peter's Creek.
214	392	James Standefer, Sr.	" "	374	On Story Creek, adjoining James Standefer, Jr.
215	413	George Carter	" "	190	On the Bull Mountain of Mayo River.
216	480	John Daniel	" "	300	On both sides of Bigg Dan River, adjoining Belcher's land.
217	482	Robert Baker	" "	205	On the waters of Green Creek, adjoining Thomas Low.
218	488	Robert Baker	" "	155	On Green Creek Waters, adjoining Archelaus Hughes.
219	493	Samuel Johnston	" "	272	On the waters of Leatherwood Creek, adjoining Dickenson, etc.
220	496	Adam Lackey	" "	900	On the head of Smith's River, Dan River and Rockcastle Creek.
221	498	John Salmon	" "	81	On the branches of Marrowbone Creek, adjoining Harmour's land.
222	500	Richard Dickens	" "	594	On a creek called Grey's Creek, adjoining Grey's Order land.
223	501	Isham Hodges	" "	249	On the branches of Chestnut Creek and adjoining Dickenson's land.
224	528	Josiah Smith	" "	343	On Mayo River, adjoining Jordan's land.

HENRY COUNTY COMMONWEALTH'S GRANTS OR PATENTS—Continued

BOOK D

	Page	Name	Date	Acres	Location
225	531	Henry Tate	1 Feb. 1781	172	On the branches of Smith's River and adjoining Randolph's land.
226	533	George Hairston, John Marr and Thomas Bedford	"	584	At a place called the Timber Level, adjoining Powers and Company's line, etc.
227	545	Archelaus Hughes	"	315	On Mill Creek of Mayo River.
228	566	John Jones	" Mar.	391	On the branches of Turner's Creek and Nicholas's Creek, adjoining Thomas Jones.
229	507	James Taylor	" Feb.	422	On the South Fork of Nobusiness Fork of Mayo River.
230	582	John Simmons	" Mar.	638	On the Grassy Creek of Smith's River, adjoining John Rowland.
231	583	James Shard	"	432	On Mayo waters, adjoining George Taylor.
232	510	Robert Pedigrow	" Feb.	206	On Beaver Creek waters.
233	585	George Hairston	" Mar.	442	On the waters of Smith's River.
234	586	Thomas Chowning	"	185	On Smith's River, Drag Creek and Turkey Cock Creek.
235	587	Jesse Willingham	"	185	On the branches of Marrowbone Creek.
236	588	John Sims	"	172	On both sides of South Mayo River, adjoining Fountain, Walton, etc.
237	593	John Colyer	"	351	On the branches of Leatherwood Creek, adjoining James Blivers.
238	598	Richard Runnolds	"	312	On Smith's River, adjoining Matthew Small's land.
239	599	John Mitchell	"	379	On the branches of Rockey Branch of Sandy River.
240	600	Henry Sumpter	"	1,494	On Rock Run and Ramsey's Creek.
241	605	John Richardson	"	129	On the branches of Marrowbone Creek, adjoining John Hardiman.
242	606	Jemmy and John James	"	400	On both sides of Turkey Cock Creek.
243	608	David Chadwell	"	110	On the south side of Smith's River, adjoining his own land.
244	614	Francis Gilley	"	444	On Turkey Cock Creek.
245	616	Francis Kerby	"	584	On the Pole Cat Branch of Pigg River on Coon's Creek.
246	617	Robert Bolton	"	1,819	On both sides of Snow Creek, adjoining Copeland's Order line.
247	620	Thomas Hollingsworth	"	52	On both sides of Blackberry Creek.
248	623	Thomas Chowning	"	200	On the branches of Turkey Cock Creek of Smith's River, adjoining James Bowling's land.
249	636	James Wilson	"	176	On Smith's River, adjoining land of Lomax, Webb, etc.
250	639	Miles Jennings	"	453	On Mayo River, adjoining Daniel Goodsby.

HENRY COUNTY COMMONWEALTH'S GRANTS OR PATENTS—Continued

BOOK D

	Page	Name	Date	Acres	Location
251	647	George Hairston.......—....	1 Mar. 1781	467	On the north side of Smith's River, adjoining Copeland's line.
252	667	Ralph Shelton, Jr.......	"	78	On both sides of Dan River.
253	669	Charles Cox........	"	271	On Turkey Pen Branch.
254	674	Charles Cox........	"	271	On Turkey Pen Branch. This grant appears to be recorded twice. See Page 69.
255	683	John Wells........	10 Apr. "	300	Being late the property of James Smith, a British subject, and sold by Abraham Penn, Escheator, to said Wells.
256	702	Bradley Smith......	1 Mar. 1781	244	On the branches of Mayo River, adjoining George Taylor.
257	715	Rowland H. Burke......	"	199	On Goblingtown Creek.
258	717	Josiah Hodges........	"	173	On both sides of Pigg River, adjoining Richard Whitton.
259	731	Palliah Shelton......	"	310	On the South Fork of Russell's Creek, adjoining David Rogers.
260	746	Jesse Heard........	"	183	On the north side of Pigg River, adjoining Darby Ryon.
261	775	John Fontaine........	"	109	On the waters of Smith's River and Leatherwood Creek.
262	799	Anthony Smith........	10 Apr. "	440	On Horse Pasture and Mayo waters, adjoining Josiah Smith.
263	800	Daniel Newman......	"	205	On Stone's Creek, adjoining Jacob Cogar, etc.
264	805	Stephen Heard........	"	397	On the Meadow Branch and Foul Ground Branch.
265	811	John Marr........	"	142	On the south side of North Mayo River.
266	816	Hamon Critze........	"	200	On both sides of Spoon Creek, adjoining Keetin's land.
267	818	Hamon Critze........	"	48	On Spoon Creek, adjoining Robert Barrett's land.
268	820	William Halbert......	"	486	On Russell Creek waters, adjoining John Parr's land.
269	821	Bartlet Renalds......	"	367	On Stone's Creek.
270	825	Benjamin Hawkins.....	"	309	On Stone's Creek, adjoining the land of William Taylor.
271	830	Thomas Morrison.....	"	180	Adjoining his own land.
272	833	John Newman........	"	182	On Stone's Creek, adjoining Daniel Newman.
273	841	Nehemiah Prawther......	"	160	On the branches of Mayo, adjoining Thomas Stockton.
274	850	Augustine Brown......	"	162	On the waters of Peter's Creek, adjoining the county line.
275	862	James East........	"	286	On the south side of Horse Pasture Creek, adjoining Watson's land.
276	863	George Poor........	"	351	On Fusy's Fork, adjoining Shelton's land.
277	874	Frederick Fulkerson......	"	189	On the north side of South Mayo River, adjoining his own and Roberts's land.
278	876	James Mankin........	"	290	On both sides of Russell's Creek.
279	883	Deberix Gillum........	"	202	On the North Branches of North Mayo River, adjoining Randolph and Company.

HENRY COUNTY COMMONWEALTH'S GRANTS OR PATENTS—Continued

BOOK D

	Page	Name	Date	Acres	Location
280	888	Thomas Hamilton	10 Apr. 1781	198	On the waters of Stone's Creek, adjoining Jacob Cogar.
281	890	Hayman Critre	"	347	On Mill Creek, adjoining Archelaus Hughes.
282	891	Hayman Critre	"	210	On the branches of Mill Creek, adjoining Hughes' land.
283	893	John Ross	"	184	On the south side of Smith River, adjoining Turner's land.
284	895	Abraham Frazer	"	286	On Spoon Creek, adjoining the land of James Dickenson.
285	900	John Grisham, Jr.	"	350	On Spoon Creek, adjoining Parr's land.
286	902	James East	"	670	On the north side of Big Pasture Creek, adjoining John Watson.
287	903	Richard Adams	"	434	On the waters of Mill Creek, adjoining Haymon Critre.
288	905	Philip Buzzard	"	383	On the waters of Spoon Creek, adjoining William Wilson.
289	909	Henry Parr	"	445	On the branches of the South Mayo River, adjoining his own land.
290	911	John Parr, Sr.	"	148	On the Mayo River, adjoining his own land.
291	913	Daniel Newman	"	442	On Stone's Creek, adjoining Jacob Cogar.
292	918	John Parr, Sr.	"	391	On the north side of the South Mayo River.
293	920	James Lyon	"	360	On the branches of Russell's Creek.
294	921	Thomas Adams	"	428	On Mill Creek, adjoining Richard Adams.
295	928	William Perkins	"	492	On Poplar Camp Creek, adjoining Charles Thomas.
296	930	Daniel Ross	"	260	On the north side of Smith's River, adjoining his own land.

BOOK E

	Page	Name	Date	Acres	Location
297	77	Stephen Heard	20 July 1780	1,245	On the branches of Camp Branch and Cedar Run, between Pigg River and Blackwater River.
298	108	John Ward	"	89	On both sides of Buffaloe, a creek of the Irvin River.
299	121	John Ward	"	87	On the branches of the Flat Creek of the Irvine River.
300	123	John Ward	"	135	On the North Fork of Turkey Cock Creek and the branches of Runnett Bag.
301	104	John Ward	"	111	On Turkey Cock Creek.
302	128	John Ward	"	217	On the head branches of Wagion Creek.
303	130	John Ward and John Callaway	"	1,170	On both sides of Smith's River and Jointcrack Creek.
304	132	John Ward	"	200	Both sides Smith River, adjoining his own land.

HENRY COUNTY COMMONWEALTH'S GRANTS OR PATENTS—Continued

BOOK E

	Page	Name	Date	Acres	Location
305	133	Thomas M. Randolph, John Harmer and Walter King.	31 July 1780	1,155	On both sides of the North Fork of Mayo River.
306	134	Thomas M. Randolph, John Harmer and Walter King.	"	890	On Jordon's Creek and its branches.
307	135	John Ward	20 "	318	On the south side of Runnett Bag Creek of Smith's River.
308	138	Edward Choat, Jr.	"	253	On the South Fork of Doe Run.
309	141	Edward Choat	"	485	On Doe Run.
310	142	Archibald Grayham	"	900	On Chestnut Creek, adjoining Robert Hill's land.
311	145	Smith Webb	"	129	On Doe Creek, adjoining his own land.
312	146	Jeremiah Earley and James Callaway.	"	374	On both sides of Puping Creek of Pigg River.
313	149	Edward Choat	"	295	On the south branches of Pigg River, adjoining John Holloway.
314	152	Jeremiah Earley and Company.	"	1,196	On the branches of Blackwater River and Pigg River, adjoining John Savarywood.
315	153	Jeremiah Earley and James Callaway.	"	1,057	On Pigg River and north branches thereof, adjoining Robertson, Hill, etc.
316	154	Jeremiah Earley and James Callaway.	20 " 1781	2,256	On the branches of Pigg River and Blackwater, adjoining Manifee.
317	157	Jeremiah Earley and James Callaway.	"	533	On the south branch of Pigg River, adjoining John Furguson.
318	172	Gasper Houser	"	426	On the North Fork of Grassy Fork of Chestnut Creek, adjoining James Martin.
319	176	Robert Hodges	"	193	On Chestnut Creek, adjoining Samuel Patterson.
320	321	Jonathan Davis	"	530	On the waters of Chestnut Creek, adjoining Patterson, etc.
321	432	John Davis	1 Sept. 1780	289	On Owne's Creek of Pigg River, adjoining his own land.
322	481	Butler Stone Street	"	133	On both sides of Leatherwood Creek, adjoining Merry Webb.
333	501	Richard Parsley	"	200	On Beaver Creek.
334	521	Daniel Ramey	"	159	On the waters of Smith's River, adjoining William Alexander.
335	541	William Bohannon	"	300	On the head branches of Butramstown Creek, adjoining Key's land.
336	555	Samuel Fox	"	119	On Little Otter Creek, adjoining Christopher Choat.
337	558	Robert Hill	"	313	On both sides of Pigg River.

HENRY COUNTY COMMONWEALTH'S GRANTS OR PATENTS—Continued

BOOK E

	Page	Name	Date	Acres	Location
338	561	Capt. Thomas Jones	1 Sept. 1780	393	On Turner's Creek and Nicholas's Creek.
339	562	John Grimmet	"	800	On the south side of Pigg River and adjoining Robert Hill.
340	586	George Carter	"	53	On the North Fork of the North Fork of Mayo River.
341	587	Luke Foley	"	146	On Goblingtown Creek.
342	588	George Carter	"	200	On Russell's Creek, adjoining Hanby's land.
343	591	Jacob Cox and John Cantwell	"	293	On the south side of the South Mayo, adjoining Walton's land.
344	601	James Standifer	"	411	On the head branches of the South Fork of Story Creek, adjoining Luke Standefer.
345	610	Isham Solomon	"	87	On Elk Creek, adjoining Bell's land.
346	620	John Jones	"	110	On both sides of the South Fork of Pigg River.
347	621	John Bibe	"	82	On both sides of Daniels Mill Creek of Blackwater River.
348	625	Daniel Smith	"	190	On both sides of Butramstown Creek.
349	628	Henry Sumter	"	278	On the waters of Smith's River, adjoining Woodson and Randolph's land.
350	629	William Bohannon	"	174	On Town Creek.
351	631	Robert Kelly	"	70	On the draughts of Nicholas's Creek.
352	632	Thomas and Swinkfield Hill, Executors and Legatees of Robert Hill, dec'd.	"	159	On both sides of Blackwater River, adjoining John Stephenson.
353	633	James Standeford	"	177	On the branches of Story Creek.
354	634	Jesse Clay	"	142	In the Parish of Saint Patrick, on Blackwater River, adjoining Stephen Heard.
355	637	James Edwards	"	142	On the branches of Smith's River, adjoining James Poteet.
356	639	Thomas Jones	"	147	On both sides of Turner's Creek of Pigg River, adjoining his own land.
357	643	George Reaves	"	138	On both sides of Butramstown Creek, adjoining Childs land.
358	647	Thomas Hail	"	200	On Pigg River, adjoining Mavity's land.
359	649	Joshua Rentfroe	"	110	On the branches of Blackwater River, adjoining William Cook.
360	650	George Reives	"	106	On Smith's River, adjoining the land of William Cox.
361	653	Bartholomey Folin	"	219	On the draughts of Smith's River.
362	655	William Haynes	"	110	On the Grassy Fork of Bull Run.
363	657	John Small	"	188	On the branches of Gills Creek and Rockcastle Creek.

HENRY COUNTY COMMONWEALTH'S GRANTS OR PATENTS—Continued

BOOK E

	Page	Name	Date	Acres	Location
364	660	Edmond Edwards	1 Sept. 1780	263	On Steward's Creek.
365	748	Patrick Henry	28 Nov. "	949	On Smith's River and Leatherwood Creek, adjoining Thomas Wilson, etc.
366	776	Robert Pedigow	1 Jan. 1782	1,214	On the branches of Leatherwood and Talbot's Creek.
367	787	Thomas Edwards	1 Sept. 1780	315	On the draughts of Toulout Creek, adjoining William Edwards.
368	813	William Smith	20 Aug. 1783	139	On Little Peters' Creek.
369	814	George Carter	1 Sept. 1780	344	On South Mayo River, adjoining his own land.
370	838	Thomas Medkiff	20 Aug. "	129	On the branches of Peters' Creek, adjoining his own land.
371	844	Joel Ragland	11 Dec. "	160	On a branch of Pigg River called Turner's Creek, adjoining Mavily's land.
372	845	Joel Ragland	" "	441	On the branches of Pigg River, adjoining William Mavily's land.
373	846	John Murphy	" "	336	On the waters of Pigg River near the Great Mountain, adjoining Joseph Hail.
374	851	John Brammer	" "	248	On White Oak Creek.
375	852	Richard Macoy	" "	377	On branches of Blackwater River.
376	853	Philip Thomas	" "	212	On Smith's River.
377	890	Samuel Allen	1 Sept. "	107	On both sides of the North Fork of Jacke's Creek.
378	891	William Stephens	" "	188	On the branches of Home Creek. (Name of county omitted in the record of this grant, upon examining the survey it appears to be in Henry County.)
379	892	Robert Peregoy	1 Jan. 1782	291	On Camp Branch of Leatherwood Crk., adjoining Elkin's land.
380	895	John Acuff	1 Sept. 1780	450	On the branches of Leatherwood Creek, adjoining Christopher Bowling.
381	901	George Rogers	1 Feb. 1781	225	On the branches of Russell's Creek, adjoining George Carter.
382	902	John Fuson	" "	235	On the North Fork of Story Creek and adjoining James Smith's land.
383	906	Luke Foley	" "	176	On the waters of Great Sycamore Creek.
384	907	Luke Foley	" "	346	On the waters of Goblingtown Creek, adjoining Adams' Order line.

BOOK F

	Page	Name	Date	Acres	Location
385	1	Henry Smith	10 Apr. "	207	On the north branches of Russell's Creek, adjoining Shelton, Lyons, etc.

HENRY COUNTY COMMONWEALTH'S GRANTS OR PATENTS—Continued

BOOK F

	Page	Name	Date	Acres	Location
386	7	Eliphaz Shelton	10 Apr. 1781	365	On the waters of Mayo River.
387	20	James Lyon	" "	153	On the waters of Russell's Creek, adjoining Parr, Walton, etc.
388	22	James Lyon	" "	300	On both sides of Mathews' Creek and adjoining Shelton's land.
389	28	Joseph Anthony	" "	372	On the branches of Marrowbone Creek, adjoining land of Burns, Randolph, etc.
390	31	Samuel Buckley	" "	400	On the branches of Marrowbone Creek, adjoining Meredith, Webb, etc.
391	33	John Dickenson	" "	1,063	On Leatherwood Creek, adjoining Daniel Hankin, etc.
392	37	James Dickenson	" "	361	On Spoon Creek waters, adjoining his own lines.
393	40	August Browne	" "	680	On the waters of Peters' Creek, adjoining George Rogers.
394	46	Stephen Heard	" "	106	On the branches of Poplar Camp Creek.
395	49	Daniel Hankins	" "	316	On the waters of Turkey Cock Creek, adjoining William Hankins.
396	50	Stephen Heard	" "	303	On the branches of Blackwater River, adjoining Blankinship's land.
397	51	Thomas Heard	" "	100	On both sides of Sacks Creek.
398	54	Moses Runnalds	" "	157	On Nobusiness Fork of Mayo River, adjoining Cogar's land.
399	62	John Wills	" "	297	On the south branches of Leatherwood Creek, adjoining Lomax and Company's line.
400	65	John Parr, Jr.	" "	241	On Russell's Creek, adjoining the land of Azariah Shelton.
401	67	John Parr, Sr.	" "	374	On the north branches of South Mayo River, adjoining his own land.
402	68	William Poor	" "	391	On the waters of Spoon Creek, adjoining John Grisham.
403	72	John Grisham	" "	344	On branches of Spoon Creek, adjoining John Parr.
404	97	Stephen Heard	" "	293	On Poplar Camp Creek and Fould Ground Branch.
405	124	John Bookerhoy	1 June 1782	253	On the waters of Jennings Creek.
406	151	John Marr	" "	464	On the north branches of North Mayo River, adjoining Randolph.
407	153	William Hankins	" "	838	On waters of Turkey Cock Creek, adjoining Twitty's land.
408	160	James East	" "	287	On south branches of Horse Pasture Creek.
409	162	John O'Bryan	" "	178	On waters of Nicholas's Creek, adjoining Dennis O'Bryan.
410	167	William Taylor	" "	85	On the branches of Horse Pasture Creek, adjoining Hooker's land.
411	168	Darby Rion	" "	270	On both sides of Widgeon Creek, adjoining Harbour's land.
412	190	Robert Grimmet	" "	195	On branches of Chestnut Creek.

HENRY COUNTY COMMONWEALTH'S GRANTS OR PATENTS—Continued

BOOK G

	Page	Name	Date	Acres	Location
413	142	John Watson	1 Sept. 1782	190	On the head branches of Ramsey's Creek, adjoining Dillian and others.
414	148	Thomas Evans	" "	378	On the branches of Blackwater and Pigg Rivers.
415	153	John Watson	" "	400	On the head branches of Horse Pasture Creek, adjoining Dillian, etc.
416	154	John Watson	" "	81	On the south branches of Horse Pasture Creek, adjoining Vaughan's land.
417	159	Benjamin Murrell	" "	154	On both sides of Beard's Creek.
418	198	Robert Hairstone	" "	153	Adjoining his own lines on Running Bag Creek.
419	199	William French	" "	56	Adjoining Harmon and King.
420	204	Samuel Patterson	" "	140	On Gap Branch of Chestnut Creek.
421	205	Thomas Vaughan	" "	300	On the head branches of Horse Pasture Creek, adjoining Redmond's line.
422	205	Thomas Jameson	" "	315	On the south branches of Marrowbone Creek, adjoining Lumkin's Order line.
423	206	William Cook	1 June	107	On the North Fork of Pigg River, adjoining James Rentfroe.
424	207	Joel Barker	" "	288	On the branches of Mayo River, adjoining Randolph, Dickens, etc.
425	207	John Barker	" "	458	On the North Fork of Spoon Creek.
426	208	Humphrey Posey	" "	30	On the north side of Smith's River, adjoining Gray's land.
427	209	Joseph Davis	" "	566	On the branches of Nicholas's Creek.
428	209	Samuel Hairstone	" "	236	On the branches of Nicholas's Creek, adjoining James Standifer.
429	210	Samuel Patterson	" "	333	On Hades Gap, a branch of Chestnut Creek.
430	211	William Cook	" "	187	On Hatchett Run, adjoining the land of Callaway.
431	212	John Heard	" "	413	On the Fould Ground Branch, adjoining Gilmore, Hartwell, etc.
432	212	Luke Thornton	" "	237	On Chestnut Creek, adjoining Walton's Order line.
433	213	John Kendrick	" "	348	On Smith's River, adjoining Captain Ward's land.
434	214	John Small	" "	164	On the branches of Gills Creek.
435	214	Samuel Cox	" "	400	On the Dan River near the Pinnacles, adjoining his own land.
436	215	Robert Hairstone	" "	132	On the waters of Runnett Bag Creek, adjoining his own land.
437	215	James Edmundson	" "	180	On the south side of Blackwater River on both sides of Standefer's Creek.
438	216	Robert Hairstone	" "	774	On Runnett Bag Creek, adjoining Mead's land.
439	218	Lansford Hall	" "	202	On the north side of Pigg River, adjoining Dickenson.

HENRY COUNTY COMMONWEALTH'S GRANTS OR PATENTS—Continued

BOOK G

	Page	Name	Date	Acres	Location
440	246	William Warrain	1 Nov. 1782	313	On the branches of Chestnut Creek, adjoining Johnston.
441	246	Richard Welch	1 June "	147	On Stone's Creek, adjoining Robert Hooker.
442	250	Daniel Ross	1 Nov. "	260	On the north side of Smith's River and on Nicholas's Creek.
443	306	William and Janes Robertson.	21 Dec. "	1,142	Adjoining the land of Randolph, Harmer, etc.

BOOK H

	Page	Name	Date	Acres	Location
444	9	Stephen Heard	7 May 1783	460	On the south side of Blackwater River, adjoining Richard Bailey.
445	10	Stephen Heard	" " "	269	On the south side of Blackwater River, adjoining Bennian's line.
446	62	Henry Tate	27 "	200	On the north side of Smith's Creek, adjoining Randolph otherwise Hairston.
447	176	James McCraw	27 June "	164	On the branches of Horse Pasture Creek, adjoining the lines of Randolph and Company.
448	230	William Rentfrow	30 "	145	On Runnett Bag Creek.
449	243	Daniel Prilleman	17 "	285	On the waters of Nicholas's Creek, adjoining Dennis O'Brian.
450	251	Nathan Sellars	3 July "	164	On the Pine Spur on the top of the Blue Ridge.
451	255	Israel Standefer	30 June "	419	On the head branches of Bull Run and Standefer's Creek.
452	258	James Phips	16 "	335	On both sides of the Meadow Creek, a north branch of Pigg River.
453	263	Joseph Davis	" "	536	On Otter Creek, adjoining William Tharp.
454	297	Aaron Wousley	3 July "	286	On the waters of Nicholas's Creek.
455	299	William Mavity	5 "	223	On a branch of Otter Creek and adjoining Davis.
456	304	Joseph Davis	17 June "	179	On a branch of Otter Creek.
457	326	Shadrack Woodson	" "	134	On the rich run of Blackwater River.
458	367	David Barton	26 May "	443	On the South Fork of Otter Creek, adjoining Nelley Cummings' land.
459	369	Robert Stogdan	30 June "	662	On Nicholas's Creek, adjoining the land of Dennis O'Bryan.
460	372	Archelaus White	25 "	122	On the south branches of the North Fork of Blackwater River, adjoining his own land.
461	390	Samuel Packwood	13 "	273	On the Northwest Fork of Mill Creek of Smith's River.
462	400	Blackmore Hughs	27 Aug. "	300	On the south side of Smith's River.
463	402	James Elkins	" "	442	On Smith's River, adjoining Poteet's land.

HENRY COUNTY COMMONWEALTH'S GRANTS OR PATENTS—Continued

BOOK H

	Page	Name	Date	Acres	Location
464	405	Benjamin Handy	27 Aug. 1783	188	On the waters of Beard's Creek.
465	409	James Ecton	"	321	On the branches of the Nobusiness Fork of Mayo River.
466	411	William Farguson	"	664	On the branches of Nicholas's Creek, adjoining William Standefer.
467	438	William Kelley	1 Sept.	158	On the Fork of Blackwater River, adjoining Stout's land.
468	440	Cornelius Keeth, Sr.	"	130	On the branches of Stewart's Creek.
469	446	Thomas Jones, Jr.	"	162	On the south branch of Otter Creek, adjoining David Barton.
470	447	Thomas Jones	"	275	On the South Fork of Otter Creek, adjoining David Barton.
471	452	Cornelius Keeth, Jr.	"	133	On the waters of Fish River.
472	453	John Keile	"	444	On the branches of Nicholas's Creek, adjoining Robert Stockton.
473	456	Charles Foster	"	332	On both sides of Puppy Creek of Smith's River.
474	459	Joseph Lewis	"	257	On the head branches of Pigg River, beginning where Beck's line adjoins Greer's.
475	461	Joseph Lewis	"	174	On the head branches of Pigg River, adjoining his new survey.
476	507	John Lumsden	"	409	On the branches of Blackwater River, adjoining John Nowlin.
477	517	John Hilton	3 Oct	200	On both sides of Blackwater River, beginning at Randolph's corner.
478	520	Edward Choat	1 Sept.	307	On the branches of Doe Creek, adjoining Edward Choat, Jr.
479	531	James McCraw	8 Oct.	258	On both sides of Fall Creek of Horse Pasture, adjoining Randolph's line.
480	572	Samuel Patterson and William Ryan	4 "	900	On the branches of Pigg River and Doe Creek, adjoining Holloway's line.
481	634	John Marr	3 Nov.	400	On both sides of Dan River, adjoining Shelton's land.

BOOK I

	Page	Name	Date	Acres	Location
482	13	Jacob Brillemon	23 May	250	On the south branch of Blackwater, adjoining Daniel Donohoo.
483	106	John Marr	3 Nov.	34	On the north side of Big Dan River, adjoining his own land.
484	107	John Marr	"	300	On the south side of the Areseat River.
485	109	John Marr	"	221	On the west side of Dan River on both sides of Rock Creek, adjoining Bell's Order line.

HENRY COUNTY COMMONWEALTH'S GRANTS OR PATENTS—Continued

BOOK I

	Page	Name	Date	Acres	Location
486	153	Abraham Eades	4 Nov. 1783	344	On Archey's Creek.
487	231	Robert Jones, Sr.	6 Dec. "	160	On the South Fork of Pigg River, adjoining his own land.
488	233	Blackmore Hughes	" "	687	On Buffalo Creek and branches of Smith's River.
489	236	Jacob Preliman, Jr.	" "	65	On the north side of the South Fork of Blackwater River.
490	237	William Lynch	" "	295	On the branches of Mayo River, adjoining Randolph's line.
491	241	John Wimbish	10 "	285	On the branches of Cascade Crk., adjoining Russell, Rice, etc.
492	259	Edward Tatum	9 "	550	On the south side of Bartlett's Branch, a South Fork of Dan River.
493	261	Edward Tatum	8 "	106	On both sides of Little Peters' Creek, adjoining Hanley.
494	263	Robert Stocton	" "	192	On both sides of Beard's Creek, beginning in John Handy's line.
495	342	Susanna Cameron	23 Jan. 1784	231	On the branches of Stone's Creek, adjoining John Cogar.
496	347	Edward Baker	5 Feb. "	323	On both sides of Smith's River.
497	349	John Witt	7 " "	222	On the branches of Blackberry Creek, adjoining John Gowin.
498	351	Obed Baker	7 "	680	On the south branches of the Pinnacle Fork of Dan River.
499	352	William Farguson and William Mavity	9 "	1,450	On Story Creek, adjoining Ryon's land.
500	357	James Callaway	" "	402	On the branches of Blackwater and Pigg River, adjoining his own and Bird's land.
501	360	James Spencer	12 "	114	On the bold branch of Marrowbone Creek, adjoining Taylor's line.
502	362	Richard Baker	11 "	218	On both sides of Bowins Creek, adjoining Richmons line.
503	363	Nehemiah Prayther	14 "	175	Adjoining Runnolds' land.
504	368	Richard Tucker	14 "	370	On the north side of Smith's River.
505	370	John Henderson	17 "	122	On the south branches of the North Fork of Blackwater, adjoining his own line.
506	372	Thomas Jones	" "	400	On the South Fork of Pigg River, adjoining Robert Jones, Sr.
507	374	Marvil Nash	" "	302	On the waters of Mayo River, adjoining Prayther's land.
508	376	Hugh McWilliams	16 "	443	On both sides of Reedy Creek.
509	380	Eliphas Shelton	18 "	531	On the waters of Mayo River, beginning, etc. Carters' Corners.
510	383	Edmund Sweeny	24 "	346	On both sides of Nicholas's Creek, adjoining O'Brian's and Ross's land.
511	385	John Rentfro	21 "	300	On the north branches of Pigg River, adjoining Jones, Geerhart, etc.

HENRY COUNTY COMMONWEALTH'S GRANTS OR PATENTS—Continued

BOOK I

	Page	Name	Date	Acres	Location
512	390	John Farrel	25 Feb. 1784	565	On Sycamore Creek, adjoining the land of Bartley Folie.
513	394	Robert Stockton	"	52	On the waters of Nicholas's Creek, adjoining his own land.
514	400	William Harrison	3 "	111	On both sides of Shooting Creek.
515	401	Henry Cogar	4 "	256	On the branches of Stoner Creek, adjoining Thos. Hambleton.
516	408	William Read	16 "	259	On both sides of Blackberry Creek.
517	410	Marvil Nash	14 "	445	On both sides of the Prayther Fork of Mayo River, adjoining Stockton.
518	414	James Doak	20 "	300	On the head of the South Fork of Johnson's Creek.
519	423	Gideon Smith	18 "	455	On the branches of Otter Creek, adjoining Daniel Smith.
520	426	George Reaves	21 "	254	On the branches of Weding Creek.
521	437	John Dickenson	28 "	50	On Little Dan River, adjoining Ivie's land.
522	438	John Henderson	"	172	On the Blue Ridge, including some of the branches of Blackwater Run, adjoining land of Huff, etc.
523	440	George Wadkins	"	37	On the west side of Little Dan River and on both sides of John's Creek.
524	441	Isaac Cloud	"	167	On Elk Creek, adjoining land of Marr and Hanley.
525	443	George Hairston	27 "	400	On the south side of Smith's River and adjoining his own land.
526	445	Robert Stockton	"	350	On the waters of Beard's Creek, adjoining his own land.
527	447	Robert Stockton	"	286	On the waters of Nicholas's Creek, adjoining his own land.
528	482	William Webb	1 Mar.	206	On the branches of Paul's Creek on the southwest side of the Good Spur.
529	489	William Hickingbottom	28 Feb.	106	On both sides of Sun's Run, a branch of the Arrat River.
530	491	William Woods	"	450	On one of the North Forks of Johnston's Creek, adjoining Baker's land.
531	493	William Woods	"	211	On the branches of Little Peters' Creek, adjoining Medkiff's land.
532	517	Jacob McCraw	18 Mar.	300	On the head of Loving's Creek in a cove of the Mountain known by the name of Spice Cove.
533	518	Jacob McCraw	"	111	On a branch of Loving's Creek near Ward's Gap.

BOOK K

	Page	Name	Date	Acres	Location
534	58	Jesse Hilton	6 Dec. 1783	336	On the South Fork of Jack's Creek.
535	71	James Lyon	8 "	222	On the south branches of Russel's Creek, adjoining his own line.

HENRY COUNTY COMMONWEALTH'S GRANTS OR PATENTS—Continued

BOOK K

	Page	Name	Date	Acres	Location
536	101	Benjamin Hale	6 Dec. 1783	190	On the north side of the South Fork of Pigg River.
537	163	Joseph Street	24 Jan. 1784	133	On both sides of Goblingtown Creek, adjoining Rowland H. Birk.
538	165	John Farrie	"	155	On Sycamore Creek, adjoining Folie's land.
539	166	Josiah Halkin	"	288	On both sides of Reedy Creek, adjoining Williams' land.
540	168	Stephen Heard	22 "	397	On the Meadow Branch and Foul Graise Ground.
541	169	Nathan Hall	23 "	456	On the waters of Smith's River, adjoining his own land.
542	172	John Cogan	"	386	On the branches of Mayo River, adjoining Jourdan's line.
543	177	John Briscoe	24 "	289	Adjoining King's Order line of his Marrowbone Tract.
544	181	Elijah Donathan	26 "	80	On Richard Bennett's Mill Creek, a South Fork of Little Dan River.
545	184	George Allen	"	126	On both sides of King's Run, a South Fork of the Ararat River.
546	185	Samuel Allen	"	112	On the North Fork of Jack's Creek.
547	186	Jonathan Hanby	"	110	On the branches of South Mayo River, adjoining his own land.
548	188	Charles Thomas	"	394	On the branches of Joint Craik Creek.
549	189	William Wann	"	114	On the North Fork of Johnson's Creek.
550	192	John Gussell	29 "	446	On Blackberry Creek, adjoining land of Thomas Halland.
551	196	Benjamin Garrett	3 Feb.	400	On both sides of Big Dan River near the Pinnacle, adjoining Samuel Cox.
552	198	Obed Baker	"	800	On the branches of Johnson's Creek.
553	199	Peter Huff	"	26	On both sides of the South Fork of Blackwater River, adjoining his own line.
554	201	John Farrall	4 "	139	On Sycamore Creek.
555	202	John Loyd	3 "	325	On Elk River, adjoining Cloud's line.
556	205	George Sumpter	4 "	277	On the head of Horse Pasture Creek and adjoining John Watson.
557	206	John Hickey	5 "	193	On the head of Reed Creek and Town Creek waters.
558	210	George Hairston	6 "	219	On the branches of Little Marrowbone Creek, adjoining Gray's line.
559	212	George Carter	7 "	211	On the waters of Mayo River, adjoining Logan's line.
560	215	William Carter and Jonathan Jennings	" "	528	On Russell's Creek, adjoining John Barrott's line.
561	217	Aaron Waldon	10 "	330	On the branches of Smith's River and Goblingtown Creek.
562	220	Edward Pedigow	13 "	50	On the Grassy Creek, adjoining his own land.

HENRY COUNTY COMMONWEALTH'S GRANTS OR PATENTS—Continued

BOOK K

	Page	Name	Date	Acres	Location
563	221	Walter McCoy	14 Feb. 1784	96	On Turner's Creek, a branch of Pigg River, adjoining Smith's land.
564	223	William Weeks	12 "	208	On both sides of Runnett Bag Creek, adjoining William Kennedy.
565	232	Darby Ryon	23 "	146	On Nicholas's Creek, adjoining his own and Robert Jones' land.
566	234	John Randolph	"	219	On Mayo Waters, adjoining Nashes' land.
567	235	William Skeefe and Alexander Donelson	24 "	218	On both sides of John's Creek.
568	243	James Taylor	29 Jan.	145	On the head branches of the North Fork of Spoon Creek, and the head of the Nobusiness Fork of Mayo River.
569	244	Nicholas Baker	24 "	400	On the Blue Ridge opposite to the head of Doe Run and some of the branches of Johnson's Creek.
570	246	John Barker	"	181	On the branches of Spoon Creek.
571	247	Benjamin Dillian	6 Feb.	315	On the branches of Ramsey's Creek, adjoining Henry Dillian.
572	248	John Barrott	"	262	On Russell's Creek, adjoining Walton's Order Line.
573	250	Jacob Adams	7 "	971	On the branches of the Mayo, called the Roundabout, adjoining Barton's line.
574	258	Rowland Tankesley	10 "	265	On the branches of Leatherwood Creek, adjoining Hamilton's land.
575	259	Charles Burnett	"	147	On the branches of Beaver Creek, adjoining Cooper's line.
576	263	John Randolph	18 "	291	On Mayo Waters.
577	264	William Reed	16 "	270	On both sides of Blackberry Creek.
578	268	Thomas Smith	20 "	359	On Mayo Waters, adjoining Chiles's line.
579	272	William Skeefe and Alexander Donelson	24 "	117	On both sides of John's Creek and adjoining the county line.
580	274	Zadock Smith	"	338	On the branches of the North Mayo River.
581	278	Eliphas Shelton	28 "	72	On the Blue Ridge, including some of the branches of Johnson's and Loving's Creek.
582	279	William Cloud	"	196	On the branches of Elk and Turkey Cock Creek, adjoining Joseph Cloud.
583	281	Palitiah Shelton	"	251	On Wigeon Creek, adjoining land of Jones, Ward, etc.
584	304	Jacob Adams	1 Mar.	295	On both sides of Bourn's Creek.
585	325	William Webb	"	108	On the branches of Paul's Creek.

HENRY COUNTY COMMONWEALTH'S GRANTS OR PATENTS—Continued

BOOK K

	Page	Name	Date	Acres	Location
586	326	John Gowin	1 Mar.1784	374	On both sides of Blackberry Creek, adjoining his own land.
587	338	Palitiah Shelton	28 Feb. "	90	On the south side of the Rockey Mountain, including some of the branches of the South Mayo River.
588	339	Richard Davison	" "	113	On the branches of Elk Creek.
589	341	Samuel Street	" "	298	On both sides of the Widow's Fork of North Fork of Elk Creek, adjoining Midkiff's land.
590	343	John Pilfree	" "	176	On the south side of Smith's River, adjoining Hairston line.
591	352	Eliphaz Shelton	" "	590	On both sides of the North Mayo River, adjoining John Shelton.
592	358	Robert Pedigow	18 Mar. "	776	On branches of Beaver Creek, adjoining Copland, etc.
593	361	Robert Pedigow	" "	236	On branches of Leatherwood Creek, adjoining Lomax and Company's lines.
594	526	Benjamin Harrison, Jr	7 Apr. "	1,150	On the forks of Dan River, beginning on the North Fork.
595	555	Dutton Lane	20 " "	642	On Horse Pasture Creek, adjoining Randolph and Company's line.
596	581	Samuel Hairston	7 " "	1,044	On the branches of Nicholas's Creek, adjoining his own and Darby Ryon's land.

BOOK L

	Page	Name	Date	Acres	Location
597	104	German Baker and David Jameson	1 May "	852	On Grassy Hill, adjoining Duff's land and John Donelson.
598	538	Daniel Hankins	15 June "	400	On Leatherwood and Turkey Cock Creek, adjoining Joseph Dickenson.
599	561	Philemon Sutherland	1 May "	265	On waters of Bull Run, adjoining William Swanson, etc.

BOOK M

	Page	Name	Date	Acres	Location
600	55	John Dickenson	1 May "	257	On waters of Leatherwood Creek, adjoining Benjamin McCraw, etc.
601	56	Robert Pedigow	" "	292	On Tolbot's Creek, adjoining his own and Bouldin's land.
602	152	John Craghead	" June "	270	On the south side of Blackwater River, adjoining Samuel Smith.
603	179	William Thorp	" "	157	On Otter Creek.
604	180	William Thorp	" "	102	On the branches of Otter Creek.
605	205	Jacob Cayton	" "	560	On both sides of Stewart's Creek, adjoining Edward's land.

HENRY COUNTY COMMONWEALTH'S GRANTS OR PATENTS—Continued

BOOK M

	Page	Name	Date	Acres	Location
606	225	Samuel Patterson	1 June 1784	400	On the South Fork of Doe Run, adjoining Smith's land.
607	244	William Tanzey	" "	351	On the South Fork of Bowin's Creek.
608	305	John Ward	10 July "	100	On the waters of Jack's Creek.
609	314	David Chadwell	" "	380	On the south side of Smith's River, adjoining Hailey's land.
610	429	Peter Copeland	1 Oct.	407	On waters of Beaver Creek and adjoining his own land.
611	431	Peter Copeland	" "	310	On branches of Beaver Creek.
612	432	Peter Copeland	" "	356	On the north side of Ready Creek.
613	442	George Hairston	12 "	201	On waters of Smith's River, adjoining Randolph's line.
614	511	Joseph Paxton	20 Sept.	192	On both sides of Paul's Creek and adjoining the county line.
615	551	John Smallman	1 Oct.	200	On waters of Goblingtown Creek, adjoining James Ingram.
616	658	Thomas Bouldin	20 Nov.	200	On Jourdan's Creek and Grassy Creek, adjoining Salmon's line.
617	599	Daniel Rogers	1 Dec.	378	On Russell's Creek waters, adjoining George Rogers.
618	652	Edward Richards	16 "	252	On both sides Edge's Branch, the north waters of Chestnut Creek.
619	657	Woody Burge	10 "	160	On both sides of Peters' Creek, adjoining Smith's land.

BOOK N

	Page	Name	Date	Acres	Location
620	148	Jacob Cayton	1 June "	460	On both sides of Stewart's Creek and the branches of Drag Creek.
621	237	John Booth	10 July "	206	On Leatherwood Creek, adjoining Lomax and Company's Order line.
622	386	Thomas Bouldin	20 Nov. "	212	On Grassy Creek, adjoining his own land.
623	401	George Hairston	4 Dec. "	148	On Reed Creek, adjoining his own and Murphey's land.
624	468	Patrick Henry	1 Jan. 1785	2,125	On branches of Mulberry Creek, Rugg Creek, Smith's River and Beaver Creek.
625	492	John Ward	16 Dec. 1784	166	On the branches of Town Creek called the branches of the Grassy Mountain or Brown Hills.
626	497	Woodey Burge	" "	43	On the branches of Peters' Creek, adjoining Brown's land.
627	503	Thomas Garrison	10 " "	122	On Rockcastle Creek.
628	505	Brice Martin and Mordecai Hord	10 " "	190	On the south side of Jourdon's Creek and adjoining Salmon's line.

HENRY COUNTY COMMONWEALTH'S GRANTS OR PATENTS—Continued

BOOK O

	Page	Name	Acres	Date	Location
629	162	David Peck	98	1 Apr. 1784	On the branches of Chestnut Creek, adjoining Archibald Grayham.
630	303	Charles Thomas	60	30 Mar. 1785	On the branches of Smith's River, adjoining Sylas Ralliff.

BOOK P

631	91	Thomas and Swinfield Hill, heirs of Robert Hill, deceased.	391	10 July 1784	On the branches of Blackwater River and adjoining Thomson's line.
632	98	Joseph Lyall	166	5 "	On the branches of Turkey Cock Creek, adjoining Twitty's land.

BOOK R

633	12	John Dickenson	396	11 Aug. 1785	On both sides of Snow Creek, adjoining Joshua Brock's land.
634	380	Solomon Davis	85	20 Sept. "	On both sides of Snow Creek, adjoining Joshua Brock's land.
635	402	Isham Webb	25	" "	On Matthew's Branch.
636	420	Harrison Hubbard	47	" "	On the north side of Smith's River, beginning at the mouth of Bowing Creek.
637	422	William Halbert	66	" "	On the south side of Russell's Creek, adjoining his own line.
638	423	Jacob Johnson	45	" "	On both sides of Loving's Creek.
639	432	Jessee Witt	68	" "	On a north branch of Horse Pasture Creek, adjoining Randolph and Taylor's line.
640	434	George Yates	92	" "	On the South Fork of Johnson's Creek.
641	439	William Adams	20	27 "	On the north branch of Mill Creek of North Mayo River and adjoining Richard Adams's, etc.

BOOK S

642	105	Joseph Hodges	50	4 Aug. 1785	On the south side of Pigg River, adjoining Richard Wilton, etc.
643	383	John Thomas	131	29 Sept. "	Adjoining Landsford Hall, James Cowden, etc.
644	475	John Small	58	26 Oct. "	On the branches of Jill's Creek and adjoining his own land.

HENRY COUNTY COMMONWEALTH'S GRANTS OR PATENTS—Continued

BOOK U

	Page	Name	Date	Acres	Location
645	611	Augustine Brown........	2 Dec. 1785	330	On the south side of the North Fork of Little Dan River.
646	701	Anthony Tittle.........	" "	415	On both sides of Goblingtown Creek and adjoining Adam's Order line.
647	746	William Isham..........	" "	271	On Little Sycamore Creek, adjoining Thomas Morrow.

BOOK V

648	572	James Prunty..........	2 Dec. 1785	400	On both sides of Ditto's Creek of Snow Creek, adjoining Caldwell's line.
649	694	George Rogers.........	" "	242	On Russell's Creek, adjoining Carter and Jenning's survey.
650	725	Robert Stockdell......	" "	209	On the branches of Leatherwood and Beaver Creek, adjoining Hicks, etc.

BOOK W

651	266	John Lumsden.........	31 Mar. 1786	440	On the Maple Swamp, a branch of Blackwater River.
652	270	John Dickenson.......	" "	162	On the north side of Pigg River, adjoining Solomon Davis, etc.
653	272	John Jones............	" "	132	On the South Fork of Back Creek of Yadkin River.
654	276	William Donathan.....	" "	261	On both sides of Squirrel Creek, a south branch of Dan River.
655	280	Palatiah Shelton.......	" "	309	On the head branches of the Middle Fork of Little Dan River.
656	281	John Botetourt........	" "	395	On the north branches of Mayo River, adjoining his own line.
657	283	Isham Webb...........	" "	193	On the head branches of Paul's Creek and east side of the Main Mountain.
658	580	Anthony Tittle.........	5 Apr.	201	On Goblingtown Creek, adjoining land of Foley, Harbour, etc.
659	586	Bailey Carter..........	7 "	100	On a north branch of Otter Creek, adjoining his own land.

BOOK X

660	17	Isaac Cloud...........	2 Dec. 1785	101	On the Blue Ridge, including some of the branches of Squirrel Creek.
661	57	Isaac Cloud...........	" "	135	On the waters of Fall Creek on the east side of Bell's Spur, adjoining his own line.

HENRY COUNTY COMMONWEALTH'S GRANTS OR PATENTS—Continued

BOOK X

	Page	Name	Acres	Date	Location
662	76	Jacob Coger	117	2 Dec. 1785	On Stone's Creek, adjoining Richard Welch's land.
663	109	Charles Barnard	360	"	On Sycamore Creek, adjoining Luke Foley.
664	133	Wooddy Burge	128	"	On the south side of Peter's Creek, adjoining the county line.
665	138	Francis Barrott	889	"	On the waters of Mayo River and adjoining Azariah Shelton.
666	154	Shadrack Barrott	190	"	On the branches of Russell's Creek and adjoining Henry Smith.
667	170	Augustine Brown	320	"	On branches of Little Peter's Creek, adjoining Lawson, etc.
668	232	Azariah Shelton	933	"	Adjoining Jacob Adam's land, etc.
669	329	John Stephens	236	"	On the branches of Home Creek and adjoining James Roberts, etc.
670	364	John Geey	391	"	On Smith's River and both sides of Buffalo Creek.
671	442	Thomas Henderson	336	"	On both sides of Smith's River, adjoining John Henderson, Samuel Helton, etc.
672	481	Samuel Hilton	364	"	On Jack's Creek and Turnip Creek waters.
673	483	Daniel Howell	118	"	On Smith's River, adjoining John Henderson and Thomas Henderson.
674	529	Bartlett Foley	491	"	On Sycamore Creek, adjoining his own and land of Luke Foley, etc.
675	582	William Forkner	178	"	On both sides of Fall Creek of Dan River, adjoining Mar's land.
676	683	Peter Rigg	183	"	On the head of South Marrowbone Creek, adjoining Thomas Webb.

BOOK Y

	Page	Name	Acres	Date	Location
677	23	James Callaway	12,800	20 Dec. 1785	In the counties of Bedford and Henry on Blackwater River, adjoining James Stephens, etc.
678	264	William Fain	292	31 Mar. 1786	On both sides of Spoon Creek, adjoining Shelton, Parr, Ward, etc.
679	490	Benoni Perryman	400	19 July "	On the branches of Blackwater River, adjoining Richard Perryman.

BOOK Z

	Page	Name	Acres	Date	Location
680	10	William Alexander	354	2 Dec. 1785	On the south side of Smith's River and both sides of Marrowbone Creek.

HENRY COUNTY COMMONWEALTH'S GRANTS OR PATENTS—Continued

BOOK Z

	Page	Name	Date	Acres	Location
681	335	George Evans	2 Dec. 1785	300	On the south side of Paul's Creek, and on the side of the Main Mountain.
682	446	Samuel Allen	"	174	On waters of Goblingtown Creek, adjoining Luke Folie's land.
683	447	William Austin	"	600	On top of the Main Mountain and on the waters of Dan River.
684	456	Phillip Anglin	"	131	On the north side of Fall Creek and north side of North Mayo River.
685	459	Phillip Anglin	"	157	On both sides of the North Fork of Fall Creek, adjoining Medlock's line.
686	467	John Hammon	"	202	On both sides of Johnson's Creek, adjoining John McGown.

BOOK No. 1

	Page	Name	Date	Acres	Location
687	155	Daniel Hankins	11 Apr. 1786	4,822	On the branches of the South Fork of Sandy River and Leatherwood Creek.

BOOK No. 3

	Page	Name	Date	Acres	Location
688	112	William Hudspeth, William Griffin and Henry Biggs	22 June 1786	465	On the branches of the Ararat, adjoining Marr's Order line, etc.
689	132	Hugh Innes	"	933	On both sides of Snow Creek and adjoining Randolph's line.
690	168	Thomas Edwards	5	550	On the north side of Smith's River and on both sides of Home Creek.
691	183	Griffith Dickerson	"	246	On the north side of Smith's River.
692	293	George Adams	"	260	On both sides of Leatherwood Creek, adjoining Randolph and Company's line.
693	298	Benoni Perryman	15 July	340	On the branches of Blackwater River, adjoining Israel Standafer.
694	612	Page White	26 June	400	On the south branches of Bull Run, adjoining David's line.
695	699	James Edwards	5 July	702	On Smith's River, adjoining James Robertson, etc.

BOOK No. 5

	Page	Name	Date	Acres	Location
696	165	Thomas Jones	5 July 1786	600	On branches of Runnett Bag Creek, adjoining John Mead.

HENRY COUNTY COMMONWEALTH'S GRANTS OR PATENTS—Continued

	Page	Name	Date	Acres	Location
			BOOK No. 7		
697	619	William Anderson	16 Aug. 1787	38	On both sides of Roaring Branch of South Fork of Blackwater.
			BOOK No. 8		
698	203	Joel Walker	11 Jan. 1787	226	On branches of the North Fork of Pigg River, adjoining Joseph Lewis.
699	395	Ashford Napier	23 "	188	Near the head of the Maple Branch of Snow Creek, adjoining the land of David Prewet.
700	498	James Taylor	6 Feb. "	207	On Marrowbone Creek, adjoining his own land.
701	642	John Wilson	14 May "	36	On the South Fork of Blackwater River.
			BOOK No. 9		
702	108	William Farguson	14 Apr. 1787	112	On branches of Nicholas's Creek, adjoining Samuel Hairston, etc.
703	119	William Farguson	15 "	276	On the south branches of Pigg River.
704	348	Joseph Lewis	15 May "	40	On the waters of the North Fork of Pigg River, adjoining his own land.
705	487	Joseph Martin	21 June "	435	On Rugg Creek, adjoining his own land, etc.
706	557	Frederick Fitzgerald	19 "	77	On the north side of South Mayo River and both sides of Spoon Creek.
707	687	Jonathan Peck	17 July "	120	On Mill Branch of Runnett Bag Creek.
708	695	John Smith	16 "	187	On branches of Beard's Creek, adjoining his own line.
709	709	William Mills	17 "	223	On the branches of Matrimony Creek, adjoining Fountain, etc.
710	729	John Smith	16 "	300	On Little Otter Creek.
711	737	William Weatherspoon	23 "	249	On the branches of the Middle Fork of the South Mayo.
			BOOK No. 10		
712	366	William Kennady, Sr.	21 June 1787	551	On head branches of Runnett Creek, adjoining Jones' land.
713	399	George F. Harris	25 "	78	On branches of Cascade Creek, adjoining James Roberts and others.

BOOK No. 10

	Page	Name	Date	Acres	Location
714	448	Allen Brock	3 Aug. 1787	11	On waters of Snow Creek, adjoining Copeland, Heard, etc.
715	453	William Kelly	" "	60	On branches of Blackwater River, adjoining Price's land.
716	478	William Brown	9 "	170	On the South Fork of Leatherwood Creek, adjoining Williams' line.
717	482	Daniel Wilson	7 "	336	On Home Creek, adjoining Thomas Edwards.
718	602	John Dickenson	10 Sept. "	66	On both sides of Bushey Fork of Stewart's Creek, near where it crosses the county line.
719	605	Samuel Patterson	13 "	235	On both sides of North Fork of Chestnut Creek, adjoining Callaway's line.
720	626	Samuel Dust	1 Oct. "	13	On the south side of the North Fork of Stoney Creek, adjoining Fuson and others.
721	627	James Callaway and John Earley.	8 "	200	On the north side of Pigg River, adjoining Swinfield Hill, etc.
722	628	Adam Turner	10 Sept. "	45	On the north side of Rock Castle Creek.
723	629	Andrew Thompson	" "	148	On the South Branches of Stoney Creek, adjoining William Thompson.
724	631	Stephen Raney	1 Oct. "	268	On the branches of Home Creek, adjoining John Stephens, Peter Perkins, etc.

BOOK No. 11

	Page	Name	Date	Acres	Location
725	28	Samuel Patterson	6 Feb. 1787	510	On the South Branches of Chestnut Creek.
726	362	Philip Buzzard	19 June "	198	On the north side the South Mayo River, adjoining Walton's line.
727	392	George F. Harriss	25 "	191	On the waters of Home Creek and Cascade, adjoining William Stephens, etc.
728	460	Joseph Sowell	11 July "	56	On the waters of Stone's Creek, adjoining James East.
729	485	William Weatherspoon	23 "	317	On the Orchard Fork of Mayo River.
730	494	Reubin Hill	" "	404	On both sides of Prather's Fork of the North Mayo River.
731	495	Janey Davis	20 "	103	On both sides of Doe Creek, adjoining Smith, etc.
732	499	David Payne	23 "	212	On branches of Stewart's Creek, including the Poplar Cove.
733	512	Jacob Coger	" "	257	On Stone's Creek, adjoining his own line.
734	513	William Weatherspoon	" "	64	On both sides of the South Mayo, adjoining Hanley's line.
735	543	Benjamin Neel	24 "	180	On the head branch of the Grassy Fork of the North Mayo River and adjoining his own land.

HENRY COUNTY COMMONWEALTH'S GRANTS OR PATENTS—Continued

BOOK No. 11

	Page	Name	Date	Acres	Location
736	555	Reubin Hill	23 July 1787	249	On the branches of Prather's Fork of the Mayo River, adjoining John Randolph's line.
737	556	William Sharp	"	90	On the branches of the North Mayo River, adjoining Murry's line.
738	579	George Turnbull	21 "	254	On the head branches of Runnett Bag Creek.
739	604	William Smith	1 Aug.	1,178	On Peters' Creek, including 225 acres granted to said Smith by patent.
740	608	Isaac Bates	17 July "	126	On the north side of the South Fork of Blackwater River, adjoining Alias Price.
741	609	Edward Cockerham	30 "	165	On the south branch of Stewart's Creek, adjoining Jacob Caton.
742	619	James Armstrong	"	32	On the south side of the Nettle Cove Branch, a branch of Loving's Creek.
743	631	Rachel Fee	1 Aug.	51	On the South Mayo River.
744	642	Jonathan Hanby	" "	880	On Peters' Creek, adjoining his own land.
745	679	David Chadwell	23 July "	340	On the north side of Smith's River, adjoining Hairston's line.
746	727	Woolman Studham	3 Aug. "	187	On the South Fork of Jack's Creek.

BOOK No. 12

	Page	Name	Date	Acres	Location
747	233	George Hairston	1 Aug. 1787	195	On the south branches of Marrowbone Creek, adjoining his own land.
748	244	Frederick Fulkerson	5 July "	93	On the north side of the South Mayo River, adjoining his own line.
749	277	William Kellum	1 Aug. "	311	On the branches of Mayo River.
750	281	Charles Davis	18 July "	155	On the east branches of Reedy Creek, adjoining Jourdan's Order line.
751	339	William Kelley	3 Aug. "	81	On branches of Lazy Run of Blackwater River, adjoining Kingerie's line.
752	350	Ambria Jones	2 "	532	On the branches of Beaver Creek.
753	386	William Kelley	3 "	160	On the head branches of Lick Run of Blackwater River.
754	397	Mumford Smith	1 "	70	On both sides of Burd's Run, a South Fork of the Ararat River.
755	442	John Ingram	" "	70	On both sides of Smith's River, adjoining Callaway's line.

HENRY COUNTY COMMONWEALTH'S GRANTS OR PATENTS—Continued

BOOK No. 12

	Page	Name	Date	Acres	Location
756	489	James Armstrong	2 Aug. 1787	169	On both sides of Loving's Creek, adjoining his own land.
757	528	George Hairston	" "	112	On the branches of Marrowbone Creek, adjoining Randolph's Order line.
758	596	Thomas Nunn	10 Sept. "	120	On the north side of Smith's River and both sides of Rock Run.
759	729	Samuel Patterson	13 "	323	On the branch of Chestnut Creek, adjoining Ramsey's line and others.
760	731	William Adams	27 July "	1,365	On the south side of Irvin's River and on both sides of Puppy Creek and Goblingtown Creek.

BOOK No. 13

	Page	Name	Date	Acres	Location
761	285	William Adams	27 July 1787	360	On the waters of Goblingtown Creek.
762	374	William Willis	23 "	339	On the South Fork of Russell's Creek, adjoining Grey's Order line.
763	392	John Willis	31 "	628	On Cole's Creek, a branch of Blackwater River.
764	488	Francis Turner	10 Sept. "	140	On the mountain called the Blue Ridge, including some of the branches of Rock Castle Creek.
765	557	Francis Turner	12 "	386	On both sides of Flat Creek of Smith's River, adjoining his own land.

BOOK No. 14

	Page	Name	Date	Acres	Location
766	3	Samuel Patterson	13 Sept. 1787	341	On the Gap Branch of Chestnut Creek.
767	538	George Currie	3 Aug. "	400	On both sides of the South Fork of Leatherwood Creek.
768	613	Samuel Patterson	13 Sept. "	345	On the north branch of Smith River, adjoining Richard Runnolds.
769	615	Robert Perryman	3 Aug. "	226	On Mill Creek.

BOOK No. 15

	Page	Name	Date	Acres	Location
770	525	John Radford	17 Mar. 1788	256	On the south branches of Smith's River, beginning at Ingram's corner.
771	611	Jesse Corne	24 "	174	On the north side of Sycamore Creek, adjoining Mead and Company's line.

HENRY COUNTY COMMONWEALTH'S GRANTS OR PATENTS—Continued

	Page	Name	Date	Acres	Location
			BOOK No. 15		
772	642	James Ingram	15 Mar. 1788	450	On both sides of Smith's River, part in Franklin County.
773	372	John Stuart	17 Sept. 1787	50	On the branches of Stewart's Creek.
			BOOK No. 16		
774	40	William Anderson	16 Aug. 1787	37	On the south side of the South Fork of Blackwater River, adjoining Joseph Stout.
775	90	Daniel Carlin	17 Sept. "	250	On both sides of Elk Creek of the Yadkin River.
776	109	Harmon Critz, Jr.	10 Oct. "	266	On the branches of Spoon Creek.
777	149	Blizard Magruder	8 Nov. "	1,000	On both sides of Beaver Creek.
778	589	John Gowin	16 Apr. 1788	79	On the waters of Blackberry Creek.
779	591	William Alexander	17 " "	100	On the south side of the South Fork of Rock Castle Creek.
780	630	William Witt	16 " "	170	On the south branches of Blackberry Creek, adjoining his own land.
781	632	Hayman France	18 " "	328	On the branches of Mill Creek of North Mayo River.
782	634	Thomas Murrough	16 " "	86	On the branches of Little Sycamore Creek, adjoining Mead's land.
783	700	Walter Barnard	23 " "	235	On both sides of Loving's Creek of Yadkin River.
			BOOK No. 17		
784	7	Thomas Morrow	16 Apr. 1788	187	On the branches of Sycamore Creek, adjoining his own land.
785	231	George Poor	26 June "	90	On both sides of South Mayo River.
786	278	Jacob Prilleyman	" "	70	On the South Fork of Blackwater River.
787	414	Abraham Ritter	9 July "	150	On the branches of Lick Run of Blackwater River, adjoining Callaway, etc.
788	473	Richard Oakley	21 " "	424	On both sides of Matrimony Creek, adjoining Smith's land.
789	513	Samuel Woodson	" "	440	On North Fork of Matrimony Creek, adjoining Mill's land.
790	534	George Hairston	" "	400	On branches of Fall Creek and adjoining Harbour's line.
791	586	Jesse Murphey	30 " "	215	On the branches of Matrimony Creek.
			BOOK No. 18		
792	14	Isham Hall	26 June 1788	318	On waters of Little and Big Jack's Creek, adjoining Hancock, Parrott, etc.
793	583	Blizard Magruder	8 Nov. "	384	On Leatherwood, adjoining Watson's and Lomax and Company's line.

HENRY COUNTY COMMONWEALTH'S GRANTS OR PATENTS—Continued

BOOK No. 19

	Page	Name	Date	Acres	Location
794	35	Blizard Magruder	8 Nov. 1788	441	Adjoining the land of Pedigow.
795	290	James Bartlett	30 Mar. 1789	266	On both sides of Storton's Creek, a North Fork of North Mayo River and adjoining Stockton's land.
796	297	David Gowin	" "	94	On Spoon Creek, adjoining John Ward's land.
797	307	David Gowin	" "	185	On the south side of Spoon Creek, adjoining Collier's line.
798	311	Adam Lackey	29 "	115	On the north side of Smith's River and on the south side of Rockcastle Creek, adjoining Mayo's line.
799	329	John Staples	27 "	80	On the north side of the Mayo River, adjoining Smith and Company,
800	394	Hugh Armstrong	11 Apr. "	70	On the east side of a mountain, including some of the branches of Loving's Creek of the Yadkin River.
801	603	Stephen Senter	31 Aug. "	300	On both sides of Back Creek, adjoining James Charles' land.

BOOK No. 20

	Page	Name	Date	Acres	Location
802	260	Jacob Pillemon	18 Mar. 1789	167	On the branches of Blackwater and Pigg Rivers.
803	316	Hugh Armstrong	11 Apr. "	250	On both sides of Loving's Creek.
804	330	William Webb	15 "	78	On the head branches of Paul's Creek.
805	346	Thomas Edwards, Sr.	" "	343	On the north side of Smith's River, adjoining his own and Dickinson's land.
806	347	John Medley	25 "	167	On waters of Nobusiness Fork of Mayo River, adjoining James Taylor.
807	350	James Walker	" "	89	On the branches of the North Fork of Mayo River.
808	352	William Webb	15 "	124	On the branches of Stony Creek.
809	361	Luke Foley	25 "	629	On branches of Goblingtown Creek, adjoining Adams's Order line.

BOOK No. 21

	Page	Name	Date	Acres	Location
810	178	John Borman	17 Aug. 1789	300	On the south side of the South Fork of Squall Creek, a south branch of Dan River.
811	247	James Charles	31 "	155	On both sides of Back Creek.
812	279	John Koger	21 Sept. "	262	On the north side of the South Fork of Goblingtown Creek, adjoining his own land.

HENRY COUNTY COMMONWEALTH'S GRANTS OR PATENTS—Continued

BOOK No. 21

	Page	Name	Date	Acres	Location
813	292	Aquilla Greer	24 Sept. 1789	336	On the north side of Little Bull Run, adjoining William Greer.
814	316	James Laremore	1 Oct. "	210	On branches of Marrowbone Creek and Mayo Waters, adjoining Moor and Chandler's land.
815	390	Matthew Scott	31 " "	103	On Daniel's Run, adjoining land of Bibey and Prilleyman.
816	568	Benjamin Cook	19 Jan. 1790	165	On Keeton's Creek, a branch of Snow Creek.
817	714	John Smallman	10 Mar. "	259	On both sides of the Cow Branch, a south branch of Smith's River.
818	724	James Pigg	9 " "	200	On the North Fork of the North Mayo River, adjoining his own and the land of Stockton, etc.

BOOK No. 22

	Page	Name	Date	Acres	Location
819	40	William Austin	1 Feb. 1790	1,585	On the branches of Dan River near the Meadows of Dan.
820	41	William Austin	" " "	33	On the head branches of Little Dan and Ivey Creek.
821	96	John Morgan	4 Mar. "	310	On north side of Smith's River, adjoining land of Lucas.
822	471	Lucy Barnett	31 July "	231	On branches of Goblingtown Creek, adjoining Richard Adams.
823	472	Patrick Coleman	2 Aug. "	40	On branches of Jack's Creek, adjoining Allen's line.
824	473	Joshua Hutson	31 July "	355	On the waters of Russell's Creek, adjoining his own and Carter's lines.
825	475	Diah Hutson	13 " "	268	On both sides of Little Dan River, adjoining his own and Marr's lines.
826	476	Russell Cox	31 " "	674	On both sides of Bold Branch of Leatherwood, adjoining George Runnold's land.
827	641	Blizard Magruder	1 Dec. "	1,384	On branches of Leatherwood and Beaver Creeks, adjoining the land of Williams, Watson, etc.
828	648	William Perkins	4 " "	111	On both sides of White Oak Creek of Smith's River, adjoining Perkin's land.
829	701	John Matthis	24 Jan. 1791	252	On the south side of North Mayo River, adjoining Randolph & Company's Order line.
830	709	William Dillian	7 " "	700	On the side of Smith's River, adjoining Jacob Stalling's land.

HENRY COUNTY COMMONWEALTH'S GRANTS OR PATENTS—Continued

BOOK No. 23

	Page	Name	Date	Acres	Location
831	46	William Austin	1 Feb. 1790	294	On the head branches of Dan River westwardly of the Main Mountain, adjoining Mead and Company's line.
832	161	Augstine Thomas	11 May "	320	On both sides Gray's Branch, a south branch of the North Mayo River, adjoining Hugh's line.
833	387	Blizard Magruder	1 Dec. "	3,126	On the north side of South Mayo River and on the waters of Green Creek and Spoon Creek, Mill Creek of Mayo.
834	340	Blizard Magruder	29 Nov. "	3,892	On both sides of South Mayo River, adjoining Hugh's land and Buzard's Spoon Creek Survey.
835	610	Daniel Carlin	1 June "	381	On both sides of Stewart's Creek of the Yadkin River, adjoining his own land.
836	730	Henry Tuggle	25 July "	280	On both sides of Rock Castle Creek.
837	739	James Anthony	26 " "	590	On the waters of Little Beaver Creek, adjoining George Hairston.
838	750	William Pace	" "	152	On the south side of Smith's River, adjoining Newson Pace, etc.

BOOK No. 24

	Page	Name	Date	Acres	Location
839	111	Edmund Winston	30 Mar. 1791	84	On the west branches of Horse Pasture, adjoining Randolph, and Company's land.
840	112	Edmund Winston	7 Apr. "	500	On both sides of Jennings Creek, adjoining Nicols, etc.
841	114	Balenger Wade	30 Mar. "	122	On the south side of North Mayo River, adjoining George Taylor, etc.
842	298	George Britton	1 Sept. "	195	In the Counties of Pittsylvania and Henry on Cascade Creek adjoining David Stephens.
843	311	William Eubanks	8 " "	321	On branches of Pigg River, adjoining Hill and Hutching's lines.
844	361	Moses Reynolds	18 Nov. "	117	On a south branch of Gray's Fork of North Mayo River, adjoining Francis's line.
845	460	John Dickinson	1 Oct. "	263	On the south side of Smith's River, adjoining the land of Turner and Baker.
846	555	Charles M. Talbott, John Callaway and Henry Ward	23 Mar. 1792	930	On both sides of Flat Creek, adjoining John Ward, etc.
847	557	John Callaway	" "	186	On both sides of Little Wigeon and on the north side of Rock Castle Creek.

HENRY COUNTY COMMONWEALTH'S GRANTS OR PATENTS—Continued

BOOK No. 25

	Page	Name	Date	Acres	Location
848	10	Thomas Cooper	26 July 1791	420	On both sides of Beaver Creek, adjoining Lomax and Company.
849	120	George Poor, Sr.	1 Oct.	198	On the branches of Ferry's Fork of Russell Creek, a South Fork of South Mayo River.
850	123	George Poor, Sr.	"	208	On the South Mayo River.
851	126	Robert Heedspath	3 "	139	On the head branches of Johnson's Creek.
852	128	Philip Anglin	" "	86	On the east branches of North Mayo River, adjoining Rigs, Golsby, etc.
853	179	William Allen	1 "	400	On one of the head branches of Paul's Creek on the north side of the Good Spur under the Main Mountain.
854	208	Thomas Hill	30 Sept.	46	On the branches of Stewart's Creek.
855	212	Hugh Woods	" "	560	On the north side of Smith's River, adjoining Wilson's land.
856	215	Thomas Hill	" "	86	On both sides of Back Creek, adjoining Senter's land.
857	386	John Dickinson	1 Oct.	400	On the head branches of the Rockey Fork of Sandy River.

BOOK No. 26

	Page	Name	Date	Acres	Location
858	43	Blizard Magruder	15 Mar. 1792	2,984	On the branches of Leatherwood, Snow and Beaver Creeks.
859	45	Blizard Magruder	" "	467	On both sides of Little Spoon Creek, adjoining Samuel Clark.
860	46	Blizard Magruder	14 "	634	On the south side of Russell's Creek, adjoining his own land, George Poor, etc.
861	85	John Callaway	22 "	71	On both sides of Nicholas's Creek, adjoining Dennis O'Bryant.
862	154	George Hairston	30 "	336	On the north branches of Smith's River, adjoining Stark Brown.
863	156	George Hairston	" "	1,132	On the waters of Matrimony Creek, Toeclout, Turkey Cock Creek and the White Oak Fork.
864	163	John Ward	23 "	380	On branches of Rock Castle and Widgeon.
865	613	William Austin	10 July	234	On the head branches of Sycamore Creek, adjoining Hancock, Bennett, etc.

BOOK No. 27

	Page	Name	Date	Acres	Location
866	172	Joseph Martin	6 Oct. 1792	126	On the north branches of Smith's River, adjoining Lomax and Company's line.

HENRY COUNTY COMMONWEALTH'S GRANTS OR PATENTS—Continued

BOOK No. 27

	Page	Name	Date	Acres	Location
867	260	William Gardner	3 Nov. 1792	230	On the branches of the North Fork of Flat Creek of Smith's River.
868	384	Parish Sims, heir at law to James Sims, dec'd.	26 Dec. "	47	On Sims' Fork of Mayo River.
869	388	John Smith	28 " "	65	On the branches of Horse Pasture Creek, adjoining Randolph's line.
870	664	Edward Tatum	7 Apr. 1793	282	On the north waters of Peters' Creek, adjoining his own and Jonathan Hanby's land.

BOOK No. 28

	Page	Name	Date	Acres	Location
871	71	John Grogan	8 Oct. 1792	143	On the branches of Matrimony Creek, adjoining Edwards, May, etc.
872	178	John Jones	19 Dec. "	52	On the waters of Paul's Creek, adjoining his own land.
873	179	John Ingram	15 " "	42	On south side of Smith's River, adjoining his own land.
874	184	James Armstrong	" "	191	On both sides of Loving's Creek, adjoining his own land.
875	185	William Hickembotom	" "	42	On both sides of Loving's Creek, adjoining Harrington, etc.
876	186	Joseph Johnson	" "	29	On both sides of Loving's Creek.
877	187	Joseph Johnson	17 " "	57	On both sides of the North Fork of Loving's Creek, adjoining James Harrington.
878	188	Thomas Mace	" "	54	On the head branches of Loving's Creek.
879	189	Betheny Haynes	" "	175	On the north branches of Paul's Creek.
880	190	Daniel Barnett	19 " "	40	On the branches of Loving's Creek.
881	192	James James	" "	317	On the head waters of Loving's Creek.
882	194	Benjamin Yates	20 " "	124	On the South Fork of Johnson's Creek.
883	195	Haman Critz, Jr.	19 " "	262	On both sides of Spoon Creek of Mayo River, adjoining his own land.
884	10	William Reed	17 June 1793	170	On the branches of Stockton's Creek, adjoining Stockton's line.
885	423	Samuel Paterson	18 " "	125½	On the upper Gap Branch of Chestnut Creek.
886	456	James Larimore	29 " "	220	On waters of Marrowbone and Jenning's Creek, adjoining James Taylor, etc.
887	460	Stephen Senter	" "	60	On the north branch of Paul's Creek of the Ararat.
888	516	Benjamin Wade	8 July "	454	On both sides of Young's Branch of Horse Pasture Creek, adjoining Jesse Witt's line, etc.

HENRY COUNTY COMMONWEALTH'S GRANTS OR PATENTS—Continued

BOOK No. 28

	Page	Name	Date	Acres	Location
889	523	Francis Turner	9 July 1793	116	On both sides of the Haw Branch of Smith's River, adjoining James Denney's line.
890	581	James Taylor	26 July "	100	On both sides of the South Fork of the North Mayo River, adjoining Smith's land.
891	595	Blackmore Hughes	19 "	254	On the head branches of Buffalo Creek.
892	621	William Johnson	23 "	200	On both sides of Mill Creek, adjoining Webster's line.
893	622	Andrew Rhea	26 "	45	On the east branches of North Mayo River, adjoining his and Anglin's line.
894	655	Benjamin Kinsey	22 "	48	On the north side of Rock Castle Creek.

BOOK No. 29

	Page	Name	Date	Acres	Location
895	31	Thomas Chawning	7 May 1793	200	On the north side of Smith's River and on the east side of Middle Creek.
896	172	George Hairston	6 June "	115	On both sides of Shooting Creek, adjoining Nathan Hall, etc.
897	202	Thomas P. Jordan	26 July "	200	On both sides of Wigion Creek, adjoining Ward's line.
898	225	Joshua Agee	27 Sept. "	408	On the draughts of Potter's and Bull's Creek, adjoining Nathaniel Christian.
899	231	John Camron	16 " "	115	On both sides of North Mayo River, adjoining John Pulliam.
900	232	William Carter	" "	145	On the Cloud Break Mountain, a Spur of the Bull Mountain, adjoining Eliphas Shelton.
901	238	William Heard	18 "	450	On the branches of the Grassy Fork of Town Creek, adjoining John Hickey.
902	238	William Hudspeath	12 "	103	On the head branches of Mill Creek of Ararat River, adjoining Nicholas Baker.
903	239	William Hulet	17 "	162	On the south side of Smith's River, adjoining his own and Wilson's lines.
904	240	William Moore	" "	100	On the south branches of Marrowbone Creek, adjoining George Hairston.
905	259	Henry Sumpter	18 Nov. "	507	On both sides of Smith's River.
906	262	William West	12 Sept. "	78	On a head branch of Johnson's Creek, adjoining his own line.
907	263	Thomas Cooper	" "	348	On the branches of Reedy Creek and Donald's Creek.
908	264	Thomas Cooper	" "	308	On the waters of Reedy Creek, Daniels Creek and Smith's River, adjoining Murphey's line.

HENRY COUNTY COMMONWEALTH'S GRANTS OR PATENTS—Continued

BOOK No. 29

	Page	Name	Date	Acres	Location
909	265	Samuel Croutcher	12 Sept. 1793	104	On the west side of Gray's Fork of Mill Creek, adjoining his own and Farris's line.
910	266	Thomas Hamilton	" "	130	On both sides of Stone's Creek, adjoining Abraham Penn.
911	268	Frederick Hutchins	" "	67	On the north side of South Mayo River, adjoining William Haze's line.
912	538	Thomas Crutcher, Guy Smith, John Ferguson and George Ferguson	21 Nov. "	2,922	In the Counties of Franklin and Henry on the waters of Chestnut and Reed Creeks.

BOOK No. 30

	Page	Name	Date	Acres	Location
913	115	Samuel Paterson	14 Aug. 1793	1,300	On the waters of Doe Creek and of Chestnut Creek, adjoining the land of Dickerson.
914	219	Isham Webb	5 May 1794	176	On the branches of Paul's Creek.
915	219	Charles Thomas	14 " "	168	On Grassy Creek, adjoining his own land.
916	229	Hugh McWilliams	19 Aug. "	35	On the north branches of Snow Creek.
917	232	Francis Jenkins	18 " "	285	On head branches of Marrowbone Creek, adjoining land of Harbour, Witts, etc.
918	237	Charles Thomas	14 May "	158	On the north waters of Poplar Camp Creek.
919	252	Kenney McKenney	" "	163	On the south side of Smith's River, adjoining his own land.
920	401	John Phillpot	27 Aug. "	241	On the south side of Smith's River, adjoining Hairston's land.
921	404	William Watson	" "	356	On the branches of Stuart's Creek of Smith's River, adjoining William Cayton.
922	406	Jacob Critz	" "	319	On the south waters of the North Mayo River, adjoining John Matthis.
923	413	George Stutts	23 "	96	On both sides of Furie's Fork, a South Fork of Russell's Creek.
924	419	George Taylor	14 "	89	On the north branches of South Mayo River, adjoining William Fee's land, etc.
925	497	Blizard McGruder	7 May "	235	On the head waters of Little Dan River.
926	505	William Jessop	20 June "	64	On the branches of John's Creek.
927	507	Matthew Small	9 May "	88	On the south side of Smith's River, adjoining Joseph Reynolds.
928	515	John Dillion	20 Nov. "	212	On both sides of Rock Run of Smith's River, adjoining John Barksdale.

HENRY COUNTY COMMONWEALTH'S GRANTS OR PATENTS—Continued

BOOK No. 30

	Page	Name	Date	Acres	Location
929	519	William Fee	18 Aug. 1794	286	On the north branches of South Mayo River, adjoining George Taylor.
930	579	William C. Rea	27 Nov. "	249	On both sides of Little Marrowbone Creek, adjoining Cooper's line.
931	582	Thomas Cooper	" "	95	On both sides of Little Marrowbone Creek, adjoining James Rea.
932	588	John Dillender	" "	181	On the waters of Turkey Cock Creek, of Smith's River, adjoining Grogen's line.
933	632	John Yates	23 July "	100	On a branch of the North Fork of Loving's Creek and including a place known by the name of the Poplar Cove.
934	633	Peter France	20 May "	124	On the north branches of Mill Creek, adjoining Henry Francis' land.

BOOK No. 31

	Page	Name	Date	Acres	Location
935	45	Hugh Woods	22 Nov. 1793	126	On the head branches of Chestnut Creek, adjoining Robert Woods.
936	101	James Cox	1 May 1794	99	On the north branches of Smith's River, adjoining William Furon.
937	115	Adam Turner	23 July "	116	On the south side of Smith's River, adjoining Matthew Small.
938	116	Thomas Nun	1 Dec. "	142	On both sides of Rock Run of Smith's River, adjoining Randolph and Company's line.
939	158	Edward Pedigo	21 July "	145	On both sides of Poplar Camp Creek, adjoining his own line.
940	220	Blizard Magruder	12 Aug. "	1,225	On both sides of South Mayo River, adjoining Walton's Order line.
941	244	Abraham Maze	9 Feb. 1795	227	On the head branches of Blackberry Creek, adjoining John Witt, etc.
942	247	George Hairston	" "	2	Being an Island of Smith's River called the Breaky Reed Island, opposite the land of Joseph Goading.
943	247	William Wells	7 "	195	On both sides of Little Reed Creek, beginning on Copeland's line above Burkett's Mill.
944	248	John Witt	9 "	84	On the north branches of Blackberry Creek, adjoining his own line.

HENRY COUNTY COMMONWEALTH'S GRANTS OR PATENTS—Continued

BOOK No. 31

	Page	Name	Date	Acres	Location
945	249	Ignatius Redman	9 Feb. 1795	70	On the southwest side of Stone's Creek, adjoining Marr, Penn and others.
946	256	Blizard Magruder	12 " "	2,000	On the north side of Mayo River and head branches of Marrowbone Creek.
947	317	William Stone	23 May "	174	On the North Fork of Spoon Creek, adjoining Ward, Barker, etc.
948	574	James McVey	22 " "	109	On the branches of Lick Run and Blackwater River, adjoining the land of Jacob Kingery.
949	577	Abraham Eads	" "	105	On both sides of the South Fork of Russell's Creek, adjoining Wilson, John Parr, etc.

BOOK No. 32

	Page	Name	Date	Acres	Location
950	40	John Lee	22 May 1794	62	On both sides of Joint Crack Crk. and adjoining his own land.
951	53	Isham Webb	2 " "	50	On the head branches of Poul's Creek.
952	245	John Philpot	14 " 1795	80	On the north side of Smith's River, adjoining Ingram's line.
953	246	Jonathan Cummings	26 " "	364	On both sides of Spoon Creek, including some of the branches of Matthew's Creek.
954	251	Moses Runnolds	14 " "	202	On the branches of North Mayo River, adjoining Cameron's line.
955	319	Blizard McGruder	21 July "	2,122	On the head waters of Marrowbone, Grassy, Jordans, Horse Pasture and Jenning's Creeks.
956	418	Jesse Corn	9 Nov. "	64	On the head branches of Sycamore Creek, adjoining Samuel Corn, etc.
957	433	David Weatherford	19 " "	100	On the branches of Leatherwood and Fall Creek, adjoining Lomax and Company's line, etc.
958	434	Philip Boshears, Sr.	" "	97	On the branches of Turkey Cock Creek of Smith's River, adjoining his own and the land of Gillis, Wilson and others.
959	434	Preston Kendrick	" "	42	On the south branches of Smith's River, adjoining his own and Edward's line.
960	435	William Cayton	" "	31	On the waters of Drag Creek and Stuard's Creek of Smith's River and adjoining Watson's line.
961	436	Jacob Cayton	" "	26	On both sides of Stuard's Creek of Smith's River.

HENRY COUNTY COMMONWEALTH'S GRANTS OR PATENTS—Continued

BOOK No. 32

	Page	Name	Date	Acres	Location
962	494	Isaac Maberry	22 Dec. 1795	183	On the south side of Robertson's Creek of Dan River, adjoining Irvin's line.
963	505	James Rea	4 Aug. "	146	On a south branch of Smith's River and adjoining Gray's Order line and Hairston's land.

BOOK No. 33

	Page	Name	Date	Acres	Location
964	510	William West	16 Nov. 1796	118	On a north branch of the South Fork of Johnson's Creek.
965	513	Alexander Hunter	17 " "	632	On the branches of Smith's River and Blackberry Creek, adjoining his own and James Baker's line.
966	514	William Heard	" "	114	On the waters of Little Reed Creek, adjoining Copeland.
967	515	Ignatious Simms	" "	152	On the North Fork of Flat Creek.
968	516	Hugh Woods	" "	40	On the south branch of Flat Creek.
969	576	Abraham Penn	9 Apr. "	1,024	On the waters of Blackberry, Horse Pasture and Coger's Creeks.
970	578	Abraham Penn	8 "	91	On head branches of Kogar's Creek, adjoining Joseph Newman.

BOOK No. 34

	Page	Name	Date	Acres	Location
971	141	Peter Duprad	11 Apr. 1796	38	On both sides of Johnson's Creek, adjoining Michael Kelley, etc.
972	143	Hugh Woods and Robert Stockton	"	200	On the branches of the Ararat and Dan Rivers, adjoining Cloud's line.
973	156	Thomas Gee	14 "	117	On the north side of Rock Castle Creek.
974	441	William Robinson	18 July "	56	On the south side of Smith's River, adjoining Francis Gilley.
975	443	John Alexander	" "	151	On the head branches of Little Marrowbone and Grassy Creek.
976	444	Thomas Steward	" "	34	On the branches of Leatherwood Creek of Smith's River, adjoining Robertson's land.
977	534	John Hammonds	27 "	60	On the north branches of Leatherwood Creek, adjoining his own and the land of Wilson, Weatherford, etc.
978	561	George Hairston	5 Sept. "	294	On the waters of Sandy River, adjoining Robinson's line.
979	573	Thomas Baldwin	31 Aug. "	542	On both sides of Grassy Creek, adjoining his own land.
980	578	George Hairston	1 "	362	Adjoining William Cayton, John Kelley and others.
981	673	William C. Rea	26 Sept. "	33	On Marrowbone Creek, adjoining William Dillon.

HENRY COUNTY COMMONWEALTH'S GRANTS OR PATENTS—Continued

BOOK No. 35

	Page	Name	Date	Acres	Location
982	107	George Hairston	4 Apr. 1796	213	On both sides of the North Fork of the South Mayo River.
983	116	Abraham Penn	9 "	212	On the north side of North Mayo River, adjoining his own land.
984	117	Abraham Penn	"	298	On both sides of Bull Run of Cogar's Creek, adjoining Henry Cogar, etc.
985	120	William Sowell	"	50	On the east side of Cogar's Creek, adjoining land of Marr, Cooksey, etc.
986	131	William Woods	14 "	50	On the branches of Stewart's Creek.
987	143	William McPeek	" "	124	On the north side of the North Fork of Jack's Creek, adjoining Allen's line.
988	146	Thomas Chowning	16 "	355	On the south branch of Smith's River, adjoining his own and the land of Kelley, etc.
989	153	John Going	14 "	153	On both sides of Little Blackberry Creek, adjoining his own land.
990	512	John Waller	23 Aug.	4½	An island in Smith's River, opposite the lands of said Waller.
991	528	John Waller	"	182	Beginning in Randolph and Company's line on the south side of Smith's River.
992	717	Joseph Garratt	13 Oct.	50	On south side of a spur of the Blue Ridge, adjoining his own land.
993	718	Thomas Cooper	20 Sept.	110	Adjoining Harmour and Company, Webb and others.

BOOK No. 36

	Page	Name	Date	Acres	Location
994	182	George F. Harris	18 Nov. 1796	95	Adjoining Barnard Clay and Dickenson's lands.
995	268	Thomas Jamison	20 Sept. "	56	On both sides of a south branch of Marrowbone Creek, adjoining his own and William Smith's land.
996	479	William Hooker	3 Aug. 1797	67	On the north side of the South Fork of Little Dan River.

BOOK No. 37

	Page	Name	Date	Acres	Location
997	99	Henry Fee	26 Sept. 1796	78	On the north side of the South Mayo River, adjoining his own land.
998	127	John Kelley	" "	250	On both sides of Drag Creek of Smith's River, adjoining Clayton's line.

HENRY COUNTY COMMONWEALTH'S GRANTS OR PATENTS—Continued

BOOK No. 37

	Page	Name	Date	Acres	Location
999	211	George Hairston	3 Aug. 1796	1,213	On the south branches of Smith's River, adjoining Coles, Dillen, etc.
1000	343	James Gowin	2 " 1797	61	On both sides of Little Dan River, adjoining Augustine Brown, etc.
1001	471	George Hairston	20 Oct. "	200	On the waters of Middle Creek and Home Creek, adjoining Wilson Barnard's line, etc.
1002	582	Daniel Wilson	16 Dec. "	86	On the branches of Home Creek.
1003	611	John Hord	8 Feb. 1798	9½	Being an island in Smith's River.
1004	613	John Cook	3 " "	203	On the waters of Leatherwood Creek.

BOOK No. 38

	Page	Name	Date	Acres	Location
1005	63	Henry Hefflefinger	16 Dec. 1797	166	On the waters of Leatherwood Creek, adjoining Joseph Boulden, etc.
1006	117	George Hairston	20 Mar. 1798	3,526	On the waters of Marrowbone Creek, Grassy Creek and Jordan's Creek and Smith's River.
1007	204	George Hairston	30 Apr. "	1,375	On Middle Creek and the waters of Smith's River, adjoining Rice, Goodwin, etc.
1008	206	Mary Hickey	28 " "	120	On the waters of Butramstown Creek, adjoining Hickey's Old Survey.
1009	276	William Stokes	6 June "	197	On the west side of Rug Creek, adjoining George Hairston, etc.
1010	319	Thomas Wilson, Jr.	10 July "	50	On Grassy Fork of Turkey Cock Creek.
1011	409	George Hairston	20 Oct. "	488	On the Bold Branch of Leatherwood Creek, adjoining Henry's and Callaway's lines.
1012	410	George Hairston	" "	321	On the waters of Matrimony Creek, adjoining Jesse Murphey, etc.
1013	560	William Fee	9 Apr. "	20	Adjoining Henry Franse's land.
1014	581	George Hairston	16 " "	434	On the waters of Fall Creek, adjoining Barnard, etc.
1015	585	George Hairston	17 " "	259	On the headwaters of Marrowbone Creek and Matrimony.
1016	590	Robert Stockton	4 May 1799	328	On the waters of Leatherwood Creek and adjoining Jesse Crouch's land.

BOOK No. 39

	Page	Name	Date	Acres	Location
1017	258	Thomas Nunn	29 May 1797	331	On the waters of Little Rock Run.
1018	274	George Runnolds	15 " "	462	Beginning on the head of Bold Branch of Leatherwood Creek at William Bernard's corner.

HENRY COUNTY COMMONWEALTH'S GRANTS OR PATENTS—Continued

BOOK No. 39

	Page	Name	Date	Acres	Location
1019	503	Daniel Carlin	4 Aug. 1797	30	On a branch of Stewart's Creek, adjoining his own land.
1020	544	John Nunn	18 "	64	On both sides of the Little Dan River and adjoining Brown's land.

BOOK No. 40

	Page	Name	Date	Acres	Location
1021	198	George Washington, Tent Marr, John Marr, William Miller Marr, Sarah Marr, Constant Hardin, Perkins Marr, Peter Nicholas Marr and Agatha Anna Marr, Heirs and Representatives of John Marr, deceased.	22 May 1798	162	On the South Fork of Little Dan River.
1022	195	George Washington, Tent Marr, John Marr, William Miller Marr, Sarah Marr, Constant Hardin, Perkins Marr, Peter Nicholas Marr and Agatha Anna Marr, Heirs and Representatives of John Marr, deceased.	"	560	On the branches of Home's Creek of Cascade and Smith's River, adjoining Adam's, etc.
1023	244	Fuller Harris	29 June "	19½	On the waters of Cascade, adjoining David Harris.
1024	251	Goodwin Mayse	3 July "	100	On the waters of Matrimony Creek, adjoining Jesse Murphey.
1025	283	Isham Craddock	20 "	311	On the waters of Rock Run, adjoining Henry Sumpter.
1026	284	Daniel Wilson	13 "	427	On the waters of Home Creek and Cascade, adjoining Henry Lansford, etc.
1027	293	William Jenkins	12 "	132	On the waters of Marrowbone Creek, adjoining George Hairston, etc.
1028	335	John Redd	8 Aug. "	50	On the waters of Reed Creek and Daniel's Creek, adjoining Towlin's line, etc.

HENRY COUNTY COMMONWEALTH'S GRANTS OR PATENTS—Continued

BOOK No. 40

	Page	Name	Date	Acres	Location
1029	386	John Redd...............	8 Aug. 1798	307	On the waters of Reed Creek, adjoining Meredith's, Donalds' and his own land.
1030	506	George Hairston..........	20 Oct. "	290	On the waters of Middle Creek, adjoining his own and Lomax and Company's lines.
1031	507	George Hairston..........	22 " "	297	On the waters of Turkey Scratch Creek.
1032	508	George Hairston..........	" "	574	On the waters of Sandy River, adjoining Mitchell, Dickerson and others.

BOOK No. 41

1033	83	William Heard............	8 Mar. 1799	91	On both sides of the Grassy Fork of Town Creek, adjoining Hickey's line, etc.
1034	169	George Hairston..........	13 Apr. "	394	On the waters of Matrimony Creek, adjoining land of Mills, Cox, etc.
1035	181	Henry Fee................	9 " "	62	Beginning on the north side of South Mayo River, adjoining Manning Hill, George Taylor, etc.
1036	198	John Minter..............	16 " "	249	On the waters of Leatherwood Creek, adjoining Delozer's land and Lomax's Order line.

BOOK No. 42

1037	286	Charles Hicks and John Hicks, Executors of James Hicks, deceased.	30 Mar. 1799	154	On the waters of Beaver Creek, adjoining James Hicks' own land.
1038	297	Martin Dunkin............	18 " "	50	On both sides of Little Dan River, beginning on the east side of the creek.

BOOK No. 43

1039	138	Thomas Bouldin, Jr.......	30 Dec. 1799	150	On the waters of Grassy Creek and Jourdan's Creek, adjoining land of Hord and others.
1040	485	John Lee.................	8 Mar. 1800	176	On the branches of Jack's Creek.
1041	523	Abraham Penn............	28 " "	767	On the north side of Beaver Creek, adjoining his own land.
1042	590	George Hairston..........	22 Apr. "	2,470	On the Grassy Fork of Town Creek, adjoining Hickey's Old Survey, etc.

HENRY COUNTY COMMONWEALTH'S GRANTS OR PATENTS—Continued

	Page	Name	Date	Acres	Location
BOOK No. 45					
1043	468	David Morgan	17 May 1800	59	On the south branches of Jack's Creek, adjoining James Dennei.
1044	483	William Dillen, Jr.	19 "	48	On waters of Jourdan's Creek, adjoining Powers' and Jourdan's lines.
BOOK No. 46					
1045	480	Joseph Jones	8 Dec. 1800	39	Adjoining land of George F. Harris, Hixes and his own land.
1046	486	Joseph Jones	" "	306	On the waters of Sandy River, adjoining his own and the land of Mitchell, Dickenson, etc.
BOOK No. 47					
1047	535	John Watson	20 Mar. 1801	48	On waters of Ramsey's Creek, adjoining Watson, Sumpter, etc.
1048	536	Doctor John Watson	" "	102½	On waters of Horse Pasture Creek, adjoining James East's Survey and land of Henry Dillen, etc.
BOOK No. 48					
1049	191	Doctor John Watson	20 Mar. 1801	118	On the waters of Jourdan's Creek, adjoining land of Dillen, Jourdan and others.
BOOK No. 49					
1050	39	John Redd	17 Apr. 1801	713	On waters of Butramstown Creek, adjoining Reaves' land, etc.
1051	77	George Hairston	24 "	125	On waters of Leatherwood Creek, adjoining Joseph Gravley.
1052	81	George Hairston	" "	689	On the waters of Butramstown Creek and Smith's River, adjoining Daniel Smith.
1053	90	George Hairston	" "	1,462	On waters of Reed and Beaver Creeks, adjoining his own land.
1054	571	William Sharp	12 Dec. "	264	On the south branch of Goblingtown Creek, adjoining Anthony Tittle's land.

HENRY COUNTY COMMONWEALTH'S GRANTS OR PATENTS—Continued

BOOK No. 50

	Page	Name	Date	Acres	Location
1055	64	Robert Hunter and George Waller.	31 May 1802	430	On the south waters of Smith's River, beginning where Philpot's line intersects Alexander Hunter's Horse Shoe Tract.
1056	65	George Waller, Jr., and Joel Motley.	" "	213	On waters of Blackberry Creek, adjoining land of Hunter, Witt, etc.
1057	86	Philip Anglin	3 June	68	Adjoining the land of West, Harbour, etc.
1058	363	Henry Morris, Sr.	30 Dec.	22½	On the waters of Leatherwood Creek, adjoining Lomax and Company's Order line.
1059	563	James Howard	30 July 1803	45	On waters of Beaver Creek, adjoining the lands of Phillpot, Woodson and others.
1060	612	John Cock and David Wilis.	11 Oct.	724	In the Counties of Henry and Franklin, on the waters of Reedy Creek.

BOOK No. 53

	Page	Name	Date	Acres	Location
1061	50	Reubin Nance	25 Apr. 1804	133	On waters of Leatherwood Creek, adjoining Pedigoe's land.
1062	51	John Pace	" "	239	On north side of Smith's River, adjoining Lomax and Company and Fountain's lines.
1063	56	John King, Jr.	24	14	On the Southwest Fork of Leatherwood Creek, adjoining his own and land of Sympson, etc.
1064	57	Robert Smith	"	224	On the waters of Fall Creek and Bold Branch of Leatherwood Creek, adjoining Bernard's Order line, etc.
1065	60	Stephen King	"	121	On waters of Reedy Creek adjoining John Redd and William Herd.
1066	108	John P. Pyrtle	2 May	48	On waters of Little Reedy Creek, adjoining Copeland and McDonald.
1067	108	John P. Pyrtle	"	64	On Little Reedy Creek, adjoining Hairston and McDonald.
1068	310	John Phillpott	23 Aug.	145	On Town Creek, adjoining his own and Redd's land.

BOOK No. 54

	Page	Name	Date	Acres	Location
1069	175	George Hairston, Jr.	14 Aug. 1805	98	On the branches of Matrimony Creek, adjoining land of Mill's and George Hairston, Sr.
1070	176	George Hairston, Jr.	" "	29	On waters of Matrimony Creek, adjoining Price, Cox, etc.

HENRY COUNTY COMMONWEALTH'S GRANTS OR PATENTS—Continued

BOOK No. 54

	Page	Name	Date	Acres	Location
1071	177	George Hairston, Jr.	14 Aug. 1805	55	On Toeclout, a branch of Matrimony Creek, adjoining John Price, etc.
1072	178	George Hairston, Jr.	" "	649	On branches of Reedy Creek, a branch of Smith's River, adjoining land of Warren, Cook, etc.
1073	248	Jesse Carter	22 "	126	On the south side of Smith's River, adjoining John Pelphrey.
1074	329	Thomas Nunn	4 Oct.	77	On the north branches of Smith's River, adjoining Henry Barksdale.
1075	330	Henry Morris	8 "	50½	On waters of Leatherwood Creek, adjoining Proctor, Deshaze, etc.
1076	332	Joseph Boulden	" "	72	On waters, of the Muster Branch of Leatherwood Creek, adjoining Ramy, etc.
1077	333	Thomas Nunn	" "	144	On waters of Smith's River, adjoining William Stone, etc.
1078	335	William Hail	" "	5	On Mulberry Creek, adjoining Jacob Mastiff's land.

BOOK No. 55

	Page	Name	Date	Acres	Location
1079	193	Thomas C. Boulden	22 Apr. 1805	3	On the west side of Lomax and Company's Leatherwood Order, adjoining Joseph Boulden, Sr.
1080	278	Thomas Childers	12 "	188	On the north side of the South Fork of Mayo River, adjoining the land of Hutchings, Henry Fee, etc.

BOOK No. 56

	Page	Name	Date	Acres	Location
1081	87	George Hairston, Jr.	15 Aug. 1806	52	On the waters of Rug Creek and Stewart's Creek, adjoining William Norman, etc.
1082	89	George Hairston	" "	12	On Leatherwood Creek, adjoining land of Dunn and Lomax and Company's lines.
1083	90	George Hairston, Jr.	" "	226	On the waters of Reedy Creek and adjoining George Hairston, Sr.
1084	91	George Hairston	" "	156	On waters of Marrowbone Creek, adjoining Buckley's land.
1085	93	George Hairston	" "	324	On the waters of Beaver Creek and Mulberry Creek, adjoining James Howard.

HENRY COUNTY COMMONWEALTH'S GRANTS OR PATENTS—Continued

	Page	Name	Date	Acres	Location
			BOOK No. 56		
1086	94	George Hairston	15 Aug. 1806	245	On the waters of Marrowbone and Matrimony Creeks, adjoining his own and Taylor's Order line.
1087	451	John Morgan	12 July 1808	496	On the north side of Smith's River, adjoining his own and Dickinson's lines.
			BOOK No. 57		
1088	272	Thomas Dix	21 June 1808	2¼	On waters of Little Bold Branch of Leatherwood Creek.
1089	274	John Redd	" " "	620	On the north side of Smith's River and Rock Run, adjoining John Philpott's.
			BOOK No. 59		
1090	7	Young Burchet and William Warren	26 July 1809	611	On waters of Reedy Creek, adjoining Fauguson's land.
			BOOK No. 61		
1091	436	Mary Stockton	27 Mar. 1811	858	In the Counties of Pittsylvania and Henry, the greater part in Pittsylvania on the south side of Turkey Cock Mountain and on branches of Turkey Cock Creek.
1092	470	Benjamin Davis	4 May "	703	On waters of Reedy Creek, adjoining George Hairston and others.
			BOOK No. 62		
1093	180	Manin Hill	1 Oct. 1811	20	On the waters of Mayo River, adjoining land of Ray, Taylor, etc.
			BOOK No. 63		
1094	342	George Hairston	22 Feb. 1813	1,122	On waters of Sandy River and Leatherwood Creek, adjoining Dickenson.

HENRY COUNTY COMMONWEALTH'S GRANTS OR PATENTS—Continued

	Page	Name	Date	Acres	Location
					BOOK No. 65
1095	491	George Hairston	17 June 1816	44	Adjoining Pedigoe's and Henry's Surveys.
					BOOK No. 66
1096	40	John Minter	17 July 1816	400	On the waters of Leatherwood.
1097	349	John Cox	20 June 1817	280	On the waters of Ramsey's Creek, adjoining Powers and Company's line.
1098	350	John Cox	" "	26	On the south waters of Smith's River, adjoining Powers and Jordan's lines.
					BOOK No. 68
1099	86	Joseph Jones	1 Dec. 1818	40	On the Rocky Fork of Sandy River.
1100	108	William Deshazo	25 Feb. 1819	45	On the branches of Leatherwood, beginning, etc., corner of Richardson's and Davis' land.
1101	368	George Hairston	26 Oct. "	68	Beginning at Edward Cockram's corner white oak.
1102	369	Richard B. Beck	" "	521	In the Counties of Henry and Pittsylvania, the greater part in Henry, on waters of Turkey Cock Creek.
1103	407	Joseph Jones	" "	22	Beginning, etc., on the north side of a bold branch of Marrowbone Creek, in Jameson's and Anderson's lines.
					BOOK No. 69
1104	69	David Mayo	30 Dec. 1819	16	On the south branches of Marrowbone Creek, beginning on Richard Watson's corner post oak.
1105	480	George Hairston, Jr.	11 Nov. 1820	120	Beginning, etc., a corner of George Hairston, Sr., in John Oakley's line.
					BOOK No. 70
1106	241	Thomas Harbour and Eli Watkins	30 July 1821	273	Beginning, etc., on Hairston's and Anderson's corner red oak Lumpkin's old line.

HENRY COUNTY COMMONWEALTH'S GRANTS OR PATENTS—Continued

	Page	Name	Date	Acres	Location
			BOOK No. 73		
1107	220	Archibald Perkinson......	12 July 1824	5	On the waters of Leatherwood.
1108	250	George Hairston............	22 " "	937	On the branches of Cascade and branches of Smith's Run.
1109	285	Lewis Jones...............	6 Aug. "	72	On Grassy Fork waters of Leatherwood Creek.
			BOOK No. 74		
1110	249	Henry Fee..............	8 Oct. 1825	10	On the north side of South Mayo River.
1111	250	John Burriss..............	" " "	3	Near the waters of Mayo.
1112	442	Thomas S. Shelton.........	21 Nov. "	52	.... East side of Smith's River.
1113	447	Stephen Walker...........	" " "	42	
1114	456	John Price...............	" " "	65	Abraham's Creek.
1115	476	Hezekiah Perkinson.......	26 " "	8¼	Leatherwood Run.
			BOOK No. 75		
1116	123	George Hairston.........	12 July 1825	425	Beaver Creek.
1117	344	Jacob Hefflefiner and W. } Perkins.	16 Sept. "	1	Smith River.
			BOOK No. 76		
1118	266	George Hairston, Jr.......	8 Aug. 1827	26	On Marrowbone.
1119	330	George Hairston, Jr.......	28 " "	14	.... Little Reed Creek.
1120	...	John P. Pyrtle...........	29 Dec. "	55	
			BOOK No. 78		
1121	68	Thomas Boulden..........	20 Jan. 1829	160	Beaver Creek.
1122	80	Edward Pease............	19 Feb. "	440	Read Creek.
1123	242	John Cobler..............	21 July "	35	Smith River.
			BOOK No. 79		
1124	238	James Bradbury..........	1 Sept. 1830	6	On waters of Rock Run Creek.
1125	241	Thomas Turner, Assignee..	" " "	5	On waters of Grassy Fork of Toron Creek.

HENRY COUNTY COMMONWEALTH'S GRANTS OR PATENTS—Continued

BOOK No. 79

	Page	Name	Date	Acres	Location
1126	568	Thomas C. Boulden	1 July 1831	12	On waters of Jourdan's Creek.
1127	570	Thomas C. Boulden	" " "	26	On Matrimony Creek.
1128	569	John P. Pyrtle	" " "	82	On the ridge between Beaver and Reed Creeks.

BOOK No. 81

1129	15	Nelson Norman	20 Sept. 1832	4	An island in Smith River.
1130	112	Tarleton King	1 Nov. "	7	On waters of Beaver Creek.

BOOK No. 84

1131	190	Thomas Nunn	23 Feb. 1835	15	On Marrowbone Creek.
1132	413	Jabez Graveley	25 July "	91	On waters of Leatherwood Creek.

BOOK No. 92

1133	502	Henry Laurence	10 May 1842	150	On the branches of Turkey Cock Creek.
1134	503	John T. Cole	" " "	21	On the waters of Turkey Cock Creek.
1135	504	John T. Cole	" " "	190	On the waters of Turkey Cock Creek.
1136	644	Samuel Gilbert	20 July "	100	On the waters of Leatherwood Creek.
1137	645	James Carter	" "	52	On the waters of Leatherwood Creek.

BOOK No. 93

1138	503	Joseph Eddes	31 Oct. 1842	208	On the waters of Leatherwood Creek.
1139	504	Joseph Eddes	" "	178	On the waters of Leatherwood Creek.

BOOK No. 95

1140	47	George Waller	30 Nov. 1743	5	On the waters of Horse Pasture Creek.
1141	424	James Carter	31 July 1844	41	On the headwaters of Leatherwood Creek.

HENRY COUNTY COMMONWEALTH'S GRANTS OR PATENTS—Continued

	Page	Name	Date	Acres	Location
			BOOK No. 96		
1142	9	Edmund B. Redd	30 Sept. 1844	78	On the waters of the South Fork of Marrowbone Creek, called Webb's Fork.
			BOOK No. 97		
1143	85	Thomas C. Boulden	30 Sept. 1845	56	On the waters of Marrowbone Creek.
1144	294	William A. Dandridge	4 Apr. 1846	46	On both sides of the dividing ridge between Horse Pasture and Jourdan's Creek.
1145	427	Barton Pyrtle	30 June "	7	On the east side of Reedy Creek.
			BOOK No. 100		
1146	176	Thomas Stanley	30 June 1848	43	On Smith's River and its branches.
			BOOK No. 102		
1147	235	Thomas Nunn	1 Oct. 1849	14	On waters of Little Marrowbone Creek.
1148	680	Jesse Strange	1 Apr. 1850	58	On north side of Smith's River.
			BOOK No. 103		
1149	74	John F. Hairston and George Carter }	1 July 1850	4½	Adjoining James Zeigler and Trent.
1150	75	Barton Pyrtle	" " "	14	On both sides of Big Reedy Creek.
			BOOK No. 108		
1151	5	Thomas Vernon	1 Nov. 1852	19½	On north side of Turkey Cock Creek Mountain.
1152	278	Warren and William Norman }	1 Mar. 1853	116	Beginning at Martin's corner in Bernard's Order line.
			BOOK No. 113		
1153	627	Thomas East	1 May 1857	83	On waters of Horse Pasture Creek.
1154	628	Thomas East	" "	75	On both sides of Horse Pasture Creek.
1155	704	Alexander Hodges	" June "	136½	On the headwaters of the North Fork of Leatherwood Creek.

HENRY COUNTY COMMONWEALTH'S GRANTS OR PATENTS—Continued

	Page	Name	Date	Acres	Location
			BOOK No. 114		
1156	117	Samuel Manning..........	1 Sept. 1857	92	On waters of Turkey Cock Creek.
			BOOK No. 115		
1157	690	Samuel Good..............	1 Jan. 1859	100	On waters of Smith's River.
			BOOK No. 116		
1158	377	Pleasant W. Grigg........	1 Aug. 1859	406	On Turkey Cock Creek.
1159	414	Andrew J. and Patrick F. Jarrett.	1 Sept. "	30	On waters of Blackberry Creek.
1160	857	James A. Mitchell.........	1 Oct. "	1,316 and 123/160	The greater part in Franklin County on Turkey Cock Mountain and on waters of Turkey Cock Creek.
			BOOK No. 117		
1161	655	Willis Gravely.............	1 Mar. 1861	42½	On waters of Leatherwood Creek.
			BOOK No. 118		
1162	411	Henry Bousman............	1 Sept. 1864	62	On the waters of Leatherwood Creek.
1163	627	Marshal Harriston.........	1 Mar. 1872	7,317	On Beaver and Reed Creeks.
			BOOK No. 119		
1164	322	Granville L. Carter........	2 Apr. 1878	10	On the waters of Leatherwood.
1165	341	John Prunty..............	31 Aug. "	23	On the waters of Blackberry Creek.
1166	579	James A. Grogan..........	15 Nov. 1881	100	At pointers where Grogan intersects Fry's line.
			BOOK No. 120		
1167	54	B. K. and J. K. Terry.....	14 Sept. 1883	46	On Cascade Creek.

PATRICK COUNTY COMMONWEALTH'S GRANTS OR PATENTS

BOOK No. 28

	Page	Name	Date	Acres	Location
1	519	James Harris..............	8 July 1793	85	On the south branches of North Mayo River.

BOOK No. 31

	Page	Name	Date	Acres	Location
2	171	Edward Pedigo............	21 July 1794	31	On the waters of Poplar Camp Creek, adjoining Charles Thomas.
3	246	George Hairston...........	9 Feb. 1795	150	On the waters of the North Mayo River, adjoining John Pulliam.
4	363	John Hook................	17 Mar. "	1,190	In the Counties of Montgomery and Patrick on the waters of the South Fork of Little River, a branch of New River, adjoining William Walker, Benjamin Howell, etc.
5	378	John Hook................	16 "	394	In the Counties of Montgomery and Patrick on the dividing ridge including the heads of Howell's Creek, the South Fork of the Little River and the head of the North Fork of Rockcastle.
6	595	George Hairston...........	16 June "	729	On the waters of Stone's Creek, adjoining Jacob Goalden, William Taylor.

BOOK No. 32

	Page	Name	Date	Acres	Location
7	173	David Lawson.............	4 Apr. 1795	598	On Hicks' Fork, adjoining land of Brown and Mideaph.
8	495	James Lyon, Sr............	22 Dec. "	97	On the south waters of South Mayo River, adjoining Miller Easley and William Gilliam.
9	495	James Lyon, Sr............	" "	118	Beginning in his old line on the north side of South Mayo River, adjoining Hezekiah Shelton.
10	565	Joseph Gallego and John Augustus Chevallie. }	25 Jan. 1796	8,000	On the head waters of Dan River and Smith's River, adjoining Twitty and Ward.
11	619	Benjamin Chambers......	15 "	40,194½	On the waters of Stewart's, Paul's, Loving's and Reed Island Creeks.

BOOK No. 33

	Page	Name	Date	Acres	Location
12	249	John Hall.................	3 Aug. 1795	261	On the south waters of Goblingtown Creek, adjoining Allen and Anderson.
13	377	James Lyon, Sr............	26 Dec. "	23	On the south side of the South Mayo River, adjoining his own land.

PATRICK COUNTY COMMONWEALTH'S GRANTS OR PATENTS—Continued

BOOK No. 33

	Page	Name	Date	Acres	Location
14	424	John A. Chevallie and Joseph Gallego.	24 Jan. 1796	32,000	On the waters of the North and South Mayo Rivers and Smith River, adjoining Magruder, etc.
15	457	Jedediah Leeds	" 17 Feb.	24,265	On the waters of Dan River, Ivory Creek and South Mayo River waters.
16	577	Miller Easley	" 11 Apr.	122	On the south waters of South Mayo River, adjoining William Gilliam.

BOOK No. 34

	Page	Name	Date	Acres	Location
17	20	James Ternan	27 Feb. 1796	45,000	On the waters of Dan and Arratt Rivers, adjoining William Carter.
18	332	Adam Turner	" 4 June	73	On the waters of Smith River, adjoining land of Ferrel.
19	333	Jacob Adams	" "	165	On the north branches of the South Mayo River.
20	333	John Burnett	" "	39	On the north waters of Sycamore Creek, adjoining Richard Adams.
21	384	Thomas Southcomb	" 7 July	14,000	On the south waters of Smith's River and adjoining Pollard.
22	388	William Bowyer and William Breckenridge.	" 5	65,000	On the waters of Dan and Arratt Rivers, adjoining John Miller, John Creek, McLane, etc.
23	392	James Poteet, Jr.	" 28 June	137	On Goblingtown Creek.
24	517	Joseph Reynolds	" 17 Aug.	209	On the headwaters of Wegen Creek and adjoining William Lee.
25	518	William Deal	" 18	55	On the south waters of the North Mayo River, adjoining John Clarke.
26	523	Augustine Thomas	" "	47	On the north waters of South Mayo River, adjoining James Fulkerson, William Gray, etc.

BOOK No. 34

	Page	Name	Date	Acres	Location
27	569	John Armstrong	11 Oct. 1796	4,400	On Loving's Creek and the waters thereof, adjoining William Cloud.
28	694	William Coleman and Horatio Gates Haveland.	" 25 Dec.	25,000	On the waters of North Mayo River, beginning on Spoon Creek in Galligoe's line.
29	644	Clement Rogers	" 10 Oct.	55	On the north waters of Russell's Creek, adjoining Lyon's.
30	644	John Tompson	" "	58	On Paul's Creek.
31	645	Moses Reynolds	" "	57	On the Business Fork of North Mayo River.

PATRICK COUNTY COMMONWEALTH'S GRANTS OR PATENTS—Continued

BOOK No. 34

	Page	Name	Date	Acres	Location
32	646	Lawrence Lee	10 Oct. 1796	316	On the head branches of Loving's Creek, including a place called Ward's Gap.
33	646	John Dillian	"	40	On Smith's River, beginning, etc., to Town Creek.
34	143	Hugh Woods and Robert Stockton	11 Apr. "	200	On the branches of the Ararat and Dan Rivers. The land stated to lie in the County of Patrick.

BOOK No. 35

	Page	Name	Date	Acres	Location
35	22	John Barclay	3 Mar. 1796	35,123	On the waters of Johnston's Creek, adjoining Bell's Order line and on the headwaters of Ararat River.
36	25	John Barclay	5 "	24,090½	On the waters of Shooting Creek and Poplar Camp Creek.
37	61	William Thorp	17 "	101	On Smith's River, adjoining James Elkins, Nathan Hall, etc.
38	128	David Robertson	14 Apr. "	422	On the waters of Jack's Creek and Jill's Creek, adjoining Darby Rion, Samuel Helton, etc.
39	152	Joseph Reynolds	13 "	18	On the north waters of Smith's River, adjoining Matthew Small, etc.
40	164	Joseph Reynolds	13 "	150	On the north waters of Smith's River, adjoining Joel Harbour, etc.
41	169	Joseph Reynolds	28 "	312	On the north waters of Smith's River, adjoining William Isam, Joel Harbour, etc.

BOOK No. 36

	Page	Name	Date	Acres	Location
42	34	William Bowyer and William Breckenridge	5 July 1796	35,000	On the south waters of Smith's River, beginning at Joseph Gallego's corner on Goblingtown Creek.
43	117	James Perkins, Samuel Blagge, Gardiner L. Chandler and William Coleman	3 Oct. "	14,700	On Peters' Creek, adjoining Miller Hughes, the North Carolina Line, etc.
44	302	Henry Lee	21 "	70,000	On the waters of Big and Little Dan Rivers and South Mayo River waters.
45	407	Blizard Magruder	29 Aug. "	1,843	On the waters of South and North Mayo Rivers, adjoining Samuel Clark, John Parr, Sr., etc.
46	484	Bodham Moore	4 " 1797	21	On the headwaters of Ararat River, adjoining Bell's Order line.

PATRICK COUNTY COMMONWEALTH'S GRANTS OR PATENTS—Continued

BOOK No. 36

	Page	Name	Date	Acres	Location
47	484	Bartemus Reynolds	5 Aug. 1797	232	On the North Mayo River, adjoining Smith, Taylor, etc.
48	486	Michael Ahart	7 " "	147	Beginning at Stephen Senter's corner on the east side of Paul's Creek, adjoining John Burras, etc.
49	488	William Williams	" "	22	On the waters of Big Dan River, adjoining his own land.
50	506	John Ogle	17 " "	79	On the west branch of Johnson's Creek, adjoining Benjamin Yates.
51	539	Joshua Haynes	5 Sept. "	93	On the headwaters of Indian Fork of Loving Creek.
52	543	John Hook	7 " "	3,023	On Dan River and its waters, beginning in Patterson's Order line where it crosses the Meadows of Dan River.
53	543	John Hook	" "	100	On Jill's Creek, adjoining John Henry, Thomas McDaniel, etc.
54	545	John Hook	8 " "	124	On the waters of Jack's Creek, adjoining the land of Nathaniel N. Hilton.
55	546	John Hook	" "	231	On the north waters of Smith's River, adjoining Patterson's Order line.

BOOK No. 37

	Page	Name	Date	Acres	Location
56	57	Owen Ruble	27 July 1796	669	On the north waters of Smith's River, adjoining Richard Stone, Rawlins, etc.
57	342	Elihu Ayrs	1 Aug. 1797	170	On the waters of Johnson's Creek.
58	346	Francis Turner and Robert Rowan	3 " "	1,223	On the headwaters of Smith's River, adjoining land of Sims, and Patterson's Order line.
59	356	George Carter	10 " "	145	On Cluds Creek Mountain, a Spur of the Bull Mountain, adjoining Eliphaz Shelton.
60	370	Tedrick Ewes	16 " "	86	On both sides of Mall Branch of Loving's Creek.
61	396	William Fuson	6 Sept "	41	On the south waters of Smith's River, adjoining his own line.
62	397	Benjamin Garrott	" "	142	On both sides of Stone's Mountain, an arm of the Allegany Mountain, and both sides of the South Fork of Dan River.
63	398	Joshua Haynes	" "	71	On the waters of Indian Fork.
64	400	John Hook	8 " "	13,402	On Dan River, beginning on the east side.
65	532	Levi Jones	" "	222	On the west waters of Loving's Creek, adjoining William Cloud and the North Carolina line.
66	582	Thomas Dodson	23 Jan. 1798	47	On the south waters of North Mayo River.

PATRICK COUNTY COMMONWEALTH'S GRANTS OR PATENTS—Continued

BOOK No. 37

	Page	Name	Date	Acres	Location
67	585	Jonathan Shipman and Asher Waterman.	26 Jan. 1798	700	On the headwaters of Smith's River and South Mayo River, adjoining William Carter, Shelton, etc.

BOOK No. 38

	Page	Name	Date	Acres	Location
68	1	Benjamin Haskell	16 Feb. 1797	25,000	On Smith's River and the waters thereof.
69	72	James Perkins, Samuel Blagge, Gardiner L. Chandler and William Coleman.	23 Dec. "	12,095	On the north waters of South Mayo River, adjoining Colonel Critz, etc.
70	229	William Armstrong	4 May 1798	120	On the waters of Paul's Creek.
71	248	George Hairston	2 June	70	On the waters of North Mayo River, adjoining Randolph and Farris.
72	248	George Hairston	2 June	104	On the headwaters of Blackberry Creek.
73	249	George Hairston	4 June	143	On both sides of Blackberry Creek, adjoining Thomas Hollandsworth.
74	254	George Hairston	"	228	On the north waters of North Mayo River, adjoining Abraham Penn.
75	263	George Hairston	2 "	30	On the east side of Kroger's Creek, adjoining William Sowell.
76	267	George Hairston	"	133	On the headwaters of South Mayo River.
77	268	William Armstrong	4 May	50	On the waters of Paul's Creek, adjoining Waller and You's land.
78	268	William Armstrong	4 "	55	On the waters of Paul's Creek.
79	272	Jonathan Shipman and Asher Waterman.	1 Apr.	2,000	On the headwaters of Ararat River, adjoining Patterson's Order line and Isaac Mayberry.
80	314	Beverley Spencer	13 July	150	On the headwaters of Gray's Fork, adjoining George Penn, Sr., Moses Reynolds, etc.
81	323	James Turner	"	400	On Rockcastle Creek and its waters, adjoining Richard Pilson, James Lackey, etc.
82	367	William Scott	20 Aug.	200	On the Doe Run and its waters, adjoining William Griffin.
83	371	Benjamin Hancock	" "	75	On the waters of Goblintown Creek and adjoining John Kogar.
84	372	George Carter	21 "	145	On the Cloud Brake Mountain, a spur of the Bull Mountain.
85	566	George Penn	10 Apr. 1799	3,156	Adjoining the land of Edward Tatum, Robert Hall, Archelaus Hughes, etc.

PATRICK COUNTY COMMONWEALTH'S GRANTS OR PATENTS—Continued

BOOK No. 39

	Page	Name	Date	Acres	Location
86	40	Harman Critz, Jr	16 Aug. 1796	96	On the north waters of Spoon Creek, adjoining his own land.
87	43	Jesse Com	10 Oct. "	86	On Rich Run, a branch of Smith's River, adjoining Ward, Butterworth, etc.
88	54	William Hamlett, Jr	16 "	120	On the south side of the South Mayo River, adjoining Shelton; and Walton's Order line.
89	90	Terry Hughes	26 Sept. "	83	On the north branches of Russell's Creek, adjoining Lyons.
90	272	James Perkins, Samuel Blagge, Gardiner L. Chandler and William Coleman.	16 May 1797	65,000	On the waters of Smith's River, adjoining William Perkins and others.
91	487	Joseph Jackson	1 Aug. "	58	On the headwaters of Loving Creek, adjoining Joseph R. Johnson.
92	491	John Davis	" "	57	On the south waters of Paul's Creek, adjoining Isham Webb, etc.
93	493	Jacob Talbott	2 "	50	On the headwaters of Johnson Creek, adjoining his own land.
94	495	Martin Dickinson	" "	150	On the headwaters of the Anall River.
95	495	James Dickinson	" "	137	On the north branches of Johnson's Creek.
96	496	John Stott	" "	72	On the headwaters of Paul's Creek.
97	498	Palmer Scritchfield	3 "	50	On the waters of Paul's Creek.
98	498	Joseph Johnson	" "	159	On Paul's Creek, adjoining his own land.
99	504	Daniel Carlan	5 "	96	On both sides of Naked Creek, adjoining his own land.
100	512	William Allen	8 "	88	On the north waters of Paul's Creek, adjoining John Allen.
101	542	Rhodham Moore	17 "	56	Beginning in Bell's Order line on the headwaters of Aratt River.
102	543	Stephen Senter	" "	43	On the west waters of Paul's Creek, adjoining his own land.
103	587	John Hook	6 Sept. "	450	On the waters of Rockcastle Creek, adjoining Turner, etc.
104	587	Benjamin Garrott	" "	42	On both sides of Dan River, adjoining his own land.
105	588	John Hook	7 "	616	On the headwaters of Widgeon Creek, a branch of Smith River.
106	589	Joshua Hayes	" "	134	On both sides of Brushy Fork of Paul's Creek.
107	590	John Hook	" "	400	On Rockcastle Creek waters of the North Fork of Smith's River, adjoining Patterson's Order line.
108	591	John Hook	" "	1,755	On the south waters of Smith's River, adjoining Jacob Critz, Patterson's Order line, etc.

PATRICK COUNTY COMMONWEALTH'S GRANTS OR PATENTS—Continued

BOOK No. 39

	Page	Name	Date	Acres	Location
109	592	John Hook	8 Sept. 1797	89	On the waters of Jack's Creek, adjoining Murrell's land.
110	593	John Hook	" "	212	On the headwaters of Dan River, adjoining Patterson's Order line, etc., Tuggle and Turner's land.

BOOK No. 40

	Page	Name	Date	Acres	Location
111	29	George Hairston	20 Oct. 1797	107	On the waters of Blackberry and Rockrun Creeks, adjoining John Goings, Henry Sumpter, etc.
112	29	George Hairston	" "	228	On the north waters of the North Mayo River, adjoining Abraham Penn.
113	141	William Armstrong	3 May 1798	65	On the waters of Johnson's Creek.
114	181	William Armstrong	" "	1,450	On the headwaters of Paul's Creek.
115	192	George Washington, Tent Marr, John Marr, William M. Marr, Sarah Marr, Constant H. P. Marr, Peter N. Marr, and Agatha A. Marr, Heirs and Representatives of John Marr, dec'd.	22	261	On the south waters of Big Dan River, adjoining Bell's Order line.
116	194	George Washington, Tent Marr, John Marr, William M. Marr, Sarah Marr, Constant H. P. Marr, Peter N. Marr, and Agatha A. Marr, Heirs and Representatives of John Marr, dec'd.	22 May	232	On the waters of Big Dan River, adjoining Paul Howel, etc.
117	214	Richardson Herndon	31	160	On the north waters of the North Mayo River, adjoining George Hairston, Conrad, etc.
118	218	Richardson Herndon	"	56	On the south waters of the North Mayo River, adjoining Stovall and Hairston.

PATRICK COUNTY COMMONWEALTH'S GRANTS OR PATENTS—Continued

BOOK No. 40

	Page	Name	Date	Acres	Location
119	292	Nathaniel Anderson	25 July 1798	5,000	On Dan River and the waters thereof, adjoining Jonathan Shipman, John Miller, etc.
120	303	Benjamin Mize	16 "	29	On the waters of Goblentown Creek, adjoining Anthony Street, John Ingram, etc.
121	314	John Koger	"	334	On the waters of Goblentown Creek.
122	316	Robert Rowan	17 "	70	On Sim's Fork of South Mayo River.
123	374	James Bartlett	30 "	90	On the north side of Smith's River, adjoining land of Ward, Thomas, etc.
124	419	William Carter	21 Aug.	37	On the Mill House Fork of South Mayo River, adjoining Walton, etc.
125	420	Martin Dickinson	20 "	200	On the north waters of Johnson's Creek and adjoining James Dickinson.
126	421	Rodham Moore	" "	141	On the north waters of Ararat River, adjoining Bell's Order line.
127	422	Elihu Ayres	21 "	100	On the South Fork of Johnson's Creek, adjoining Thomas Ayres.
128	422	Robert Harris	" "	50	Beginning on the south side of a branch. (Note: Name of branch not mentioned.)
129	423	Jonathan Hanley	20 "	50	On a branch of Squirrel Creek and on the south side of Squirrel Spur, adjoining the land of Cloud, etc.
130	426	Dedrick Ewes	" "	50	On Johnson's Creek.
131	428	Daniel Carlan	" "	183	On the headwaters of Stewart's Creek, adjoining his own land.
132	429	Charles Henegin	" "	70	On both sides of Stony Creek.
133	430	George Carter	21 "	196	On the Bushy Fork of South Mayo River.
134	432	William Carter	" "	533	On Big Dan River, adjoining land of Henry Fortner and the Widow Terry.
135	543	Samuel Packwood	17 Oct. "	63	On south side of Smith's River, adjoining Reaves and on Goblingtown Creek.

BOOK No. 41

	Page	Name	Date	Acres	Location
136	118	Joseph Stovall	19 Mar. 1799	65	On Bell's Spur and south branches of Dan River, adjoining Bell's Order line.
137	120	Jonathan Hanby	20 "	46	On the waters of Dan River.

PATRICK COUNTY COMMONWEALTH'S GRANTS OR PATENTS—Continued

BOOK No. 41

	Page	Name	Date	Acres	Location
138	120	David Harbour	20 Mar. 1799	275	On the waters of Sycamore, adjoining Adams' Order Line, John Terrel, etc.
139	122	John Johnson	19 "	70	On Loving's Creek and its waters, adjoining his own land.
140	128	Joseph Stovall	" "	60	On the waters of John's Creek.
141	130	Joseph Stovall	" "	29	On the south side of Smith River.
142	135	Abraham Penn	18 "	270	On the headwaters of North Mayo River.
143	619	John Ingram	20 Nov. "	291	On Smith's River, adjoining Zephaniah Davidson, James Ingram, etc.

BOOK No. 42

	Page	Name	Date	Acres	Location
144	109	William Ross	3 Jan. 1799	307	On the south side of Smith's River.
145	164	Archileus Hughes, Jr.	9 Nov. 1798	80	On the headwaters of Smith's River, adjoining Ward's line.
146	165	Joshua Haynes	16 Aug. "	153	On the north waters of the Brushy Fork, adjoining his own land.
147	170	Archelaus Hughes	9 Nov. "	83	On Paul's Creek, adjoining William Allen.
148	182	Adam Tittle	8 Feb. 1799	301	On the north waters of Goblingtown Creek, adjoining Callaway, Eckols, etc.
149	259	Charles Thomas	14 Mar. "	53	On the waters of Joint Crack Creek, adjoining land of Mead, Brammer, etc.
150	264	Thomas Ayres	15 "	100	On the waters of Johnson's Creek, adjoining land of Job Ross.
151	267	Jacob Johnson	20 "	68	On the east side of Loving's Creek, adjoining his own land.
152	271	Joseph Stovall	19 "	35	On the waters of John's Creek, adjoining Jessop's lines.
153	273	Jesse Reynolds	" "	140	On the South Fork of the North Mayo River, adjoining Reynolds' and Pullin's land.
154	274	Richard T. Manon	" "	113	On the waters of Smith's River, adjoining the land of Packwood.
155	278	William West	18 "	63	On the headwaters of Johnson's Creek and adjoining his own land.
156	295	Thomas Ayres, Jr.	" "	124	On both sides of Loving's Creek.
157	295	James Harris	19 "	60	On the south waters of North Mayo River, adjoining his own land.
158	299	John Walters	18 "	105	On both sides of Loving's Creek, adjoining Joseph Johnson.
159	450	Paul McMillion	19 "	70	On the headwaters of Johnson's Creek.

PATRICK COUNTY COMMONWEALTH'S GRANTS OR PATENTS—Continued

BOOK No. 43

	Page	Name	Date	Acres	Location
160	62	George Yates	16 Dec. 1799	59	On the South Fork of Johnson's Creek.
161	63	Samuel Harris	"	51	On the waters of Jack's Creek.
162	64	John Yates	"	65	On the headwaters of Johnson's Creek.
163	66	Stephen Jones	"	100	On the waters of Paul's Creek.
164	68	John Hall	13 "	145	On the waters of South Mayo River, adjoining Archalaus Hughes.
165	445	Joseph Reynolds	7 Mar. 1800	441	On Rockcastle Creek and its waters, adjoining Patterson, Callaway, etc.
166	447	Joseph Reynolds	"	223	On the south waters of Smith's River, adjoining Ward, Braden, etc.
167	462	Joseph Reynolds	"	109	On Joint Crack Creek and its waters, adjoining Ratliff, Harbour, etc.
168	467	David Harbour	8 "	50	On the south waters of Sycamore, adjoining Moses Harbour.
169	471	Joseph Reynolds	7 "	1,479	On Rockcastle Creek, adjoining Walton, Kinsey and Denny, etc.
170	504	Daniel Carlan	25 "	50	On Stewart's Creek, adjoining the North Carolina line.
171	505	Rhodam Moore	" "	93	On the east side of Johnson's Creek, adjoining the North Carolina line.
172	506	Beveridge Hughes	5 "	48	On the waters of Buffalo Creek, adjoining his own and Meade's land.
173	510	Jeremiah Jadwin	26 "	167	Beginning where Daniel Carlan's line crosses the Nasty Hill.
174	513	Thomas Ayrs	24 "	50	On the east waters of Johnson's Creek, adjoining his own land.
175	514	Thomas Ayrs, Jr.	"	124	On Meaner's Creek.
176	521	Isaac Johnson	25 "	36	On the waters of Paul's Creek.
177	540	Joseph Reynolds	10 "	672	On the waters of Jonent Crack Creek, adjoining Brammer, Lee, etc.
178	556	Joseph Reynolds	7 Feb.	379	On the waters of Rockcastle and Jill's Creeks, adjoining McAlexander, Denny, etc.
179	561	Joseph Reynolds	10 Mar.	193	On Big and Little Wedgin Creeks, adjoining Ward, McBride, etc.
180	562	John Turner	"	118	On the south waters of Smith's River, adjoining Francis Turner, Lucy Barnett, etc.

PATRICK COUNTY COMMONWEALTH'S GRANTS OR PATENTS—Continued

BOOK No. 44

	Page	Name	Date	Acres	Location
181	567	John Hill	18 June 1800	106	On the waters of Blackberry Creek, adjoining Gassett's land.
182	599	Joseph Reynolds	25 "	211	On the north side of Smith's River, adjoining Charles Rake, Burnett and others.

BOOK No. 45

	Page	Name	Date	Acres	Location
183	208	Joseph Reynolds	10 Mar. 1800	18	On the north waters of Smith's River, adjoining Joel Harbour.
184	246	Thomas Hollandsworth	29 "	56	On Blackberry Creek and its waters, adjoining Reed.
185	264	Roland Lee	10 "	46	On the headwaters of Big Wigeon Creek.
186	266	Thomas Morough	" "	108	On Sycamore Creek, adjoining William Hancock.
187	267	Jarett Branson	29 "	53	On the South Fork of Johnson's Creek, adjoining Mc-Million.
188	277	Joseph Johnson	24 "	126	On Paul's Creek and its waters, beginning where Charles Burgess' old line crosses said creek.
189	336	Peter Fry	25 "	91	On the waters of Johnson's Creek, adjoining Benjamin Yates.
190	466	Benjamin Kimsey	17 May "	395	On the headwaters of Little River, adjoining McAlexander's land.
191	587	James Cowper and Samuel Duvall	24 June "	1,000	On the south waters of Johnson's Creek, adjoining John Armstrong, Thomas Whitlocke, etc.

BOOK No. 46

	Page	Name	Date	Acres	Location
192	581	John Walters	1 Dec. 1800	389	On Paul's Creek and its waters, beginning at the Foggy Camp.

BOOK No. 47

	Page	Name	Date	Acres	Location
193	144	John Breaden, Jr.	1 Sept. 1800	21	On the north waters of Smith's River, beginning on the south side of Rockcastle Creek in the Widow Lackey's line.
194	537	John Watson, Sr.	14 Mar. 1801	89	On the headwaters of the Horse Pasture Creek, adjoining Penn, Hoaker, etc.

PATRICK COUNTY COMMONWEALTH'S GRANTS OR PATENTS—Continued

BOOK No. 47

	Page	Name	Date	Acres	Location
195	550	Abraham Hawk	24 Mar. 1801	344	On the headwaters of Paul's Creek, adjoining Carlin's line.
196	566	Joseph Cummings	" "	150	Beginning on Bowen's Creek and Hicks' Fork, adjoining Cummings, Smallman, etc.
197	571	David Taylor	" "	135	On the North Fork of North Mayo River and adjoining James Taylor.

BOOK No. 48

198	272	Joseph Gallego	18 Nov. 1801	100	On the headwaters of Spoon Creek.

BOOK No. 49

199	35	David Pannell	16 Apr. 1801	1,000	On the southwest waters of the Ararat River and Wolf Creek.
200	72	George Hairston	23 "	1,600	On the head of the South Mayo River, adjoining Thomas Gazway and Henry Arnold.
201	75	George Hairston	" "	1,000	On Goblintown Creek and its waters, adjoining Tittle, Harbour and others.
202	78	George Hairston	" "	235½	On the south waters of Russell's Creek, adjoining Willson, Poor, etc.
203	79	George Hairston	" "	303	On the waters of Russell's Creek, adjoining Gilliam, Helton and others.
204	80	George Hairston	" "	179	On the waters of South Mayo River, adjoining Jacob Critz, James Sublet, etc.
205	211	George Penn and Brett Stovall	8 June "	1,000	On the waters of Dan River and Roberson's Creek, adjoining Black, etc.
206	278	Jesse Corn	18 "	900	On both sides of Turnip Creek, adjoining Ward and Company, Butterworth and others.
207	391	Peter Saunders	11 Aug.	134	On the headwaters of Smith's River, known by the name of Jack's Creek, adjoining Thompson.
208	442	Augustine Thomas	7 "	120	On the south waters of North Mayo River, adjoining Hannah Mayo, William Fee and others.
209	493	George Hairston	22 Oct. "	29	On the south waters of South Mayo River, adjoining Miller Esley, Rentfroe, etc.

PATRICK COUNTY COMMONWEALTH'S GRANTS OR PATENTS—Continued

BOOK No. 49

	Page	Name	Date	Acres	Location
210	543	Joseph Gallego	18 Nov. 1801	200	On the headwaters of the North Mayo River, called Dotson's Creek.
211	544	Joseph Gallego	" "	100	On the headwaters of Blackberry Creek.
212	570	Talmon Harbour	12 Dec. "	147	Adjoining his own land.

BOOK No. 50

	Page	Name	Date	Acres	Location
213	39	John Creed	26 May 1802	181	On the waters of Arratt River, adjoining Bell's Order line.
214	40	John Creed	" "	72	On the waters of Arratt.
215	46	John Mankins	25 " "	134	On the waters of Paul's Creek, adjoining land of Isaac Johnson.
216	66	Benjamin Hubbard	1 July "	300	On both sides of Jack's Creek, adjoining Dehart, Ward and others.
217	89	Cornelius Buck	16 June "	425	On the waters of Arratt and Reed Island and adjoining Michaux.
218	90	Cornelius Buck	" "	294	On the waters of Sycamore Creek, adjoining John Ferrell, William Morrison and others.
219	91	Cornelius Buck	" "	316	On the waters of Sycamore Creek and Buffalo Creek, adjoining James Mayo, William Hancock and others.
220	92	Cornelius Buck	17 " "	250	On the east waters of Paul's Creek, adjoining John Dalton.
221	93	Cornelius Buck	" "	311	On the waters of Dan River, adjoining John Bowman's land.
222	94	Cornelius Buck	18 " "	109	On the waters of Big Sycamore Creek and adjoining Nathan Morrison.
223	95	Cornelius Buck	" "	1,041	On the east waters of Paul's Creek, adjoining John Dickerson, Joshua Haynes, etc.
224	96	Cornelius Buck	" "	84	On the waters of Paul's Creek, adjoining William Howell, Mitchell Thompson, etc.
225	97	Cornelius Buck	" "	325	On the waters of Buffalo Creek, adjoining William Hancock, Isham Burnett and others.
226	98	Cornelius Buck	" "	160	On the waters of Goblintown Creek, adjoining Poteet's land.
227	99	Cornelius Buck	" "	214	On Stoney Creek waters of Stewart's Creek.
228	117	John Hall	9 " "	285	On the north waters of Smith's River, beginning in Nathan Hall's line on the north side of White Oak Creek.

PATRICK COUNTY COMMONWEALTH'S GRANTS OR PATENTS—Continued

BOOK No. 50

	Page	Name	Date	Acres	Location
229	118	Isham Cockram	9 June 1802	129	On the north waters of Smith's River, adjoining Charles Rake and on Turkey Cock Creek.
230	119	Samuel Packwood, Sr.	" "	65	Beginning at the Angelicko Fawl's on the north side of Smith's River.
231	136	Abraham Hawk	16 " "	43	On the waters of Stewart's Creek, adjoining his own land.
232	546	Joseph Michaux	16 July 1803	89	On the waters of Elk Creek, adjoining William Smith and Ralph Dangers.
233	549	Joseph Michaux	" "	313	On the waters of Russell's Creek, adjoining Magruder, Shelton, etc.
234	550	Joseph Michaux	" "	96	On Elk's Creek, adjoining Collins' and Marr's land.
235	551	Joseph Michaux	" "	75	On the waters of Peters' Creek, beginning in William Smith's line on the side of the Long Branch.

BOOK No. 51

	Page	Name	Date	Acres	Location
236	42	John Spencer	16 Sept. 1802	50	On the headwaters of the North Mayo, beginning on the south side of Prather's Fork in said Spencer's own line.
237	487	Henry Tuggle	14 July 1803	160	In the Counties of Montgomery and Patrick on the waters of Howell's Creek, waters of Little River, a branch of New River, and a small part on the waters of Rock Castle.

BOOK No. 52

	Page	Name	Date	Acres	Location
238	271	William Hannah	22 Mar. 1804	42	On the headwaters of Mill Creek, adjoining Hopkins.
239	272	Samuel Philpott	" "	84	On the south side of Smith's River, adjoining his own land.
240	273	William Cloud	" "	50	On the waters of Loving's, adjoining John Ogle, Frederick Yew, etc.
241	273	Sharp Barton	23 Mar. "	11	On the waters of Mill Creek of North Mayo River, adjoining William Banks and Isaac Adams.
242	274	Gabriel Penn	" "	25	On the north waters of the South Mayo River, adjoining Keaton (otherwise said Penn's) line.
243	275	Henry Reynolds	" "	70	On the headwaters of Loving's Creek on the east side of the Blue Ridge, adjoining Ogle.

PATRICK COUNTY COMMONWEALTH'S GRANTS OR PATENTS—Continued

BOOK No. 52

	Page	Name	Date	Acres	Location
244	275	George Penn	22 Mar.1804	450	On the waters of Paul's Creek, adjoining Betheney Haynes and Joshua Haynes.
245	278	John Edwards	27 "	21	At a place called the Poplar Cove.
246	279	John Edwards	" "	335	On McCarven's Creek and its waters.
247	280	John Edwards	" "	111	On the headwaters of the Indian Fork of Loving's Creek.
248	280	Tilmon Harbour	24 "	24¼	On the north side of Goblingtown Creek, adjoining his own land.
249	281	Gabriel Penn	" "	100	On both sides of the South Mayo River, adjoining Wolverton, Rentfroe, etc.
250	282	Richard Chandler	" "	684½	On the waters of Peters' Creek, adjoining Daniel Lawson, Augustine Brown, etc.
251	284	John Hughes	4 Apr.	87	On the waters of North Mayo River, adjoining the land of Pigg, Watson and Ferrell.
252	285	John Hughes	" "	67	On the south waters of Johnston's Creek.
253	285	John Hughes	" "	151	On the waters of Blackberry Creek.
254	333	John Burnett	10 Aug.	167	On both sides of Jack's Creek, adjoining William Robertson, David Robertson, etc.
255	334	John Burnett	" "	633	On the headwaters of Rock Castle Creek, and the waters of Little River, adjoining land of Hook, Tuggle, etc.
256	335	Charles Foster, Jr	18 "	200	On the north waters of Puppy Creek, adjoining Charles Foster, Sr.
257	509	Washington Rowland	14 Nov.	600	On the south waters of Smith's River and Brown's Creek, adjoining land of Smallman, Stone and others.

BOOK No. 53

	Page	Name	Date	Acres	Location
258	30	Joseph Michaux	6 Feb. 1804	500	On the waters of Ararat and Dan Rivers, adjoining John Bowman, Benjamin Marrett, etc.
259	43	Reuben Short	19 Apr.	23	On the north waters of Smith's River, adjoining Hall's land.
260	43	Reuben Short	" "	29	On the north waters of Smith's River, adjoining Hubbard, Dehart, Pedigoy, etc.
261	112	Martin Miller, Sr	29 May	23	On the south waters of North Mayo River, adjoining Hairston's land.
262	113	George Hairston, Jr	13 June	50	On the south waters of Wolf Creek.

PATRICK COUNTY COMMONWEALTH'S GRANTS OR PATENTS—Continued

BOOK No. 53

	Page	Name	Date	Acres	Location
263	114	George Hairston, Jr.	13 June 1804	50	On both sides of Johnston's Creek, adjoining Yates and Ayrs.
264	115	George Hairston, Jr.	"	100	On waters of Jackson's Creek, adjoining Gosset's land.
265	115	George Hairston, Jr.	"	300	On the headwaters of Spoon Creek and Mathew's Creek, adjoining land of Murphey and Rowan's land.
266	116	Eliphas Shelton	9 "	200	On the waters of the Bell Mountain Fork of the South Mayo River, adjoining land of Strong.
267	154	Brett Stovall and Josiah Ferriss.	19 "	800	On the headwaters of Mill Creek of Mayo, adjoining Crutcher, Penn, etc.
268	155	Harman Critz	"	57	On Spoon Creek and its waters, adjoining Hawkins' land.

BOOK No. 54

	Page	Name	Date	Acres	Location
269	212	William Barton, Jr.	22 Aug. 1805	364	On the north side of South Mayo River, adjoining Fletcher and William Barton, Sr.
270	212	James S. Gaines	19 "	300	On the west side of Little Dan River, adjoining land of Shadrack and William Goings.
271	399	Thomas Hollandsworth	31 Oct. "	51	On the north waters of Blackberry Creek, adjoining his own and Witt's land.
272	428	John Adams	28 Feb. 1806	112	On the south waters of Goblintown Creek, adjoining Burk, Magruder and Packwood.
273	484	Joseph Michaux	27 May 1805	126	On the headwaters of Loving's Creek, adjoining Green and McDonnan.
274	487	Joseph Michaux	"	69	On the waters of Loving's Creek, adjoining Yates' land.
275	487	Joseph Michaux	"	90	On the south side the South Fork of Loving's Creek, adjoining Brown's land.
276	488	Joseph Michaux	"	112	On the headwaters of Loving's Creek, adjoining Green and Ogle.
277	489	Joseph Michaux	"	172	On the waters of the Ararat, beginning on the west side of Noheaded Branch, adjoining his own land.

BOOK No. 55

	Page	Name	Date	Acres	Location
278	411	Joseph Reynolds	17 Apr. 1806	350	Beginning on the north side of Rockcastle Creek at the mouth of a branch and adjoining his own land.

PATRICK COUNTY COMMONWEALTH'S GRANTS OR PATENTS—Continued

BOOK No. 55

	Page	Name	Date	Acres	Location
279	414	Joseph Reynolds	17 Apr. 1806	90	On the south waters of Smith's River, adjoining Barnett, Callaway, Fuson, etc.
280	480	Thomas Row Hall	15 May "	50	On Poplar Camp Creek, adjoining Hall and Short's land.
281	481	John Yates	" "	77	On the Buck Fork of Johnson's Creek, adjoining Branson's land.
282	441	William McMillion	14 "	82	On the waters of Loving's Creek, adjoining Farmer's land.
283	447	William Fuson	16 "	290	On the south waters of Smith's River, adjoining Smith, Tharp, etc.

BOOK No. 56

	Page	Name	Date	Acres	Location
284	1	Phillip Anglin	9 July 1806	216	On north Mayo River, adjoining the land of Dodson.
285	337	Thomas Murrell	14 May 1808	300	On the headwaters of Jack's Creek.
286	348	Benjamin Hancock	12 " "	70	On both sides of Puppy Creek, adjoining his own and Foster's land.
287	363	John Adams	" "	106	On the headwaters of North Mayo River, adjoining his own land.
288	431	Samuel Staples	6 June "	92	On the waters of Sandy Creek, adjoining Bell's line.
289	473	George Hairston, Sr.	7 Nov. "	156	On the north waters of Russell's Creek, adjoining his own land.
290	515	George Hairston	10 " "	100	On the north side of Goblintown Creek, beginning on Cedar Branch.
291	518	John Hall	" " "	157	On the south waters of Goblintown Creek.

BOOK No. 57

	Page	Name	Date	Acres	Location
292	190	Daniel Askew	10 May 1808	111½	On the waters of Russell's Creek, adjoining John and Alexander Askew.
293	284	Adam Turner	25 June "	53	On the south side of Smith's River and on both sides of Sycamore Creek.
294	286	Abraham Penn	5 July "	46	On the headwaters of Loving's Creek, adjoining Jacob Talbot's land.
295	287	Brett Stovall	" "	80	On the headwaters of Green Creek, adjoining Critzer and McGruder's land.

PATRICK COUNTY COMMONWEALTH'S GRANTS OR PATENTS—Continued

BOOK No. 57

	Page	Name	Date	Acres	Location
296	290	David Taylor	6 July 1808	134	On both sides of Spoon Creek, adjoining Reynolds, Heth, Finney, etc.
297	299	Hardin Hairston	13 Feb. 1809	131	On Syms's Fork of South Mayo River, adjoining Hughes and Staples.
298	400	Hardin Hairston	" "	164	On both sides of Sandy Creek, adjoining Bell's Old Order line.
299	447	George Hairston	10 Nov. 1808	4,300	On the waters of Goblingtown Creek, North Mayo River, Blackberry Creek and Bowing's Creek.
300	467	Henry Kogars	20 Dec. "	100	On the south waters of Kogar's Creek, adjoining Reynolds, Penn, etc.

BOOK No. 58

	Page	Name	Date	Acres	Location
301	90	John Hill	12 June 1809	30	On the south waters of Blackberry Creek, adjoining Gussett, Trent, etc.
302	95	Beveridge Hughes	" "	50	On the waters of North Buffalo Creek, adjoining his own and Handy's land.
303	339	John Spaulden, Sr.	4 July "	150	On the south side of Smith's River, beginning at Hallsford and adjoining Tharp and Callaway.
304	352	William Banks	" "	156	On the south waters of Mill Creek and branch of North Mayo River, adjoining land of Magruder and France.
305	395	Thomas Farmer	12 "	115	On the north waters of the North Fork of Loving's Creek, adjoining Hickingbotham, McMillion, etc.
306	412	Talmon Harbour	18 "	25	On the south waters of Goblingtown Creek and adjoining Hairston's land.
307	433	Josiah Ferress	" "	362	On the south side of Dan River, adjoining Staples and Howel's land.
308	440	Thomas Reaves	" "	232	On the north waters of Goblingtown Creek, adjoining Tenison, Adams and Pedigo.

BOOK No. 59

	Page	Name	Date	Acres	Location
309	14	David Harbour	26 July 1809	55	On both sides of Sycamore Creek, adjoining Ross, Foley, etc.
310	101	German Baker	1 Aug. "	218	On both sides of Little Blackberry Creek, adjoining Goins and Craddock.

PATRICK COUNTY COMMONWEALTH'S GRANTS OR PATENTS—Continued

BOOK No. 59

	Page	Name	Date	Acres	Location
311	106	Enoch Bredwell	1 Aug. 1809	42	On the south waters of Bowing's Creek, adjoining Hollandsworth.
312	219	James Hollandsworth	1 Sept. "	64	On the waters of Blackberry Creek, adjoining Thomas Hollandsworth.
313	223	Eusebius Stone	" "	300	On the north side of Smith's River, adjoining Philpot, Bellamy, DuVall, etc.
314	227	William Hannah	" "	63	On the south waters of North Mayo River, adjoining Anglin's land.
315	228	Thomas Hollandsworth	" "	15	On the north side of Blackberry Creek, adjoining Hairston and Cameron.
316	232	John James	" "	152	On the headwaters of North Mayo River, adjoining Adams' land.
317	234	George Penn	" "	138	On the north branches of Loving's Creek, adjoining Higginbotham and Marr.
318	235	Garrott Branson	" "	112	On the headwaters of Loving's Creek, adjoining Summers and Branson's land.
319	241	Gabriel Hanby	" "	113	On the northeast waters of Little Dan River, adjoining Shadrack Gowins.
320	242	Abraham Hawks	" "	31	On the northeast side of Elk Creek and adjoining his own land.
321	250	Burrel Smith	" "	85	On the south waters of Clark's Creek, adjoining Bartlett Smith.

BOOK No. 60

	Page	Name	Date	Acres	Location
322	166	John Hall	10 Oct. 1809	78	On the north waters of Smith's River, adjoining Edward Pedigo.
323	230	Philip Penn	1 Mar. 1810	57	On the headwaters of Loving's Creek.
324	327	William West	2 Apr. "	38	On the headwaters of Roaring Fork of Johnson's Creek, adjoining William Sizemore.

BOOK No. 61

	Page	Name	Date	Acres	Location
325	41	Thomas Penn	6 Aug. 1810	187	On the headwaters of the North Mayo River, adjoining Randolph, Anglin, James, etc.

PATRICK COUNTY COMMONWEALTH'S GRANTS OR PATENTS—Continued

BOOK No. 61

	Page	Name	Date	Acres	Location
326	44	Thomas Penn.............	6 Aug. 1810	152	On the south waters of the North Mayo River, adjoining Harris, Penn, etc.
327	46	Valentine Branson......	"	54	On the headwaters of Johnson's Creek, adjoining his own land.
328	48	Joel Chitwood...........	"	55	On the north side of the North Mayo River, adjoining Sharp, Anglin, Pigg, etc.
329	49	Richard Sharp...........	"	52	On the south waters of Sycamore Creek, adjoining his own and Burnett's land.
330	76	Francis Nowland........	13 "	17	On the north side of the South Mayo River, adjoining Penn and Carter's land.
331	95	Gabriel Penn, Jr........	"	148	On the south side of the North Mayo River, adjoining Cameron, Harris, etc.
332	103	David May..............	"	45	On the Briery Fork of Stewart's Creek.
333	170	Charles Stewart.........	"	100	On the headwaters of Stewart's Creek.
334	224	Thomas H. Watson......	17 Sept. "	52	On the North Fork of the North Mayo River, adjoining Ferrell, Lockhart, Chitwood, etc.
335	582	John Ingram............	10 June 1811	158	On both sides of Smith's River, adjoining land of Edwards, Childsm, Ingram, etc.
336	585	John Ingram............	"	125	On the headwaters of the South Mayo River, adjoining Adams and Witt's land.
337	586	John Ingram	"	45	On the north side of Smith's River, adjoining land of Adams, Cox and James' lines.

BOOK No. 62

	Page	Name	Date	Acres	Location
338	20	Richard Sharp..........	14 Aug. 1811	35	On the south side of Little Sycamore Creek, adjoining Ferrel.
339	21	Richard Sharp..........	"	138	On the waters of Smith's River, adjoining land of Houchan.
340	180	James Murphey.........	1 Oct. "	17	On the headwaters of Mathew's Creek, adjoining his own and Rowan's land.
341	181	Abraham Penn..........	"	191	On both sides of McCarver's Creek, adjoining Johnson, Haynes, etc.
342	322	John Turner	17 Mar. 1812	150	On the headwaters of Smith's River, adjoining Hock, Rowan and Peterson's land.

PATRICK COUNTY COMMONWEALTH'S GRANTS OR PATENTS—Continued

BOOK No. 62

	Page	Name	Date	Acres	Location
343	415	David Taylor	13 May 1812	100	On the north waters of the South Mayo River, beginning at the head of Mathew's Creek, adjoining Rowan.
344	455	Joshua Haynes	15 June "	250	On the south waters of Loving's Creek, adjoining Boyd's land.

BOOK No. 63

	Page	Name	Date	Acres	Location
345	13	Carrington Dillen	6 July 1812	50	On the north waters of Roger's Creek, adjoining King, Gowin, etc.
346	284	William Carter	7 Oct. "	90	On the south waters of Big Dan River.
347	287	James Dolton	" "	107	On the waters of Johnson's Creek, adjoining East, Branson, etc.
348	289	Jarrett Branson	" "	95	On the waters of Johnson's Creek, adjoining his own land.
349	290	Nathaniel Smith	" "	100	On the headwaters of Peters' Creek.
350	298	Nathaniel Smith	9 Nov. "	100	On the waters of Peters' Creek, adjoining Hanby and Tatum's land.
351	299	Nathaniel Smith	" "	180	On the North Fork of Peters' Creek, adjoining Hamilton and Brown.
352	308	Joseph Michaux and Joseph Stovall	" "	349	On the Blackberry Creek, adjoining William Read's land.
353	322	Washington Rowland and Malichiah Parmer.	25 "	100	On Smith's River.
354	410	Abraham Staples	31 May 1813	42	On the north waters of the South Mayo River, adjoining Fitzgarrald, Shelton, etc.
355	489	Jacob Nugent	25 June "	307	On the headwaters of Stewart's Creek, beginning on Bletcher's Spring Branch, adjoining land of Lundy.

BOOK No. 64

	Page	Name	Date	Acres	Location
356	118	Moses Reynolds	11 Nov. 1813	80	On the waters of the North Mayo River, adjoining Abraham Reynolds.
357	119	Jesse Reynolds	" "	50	Adjoining Deel and Anglin's land.
358	120	William Hannah	" "	26	On the north waters of the North Mayo River, adjoining John Spencer.

PATRICK COUNTY COMMONWEALTH'S GRANTS OR PATENTS—Continued

BOOK No. 64

	Page	Name	Acres	Date	Location
359	175	Abraham Reynolds	200	4 Apr. 1814	On the south waters of the Nobusiness Fork of the North Mayo River, adjoining John Finney, Moses Reynolds and Jesse Reynolds.
360	214	John Preston, Jr.	599	25 Oct. "	On Son's Run, the headwaters of the Aratt River, adjoining Michaux's land.

BOOK No. 65

	Page	Name	Acres	Date	Location
361	333	John Crum	13	25 July 1815	On the Middle Fork of North Mayo River, adjoining Penn's land.
362	364	Amos Askew	40	18 Oct. "	On the south waters of Russell's Creek, adjoining George Hairston, Sr., and John Parr.
363	487	John Bold, Sr.	62	17 June 1816	On the headwaters of Johnson's Creek, adjoining William Cock.
364	489	Adron Anglin	21	" "	On the headwaters of the North Mayo River, adjoining his own land.

BOOK No. 66

	Page	Name	Acres	Date	Location
365	130	Obediah Burnett	210	2 Sept. 1816	On the headwaters of Smith's River, adjoining his own and Staples' land.
366	131	Obediah Burnett	334	" "	On the headwaters of Smith's River, adjoining his own land.
367	134	Aaron Boman	50	" "	On the west waters of Arratt River, beginning near a place called Raven's Rock.
368	135	Obediah Burnett	451	" "	On the headwaters of Smith's River.
369	248	Moses Reynolds	47	30 Dec. "	On the Nobusiness Fork of the North Mayo River, adjoining Gabriel Penn, Cameron and others.
370	285	Jesse Mankin	78	10 May 1817	On the headwaters of Johnson's Creek, adjoining William McMillion, etc.
371	324	Basdel Nicholds	50	" "	On Bowing's Creek and the waters thereof, adjoining George Hairston, Jr., and Hagwood.
372	327	Jacob Kogar	51	" "	On the north waters of Kogar's Creek, adjoining Watson and Gowin's land.
373	327	John Abington	108	" "	On the south waters of Horse Pasture Creek, adjoining his own and French's land.

PATRICK COUNTY COMMONWEALTH'S GRANTS OR PATENTS—Continued

BOOK No. 66

Page	Name	Date	Acres	Location
374	Munford Smith, Sr.	10 May 1817	84	On the headwaters of the Arratt River, adjoining William Moores.
375	Jonathan Hanby	20 June "	60	On the south waters of Peters' Creek, adjoining Martindale, Hanby, etc.
376	Gabriel Penn, Jr.	1 July "	250	On the headwaters of the North Mayo River.
377	Zachariah King	" "	67	On the south branches of Blackberry Creek, adjoining John Wells, William Wells and others.
378	Jesse Moore	" "	50	On the headwaters of the North Mayo River, adjoining his own and Israel Martin's land.

BOOK No. 67

Page	Name	Date	Acres	Location
379	William Handy	1 Nov. 1817	160	On the waters of Beaver Tail Creek, adjoining Nancy Hughes and Beverage Hughes' land.
380	William Crum	20 "	45	On the Middle Fork of North Mayo River, adjoining Abraham Reynolds and Abraham Penn, Jr.
381	James Fulkerson	2 Mar. 1818	5	On the north waters of the South Mayo River, adjoining Fulkerson and Thomas's land.
382	Thomas Whitlock	30 "	200	On the south waters of Johnson's Creek, adjoining James Dickinson and Elihu Ayres.
383	Madison R. Hughes	6 July "	35	Beginning at his corner on the south waters of North Mayo River, adjoining land of Penn and Thomas.
384	Obediah Burns	" "	90	On the headwaters of Smith's River, beginning on Kendrick's Spur of the Blue Ridge.
385	Cornelius Thomas	1 Aug. "	25	On the north waters of Smith's River, adjoining Hall and Thomas's land.

BOOK No. 69

Page	Name	Date	Acres	Location
386	William Gray, Sr.	13 June 1820	5¾	On the headwaters of Russell's Creek.
387	Isam Green	" "	250	On the south waters of Russell's Creek, adjoins land of Burge, Poor and Gray.
388	George Penn	17 Aug. "	130	On the headwaters of Loving's Creek.
389	Valentine Burnett	10 Oct. "	160	On the headwaters of Smith's River, beginning at William Parmer's Corner.

PATRICK COUNTY COMMONWEALTH'S GRANTS OR PATENTS—Continued

BOOK No. 69

	Page	Name	Date	Acres	Location
390	451	Thomas Bowlin	10 Oct. 1820	25	On the headwaters of Spoon Creek.
391	451	Jacob Kogar	" " "	21	On the north waters of Kogar's Creek, beginning, etc., in Newman's old line now Kogar's.
392	452	John Tatum	"	56	On the north waters of Peters' Creek, beginning at Jonathan Hanby's corner red oak in William Tatum's line.
393	458	Jesse Moore	"	134	On the headwaters of the South Fork of the North Mayo River.
394	458	John Thomas	"	125	On the headwaters of Poplar Camp.

BOOK No. 70

	Page	Name	Date	Acres	Location
395	410	Isham Barnett	1 Oct. 1821	134	On Dan River and the waters thereof, beginning, etc., corner of Jonathan Hanby.

BOOK No. 71

	Page	Name	Date	Acres	Location
396	20	Micajah Martin	12 Mar. 1822	49	On the headwaters of Mill Creek, beginning, etc., on the top of Nobusiness Mountain.
397	296	Thomas R. Hall	10 Oct. "	82	Beginning at William Feston's corner chestnut tree on a branch of Smith's River.
398	297	Thomas R. Hall	"	100	Beginning at Nicholas Thomas's corner on a ridge near the waters of Poplar Camp Creek.
399	298	Thomas Teneson	"	100	On the north waters of Widgin Creek.
300	300	Jesse Jones	"	125	Beginning at Waras corner on the headwaters of Widgeon Creek.

BOOK No. 72

	Page	Name	Date	Acres	Location
301	54	William Carter, Sr.	17 Feb. 1823	162	On the South Fork of Little Dan River.
302	323	William Cannaday	10 July "	16	On the north waters of Smith River.
303	324	Henry Kogar	10 " "	300	On little Blackberry Creek.
304	325	Obediah Burnett	" "	261	On Dan and Smith Rivers.
305	326	Silas Carter	" "	25	On the waters of the South Mayo River.
306	327	Winston Newman	" "	55	On the headwaters of the South Mayo River.
307	328	Thomas Hollandsworth, Jr.	" "	32	On the north waters of Blackberry Creek.

PATRICK COUNTY COMMONWEALTH'S GRANTS OR PATENTS—Continued

BOOK No. 72

	Page	Name	Date	Acres	Location
308	482	Thomas Hollandsworth, Jr.	29 Sept. 1823	54	On the north waters of Blackberry Creek.
309	483	Thomas Hollandsworth, Sr.	" "	50	On the north waters of Blackberry Creek.
310	484	John Davis	" "	44	On the north waters of Smith's River.
311	487	Adam Ahart	" "	100	On the north waters of Johnson's Creek.
312	495	Samuel Howel	" "	70	On the headwaters of Lynn's Fork of the South Mayo River.
313	496	William Carter, Sr.	" "	300	On the headwaters of Archer's Creek.

BOOK No. 73

	Page	Name	Date	Acres	Location
314	247	William Lyon	22 July 1824	150	Headwaters of Sycamore Creek.
414	251	Thomas Harbour	" "	150	Headwaters of Widgeon Creek.
415	448	William Sharpe	28 Sept. "	380	Headwaters of Russell's Creek.
416	542	Munford Smith	24 Mar. 1825	200	South waters of Russell's Creek.

BOOK No. 74

	Page	Name	Date	Acres	Location
417	71	Jeremiah Hilton and Adderson Philpott.	6 June 1825	500	On Mathew's Fork of South Mayo River.
418	77	Dandridge Slaughter	" "	258	On the south waters of Smith's River.
419	78	James Reynolds	" "	248	On Rock Castle Creek.
420	391	Obadiah Burnett	11 Nov. "	70	On the headwaters of South Mayo River.
421	392	Nathaniel Young	" "	150	On the headwaters of Arrat River.
422	395	Robert Harriss	" "	110	On the South Fork of Little Dan River.
423	443	George W. Callaway	21 "	250	On Widgeon Creek.
424	444	George W. Callaway	" "	130	On Smith's River and the waters thereof.

BOOK No. 75

	Page	Name	Date	Acres	Location
425	73	Nathaniel Ankers	13 June 1826	27	On the waters of Smith's River.
426	74	John Flemming	" "	31	On the South Fork of Johnson's Creek.
427	75	David Boyd	" "	39	On the headwaters of Smith's River.
428	76	Nathan Hall	" "	80	On the headwaters of Little Sycamore Creek.
429	77	Thomas Hancock	" "	30	On the south waters of Gibbon-Town Creek.
430	484	William Cannaday	6 Feb. 1827	4¾	On the north waters of Smiths.
431	485	Conrod Plasters	" "	27	On the headwaters of South Mayo River.

PATRICK COUNTY COMMONWEALTH'S GRANTS OR PATENTS—Continued

	Page	Name	Date	Acres	Location
			BOOK No. 75		
432	534	Blacknon Hughes and Burbridge A. Hughes, sons and devisees of Burbridge Hughes, dec'd.	31 Oct. 1826	50	On the waters of Buffalo Creek.
			BOOK No. 76		
433	337	Thomas Bouldin	28 Aug. 1827	40	On the headwaters of Blackberry and Horse Pasture.
434	427	Jeremiah Burnett, Jr.	22 Oct. "	74	On the headwaters of Smith's River.
435	509	James Brammer	29 Dec. "	63	On the headwaters of Joint Creek.
436	414	James Duval	22 Oct. "	32	On the headwaters of North Mayo River.
437	155	Naaman Harbour	7 July "	200	On the waters of Sycamore Creek.
438	426	Thomas Morrison	22 Oct. "	42	On the south waters of Sycamore Creek.
439	151	Dandridge Slaughter	7 June "	270	On the waters of Buffalo Creek.
440	153	John Thomas	7 July "	187	On the headwaters of Wegeon Creek.
441	152	Richard Wood	" "	100	On the headwaters of Poplar Camp Creek.
442	356	James W. Warhoop	26 Sept. "	91	On the south waters of the South Fork of Johnston's Creek.
			BOOK No. 77		
443	270	Ellen F. Overley	11 Aug. 1828	107	On the south waters of Peters' Creek.
444	276	Joshua Wadkins	" "	119	On the headwaters of Little Dan River.
445	277	John Conner	" "	100	On the waters of Pack's Creek.
446	278	John Eaton	" "	100	On Sismey Creek.
447	279	John Habboard	" "	77	On waters of Jill Creek.
448	405	Joseph Cox	13 Oct. "	22	On Gobbin Town Creek.
449	453	Pleasant Thomas	12 Nov. "	200	On the headwaters of Poplar Camp Creek.
			BOOK No. 78		
450	458	John Ellegin	5 Jan. 1830	337	On the headwaters of Jack's Creek.
451	485	Conroy Plaster	17 Feb. "	112	On headwaters of Bull Mountain.
452	486	Joshua Adams	" "	28	On headwaters of the North Mayo River.
453	487	William Ayers	" "	14	On the north waters of Smith's River.
454	488	Abijah Booth	" "	25	On the north waters of Smith's River.
456	489	Jonas Plaster	" "	160	On the headwaters of the South Mayo River.
457	281	Anderson Faulks	4 Aug. 1829	300	On the waters of the South Fork of Johnson's Creek.

PATRICK COUNTY COMMONWEALTH'S GRANTS OR PATENTS—Continued

BOOK No. 79

	Page	Name	Date	Acres	Location
458	128	Aaron Bowman	1 Aug. 1830	120	On the headwaters of Fall Creek.
459	129	Washington Mitchell	" "	94	On headwaters of Elk Creek.
460	130	Washington Mitchell	" "	100	On south waters of Peters' Creek.
461	239	Notely P. Adams	1 Sept. "	74	On the south waters of Smith's River.
462	313	Samuel H. Woods	9 Oct. "	300	On Smith's River and its north waters.
463	319	Harmon Shelton	" "	90	On headwaters of Bull Mountain.
464	320	Augustin Clifton	10 "	41	On headwaters of Widgeon Creek.
465	323	Thomas Dehart	9 "	29	On headwaters of Widgeon Creek.
466	400	Aaron Dehart	14 Jan. 1831	114	On waters of Rockcastle Creek.
467	407	William Spencer	" "	100	On Grassy Fork of North Mayo River.
468	449	James and Alexander Via	17 Mar. "	125	On waters of Smith's River.
469	545	William Ayer, Sr.	20 June "	60	On headwaters of Loving's Creek.
470	546	Thomas Morrison	" "	40	On south waters of Sycamore Creek.
471	547	Dandridge Slaughter	" "	114	On headwaters of Bull Mountain.
472	582	Thomas C. Bouldin	1 July "	57	On Bull Run of Horse Pasture Creek.
473	583	Jesse Hubbard	" "	60	On headwaters of Jack's Creek.

BOOK No. 80

	Page	Name	Date	Acres	Location
474	58	James W. Wanhop	17 Oct. 1831	102	On the South Fork of Johnson's Creek.
475	65	James W. Wanhop	" "	146	On Johnson's Creek.
476	111	John Castle	27 "	30	On the west waters of Bull Mountain.
477	237	Callaway and Stovall	15 Nov. "	600	On Buffalo Creek and its waters.
478	238	George W. Callaway	" "	400	On Ivory Creek.
479	282	John Tuggle	16 "	34	On Rock Castle Creek.
480	353	Isaac Martin	24 Feb. 1832	50	On headwaters of North Mayo River.

BOOK No. 81

	Page	Name	Date	Acres	Location
481	29	Samuel Howell	29 Sept. 1832	75	On headwaters of South Mayo River.
482	98	Abram Reynolds	24 Oct. "	22	On headwaters of Mill Creek.
483	187	Obadiah Burnett	3 Nov. "	90	On headwaters of Smith's River.
484	202	Notely P. Adams	" "	90	On waters of Smith's River.
485	457	Joshua Adams	27 May 1833	400	On waters of North Mayo River.
486	458	Ranley White	30 "	1,000	On headwaters of John's Creek of Dan.

PATRICK COUNTY COMMONWEALTH'S GRANTS OR PATENTS—Continued

BOOK No. 81

	Page	Name	Date	Acres	Location
487	459	Ranley White	30 May 1832	293	On headwaters of the North Fork of Little Dan.
488	460	Ranley White	3 June "	336	On the headwaters of Little Dan River.
489	461	Joseph Furguson	5 "	150	On the three forks of Little Dan River.

BOOK No. 82

	Page	Name	Date	Acres	Location
490	30	John Eaton	29 July 1833	150	On north waters of Johnson's Creek.
491	50	Solomon Keaton	1 Aug. "	60	On the waters of North Mayo River.
492	55	Peter Havely (or Handy)	" "	100	On Descent's Creek.
493	56	John Light	" "	20	On headwaters of South Mayo River.
494	92	James M. Redd	5 "	115	On headwaters of South Mayo River.
495	93	Elijah Dehart	" "	65	On Big Widgeon Creek.
496	95	Aaron Bowman	" "	40	On waters of Dan River.
497	154	Joseph H. Edwards	15 "	68	On the headwaters of Simm's Fork.
498	210	Naaman Harbour	1 Sept. "	71	On the Cook Fork of Morrison's Creek.
499	248	Samuel Hooker	20 "	65	On the Little Fork of Little Dan River.
500	434	John Spencer, Jr.	29 Nov. "	150	On headwaters of North Mayo River.
501	449	Sarah Wright	18 Feb. 1834	75	On the south waters of Smith's River.

BOOK No. 83

	Page	Name	Date	Acres	Location
502	61	James W. Wanhoup	28 Nov. 1833	24	On the south waters of the South Fork of Johnson's Creek.
503	65	James M. Redd	" "	90	On the headwaters of South Mayo River.
504	155	William Conner	11 June 1834	120	On the headwaters of Jack's Creek.
505	156	Jacob Wade	" "	10	On Rock Castle Creek.
506	333	Elijah Dehurt	1 Sept. "	50	On headwaters of Widgeon Creek.
507	339	Gabril Critz	" "	80	On the north waters of Spoon Creek.
508	356	George Askin	" "	50	On headwaters of Rock Castle Creek.
509	474	Stephen Dihurt	10 "	50	On headwaters of Smith's River.
510	572	John Boyd	14 Nov. "	25	On waters of Johnson's Creek.
511	575	Gregory Haggood	12 "	150	On waters of Mill Creek and Smith's River.

BOOK No. 84

	Page	Name	Date	Acres	Location
512	...	Obadiah Burnet, Sr.	20 Aug. 1835	180	On north branches of South Fork of Smith's River.

PATRICK COUNTY COMMONWEALTH'S GRANTS OR PATENTS—Continued

388   HISTORY OF PATRICK AND HENRY COUNTIES

BOOK No. 85

	Page	Name	Date	Acres	Location
513	214	William Lawson	25 Aug. 1835	145	On headwaters of Rock Castle Creek.
514	215	John Brammer	"	9	On south waters of Rock Castle Creek.
515	211	William Spencer	20	68	On headwaters of Rock Castle Creek.
516	218	John B. Hudson	25	10	North Fork of Russell's Creek.
517	219	John Tuggle	"	61	On south waters of Rock Castle Creek.
518	220	Thomas Dehart	"	68	North waters of Rock Castle Creek.
519	221	Obadiah Burnett, Sr.	"	75	On headwaters of Smith's River.
520	222	Obadiah Burnett, Sr.	"	51	On south waters of Smith's River.
521	223	John Tuggle	"	182	On north waters of Rock Castle Creek.
522	224	Gabriel Hanbey and Robert Hinns.	"	42	On north waters of Peters' Creek.
523	225	Crofford Turner	"	143	On south waters of Buffalo and north waters of Sycamore Creek.
524	232	Naaman Harbour	1 Oct.	134	On waters of Little Sycamore Creek.
525	458	Brammer and Hall	1 June 1836	318	On south waters of Smith's River.
526	459	Elijah Dehurt	1 July	36	On waters of the North Fork of Jack's Creek.
527	460	Nelson Morran	"	50	On Widgeon Creek.
528	622	Benjamin J. Campbell	10 Sept.	44	On Smith's River.

BOOK No. 86

	Page	Name	Date	Acres	Location
529	272	Valentine Burnett	1 Aug. 1836	58	On headwaters of Rich Run Creek.
530	273	Maxwell Spencer	"	51	On headwaters of the North Fork of Pole Cat Branch.
531	274	Henry Crum	"	100	On the south waters of Smith's River.
532	837	Notely P. Adams	31	100	On headwaters of Rock Castle Creek.

BOOK No. 87

	Page	Name	Date	Acres	Location
533	587	Valentine Burnett	20 Oct. 1837	248	On headwaters of Rich Run.
534	538	John Gustler	"	25	On Smith's River.

BOOK No. 88

	Page	Name	Date	Acres	Location
535	28	Charles Perrow	1 Jan. 1838	928	On south waters of Smith's River.
536	315	William Lawson	30 Oct.	47	On north waters of Elk Creek.

PATRICK COUNTY COMMONWEALTH'S GRANTS OR PATENTS—Continued

BOOK No. 88

	Page	Name	Date	Acres	Location
537	316	Jesse Jones	30 Oct. 1838	129	On headwaters of Widgeon Creek.
538	317	Samuel Watkin	" "	30	On south waters of Smith's River.
539	339	Samuel Hubbert	" "	45	On headwaters of Smith's River.
540	340	Obadiah Burnett, Jr.	" "	277	On north waters of Smith's River.
541	341	Obadiah Burnett, Jr.	" "	37	On the south waters of Smith's River.
542	342	Obadiah Burnett, Jr.	" "	66	On north waters of Smith's River.
543	343	Obadiah Burnett, Jr.	" "	35	On south waters of Smith's River.
544	344	Obadiah Burnett, Jr.	" "	41	On south waters of Smith's River.
546	345	Isam Bernard	" "	150	On headwaters of Stephen's Creek.
547	405	Ewel Belton	" "	100	On waters of Elk Creek.

BOOK No. 89

	Page	Name	Date	Acres	Location
548	786	John Thompson	30 Nov. 1838	30	On headwaters of Ararat River.
549	787	Henry B. Terry	" "	12	On south waters of Smith's River.

BOOK No. 90

	Page	Name	Date	Acres	Location
550	10	Bernard M. Price	1 July 1840	70	On south waters of Smith's River.

BOOK No. 91

	Page	Name	Date	Acres	Location
551	115	Elijah Dehurt	30 Sept. 1840	250	On north waters of Rock Castle Creek.
552	116	Joseph Flippin	" "	150	On south waters of Peters' Creek.
553	117	Sampson Kenton	" "	68	On north waters of North Mayo River.
554	118	Thomas Morrison	" "	40	On south waters of Sycamore Creek.
555	119	Conrad Plaster	" "	75	On headwaters of South Mayo River.
556	120	Jonas Plaster	" "	200	On waters of Simms' Fork of South Mayo River.
557	121	Thomas Penn	" "	84	On headwaters of Blackberry Creek.
558	122	Thomas Penn	" "	35	On north waters of Rogers' Creek.
559	123	Trent and Spencer	" "	140	On North Fork of Mayo River and headwaters.
560	502	Benjamin J. Campbell	" June 1841	28	On Smith's River.

PATRICK COUNTY COMMONWEALTH'S GRANTS OR PATENTS—Continued

BOOK No. 92

	Page	Name	Date	Acres	Location
561	83	John Shelor	30 Aug. 1841	140	On the south waters of Round Meadow Creek of Dan River.
562	84	James Joyce	" "	480	On headwaters of North Mayo River.
563	85	Braxton Purdey	" "	188	On headwaters of Prater's Fork of North Mayo River.
564	86	John Spencer	" "	300	On south side of the Hogpen Mountain and on north waters of Prater's Fork of the North Mayo River.
565	87	Elisha Collins	" "	50	On the south waters of Elk Creek.
566	88	James Collins	" "	17	On the south waters of Elk Creek.
567	89	Abram Spencer	" "	150	On Prater's Fork of North Mayo River.
568	90	Ezekel Purdy	" "	98	On the headwaters of North Mayo River.
569	91	Naaman Harbour	" "	63	On Buffalo Creek.
570	92	Joshua Adams	" "	60	On headwaters of the Pole Bridge Creek of North Mayo River.
571	93	Jesse A. Ingram	" "	90	On the north waters of North Mayo River.
572	94	Joseph Moles	" "	20	On the south waters of Goblingtown Creek.
573	95	Joshua Adams	" "	50	On the headwaters of Pole Bridge Creek of North Mayo River.
574	300	Isaac Martin	" Sept.	21	On headwaters of North Mayo River.
575	301	John Thompson	" "	30	On headwaters of Ararat River.
576	302	Thomas Reynolds	" "	49	On headwaters of North Mayo River.
577	334	George Hairston, Sr.	" "	1,015	On waters of Blackberry and Bowen's Creeks.
578	496	Danderage Slaughter	10 May 1842	7	On the west waters of Big Sycamore Creek.
579	497	Meakin Reynolds	" "	31	On the Nobusiness Fork of the North Mayo River.
580	499	Henry Bearley	" "	250	On the headwaters of Elk Creek.
581	500	George W. King	" "	120	Beginning at Seaton Chandler's corner sorrelwood tree.

BOOK No. 93

	Page	Name	Date	Acres	Location
582	170	Henry Crum	30 Aug. 1842	64	Beginning at a white oak in Sarah Wright's line.
583	567	Mary Banks	30 Nov. "	87	On the headwaters of the North Mayo River.
584	568	Moses Hylton	" "	160	Beginning at Obadiah Burnett's corner white oak on Smith's River.
	569	Abraham Staples	" "	151	On the headwaters of the South Fork of Russell's Creek.

PATRICK COUNTY COMMONWEALTH'S GRANTS OR PATENTS—Continued

BOOK No. 94

	Page	Name	Date	Acres	Location
570	195	Daniel Gray	20 May 1843	100	On the south waters of Russell's Creek.
571	216	Joshua Adams	30 June "	5	On the headwaters of North Mayo River.
572	217	Henry Crim	" "	24	On the south waters of Smith's River.
573	218	Abram Spencer	" "	11	On the south waters of Prater's Fork of North Mayo River.
573	219	Peter Wood	" "	100	On the headwaters of Widgeon Creek.
575	220	William D. Young	" "	56	On the north waters of Puppy Creek.
576	460	Gabriel Critz	31 July "	140	On Spoon Creek and east waters of the Puppy Creek.

BOOK No. 95

	Page	Name	Date	Acres	Location
577	416	Nathan Hall	29 June 1844	135	Beginning on a ridge on the east side of Poplar Camp Creek.
578	637	Samuel Boyed	31 Aug. "	100	On Shooting Creek and waters thereof.
579	638	Fleming Thomas	" "	30	On the waters of Poplar Camp Creek.
580	639	Daniel Greay	" "	100	On the south waters of Russell's Creek.
581	640	Hardin Spencer	" "	20	On the headwaters of Pole Cat Branch.

BOOK No. 96

	Page	Name	Date	Acres	Location
582	456	William Marshall	30 June 1845	50	On the headwaters of Sismey's Creek.
583	457	James Rangeley	" "	143	On the South Mayo River and the waters thereof.
584	655	Charles T. Martin	31 July "	63	On the north waters of Little Peters' Creek.

BOOK No. 97

	Page	Name	Date	Acres	Location
585	216	Noteley P. Adams	30 June 1846	400	On Smith's River and the waters thereof.
586	286	Joseph McMillian	30 Apr. "	150	On the headwaters of Johnson's Creek.
587	293	George W. King	4 "	85	On the waters of Peters' Creek.
588	344	Joshua Adams	30 June "	250	On the headwaters of North Mayo River.
589	345	Palin Chapell	" "	90	On the south waters of Johnson's Creek.
590	346	Abel Lee	" "	52	On the headwaters of Jack's Creek.
591	347	William J. Robertson	" "	63	On the southeastern waters of Sycamore Creek.
592	348	Dabney W. Smith	" "	7	On the waters of Russell's Creek.
593	386	Paul C. Adams	" "	59	On the headwaters of North Mayo River.
594	425	Nathan McMillian	" "	47	On the east waters of Loving's Creek.
595	579	Arch. H. Carter	" "	30	On Dan River.

PATRICK COUNTY COMMONWEALTH'S GRANTS OR PATENTS—Continued

	Page	Name	Date	Acres	Location
		BOOK No. 97			
596	643	Benjamin Belcher	31 July 1846	10½	On the South Fork of Rock Castle Creek.
597	644	Carrington J. Dillion	" " "	66½	On the South Fork of Rock Castle Creek.
598	645	Elijah Dehart, Sr.	" " "	90	On the headwaters of Rock Castle and Widgeon Creeks.
599	646	John Walker	" " "	100	On the east waters of Elk Creek.
		BOOK No. 98			
600	111	John Joyce	31 Aug. 1846	19½	On Hix's Fork of Peters' Creek.
		BOOK No. 99			
601	394	John H. and Ira P. Pedigo	30 Sept. 1847	172	On headwaters of Ivy Creek.
602	395	Richard Harbour	" "	273	On waters of Dan River.
603	396	George Hairston, Sr.	" "	1,080	On north waters of Bowen's Creek.
604	428	Joshua Keaton	" "	88	On the Nobusiness Mountain.
605	429	John C. and Andrew W. Bolling	" Oct. "	330	On waters of Bull Mountain Fork of South Mayo River.
606	516	Samuel Moles	" "	27	On waters of Goblingtown Creek.
607	517	Munford Smith	" "	50	On Doe Run, a branch of Ararat River.
608	518	Meakin Reynolds	" "	43	On the headwaters of Pole Cat Branch of North Mayo River.
609	519	William Porter	" "	50	On waters of Bull Mountain Fork of South Mayo River.
610	551	Benjamin Spencer	" "	118	On headwaters of North Mayo and Koger's Creek.
611	552	Edward Hylton and B. A. Burnett	" "	100	On south waters of Smith's River.
		BOOK No. 100			
612	107	Peter Hancock	31 May 1848	103	On waters of Bull Mountain Fork of South Mayo River.
613	108	William Combs	" "	147	On Loving's Creek.
614	169	Samuel E. Cobbs	30 June "	66	On waters of Coger's Creek and North Mayo.
615	170	Samuel Moles	" "	23	On south waters of Goblingtown Creek.
616	171	James S. Pedigo	" "	26	On Spoon Creek.
617	172	Elijah Pedigo	" "	100	On waters of Goblingtown Creek and North Mayo.
618	173	Hardin W. Reynolds	" "	473	On headwaters of Dan River.

PATRICK COUNTY COMMONWEALTH'S GRANTS OR PATENTS—Continued

BOOK No. 100

	Page	Name	Date	Acres	Location
619	174	Hardin W. Reynolds	30 June 1848	100	On Bull Mountain Fork of South Mayo River.
620	175	James Thomas	" "	37½	On headwaters of Poplar Camp Creek.
621	343	Hardin W. Reynolds	31 July "	1,052	On Nobusiness Mountain and on branches of Mile Creek, Spoon Creek and North Mayo River.
622	469	William Hollandsworth, Sr.	31 Aug. "	100	On headwaters of North Mayo River.
623	780	Fleming Akers	30 Sept. "	30	On headwaters of Jack's Creek.
624	781	William Hollandsworth	" "	350	On headwaters of Grassy Fork of North Mayo River.
625	782	Pleasant Pucket	" "	64¼	On Loving's Creek.
626	783	Martin Webb	" "	12½	Beginning at said Webb's corner on a branch of Loving's Creek.
627	781	Josiah Hiatt	" "	78	On waters of Johnson's Creek.
628	782	Absalom and George Hylton	" "	218	On Dan River, adjoining James Ingram, etc.

BOOK No. 101

	Page	Name	Date	Acres	Location
629	44	Zadock Combs	30 Sept. 1848	70	On headwaters of Loving's Creek.
630	541	George L. Carter and Caleb Howell	30 June 1849	165	On Doe Run.
631	542	Jesse Dickins	" "	67	On headwaters of Loving's Creek.
632	617	Purris Ayres	" "	180	On Doe Run, a branch of Ararat River.
633	618	William Boyd	" "	38½	On waters of Rock Castle Creek.
634	619	James Harbour	" "	53	On Farthing's Creek, a branch of Sycamore.

BOOK No. 102

	Page	Name	Date	Acres	Location
635	21	Richard Haynes	31 Aug. 1849	108	On waters of Loving's Creek.
636	22	Richard Haynes	" "	50	On waters of Loving's Creek.
637	23	Thomas Lambert	" "	225	On headwaters of Little Dan River.
638	24	James M. Morrison	" "	45	On Sycamore Creek.
639	219	William Martin	1 Oct. "	68	On branches of Spoon Creek.
640	413	Lemuel Guinn	31 " "	55	On Indian Fork of Loving's Creek.
641	508	Enos Hiatt	" Dec. "	82	On Loving's Creek and its waters.
642	509	William Marshall	" "	22	On headwaters of Cisney's Creek.

PATRICK COUNTY COMMONWEALTH'S GRANTS OR PATENTS—Continued

	Page	Name	Date	Acres	Location
BOOK No. 102					
643	548	John Thompson	31 Dec. 1849	255	On Sun's Run and other waters of Ararat River.
644	549	Enos Hiatt and William Chapell.	" "	318	On Loving's Creek and its waters.
BOOK No. 103					
645	99	Josiah Hiatt	1 July 1850	109	On waters of Johnson's Creek.
646	100	Carrington J. Dillion	"	38½	On Rock Castle Creek.
647	732	William Boyd	" Oct.	69½	On headwaters of Smith's River.
648	733	Archibald Haynes	"	125	On Indian Fork of Loving's Creek.
649	734	Zadoch Hall	"	100	On the Blue Ridge on headwaters of Son's Run.
650	735	Edward Hylton	"	123	On the headwaters of Smith's River.
651	736	John R. Wood	"	21	On Pugh's Spur of the Blue Ridge.
BOOK No. 104					
652	68	John Stoops	1 Oct. 1850	121	On South Mayo River.
653	116	William Blackwood and Pendleton Gilbert.	"	75	On headwaters of Smith's River and Ivory Creek.
654	117	John Hatcher	"	30	On headwaters of Join Crack Creek.
655	118	William Lee	"	27	On headwaters of Join Crack Creek.
BOOK No. 105					
656	587	Benjamin T. Burnett	1 July 1851	37	On Ingram's Mill Creek, a branch of Sim's Fork.
657	588	Alexander Chappell	"	50	On waters of Johnson's Creek.
658	589	Jacob Pucket	"	245	On Renfroe's Ridge, a spur of the Blue Ridge.
659	590	William Thompson	"	54	On headwaters of King's Creek and other branches of Ararat River.
BOOK No. 106					
660	7	Notely P. Adams	1 Aug. 1851	350	On the Blue Ridge and on Dan River.
661	8	John Boyd	"	60	On a fork of Johnson's Creek.
662	9	William McMilion	"	62	On headwaters of Owen's Creek.

PATRICK COUNTY COMMONWEALTH'S GRANTS OR PATENTS—Continued

BOOK No. 106

	Page	Name	Date	Acres	Location
663	104	Jubal Wright	1 Sept. 1851	130	On both sides of Smith's River.
664	285	David Washington and Joseph Reynolds.	" Oct. "	100	On Rock Castle Creek.
665	596	Thomas D. Scott	" Dec. "	160	On Dan River and Round Meadow Creek.

BOOK No. 107

	Page	Name	Date	Acres	Location
666	321	Benjamin T. Burnett and Joseph H. Edwards.	2 Aug. 1852	52	On headwaters of Sim's Fork of South Mayo River.
667	322	Thomas Dodson	" "	110	On the Bull Mountain and on branches of Goblingtown Creek and North Mayo River.
668	592	James Richeson	1 Oct. "	24	On waters of Johnson's Creek.
669	728	James B. Taylor	1 Nov. "	16	On a ridge dividing waters of Spoon Creek from those of North Mayo.
670	729	John W. Gates	" "	55	On Snow's Branch.
671	730	William Martin	" "	22	On waters of Spoon Creek.
672	735	Wilson J. Harbour and John H. Rorer.	" "	197	On headwaters of Rody's Creek, a branch of South Mayo River.
673	736	Featherston Akers	" "	20	On waters of Widgeon Creek.

BOOK No. 108

	Page	Name	Date	Acres	Location
674	324	William F. Hall	1 Apr. 1853	79	On headwaters of Poplar Camp and Shooting Creeks.
675	404	Fielden L. Hale	2 May "	550	On waters of Indian Fork of Loving's Creek.
676	445	David Nowlin	1 June "	62	On South Branch of Rock Castle Creek.
677	499	John Thomas	" "	55	On Big Widgeon Creek.
678	742	Jonathan R. Brown	" Sept. "	112	On Johnson's Creek.
679	743	Jonathan R. Brown	" "	200	On waters of Loving's Creek.
680	744	James D. Cloud	" "	187	On waters of Johnson's Creek.
681	745	Joshua Keaton	" "	180	On both sides of Spoon Creek.
682	746	Henry Young	" "	30	On waters of Sim's Run.
683	747	Reynolds McMillion	" "	40	On waters of Johnson's Creek.
684	828	James D. Cloud	" "	555	On waters of Johnson's Creek.
685	829	Munford Smith	" "	100	On waters of Doe Run.
686	646	Fountain Howell	" Aug. "	36	On waters of South Mayo River.
687	647	Naaman Harbour	" "	21	On Coal Fork of Sycamore Creek.

PATRICK COUNTY COMMONWEALTH'S GRANTS OR PATENTS—Continued

BOOK No. 109

	Page	Name	Date	Acres	Location
688	139	James Smith	1 Nov. 1853	22	On the waters of the Ararat.
689	237	Isham Barnard, Sr.	" "	490	On north side of Big Dan River.
690	238	Isham Barnard, Sr.	" "	260	On south side of Big Dan River.
691	285	John H. Walker	" Dec. "	19	On Smith's River and its waters.
692	382	Nelson Thompson	2 Jan. 1854	150	On headwaters of Ararat River.
693	565	Josiah Hiatt	1 Apr. "	20	On south waters of Johnson's Creek.
694	639	Jesse Dickens	1 May "	75	On headwaters of Loving's Creek.
695	790	John Hensley	1 July "	55½	On headwaters of Fall Creek.
696	791	Jordan Keaton	" "	48	On waters of Rhody's Creek.
697	792	Thomas Penn	" "	34	On headwaters of Loving's Creek.
698	793	James Purdy	" "	44	On north waters of Blackberry Creek.

BOOK No. 110

	Page	Name	Date	Acres	Location
699	247	James Guinn	1 Aug. 1854	42	On waters of Loving's Creek.
700	248	Robert M. Clark and John H. Pedigo.	" "	182	On waters of Johnson's Creek.
701	454	William F. Hall	2 Oct. "	27	On headwaters of Poplar Camp Creek.
702	602	James Martin	1 Nov. "	84	On headwaters of Johnson's Creek.
703	603	Hiram Stanley	" "	32	On west side of Ararat River.
704	604	John Stanley	" "	57	On east side of Ararat River.
705	709	William Bowman	" Dec. "	50	On Squall Creek and its waters.

BOOK No. 111

	Page	Name	Date	Acres	Location
706	41	Thomas Dickens, Jr.	1 Feb. 1855	209	On headwaters of Loving's Creek.
707	88	John A. Jones	" Mar. "	84	On Indian Fork of Loving's Creek.
708	142	William F. Hall	2 Apr. "	130	On headwaters of Poplar Camp Creek.
709	143	William F. Hall	" "	55	On south side of headwaters of Poplar Camp Creek.
710	144	Peter Spencer and John L. Anglin.	" "	442	On head of Double Branch, waters of South Mayo River.
711	145	Peter J., America and Mary Thomas.	" "	105	On White Oak Creek and Shooting Creek and waters thereof.
712	242	Edward F. Jefferson	1 May "	300	On north waters of South Fork of Rock Castle.
713	243	Joseph Koger	" "	260	On Kogar's Creek and its waters.

PATRICK COUNTY COMMONWEALTH'S GRANTS OR PATENTS—Continued

BOOK No. 111

	Page	Name	Date	Acres	Location
714	244	William Moran	1 May 1855	60	On waters of Little Ivy Creek.
715	643	William Parker	" Sept. "	28	On Cares Branch near Smith's River.
716	673	John Thompson	" Oct. "	192	On King's Run and the waters of Ararat River.
717	700	Benjamin Belcher	" " "	20	On north waters of Rock Castle Creek.
718	701	William Barnard	" " "	50	On South Fork of Roaring Creek.
719	724	William Barnard	" " "	170	On waters of Squirrel Creek.

BOOK No. 112

	Page	Name	Date	Acres	Location
720	359	John Stanley	1 Apr. 1856	180	On Dan River and its waters near the little bend of said river.
721	442	John Monday	" May "	286½	On Stephen's Creek and its waters.
722	685	Greenville Scott	4 Aug. "	120	On Dan River and its waters.
723	711	John Hubbard	1 " "	13	On Jack's Creek.
724	712	James M. Morrison	" " "	133	On waters of Sycamore Creek.
725	713	Martha Pack (Widow)	" " "	41	On Roaring Creek and its waters.
726	714	John Thompson	" " "	46	On Smith's Run, waters of Ararat.
727	774	Green Ayres	" Sept. "	39	On side of Blue Ridge Mountain.

BOOK No. 113

	Page	Name	Date	Acres	Location
728	16	Martin Webb	1 Sept. 1856	82	On waters of Loving's Creek.
729	324	George Z. Edwards	1 Dec. "	288	On Long Branch waters of Peters' Creek.
730	336	James Ingrum, Sr.	1 Jan. 1857	39	Near Smith's River on south waters thereof.
731	383	Jacob Packet	" " "	14	On waters of Doe Run.
732	450	Merlin Sparger	2 Feb. "	606	On the waters of Johnson's and Wolf's Creeks.
733	507	Walter McIntosh	2 Mar. "	88	On the waters of South Mayo River.
734	517	Thomas D. Scott	" " "	87	On Round Meadow Creek and its waters.
735	25	Malinda, Elizabeth P., Ruth A., George S., John M. and Susan A. Hairston, widow and heirs of John A. Hairston, dec'd.	1 Dec. 1856	780	On waters of Goblingtown Creek, being part of 1,000 acres granted to George Hairston, April 23, 1801.

PATRICK COUNTY COMMONWEALTH'S GRANTS OR PATENTS—Continued

BOOK No. 114

	Page	Name	Date	Acres	Location
736	184	John Sharp	1 Sept. 1857	125	On waters of Elk Creek.
736	135	Daniel Epperson	" "	7	On or near the waters of Ararat River.
737	211	John W. Gates	" Oct. "	440	On Doe Run and waters of Ararat River.
738	212	John W. Gates	" " "	330	On the waters of Ararat River.
739	213	James Ingrum, Jr.	" " "	30	On the south side of Smith's River.
740	214	James Ingrum, Jr.	" " "	6	On the south side of Smith's River.
741	215	James M. Morrison	" " "	100	On waters of Sycamore Creek.
742	285	James Adams	2 Nov. "	31	On waters of North Mayo River.
743	665	Hardin W. Reynolds	1 Apr. 1858	17	On waters of North Mayo River.
744	36	Jeremiah Burnett	1 Dec. 1857	646	On south side of Smith's River.

BOOK No. 115

	Page	Name	Date	Acres	Location
745	59	Munford Smith	1 July 1858	87	On waters of Doe Run.
746	161	Joseph Thomas	2 Aug. "	53	On headwaters of Big Widgeon Creek.
747	487	Smith Parker	1 Oct. "	7	On south side of Smith's River.
748	615	Samuel Blancet	1 Nov. "	58	On headwaters of Peters' Creek.

BOOK No. 116

	Page	Name	Date	Acres	Location
749	267	Gabriel Deal	1 July 1859	140	On headwaters of North Mayo River.
750	287	Allen Mitchell	" " "	97	On waters of Peters' Creek.
751	301	Merlin Sparger	" " "	180	On the North Fork of Wolf Creek.
752	415	William J. Robertson	" Sept. "	233	On headwaters of Sycamore Creek.
753	589	William McMillion	" Nov. "	11	On headwaters of Sysney's Creek.
754	837	John and James Rangeley	2 May "	3,263	Including their own lands, beginning on Archer's Creek where North Carolina line crosses said creek.
755	636	John C. Clark	" Nov. "	65	On the waters of Johnson's Creek.
756	615	Rhoda O'Bryan, William H. O'Bryan and other heirs of A. T. O'Bryan, dec'd.	3 Jan. 1860	250	On headwaters of Three Forks of Rock Castle Creek.
757	731	John A. Friebele	1 Feb. "	36	On South Fork of Johnson's Creek.
758	732	James S. Pedigo	" " "	20	On headwaters of Spoon Creek.
759	733	Thomas Scott	" " "	200	On South Fork of Johnson's Creek.

PATRICK COUNTY COMMONWEALTH'S GRANTS OR PATENTS—Continued

BOOK No. 116

	Page	Name	Date	Acres	Location
760	734	Thomas Soyars............	1 Feb. 1860	15	On waters of Sysney's Creek in fork of Court House and Volunteer Roads.
761	735	Andrew J. Spencer......	" "	280	On south side of Hogpen Mountain.
762	736	George W. Smith and Merlin Sparger.	" "	270	On waters of Johnson's Creek.
763	737	Asa Wood..............	" "	50	On headwaters of Mathew's Creek.
764	763	Asa L. and Jos. L. Howard and C. J. Dillion.	" "	300	On north waters of South Fork of Rock Castle Creek and face of the Blue Ridge.
765	764	Andrew J. Spencer........	" "	278	On headwaters of North Mayo River.
766	791	David Washington........	" Mar. "	130	On the Three Forks of Rock Castle Creek.
767	765	Harden Spencer..........	" Feb. "	71	On headwaters of North Mayo River.

BOOK No. 117

	Page	Name	Date	Acres	Location
768	165	John Gunter.............	3 July 1860	83	On waters of Peters' Creek.
769	166	Henry Handy.............	" "	16	On headwaters of North Mayo River.
770	185	Michael A. Roarer.......	" "	173	On headwaters of South Mayo River.
771	186	Wade H. Duncan.........	" "	24	On waters of Elk Creek.
772	187	Andrew J. Spencer......	" "	230	Upon the headwaters of North Mayo River.
773	218	Samuel Bowman.........	1 Aug. "	63	On top of the mountain and headwaters of Loving's Creek.
774	219	James J. Spencer........	" "	125	On Marden Creek and south side of Bull Mountain.
775	220	Levi Spencer...........	" "	138	On Marden and Rhoda's Creek.
776	221	Naaman Harbour........	" "	88	On Bull Mountain and waters of South Mayo River.
777	230	John Spencer...........	" "	55	On headwaters of North Mayo River.
778	269	John W. Hudson and A. A. Martin.	" "	76	On waters of Peters' Creek.
779	270	Thomas Blackard........	" "	30	On Gilbert's Knob of Bull Mountain.
780	349	Wilson T. Vaughn.......	" Sept. "	90	On headwaters of Big Widgeon Creek.
781	350	Wilson T. Vaughn.......	" "	37	On headwaters of Rock Castle Creek.
782	354	Calvin Joyce...........	" "	65	On headwaters of Mathew's Creek.
783	355	James B. Smith.........	" "	111	On waters of Dan River.
784	412	Alexander Ratliff.......	" Oct. "	105	On headwaters of Cold Fork of Sycamore.
785	868	Waller R. Staples.......	" Nov. "	560	On Hughes Creek generally known as the "Well's Place" including his own lands.
786	627	John W. Gates..........	" Feb. 1861	100	On waters of Johnson's Creek.

PATRICK COUNTY COMMONWEALTH'S GRANTS OR PATENTS—Continued

BOOK No. 117

	Page	Name	Date	Acres	Location
787	679	Newell Eaton	1 Mar. 1861	5	On headwaters of Sysney's Creek.
788	794	William Marshall	" June "	9	On headwaters of Sysney's Creek.
789	816	Andrew J. Hall	" July "	34	On waters of Archer's Creek, a branch of Dan River.

BOOK No. 118

	Page	Name	Date	Acres	Location
790	45	Ewell Conner and Isaac Adams.	2 Sept. 1861	40	On waters of Rock Castle Creek.
791	46	Pleasant C. Thomas	" " "	28	On waters of White Oak Creek.
792	47	Samuel Via	" " "	63	On the headwaters of Poplar Camp Creek.
793	110	John W. Gates	1 Oct. "	231	On Cisney's Creek, waters of Ararat River.
794	172	Jordan Snow	1 Feb. 1862	45	On the waters of Doe Run.
795	271	Alexander Ratliffe	1 Oct. "	38	On the waters of the Cold Fork of Sycamore Creek.
796	264	Isaac A. Gardner	1 Sept. "	130	On the waters of Owens' Creek and Wolf Creek.
797	298	Lavinia Gardner	1 Nov. "	50	On the headwaters of Johnson's Creek.
798	324	John S. Adams and Moses Hylton.	1 Aug. 1863	244	On the headwaters of Smith's River.
799	355	Isaac A. Gardner	2 Nov. "	255½	On the headwaters of Johnson's Creek.
800	363	Floyd Smith	1 Jan. 1864	80	On the waters of Ararat River in the face of Blue Ridge Mountain.
801	364	Allen Williard	" "	35	On the waters of Russell's Creek.
802	365	German Boyd	" "	84	On the headwaters of Rhody's Creek.
803	366	Moses Martin	" "	155	On the waters of Goblingtown Creek.
804	370	Isaac A. Gardner	" Mar. "	120	On the headwaters of Johnson's Creek.
805	388	John M. Marshall	2 May "	136	On the waters of Johnson's Creek.
806	421	Hamilton Marshall	1 Oct. "	150	On the headwaters of Ararat River.
807	423	George Bowman	1 Nov. "	225	On the waters of Squirrel Creek, a branch of Dan River.
808	458	Gabriel Critz	1 Oct. 1867	13	On the waters of Mill Creek.
809	466	William Barnard	1 Nov. "	130	On Dan River and its waters.

Breinigsville, PA USA
27 December 2009
229867BV00004B/3/P